IN REMEMBRANCE OF

ADOLPH S. OCHS

(*1858–1935*)

Publisher of THE NEW YORK TIMES

*With affectionate memories of thirty
years as a friend and as a member of
the Book Review staff.* H.F.

PREFACE

In the compilation of this book I have drawn on my experience as editor of the Queries and Answers page of THE NEW YORK TIMES Book Review over a period of fifteen years. The majority of inquiries that I receive are for favorite poems, and since not a day passes that does not bring to my desk a large sheaf of letters from all parts of the country, it is only natural that I have learned something of the poetry preferences of the American people. I have used this knowledge rather than my own personal liking in the selection of these poems; but I feel free to say that there are few of the poems that I would not have included myself.

My first acknowledgments are due to Lewis Copeland, whose able help in the organization of the work greatly simplified its production, and to Edward Frank Allen who contributed the introduction and lent his valuable editorial counsel. Without their interested assistance, I should have had a much more onerous task. There are literally hundreds of people whom, collectively, I wish to thank for their replies to inquiries about poems. After all, they are the ones who have made the book possible. And, although elsewhere I make formal specific acknowledgment to authors and publishers, I wish again to express my gratefulness for the privilege of reprinting their poems.

HAZEL FELLEMAN

New York City

ACKNOWLEDGMENTS

For the privilege of reprinting poems in this book, thanks are due to:

Alice E. Allen for *My Mother's Garden.*
Mrs. Young E. Allison for *Derelict,* by Young E. Allison.
Charles Bancroft for *Tadoussac.*
John Bennett for *In a Rose Garden* and *Her Answer.*
Berton Braley for *At Your Service: The Panama Gang, Do It Now, A Prayer,* and *The Thinker.*
Hally Carrington Brent for *I Think I Know No Finer Things than Dogs,* from *Moods and Melodies* (Dorrance and Company).
Mrs. George Sargent Burgess for *America the Beautiful,* by Katharine Lee Bates.
Mrs. William Herbert Carruth for *Each In His Own Tongue,* by William Herbert Carruth.
David Cory for *Miss You,* from *Moods* (The Poet Lore Company).
Mary Carolyn Davies for *If I Had Known* and *A Prayer for Every Day.*
Louise Driscoll for *Hold Fast Your Dreams.*
Max Ehrmann for *A Prayer,* from *Poems.*
Dr. Spencer M. Free for *The Human Touch.*
Theodosia Garrison for *The Torch* and *The Closed Door.*
Strickland Gillilan for *Need of Loving, The Reading Mother,* and *Watch Yourself Go By.*
Anna B. Gruber for *My Neighbor's Roses,* by Abraham L. Gruber.
James N. Hall for *Eat and Walk.*
Robert B. Hamilton for *Along the Road.*

ACKNOWLEDGMENTS

Charles Heddon for *To My Setter, Scout,* by Frank H. Seldon.

Arthur N. Hosking for *Land of the Free.*

Mrs. James L. Hughes for *My Son* from *Life's Glories* (Hambly Brothers), by Dr. James L. Hughes.

Minna Irving for *The Wedding Gift.*

Wallace Irwin for *The Worried Skipper.*

Bertha Johnston for *Did You Ever Hear An English Sparrow Sing?* from *Lyrical Lines.*

Louise Seymour Jones for *Who Loves A Garden* from her book of the same name.

Dr. John McCrae Kilgour for *In Flanders Fields,* by John McCrae.

Mrs. Rudyard Kipling, through A. P. Watt & Son and Doubleday-Doran & Company, for the following poems by Rudyard Kipling: *Recessional* and *Boots* from *The Five Nations; If* from *Rewards and Fairies; The Vampire* from *Rudyard Kipling's Inclusive Verse; The Winners* from *Soldiers Three; The Female of the Species* from *The Years Between;* and *The Power of the Dog* from *Actions and Reactions.*

Samuel E. Kiser for *The Fighter* from *Glorious Day* (George Sully & Co.).

Yolande Langworthy for *Drifting Sands and A Caravan* from *Poems from Arabesque* (Walter J. Black).

Dr. E. O. Laughlin for *The Unknown.*

Agnes Lee for *Motherhood* from *Border of the Lake* (Sherman, French).

Everett W. Lord for *The Legend of the Admen.*

Phillips H. Lord for *You Go to Your Church and I'll Go to Mine,* from the *Seth Parker Hymnal* (Carl Fischer, Inc.).

Adelaide Love for *Walk Slowly* from *The Slender Singing Tree* (Dodd Mead & Co.).

Douglas Malloch for *It's Fine Today* (copyright 1926 by author) and *Be the Best of Whatever You Are* (copyright 1925 by the McClure Newspaper Syndicate).

Alba Rosa Malone for *Opportunity,* by Walter Malone.

Rosa Zagnoni Marinoni for *Who Are My People?* from *Behind the Mask.*

Edwin Markham for *Outwitted* and *How the Great Guest Came,* from *Shoes of Happiness; The Man with the Hoe,* from the book of the same name; *A Creed,* from *Man of the People; The Right Kind of People.*

ACKNOWLEDGMENTS

H. F. Martin for *The Birds' Ball,* by C. W. Bardeen.

Madeleine S. Miller for *How Far to Bethlehem?* from *The Merchant of Muristan* (Abingdon Press).

David Morton for *Who Walks with Beauty* from *Ships in Harbor* (G. P. Putnam's Sons).

Byron Rufus Newton for *Owed to New York.*

John Oxenham for *Where Are You Going, Greatheart?*

Luther Patrick for *Sleepin' at the Foot o' the Bed.*

Silas H. Perkins for *The Common Road* from *Down East Ballads.*

Olga Petrova for *To A Child Who Inquires.*

Nan Terrell Reed for *Life* and *Vases.*

Elsie Robinson for *Beauty As A Shield.*

Mrs. John Jerome Rooney for *The Men Behind the Guns,* by John Jerome Rooney.

Edwin Milton Royle for *Don't You Be What You Ain't.*

Sydney King Russell for *Midsummer.*

Margaret E. Sangster, granddaughter of the poet, for *Our Own* and *The Sin of Omission,* by Margaret E. Sangster.

Henry Dwight Sedgwick for *Leo to His Mistress.*

Philip Stack for *Admonition.*

William L. Stidger for *I Saw God Wash the World* from the book of the same name (Frederick Jaenicken Company).

Winifred S. Stoner for *The History of the United States* from *Facts in Jingles.*

Charles Hanson Towne for *City Roofs* and *At Nightfall.*

Isabel Valle for *A Very Minor Poet Speaks.*

Blanche Shoemaker Wagstaff for *All Paths Lead to You* and *Quiet Waters* from *Quiet Waters* (Moffat, Tard & Co.).

Franklin Waldheim for *Help Wanted,* first published in the November-December issue of *The Docket,* 1921, (West Publishing Company).

Nixon Waterman for *Making A Man, To Know All Is to Forgive All* and *Far from the Madding Crowd* from *A Rose to the Living and Other Poems.*

Myra Brooks Welch for *The Touch of the Master's Hand.*

Carolyn Wells for *An Overworked Elocutionist.*

Mary Brent Whiteside for *Who Has Known Heights* from *The Eternal Quest* (Erskine MacDonald Ltd.).

Victor Blaine Wright for *The Want of You,* by Ivan Leonard Wright.

Barbara Young for *I Hear It Said.*

D. Appleton-Century Company for permission to reprint *Prayer for a Very New Angel* from *Green of the Year*, by Violet Alleyn Storey; and *Not By Bread Alone* from *In Saadi's Rose Garden*, by James Terry White.

Bobbs-Merrill Company for permission to reprint the following poems by James Whitcomb Riley: *He Is Not Dead* and *Back to Griggsby's Station* from *Afterwhiles; An Old Sweetheart of Mine* from *Pipes o' Pan at Zekesbury; Out of the Hitherwhere* from *Armazindy*.

W. B. Conkey Company for permission to reprint the following poems by Ella Wheeler Wilcox: *Whatever Is—Is Best, You Never Can Tell, Worth While, The Winds of Fate, Will, Growing Old, I Love You, Life's Scars, Lifting and Leaning, Optimism, Progress, The Queen's Last Ride, This Too Shall Pass Away, Ad Finem, The Two Glasses*.

Dodd, Mead and Company for permission to reprint *My Madonna, The Spell of the Yukon,* and *The Men that Don't Fit In,* all of which are taken from Robert W. Service's book *The Spell of the Yukon; Vagabond House* by Don Blanding; *Kashmiri Song,* from *Indian Love Lyrics* by Laurence Hope; *Death Is a Door,* by Nancy Byrd Turner; *God, the Artist* and *Today* by Angela Morgan.

E. P. Dutton and Company for permission to reprint *Sometime, If We Knew, My Life Is a Bowl* by May Riley Smith; and *The Cry of the Dreamer* from *Moondyne,* by John Boyle O'Reilly.

Forbes and Company for permission to reprint *The Pessimist* by Ben King, from *Ben King's Verses*.

Harper and Brothers for permission to reprint *Strictly Germ-Proof* from *The Laughing Muse,* by Arthur Guiterman; *The Sycophantic Fox and the Gullible Raven* from *Mother Goose for Grown-Ups,* by Guy Wetmore Carryl; and *The Country Doctor* from *Rhymes of Our Planet,* by Will M. Carleton.

Houghton Mifflin Company for permission to reprint *Leo: A Yellow Cat* from *The Upper Slopes,* by Margaret Sherwood; *My Wage* from *The Door of Dreams,* by Jessie Belle Rittenhouse; *Out There Somewhere* from *Songs of the Outlands,* by Henry Herbert Knibbs; *To A Dog,* by Josephine Preston Peabody; *Out Where the West Begins,* by Arthur Chapman; *The Enchanted Shirt,* by John Hay; *The Things I Miss,* by Thomas W. Higginson; *A Reply to The Man with the Hoe,* by John Vance Cheney; *Ultima Veritas,* by Rev. Washington Gladden.

Little, Brown & Company for permission to reprint *October's Bright Blue Weather* from *Sonnets and Lyrics,* by Helen Hunt Jackson.

Lothrop, Lee and Shepard Company for permission to reprint *The House by the Side of the Road* and *The Coming American*, by Sam Walter Foss.

The Macmillan Company for permission to reprint *My Dog* from *Foothills of Parnassus*, by John Kendrick Bangs; and *My Garden Is a Pleasant Place* from *Garden Grace*, by Louise Driscoll.

The Penn Publishing Company for permission to reprint *If I Should Die Tonight* by Robert C. V. Meyers, from *Shoemaker's Best Selections No. 3.*

G. P. Putnam's Sons for permission to reprint *Your Mission* from *The Treasures of Kurium*, by Ellen M. H. Gates.

The Reilly and Lee Company for permission to reprint the following poems by Edgar A. Guest: *Home* and *A Friend's Greeting* from *A Heap o' Livin'*; *It Couldn't Be Done* from *The Path to Home*; *Myself* from *The Friendly Way*; *Lord, Make A Regular Man Out of Me* from *The Light of Faith.*

Charles Scribner's Sons for permission to reprint *Be Strong!* from *Thoughts for Everyday Living*, by Maltbie D. Babcock; *I Have a Rendezvous with Death*, by Alan Seeger; *The Legend of the Organ-Builder*, by Julia C. R. Dorr; *The Path that Leads to Nowhere*, by Corinne Roosevelt Robinson; *Verses Written in 1872* from *Memories of Vailima*, by Robert Louis Stevenson; *Invictus*, and *Echoes*, by William Ernest Henley; *America for Me*, *A Mile with Me* and *Envoy: The Toiling of Felix* from *Collected Poems* by Henry Van Dyke; *Bachelor Hall* from *Sharps and Flats* and *A Dutch Lullaby*, by Eugene Field.

Turner Company for permission to reprint *Let Me Grow Lovely* from *Dreamers on Horseback*, by Karle Wilson Baker.

CONTENTS

I. LOVE AND FRIENDSHIP

CONTENTS

CONTENTS

CONTENTS

CONTENTS

CONTENTS

CONTENTS

CONTENTS

CONTENTS

IV. FAITH AND REVERENCE

CONTENTS

CONTENTS

V. HOME AND MOTHER

VI. CHILDHOOD AND YOUTH

VII. PATRIOTISM AND WAR

CONTENTS

VIII. HUMOR AND WHIMSEY

CONTENTS

CONTENTS

CONTENTS

X. NATURE

CONTENTS

XI. ANIMALS

XII. VARIOUS THEMES

CONTENTS

CONTENTS

INTRODUCTION

THIS BOOK began in the heart of a little newsboy in Knoxville, Tennessee. He loved poetry.

To him poetry meant music—and ideas. It sang to him and it spoke to him.

It inspired him.

Particularly did it inspire him.

The boy grew up. He continued selling newspapers—all his life.

He was Adolph S. Ochs, publisher of THE NEW YORK TIMES.

Throughout his life Mr. Ochs loved poetry. He was keenly interested in the number of inquiries regarding it that came to the editorial rooms of THE NEW YORK TIMES Book Review, and he started the *Queries and Answers* page to handle them.

The selection of verses that are here collected under the title *Best Loved Poems of the American People* is based on the most frequently requested items that have cleared through these columns over a period of three decades.

During a large part of this time, Hazel Felleman has been the editor of *Queries and Answers*. From every state in the Union, and even beyond its borders, have come countless letters asking for this poem or that, or for the complete poem whose theme is such-and-such, or the song whose refrain is thus-and-so.

Miss Felleman has long had her finger on the poetry pulse of the nation. Its heartbeats are truly registered in this, her book.

One day, Mr. Ochs appeared at Miss Felleman's desk and said:

"There's a line that has been running through my head lately, and I wish I could get the whole poem. I read it when I was a boy, and I don't remember the author's name. It begins:

" 'I am a stranger in the land where my forefathers trod.'*

See if you can find it through your *Queries and Answers* page."

So a search was begun.

Weeks passed, and no one had answered the query. But the publisher was not satisfied. He said:

"Offer five dollars to anyone who will send a copy of the complete poem. If that doesn't produce results, offer ten dollars. And if necessary offer as high as twenty-five. I simply must have that poem—it haunts me."

For various reasons, most of them obvious, Adolph Ochs's name did not appear in connection with these offers. As in most undertakings, however, he was successful in his quest. After several months a copy of the poem, found by a reader in an old magazine in the Yale University library, was sent to Miss Felleman, who turned it over to her chief.

Today poetry is an absolute necessity. The world needs it for its vitalizing strength. Poetry came into being because of this need, and it is perpetuated for the same reason.

Poetry has nearly everything that music can give—melody, rhythm, sentiment—but it has this advantage: it can come closer to the heart. Therefore it can have a more personal and a more lasting appeal.

It satisfies a hunger for beauty that is a part of nearly every normal person's make-up.

It recaptures vanished moments and recreates scenes that have grown dim through passing years.

It stirs wholesome emotions and gives glimpses across the border that, vague as they may be, are a preview of eternal things.

It entertains, it inspires, and, in time of need, it comforts.

These, then, are the poems that America loves.

Here is a magic carpet on which one may ride back to childhood days, into the realm of fancy, through eerie castles, across uncharted seas and in spiritual places.

*The poem may be found on page 323.

For company, there are mothers, wives, sweethearts; there are men of God and worshipers; there are heroes, heroines, martyrs, laborers, schoolmasters, and a goodly company of folk who laugh.

The critic tells you what you *ought* to read. Miss Felleman, out of a knowledge of and sympathy with your likes and dislikes, has provided the poems you *want* to read.

How else have certain poems become classic except through the fact that they struck a responsive chord in the breast of the average man or woman? Some of Bobbie Burns's poems—notably the one in which he says,

> *Oh, wad some power the giftie gie us*
> *To see oursels as ithers see us——*

are not kept alive and in print by the supercritical. Nor will it be such who will some day make classics of various poems by Edgar A. Guest, Margaret E. Sangster, Ella Wheeler Wilcox, and many a lesser known poet. It is the preference of the people, after all, that gives permanency to poetry.

In a sense, this book has been edited by the American people who love poetry. Miss Felleman is the liaison officer who has co-ordinated the poetry preferences of the nation. She has assembled the results in orderly fashion and given them back in an enduring and friendly form.

EDWARD FRANK ALLEN

I. LOVE AND FRIENDSHIP

SONNET FROM THE PORTUGUESE

FIRST TIME he kissed me, he but only kiss'd
  The fingers of this hand wherewith I write;
  And ever since, it grew more clean and white,
Slow to world-greetings, quick with its "Oh, list,"
When the angels speak. A ring of amethyst
  I could not wear here, plainer to my sight,
  Than that first kiss. The second pass'd in height
The first, and sought the forehead, and half miss'd,
Half falling on the hair. Oh, beyond meed!
  That was the chrism of love, which love's own **crown**,
With sanctifying sweetness, did precede.
  The third upon my lips was folded down
In perfect, purple state; since when, indeed,
  I have been proud, and said, "My love, my own!"

ELIZABETH BARRETT BROWNING.

A WOMAN'S SHORTCOMINGS

SHE HAS LAUGHED as softly as if she sighed,
  She has counted six and over,
Of a purse well filled, and a heart well tried—
  Oh each a worthy lover!
They "give her time"; for her soul must slip
  Where the world has set the grooving:
She will lie to none with her fair red lip—
  But love seeks truer loving.

3

She trembles her fan in a sweetness dumb,
 As her thoughts were beyond recalling,
With a glance for *one,* and a glance for *some,*
 For her eyelids rising and falling;
Speaks common words with a blushful air,
 Hears bold words, unreproving;
But her silence says—what she never will swear—
 And love seeks better loving.

Go, lady, lean to the night-guitar,
 And drop a smile to the bringer,
Then smile as sweetly, when he is far,
 At the voice of an indoor singer.
Bask tenderly beneath tender eyes;
 Glance lightly on their removing;
And join new vows to old perjuries—
 But dare not call it loving.

Unless you can think, when the song is done,
 No other is soft in the rhythm;
Unless you can feel, when left by one,
 That all men else go with him;
Unless you can know, when unpraised by his breath,
 That your beauty itself wants proving;
Unless you can swear, "For life, for death!"—
 Oh fear to call it loving!

Unless you can muse in a crowd all day,
 On the absent face that fixed you;
Unless you can love, as the angels may,
 With the breadth of heaven betwixt you;
Unless you can dream that his faith is fast,
 Through behoving and unbehoving;
Unless you can *die* when the dream is past—
 Oh never call it loving!

       ELIZABETH BARRETT BROWNING.

A WOMAN'S LAST WORD

LET'S CONTEND no more, Love,
 Strive nor weep:
All be as before, Love,
 —Only sleep!

What so wild as words are?
  I and thou
In debate, as birds are,
  Hawk on bough!

See the creature stalking
  While we speak!
Hush and hide the talking,
  Cheek on cheek!

What so false as truth is,
  False to thee?
Where the serpent's tooth is,
  Shun the tree—

Where the apple reddens
  Never pry—
Lest we lose our Edens,
  Eve and I.

Be a god and hold me
  With a charm!
Be a man and fold me
  With thine arm!

Teach me, only teach, Love!
  As I ought.
I will speak thy speech, Love,
  Think thy thought—

Meet, if thou require it,
  Both demands,
Laying flesh and spirit
  In thy hands.

That shall be tomorrow,
  Not tonight:
I must bury sorrow
  Out of sight:

—Must a little weep, Love,
  (Foolish me!)
And so fall asleep, Love,
  Loved by thee.

                    ROBERT BROWNING.

5

SHE WALKS IN BEAUTY

SHE WALKS in beauty like the night
   Of cloudless climes and starry skies;
And all that's best of dark and bright
   Meets in her aspect and her eyes:
Thus mellow'd to that tender light
   Which heaven to gaudy day denies.

One shade the more, one ray the less,
   Had half impair'd the nameless grace
Which waves in every raven tress,
   Or softly lightens o'er her face—
Where thoughts serenely sweet express
   How pure, how dear their dwelling-place.

And on that cheek, and o'er that brow,
   So soft, so calm, yet eloquent,
The smiles that win, the tints that glow,
   But tell of days in goodness spent,
A mind at peace with all below,
   A heart whose love is innocent.

                        LORD BYRON.

JENNY KISSED ME

JENNY kissed me when we met,
   Jumping from the chair she sat in.
Time, you thief! who love to get
   Sweets into your list, put that in.
Say I'm weary, say I'm sad;
   Say that health and wealth have missed me;
Say I'm growing old, but add—
           Jenny kissed me!

                        LEIGH HUNT.

6

SAID THE ROSE

I AM weary of the Garden,
　　Said the Rose;
For the winter winds are sighing,
All my playmates round me dying,
And my leaves will soon be lying
　　'Neath the snows.

But I hear my Mistress coming,
　　Said the Rose;
She will take me to her chamber,
Where the honeysuckles clamber,
And I'll bloom there all December
　　Spite the snows.

Sweeter fell her lily finger
　　Than the bee!
Ah, how feebly I resisted,
Smoothed my thorns, and e'en assisted
As all blushing I was twisted
　　Off my tree.

And she fixed me in her bosom
　　Like a star;
And I flashed there all the morning,
Jasmin, honeysuckle scorning,
Parasites forever fawning
　　That they are.

And when evening came she set me
　　In a vase
All of rare and radiant metal,
And I felt her red lips settle
On my leaves till each proud petal
　　Touched her face.

And I shone about her slumbers
　　Like a light;
And, I said, instead of weeping,
In the garden vigil keeping,
Here I'll watch my Mistress sleeping
　　Every night.

7

But when morning with its sunbeams
 Softly shone,
In the mirror where she braided
Her brown hair I saw how jaded,
Old and colorless and faded,
 I had grown.

Not a drop of dew was on me,
 Never one;
From my leaves no odors started,
All my perfume had departed,
I lay pale and broken-hearted
 In the sun.

Still I said, her smile is better
 Than the rain;
Though my fragrance may forsake me,
To her bosom she will take me,
And with crimson kisses make me
 Young again.

So she took me . . . gazed a second . . .
 Half a sigh . . .
Then, alas, can hearts so harden?
Without ever asking pardon,
Threw me back into the garden,
 There to die.

How the jealous garden gloried
 In my fall!
How the honeysuckle chid me,
How the sneering jasmins bid me
Light the long gray grass that hid me
 Like a pall.

There I lay beneath her window
 In a swoon,
Till the earthworm o'er me trailing
Woke me just at twilight's failing,
As the whip-poor-will was wailing
 To the moon.

But I hear the storm-winds stirring
  In their lair;
And I know they soon will lift me
In their giant arms and sift me
Into ashes as they drift me
  Through the air.

So I pray them in their mercy
  Just to take
From my heart of hearts, or near it,
The last living leaf, and bear it
To her feet, and bid her wear it
  For my sake.

GEORGE H. MILES.

WALK SLOWLY

IF YOU should go before me, dear, walk slowly
Down the ways of death, well-worn and wide,
For I would want to overtake you quickly
And seek the journey's ending by your side.

I would be so forlorn not to descry you
Down some shining highroad when I came;
Walk slowly, dear, and often look behind you
And pause to hear if someone calls your name.

ADELAIDE LOVE.

TO ALTHEA FROM PRISON

WHEN LOVE with unconfinèd wings
  Hovers within my gates,
And my divine Althea brings
  To whisper at my grates;
When I lie tangled in her hair
  And fettered with her eye,
The birds that wanton in the air
  Know no such liberty.

9

When flowing cups pass swiftly round
    With no allaying Thames,
Our careless heads with roses crowned,
    Our hearts with loyal flames;
When thirsty grief in wine we steep,
    When healths and draughts go free,
Fishes that tipple in the deep
    Know no such liberty.

When, linnet-like confinèd,
    With shriller throat shall sing
The mercy, sweetness, majesty
    And glories of my King;
When I shall voice aloud how good
    He is, how great should be,
The enlargèd winds, that curl the flood,
    Know no such liberty.

Stone walls do not a prison make,
    Nor iron bars a cage;
Minds innocent and quiet take
    That for an hermitage:
If I have freedom in my love,
    And in my soul am free,
Angels alone, that soar above,
    Enjoy such liberty.

                              RICHARD LOVELACE.

BELIEVE ME, IF ALL THOSE ENDEARING YOUNG CHARMS

BELIEVE ME, if all those endearing young charms,
    Which I gaze on so fondly to-day,
Were to change by to-morrow, and fleet in my arms,
    Like fairy-gifts fading away,
Thou wouldst still be adored, as this moment thou art,
    Let thy loveliness fade as it will,
And around the dear ruin each wish of my heart
    Would entwine itself verdantly still.

It is not while beauty and youth are thine own,
    And thy cheeks unprofaned by a tear,
That the fervor and faith of a soul may be known,
    To which time will but make thee more dear!

No, the heart that has truly loved never forgets,
But as truly loves on to the close,
As the sunflower turns to her god when he sets
The same look which she turned when he rose!

THOMAS MOORE.

THE LAKE OF THE DISMAL SWAMP

"THEY made her a grave too cold and damp
For a soul so warm and true;
And she's gone to the Lake of the Dismal Swamp,
Where all night long, by a firefly lamp,
She paddles her white canoe.
And her firefly lamp I soon shall see,
And her paddle I soon shall hear;
Long and loving our life shall be,
And I'll hide the maid in a cypress tree,
When the footstep of death is near."

Away to the Dismal Swamp he speeds,—
His path was rugged and sore,

Through tangled juniper, beds of reeds,
Through many a fen where the serpent feeds,
And man never trod before.

And when on the earth he sank to sleep,
If slumber his eyelids knew,
He lay where the deadly vine doth weep
Its venomous tear, and nightly steep
The flesh with blistering dew!

And near him the she-wolf stirr'd the brake,
And the copper-snake breathed in his ear,
Till he starting cried, from his dream awake,
"Oh when shall I see the dusky Lake,
And the white canoe of my dear?"

He saw the Lake, and a meteor bright
Quick over its surface play'd,—
"Welcome," he said, "my dear one's light!"
And the dim shore echo'd for many a night
The name of the death-cold maid.

Till he hollow'd a boat of the birchen bark,
    Which carried him off from shore;
Far, far he follow'd the meteor spark,
The wind was high and the clouds were dark,
    And the boat return'd no more.

But oft, from the Indian hunter's camp,
    This lover and maid so true
Are seen at the hour of midnight damp
To cross the Lake by a firefly lamp,
    And paddle their white canoe!

THOMAS MOORE.

KATE KEARNEY

OH! DID you ne'er hear of Kate Kearney?
She lives on the banks of Killarney:
From the glance of her eye, shun danger and fly,
For fatal's the glance of Kate Kearney.

For that eye is so modestly beaming,
You ne'er think of mischief she's dreaming:
Yet, oh! I can tell, how fatal's the spell,
That lurks in the eye of Kate Kearney.

O should you e'er meet this Kate Kearney,
Who lives on the banks of Killarney,
Beware of her smile, for many a wile
Lies hid in the smile of Kate Kearney.

Though she looks so bewitchingly simple,
Yet there's mischief in every dimple,
And who dares inhale her sigh's spicy gale,
Must die by the breath of Kate Kearney.

SADY MORGAN.

IF I HAD KNOWN

IF I HAD known what trouble you were bearing;
What griefs were in the silence of your face;
I would have been more gentle, and more caring,
And tried to give you gladness for a space.
I would have brought more warmth into the place,
    If I had known.

If I had known what thoughts despairing drew you;
(Why do we never try to understand?)
I would have lent a little friendship to you,
And slipped my hand within your hand,
And made your stay more pleasant in the land,
    If I had known.

MARY CAROLYN DAVIES.

LOVE ME LITTLE, LOVE ME LONG

LOVE ME little, love me long,
Is the burden of my song:
Love that is too hot and strong
    Burneth soon to waste.
I am with little well content,
And a little from thee sent
Is enough, with true intent,
    To be steadfast friend.
Love me little, love me long,
Is the burden of my song.

Say thou lov'st me while thou live,
I to thee my love will give,
Never dreaming to deceive
    While that life endures:
Nay, and after death in sooth,
I to thee will keep my truth,
As now when in my May of youth,
    This my love assures.
Love me little, love me long,
Is the burden of my song.

Constant love is moderate ever,
And it will through life persever,
Give to me that with true endeavor.
    I will it restore:
A suit of durance let it be,
For all weathers, that for me,
For the land or for the sea,
    Lasting evermore.
Love me little, love me long,
Is the burden of my song.

UNKNOWN.

LOVE'S PHILOSOPHY

THE FOUNTAINS mingle with the river,
    And the rivers with the ocean;
The winds of heaven mix forever,
    With a sweet emotion;
Nothing in the world is single;
    All things by a law divine
In one another's being mingle:—
    Why not I with thine?

See! the mountains kiss high heaven,
    And the waves clasp one another;
No sister flower would be forgiven
    If it disdained its brother;
And the sunlight clasps the earth,
    And the moonbeams kiss the sea:—
What are all these kissings worth,
    If thou kiss not me?

PERCY BYSSHE SHELLEY.

AD FINEM

ON THE white throat of the useless passion
    That scorched my soul with its burning breath
I clutched my fingers in murderous fashion,
    And gathered them close in a grip of death;

14

For why should I fan, or feed with fuel,
　　A love that showed me but blank despair?
So my hold was firm, and my grasp was cruel—
　　I meant to strangle it then and there!

I thought it was dead. But with no warning,
　　It rose from its grave last night, and came
And stood by my bed till the early morning,
　　And over and over it spoke your name.
Its throat was red where my hands had held it;
　　It burned my brow with its scorching breath;
And I said, the moment my eyes beheld it,
　　"A love like this can know no death."

For just one kiss that your lips have given
　　In the lost and beautiful past to me,
I would gladly barter my hopes of Heaven
　　And all the bliss of Eternity.
For never a joy are the angels keeping,
　　To lay at my feet in Paradise,
Like that of into your strong arms creeping,
　　And looking into your love-lit eyes.

I know, in the way that sins are reckoned,
　　This thought is a sin of the deepest dye;
But I know, too, if an angel beckoned,
　　Standing close by the Throne on High,
And you, adown by the gates infernal,
　　Should open your loving arms and smile,
I would turn my back on things supernal,
　　To lie on your breast a little while.

To know for an hour you were mine completely—
　　Mine in body and soul, my own—
I would bear unending tortures sweetly,
　　With not a murmur and not a moan.
A lighter sin or a lesser error
　　Might change through hope or fear divine;
But there is no fear, and hell has no terror,
　　To change or alter a love like mine.

ELLA WHEELER WILCOX.

ALL PATHS LEAD TO YOU

ALL paths lead to you
Where e'er I stray,
You are the evening star
At the end of day.

All paths lead to you
Hill-top or low,
You are the white birch
In the sun's glow.

All paths lead to you
Where e'er I roam.
You are the lark-song
Calling me home!

BLANCHE SHOEMAKER WAGSTAFF.

THE ABIDING LOVE

IT SINGETH low in every heart,
We hear it each and all—
A song of those who answer not,
However we may call;
They throng the silence of the breast,
We see them as of yore—
The kind, the brave, the sweet,
Who walk with us no more.

'Tis hard to take the burden up
When these have laid it down;
They brightened all the joy of life,
They softened every frown;
But, Oh, 'tis good to think of them
When we are troubled sore!
Thanks be to God that such have been.
Although they are no more.

More homelike seems the vast unknown
Since they have entered there;
To follow them were not so hard,
Wherever they may fare;

They cannot be where God is **not**,
   On any sea or shore;
Whate'er betides, thy love abides,
   Our God, forever more.

          JOHN WHITE CHADWICK.

TO A FRIEND

You ENTERED my life in a casual way,
   And saw at a glance what I needed;
There were others who passed me or met me each **day,**
   But never a one of them heeded.
Perhaps you were thinking of other folks more,
   Or chance simply seemed to decree it;
I know there were many such chances before,
   But the others—well, they didn't see it.

You said just the thing that I wished you would **say,**
   And you made me believe that you meant it;
I held up my head in the old gallant way,
   And resolved you should never repent it.
There are times when encouragement means such a **lot,**
   And a word is enough to convey it;
There were others who could have, as easy as not—
   But, just the same, they didn't say it.

There may have been someone who could have done **more**
   To help me along, though I doubt it;
What I needed was cheering, and always before
   They had let me plod onward without it.
You helped to refashion the dream of my **heart,**
   And made me turn eagerly to it;
There were others who might have (I question that part)—
   But, after all, they didn't do it!

          GRACE STRICKER DAWSON.

KASHMIRI SONG

PALE HANDS I love beside the Shalimar,
   Where are you now? Who lies beneath your **spell?**
Whom do you lead on Rapture's Roadway, **far,**
   Before you agonize them in farewell?

17

Oh, pale dispensers of my Joys and Pains,
  Holding the doors of Heaven and of Hell,
How the hot blood rushed wildly through the veins
  Beneath your touch, until you waved farewell.

Pale hands, pink-tipped, like Lotus buds that float
  On those cool waters where we used to dwell,
I would have rather felt you round my throat
  Crushing out life than waving me farewell!

LAURENCE HOPE

MY LIFE IS A BOWL

MY LIFE is a bowl which is mine to brim
  With loveliness old and new.
So I fill its clay from stem to rim
    With you, dear heart,
        With you.

My life is a pool which can only hold
  One star and a glimpse of blue.
But the blue and the little lamp of gold
    Are you, dear heart,
        Are you.

My life is a homing bird that flies
  Through the starry dusk and dew
Home to the heaven of your true eyes,
    Home, dear heart,
        To you.

MAY RILEY SMITH.

A MILE WITH ME

O WHO will walk a mile with me
  Along life's merry way?
A comrade blithe and full of glee,
Who dares to laugh out loud and free,

And let his frolic fancy play,
Like a happy child, through the flowers gay
That fill the field and fringe the way
   Where he walks a mile with me.

And who will walk a mile with me
   Along life's weary way?
A friend whose heart has eyes to see
The stars shine out o'er the darkening lea,
And the quiet rest at the end o' the day,—
A friend who knows, and dares to say,
The brave, sweet words that cheer the way
   Where he walks a mile with me.

With such a comrade, such a friend,
I fain would walk till journey's end,
Through summer sunshine, winter rain,
And then?—Farewell, we shall meet again!

              HENRY VAN DYKE.

AN OLD SWEETHEART OF MINE

AN OLD SWEETHEART of mine!——Is this her presence here with me,
Or but a vain creation of a lover's memory?
A fair, illusive vision that would vanish into air,
Dared I even touch the silence with the whisper of a prayer?

Nay, let me then believe in all the blended false and true—
The semblance of the old love and the substance of the *new*,—
The *then* of changeless sunny days—the *now* of shower and shine—
But Love forever smiling—as that old sweetheart of mine.

This ever restful sense of *home* though shouts ring in the hall,—
The easy chair—the old book-shelves and prints along the wall;
The rare *Habanas* in their box, or gaunt churchwarden-stem
That often wags, above the jar, derisively at them.

As one who cons at evening o'er an album, all alone,
And muses on the faces of the friends that he has known,
So I turn the leaves of Fancy, till, in a shadowy design,
I find the smiling features of an old sweetheart of mine.

The lamplight seems to glimmer with a flicker of surprise,
As I turn it low—to rest me of the dazzle in my eyes,
And light my pipe in silence, save a sigh that seems to yoke
Its fate with my tobacco and to vanish with the smoke.

'Tis a *fragrant* retrospection,—for the loving thoughts that start
Into being are like perfume from the blossom of the heart;
And to dream the old dreams over is a luxury divine—
When my truant fancies wander with that old sweetheart of mine.

Though I hear beneath my study, like a fluttering of wings,
The voices of my children and the mother as she sings—
I feel no twinge of conscience to deny me any theme
When Care has cast her anchor in the harbor of a dream—

In fact, to speak in earnest, I believe it adds a charm
To spice the good a trifle with a little dust of harm,—
For I find an extra flavor in Memory's mellow wine
That makes me drink the deeper to that old sweetheart of mine.

O Childhood-days enchanted! O the magic of the Spring!—
With all green boughs to blossom white, and all bluebirds to sing!
When all the air, to toss and quaff, made life a jubilee
And changed the children's song and laugh to shrieks of ecstasy.

With eyes half closed in clouds that ooze from lips that taste, as well,
The peppermint and cinnamon, I hear the old school bell,
And from "Recess" romp in again from "Blackman's" broken line,
To smile, behind my "lesson", at that old sweetheart of mine.

A face of lily beauty, with a form of airy grace,
Float out of my tobacco as the Genii from the vase;
And I thrill beneath the glances of a pair of azure eyes
As glowing as the summer and as tender as the skies.

I can see the pink sunbonnet and the little checkered dress
She wore when first I kissed her and she answered the caress
With the written declaration that, "as surely as the vine
Grew 'round the stump" she loved me—that old sweetheart of mine.

Again I made her presents, in a really helpless way,—
The big "Rhode Island Greening"—I was hungry, too, that day!—
But I follow her from Spelling, with her hand behind her—so—
And I slip the apple in it—and the Teacher doesn't know!

I give my *treasures* to her—all,—my pencil—blue and red;—
And, if little girls played marbles, *mine* should all be *hers,* instead!
But *she* gave me her *photograph,* and printed "Ever Thine"
Across the back—in blue and red—that old sweetheart of mine!

And again I feel the pressure of her slender little hand,
As we used to talk together of the future we had planned,—
When I should be a poet, and with nothing else to do
But write the tender verses that she set the music to . . .

Then we should live together in a cozy little cot
Hid in a nest of roses, with a fairy garden spot,
Where the vines were ever fruited, and the weather ever fine,
And the birds were ever singing for that old sweetheart of mine.

When I should be her lover forever and a day,
And she my faithful sweetheart till the golden hair was gray;
And we should be so happy that when either's lips were dumb
They would not smile in Heaven till the other's kiss had come.

But, ah! my dream is broken by a step upon the stair,
And the door is softly opened, and—my wife is standing there;
Yet with eagerness and rapture all my vision I resign,—
To greet the *living* presence of that old sweetheart of mine.

JAMES WHITCOMB RILEY.

FELLOWSHIP

WHEN a feller hasn't got a cent
And is feelin' kind of blue,
And the clouds hang thick and dark
And won't let the sunshine thro',
It's a great thing, oh my brethren,
For a feller just to lay
His hand upon your shoulder in a friendly sort o' way.

It makes a man feel queerish,
It makes the tear-drops start.
And you kind o' feel a flutter
In the region of your heart.
You can't look up and meet his eye,
You don't know what to say
When a hand is on your shoulder in a friendly sort o' way.

Oh this world's a curious compound
With its honey and its gall;
Its cares and bitter crosses,
But a good world after all.
And a good God must have made it,
Leastwise that is what I say,
When a hand is on your shoulder in a friendly sort o' way.

UNKNOWN.

A WOMAN'S QUESTION

Do YOU KNOW you have asked for the costliest thing
Ever made by the Hand above?
A woman's heart, and a woman's life—
And a woman's wonderful love.

Do you know you have asked for this priceless thing
As a child might ask for a toy?
Demanding what others have died to win,
With the reckless dash of a boy.

You have written my lesson of duty out;
Manlike, you have questioned me.
Now stand at the bar of my woman's soul
Until I shall question thee.

You require your mutton shall be always hot,
Your socks and your shirt be whole;
I require your heart to be true as God's stars
And as pure as His heaven your soul.

You require a cook for your mutton and beef,
I require a far greater thing;
A seamstress you're wanting for socks and shirts—
I look for a man and a king.

A king for the beautiful realm called Home,
And a man that his Maker, God,
Shall look upon as He did on the first
And say: "It is very good."

22

I am fair and young, but the rose may fade
From my soft young cheek one day;
Will you love me then 'mid the falling leaves,
As you did 'mong the blossoms of May?

Is your heart an ocean so strong and deep,
I may launch my all on its tide?
A loving woman finds heaven or hell
On the day she is made a bride.

I require all things that are grand and true,
All things that a man should be;
If you give this all, I would stake my life
To be all you demand of me.

If you cannot be this, a laundress and cook
You can hire and little to pay;
But a woman's heart and a woman's life
Are not to be won that way.

LENA LATHROP.

ANY WIFE OR HUSBAND

LET us be guests in one another's house
With deferential "No" and courteous "Yes;"
Let us take care to hide our foolish moods
Behind a certain show of cheerfulness.

Let us avoid all sullen silences;
We should find fresh and sprightly things to say;
I must be fearful lest you find me dull,
And you must dread to bore me any way.

Let us knock gently at each other's heart,
Glad of a chance to look within—and yet
Let us remember that to force one's way
Is the unpardoned breach of etiquette.

So shall I be hostess—you, the host—
Until all need for entertainment ends;
We shall be lovers when the last door shuts,
But what is better still—we shall be friends.

CAROL HAYNES.

TO MY UNBORN SON

"My son!" What simple, beautiful words!
  "My boy!" What a wonderful phrase!
We're counting the months till you come to us—
  The months, and the weeks, and the days!

"The new little stranger," some babes are called,
  But that's not what you're going to be;
With double my virtues and half of my faults,
  You can't be a stranger to me!

Your mother is straight as a sapling plant,
  The cleanest and best of her clan—
You're bone of her bone, and flesh of her flesh,
  And, by heaven, we'll make you a man!

Soon I shall take you in two strong arms—
  You that shall howl for joy—
With a simple, passionate, wonderful pride
  Because you are just—my boy!

And you shall lie in your mother's arms,
  And croon at your mother's breast,
And I shall thank God I am there to shield
  The two that I love the best.

A wonderful thing is a breaking wave,
  And sweet is the scent of spring,
But the silent voice of an unborn babe
  Is God's most beautiful thing.

We're listening now to that silent voice
  And waiting, your mother and I—
Waiting to welcome the fruit of our love
  When you come to us by and by.

We're hungry to show you a wonderful world
  With wonderful things to be done,
We're aching to give you the best of us both
  And we're lonely for you—my son!

CAPTAIN CYRIL MORTON THORNE.

24

LOVE

I LOVE YOU,
Not only for what you are,
But for what I am
When I am with you.

I love you,
Not only for what
You have made of yourself,
But for what
You are making of me.

I love you
For the part of me
That you bring out;
I love you
For putting your hand
Into my heaped-up heart
And passing over
All the foolish, weak things
That you can't help
Dimly seeing there,
And for drawing out
Into the light
All the beautiful belongings
That no one else had looked
Quite far enough to find.

I love you because you
Are helping me to make
Of the lumber of my life
Not a tavern
But a temple;
Out of the works
Of my every day
Not a reproach
But a song.

I love you
Because you have done
More than any creed
Could have done

To make me good,
And more than any fate
Could have done
To make me happy.

You have done it
Without a touch,
Without a word,
Without a sign.
You have done it
By being yourself.
Perhaps that is what
Being a friend means,
After all.

ROY CROFT.

HER ANSWER

TODAY, dear heart, but just today,
   The sunshine over all,
The roses crimsoning the air
   Along the garden wall!
Then let the dream and dreamer die
   Whate'er shall be, shall be—
Today will still be thine and mine
   To all eternity.

And oh, there is no glory, dear,
   When all the world is done;
There is no splendor lasteth out
   The sinking of the sun;
There is no thing that lasts, not one,
   When we have turned to clay,
But this: you loved me—all the rest
   Fades with the world away.

So little while, so little while,
   This world shall last for us:
There is no way to keep it, dear,
   But just to spend it thus:

There is no hand may stop the sand
  From flowing fast away,
But his who turns the whole glass down
  And dreams 'tis all today!

JOHN BENNETT.

IN A ROSE GARDEN

A HUNDRED YEARS from now, dear heart,
  We shall not care at all,
It will not matter then a whit,
  The honey or the gall.
The summer days that we have known
Will all forgotten be and flown;
The garden will be overgrown
  Where now the roses fall.

A hundred years from now, dear heart,
  We shall not mind the pain;
The throbbing crimson tide of life
  Will not have left a stain.
The song we sing together, dear,
The dream we dream together here,
Will mean no more than means a tear
  Amid a summer rain.

A hundred years from now, dear heart,
  The grief will all be o'er;
The sea of care will surge in vain
  Upon a careless shore.
These glasses we turn down today
Here at the parting of the way—
We shall be wineless then as they,
  And shall not mind it more.

A hundred years from now, dear heart,
  We'll neither know nor care
What came of all life's bitterness,
  Or followed love's despair.
Then fill the glasses up again,
And kiss me through the rose-leaf rain;
We'll build one castle more in Spain,
  And dream one more dream there.

JOHN BENNETT.

SLEEP SWEET

SLEEP sweet within this quiet room,
  O thou, whoe'er thou art,
And let no mournful yesterdays
  Disturb thy peaceful heart.

Nor let tomorrow mar thy rest
  With dreams of coming ill:
Thy Maker is thy changeless friend,
  His love surrounds thee still.

Forget thyself and all the world,
  Put out each garish light:
The stars are shining overhead—
  Sleep sweet! Good night! Good night!

ELLEN M. HUNTINGTON GATES.

MIDSUMMER

You LOVED me for a little,
  Who could not love me long;
You gave me wings of gladness
  And lent my spirit song.

You loved me for an hour
  But only with your eyes;
Your lips I could not capture
  By storm or by surprise.

Your mouth that I remember
  With rush of sudden pain
As one remembers starlight
  Or roses after rain . . .

Out of a world of laughter
  Suddenly I am sad. . . .
Day and night it haunts me,
  The kiss I never had.

SYDNEY KING RUSSELL.

BILLY BOY

OH, WHERE HAVE YOU BEEN, Billy boy, Billy boy,
Oh, where have you been, charming Billy?
I have been to seek a wife, she's the joy of my young life,
She's a young thing and cannot leave her mother.

Did she ask you to come in, Billy boy, Billy boy,
Did she ask you to come in, charming Billy?
She did ask me to come in, with a dimple in her chin,
She's a young thing and cannot leave her mother.

Did she ask you to sit down, Billy boy, Billy boy,
Did she ask you to sit down, charming Billy?
She did ask me to sit down, with a curtsey to the ground,
She's a young thing and cannot leave her mother.

Did she set for you a chair, Billy boy, Billy boy,
Did she set for you a chair, charming Billy?
Yes, she set for me a chair, she's got ringlets in her hair,
She's a young thing and cannot leave her mother.

How old is she, Billy boy, Billy boy,
How old is she, charming Billy?
She's three times six, four times seven, twenty-eight and eleven,
She's a young thing and cannot leave her mother.

How tall is she, Billy boy, Billy boy,
How tall is she, charming Billy?
She's as tall as any pine and as straight 's a pumpkin vine,
She's a young thing and cannot leave her mother.

Can she make a cherry pie, Billy boy, Billy boy,
Can she make a cherry pie, charming Billy?
She can make a cherry pie, quick 's a cat can wink her eye,
She's a young thing and cannot leave her mother.

Does she often go to church, Billy boy, Billy boy,
Does she often go to church, charming Billy?
Yes, she often goes to church, with her bonnet white as birch,
She's a young thing and cannot leave her mother.

Can she make a pudding well, Billy boy, Billy boy,
Can she make a pudding well, charming Billy?

29

She can make a pudding well, I can tell it by the smell,
She's a young thing and cannot leave her mother.

Can she make a feather-bed, Billy boy, Billy boy,
Can she make a feather-bed, charming Billy?
She can make a feather-bed, place the pillows at the head,
She's a young thing and cannot leave her mother.

Can she card and can she spin, Billy boy, Billy boy,
Can she card and can she spin, charming Billy?
She can card and she can spin, she can do most anything,
She's a young thing and cannot leave her mother.

UNKNOWN.

IF YOU BUT KNEW

If you but knew
How all my days seemed filled with dreams of you,
How sometimes in the silent night
Your eyes thrill through me with their tender light,
How oft I hear your voice when others speak,
How you 'mid other forms I seek—
Oh, love more real than though such dreams were true
If you but knew.

Could you but guess
How you alone make all my happiness,
How I am more than willing for your sake
To stand alone, give all and nothing take,
Nor chafe to think you bound while I am free,
Quite free, till death, to love you silently,
Could you but guess.

Could you but learn
How when you doubt my truth I sadly yearn
To tell you all, to stand for one brief space
Unfettered, soul to soul, as face to face,
To crown you king, my king, till life shall end,
My lover and likewise my truest friend,
Would you love me, dearest, as fondly in return,
Could you but learn?

UNKNOWN.

30

NEED OF LOVING

Folk need a lot of loving in the morning;
  The day is all before, with cares beset—
The cares we know, and they that give no warning;
  For love is God's own antidote for fret.

Folk need a heap of loving at the noontime—
  In the battle lull, the moment snatched from strife—
Halfway between the waking and the croontime,
  While bickering and worriment are rife.

Folk hunger so for loving at the nighttime,
  When wearily they take them home to rest—
At slumber song and turning-out-the-light time—
  Of all the times for loving, that's the best.

Folk want a lot of loving every minute—
  The sympathy of others and their smile!
Till life's end, from the moment they begin it,
  Folks need a lot of loving all the while.

STRICKLAND GILLILAN.

IF YOU'RE EVER GOING TO LOVE ME

If you're ever going to love me love me now, while I can know
All the sweet and tender feelings which from real affection flow.
Love me now, while I am living; do not wait till I am gone
And then chisel it in marble—warm love words on ice-cold stone.
If you've dear, sweet thoughts about me, why not whisper them to me?
Don't you know 'twould make me happy and as glad as glad could be?
If you wait till I am sleeping, ne'er to waken here again,
There'll be walls of earth between us and I couldn't hear you then.
If you knew someone was thirsting for a drop of water sweet
Would you be so slow to bring it? Would you step with laggard feet?
There are tender hearts all round us who are thirsting for our love;
Why withhold from them what nature makes them crave all else above?
I won't need your kind caresses when the grass grows o'er my face;
I won't crave your love or kisses in my last low resting place.
So, then, if you love me any, if it's but a little bit,
Let me know it now while living; I can own and treasure it.

UNKNOWN.

31

I'LL REMEMBER YOU, LOVE, IN MY PRAYERS

WHEN the curtains of night are pinned back by the stars,
  And the beautiful moon leaps the skies,
And the dewdrops of heaven are kissing the rose,
  It is then that my memory flies
As if on the wings of some beautiful dove
  In haste with the message it bears
To bring you a kiss of affection and say:
  I'll remember you, love, in my prayers.

Chorus:

Go where you will, on land or on sea,
  I'll share all your sorrows and cares;
And at night, when I kneel by my bedside to **pray**
  I'll remember you, love, in my prayers.

I have loved you too fondly to ever forget
  The love you have spoken to me;
And the kiss of affection still warm on my lips
  When you told me how true you would be.
I know not if fortune be fickle or friend,
  Or if time on your memory wears;
I know that I love you wherever you roam,
  And remember you, love, in my prayers.

When angels in heaven are guarding the good,
  As God has ordained them to do,
In answer to prayers I have offered to Him,
  I know there is one watching you.
And may its bright spirit be with you through life
  To guide you up heaven's bright stairs,
And meet with the one who has loved you so true
  And remembered you, love, in her prayers.

UNKNOWN

IS IT A SIN TO LOVE THEE?

Is IT a sin to love thee? Then my soul is deeply dyed,
For my lifeblood, as it gushes, takes its crimson from love's tide;
And I feel its waves roll o'er me and the blushes mount my brow
And my pulses quicken wildly, as the love dreams come and go:

I feel my spirit's weakness; I know my spirit's power;
I have felt my proud heart struggle in temptation's trying hour;
Yet, amid the din of conflict, bending o'er life's hallowed shrine,
Yielding all, my soul had murmured, I am thine, forever thine!

Is it a sin to love thee? What were existence worth,
Bereft of all the heaven that lingers still on earth!
Friendship's smiles, like gleams of sunlight, shed their feeling o'er the
    heart,
But the soul still cries for something more than friendship can im-
    part.
Frozen hearts, like ice-bound eyries, that no summer ray can melt,
Vainly boast their power to conquer what their hearts have never felt;
But envy not their glory, 'mid the rapture that is mine,
When with earnest soul I tell thee I am thine, forever thine!

Is it a sin to love three? Gentle voices round me fall,
And I press warm hearts about me—but I've given thee my all.
What though stern fate divides us, and our hands, not hearts, be
    riven—
My all of earth thou hast—wilt more? I dare not offer heaven!
But in some blessed moment, when our dark eyes flashing meet,
When I feel thy power so near me, feel thy heart's quick pulses beat,
Then I know—may God forgive me!—I would everything resign
All I have, or all I hope for—to be thine—forever thine.

Is it a sin to love thee? I remember well the hour
When we would our love to conquer, resist temptations' power;
When I felt my heart was breaking and my all of life was gone;
When I wept the hour I met thee, and the hour that I was born;
But a hidden storm was raging, and amid the muffled din
I flung my arms upon thy bosom, with thy warm hands clasped in mine,
I smiled through tears and murmured: I am thine, forever thine.

Is it a sin to love thee? with love's signet on thy brow?
Though thy lot be dark as Hades I'll cling to thee as now;
Not mine the heart to fail thee, when other cheeks grow pale;
We have shared the storm together; I'll stand by thee through the gale.
Though our bark may drift asunder, yet, with true hearts beating high,
Let the golden sunlight cheer us, or the angry storm clouds fly.
From our helms with steady brightness our beacon lights shall shine,
And the watchwords on our pennons shall be—thine, forever thine.

Is it a sin to love thee? When I bend the knee in prayer,
And before a High Omniscience my burdened heart lay bare,

On the breath of love to heaven ascends thy blessed name,
And I plead weak and erring nature, if loving thee be shame.
Heaven knows 'tis no light sacrifice I've offered up to thee,
No gilded dream of fancy, but my being's destiny.
Since our fates we may not conquer here, divide thy lot from mine—
In the starlit world above us, call me thine—forever thine!

UNKNOWN.

WE HAVE LIVED AND LOVED TOGETHER

WE HAVE LIVED and loved together
 Through many changing years;
We have shared each other's gladness
 And wept each other's tears;
I have known ne'er a sorrow
 That was long unsoothed by thee;
For thy smiles can make a summer
 Where darkness else would be.

Like the leaves that fall around us
 In autumn's fading hours,
Are the traitor's smiles, that darken
 When the cloud of sorrow lowers;
And though many such we've known, love,
 Too prone, alas, to range,
We both can speak of one love
 Which time can never change.

We have lived and loved together
 Through many changing years,
We have shared each other's gladness
 And wept each other's tears.
And let us hope the future,
 As the past has been will be:
I will share with thee my sorrows,
 And thou thy joys with me.

CHARLES JEFFERYS.

WILL YOU LOVE ME WHEN I'M OLD?

I WOULD ASK of you, my darling,
 A question soft and low,
That gives me many a heartache
 As the moments come and go.

34

Your love I know is truthful,
  But the truest love grows cold;
It is this that I would ask you:
  Will you love me when I'm old?

    Life's morn will soon be waning,
      And its evening bells be tolled,
    But my heart shall know no sadness,
      If you'll love me when I'm old.

Down the stream of life together
  We are sailing side by side,
Hoping some bright day to anchor
  Safe beyond the surging tide.
Today our sky is cloudless,
  But the night may clouds unfold;
But, though storms may gather round us,
  Will you love me when I'm old?

When my hair shall shade the snowdrift,
  And mine eyes shall dimmer grow,
I would lean upon some loved one,
  Through the valley as I go.
I would claim of you a promise,
  Worth to me a world of gold;
It is only this, my darling,
  That you'll love me when I'm old.

                              UNKNOWN.

YOU AND I

My hand is lonely for your clasping, dear;
  My ear is tired waiting for your call.
I want your strength to help, your laugh to cheer;
  Heart, soul and senses need you, one and all.
I droop without your full, frank sympathy;
  We ought to be together—you and I;
We want each other so, to comprehend
  The dream, the hope, things planned, or seen, or wrought.
Companion, comforter and guide and friend,
  As much as love asks love, does thought ask thought.
Life is so short, so fast the lone hours fly,
  We ought to be together, you and I.

                              HENRY ALFORD.

HE AND SHE

"SHE is dead!" they said to him; "come away;
Kiss her and leave her—thy love is clay!"

They smoothed her tresses of dark brown hair;
On her forehead of stone they laid it fair;

With a tender touch they closed up well
The sweet thin lips that had secrets to tell;

About her brows and beautiful face
They tied her veil and her marriage lace;

And over her bosom they crossed her hands,
"Come away!" they said; "God understands."

And they held their breath till they left the room,
With a shudder, to glance at its stillness and gloom.

But he who loved her too well to dread
The sweet, the stately, the beautiful dead,

He lighted his lamp and took the key
And turned it—alone again, he and she.

He and she; yet she would not smile,
Though he called her the name she loved erewhile.

He and she; but she would not speak,
Though he kissed, in the old place, the quiet cheek.

He and she; still she did not move
To any one passionate whisper of love.

Then he said: "Cold lips and breast without breath,
Is there no voice, no language of death,

"Dumb to the ear and still to the sense,
But to heart and to soul distinct, intense?

"See now; I will listen with soul, not ear.
What was the secret of dying, dear?

36

"Was it the infinite wonder of all
That you ever could let life's flower fall;

"Or was it a greater marvel to feel
The perfect calm o'er the agony steal?

"Was the miracle greater to find how deep
Beyond all dreams sank downward that sleep?

"Did life roll back its records, dear;
And show, as they say it does, past things clear?

"And was it the innermost part of the bliss
To find out so, what a wisdom love is?

"O perfect dead! O dead most dear,
I hold the breath of my soul to hear!

"There must be pleasure in dying, sweet,
To make you so placid from head to feet!

"I would tell you, darling, if I were dead,
And 't were your hot tears upon my brow shed—

"I would say, though the Angel of Death had laid
His sword on my lips to keep it unsaid.

"You should not ask vainly, with streaming eyes,
Which of all deaths was the chiefest surprise,

"The very strangest and suddenest thing
Of all the surprises that dying must bring."

Ah, foolish world! O most kind dead!
Though he told me, who will believe it was said?

Who will believe that he heard her say,
With the sweet, soft voice, in the dear old way;

"The utmost wonder is this—I hear,
And see you, and love you, and kiss you, dear;

"And am your angel, who was your bride,
And know that, though dead, I have never died."

SIR EDWIN ARNOLD.

LIGHT

THE NIGHT has a thousand eyes,
    The day but one;
Yet the light of the bright world dies
    With the dying sun.

The mind has a thousand eyes,
    And the heart but one;
Yet the light of a whole life dies
    When its love is done.

FRANCIS W. BOURDILLON.

REWARD OF SERVICE

THE SWEETEST lives are those to duty wed,
Whose deeds both great and small
Are close-knit strands of an unbroken thread,
Where love ennobles all.
The world may sound no trumpets, ring no bells,
The Book of Life the slurring record tells.

Thy love shall chant its own beatitudes,
After its own like working. A child's kiss
Set on thy singing lips shall make thee glad;
A poor man served by thee shall make thee rich;
A sick man helped by thee shall make thee strong;
Thou shalt be served thyself by every sense
Of service which thou renderest.

ELIZABETH BARRETT BROWNING.

OSSIAN'S SERENADE

OH, COME WITH ME in my little canoe,
Where the sea is calm, and the sky is blue!
Oh, come with me, for I long to go
To those isles where the mango apples grow!

Oh, come with me and be my love!
For thee the jungle depth I'll rove;
I'll gather the honeycomb bright as gold,
And chase the elk to its secret hold.

Refrain:

I'll chase the antelope over the plain,
The tiger's cub I'll bind with a chain,
And the wild gazelle, with its silvery feet,
I'll give thee for a playmate sweet.

I'll climb the palm for the bia's nest,
Red peas I'll gather to deck thy breast;
I'll pierce the cocoa's cup for its wine,
And haste to thee, if thou'lt be mine.
Then come with me in my light canoe,
While the sea is calm and the sky is blue,
For should we linger another day,
Storms may arise and love decay.

Oh, come if the love thou hast for me
Is pure and fresh as mine for thee—
Fresh as the fountain under ground,
When first 'tis by the lapwing found!
Our sands are bare, and down their slope,
The silvery-footed antelope,
As gracefully and gaily springs,
As o'er the marble courts of kings.

MAJOR CALDER CAMPBELL.

AMONG THE BEAUTIFUL PICTURES

AMONG the beautiful pictures
    That hang on Memory's wall,
Is one of a dim old forest,
    That seemeth best of all;
Not for its gnarled oaks olden,
    Dark with the mistletoe:
Not for the violets golden
    That sprinkle the vale below;

39

Not for the milk-white lilies,
   That lean from the fragrant ledge,
Coquetting all day with the sunbeams,
   And stealing their golden edge;
Not for the vines on the upland,
   Where the bright red berries rest,
Nor the pinks, nor the pale sweet cowslip,
   It seemeth to me the best.

I once had a little brother
   With eyes that were dark and deep;
In the lap of that dim old forest
   He lieth in peace asleep;
Light as the down of the thistle,
   Free as the winds that blow,
We roved there the beautiful summers,
   The summers of long ago;
But his feet on the hills grew weary,
   And one of the autumn eves,
I made for my little brother
   A bed of the yellow leaves.

Sweetly his pale arms folded
   My neck in a meek embrace,
As the light of immortal beauty
   Silently covered his face;
And when the arrows of sunset
   Lodged in the treetops bright,
He fell, in his saintlike beauty,
   Asleep by the gates of light.

Therefore, of all the pictures
   That hang on Memory's wall,
The one of the dim old forest
   Seemeth the best of all.

ALICE CARY.

CLEOPATRA DYING

SINKS the sun below the desert,
   Golden glows the sluggish Nile;
Purple flame crowns Spring and Temple,
   Lights up every ancient pile

Where the old gods now are sleeping;
  Isis and Osiris great,
Guard me, help me, give me courage
  Like a Queen to meet my fate.

"I am dying, Egypt, dying,"
  Let the Caesar's army come—
I will cheat him of his glory,
  Though beyond the Styx I roam;
Shall he drag this beauty with him—
  While the crowd his triumph sings?
No, no, never! I will show him
  What lies in the blood of Kings.

Though he hold the golden scepter,
  Rule the Pharaoh's sunny land,
Where old Nilus rolls resistless
  Through the sweeps of silvery sand—
He shall never say I met him
  Fawning, abject, like a slave—
I will foil him, though to do it
  I must cross the Stygian wave.

Oh, my hero, sleeping, sleeping—
  Shall I meet you on the shore
Of Plutonian shadows? Shall we
  In death meet and love once more?
See, I follow in your footsteps—
  Scorn the Caesar in his might;
For your love I will leap boldly
  Into realms of death and night.

Down below the desert sinking,
  Fades Apollo's brilliant car;
And from out the distant azure
  Breaks the bright gleam of a star.
Venus, Queen of Love and Beauty,
  Welcomes me to death's embrace,
Dying, free, proud, and triumphant,
  The last sovereign of my race.

Dying, dying! I am coming,
  Oh, my hero, to your arms;
You will welcome me, I know it—
  Guard me from all rude alarms.

Hark! I hear the legions coming,
  Hear the cries of triumph swell,
But, proud Caesar, dead I scorn you—
  Egypt, Antony, farewell.

THOMAS STEPHENS COLLIER.

MISS YOU

Miss you, miss you, miss you;
Everything I do
Echoes with the laughter
And the voice of You.
You're on every corner,
Every turn and twist,
Every old familiar spot
Whispers how you're missed.

Miss you, miss you, miss you!
Everywhere I go
There are poignant memories
Dancing in a row.
Silhouette and shadow
Of your form and face,
Substance and reality
Everywhere displace.

Oh, I miss you, miss you!
God! I miss you, Girl!
There's a strange, sad silence
'Mid the busy whirl,
Just as tho' the ordinary
Daily things I do
Wait with me, expectant
For a word from You.

Miss you, miss you, miss you!
Nothing now seems true
Only that 'twas heaven
Just to be with You.

DAVID CORY.

42

FRIENDSHIP

OH, THE COMFORT—the inexpressible comfort of feeling safe with a
  person,
Having neither to weigh thoughts,
Nor measure words—but pouring them
All right out—just as they are—
Chaff and grain together—
Certain that a faithful hand will
Take and sift them—
Keep what is worth keeping—
And with the breath of kindness
Blow the rest away.

DINAH MARIA MULOCK CRAIK.

NON SUM QUALIS ERAM BONAE SUB REGNO CYNARAE

LAST NIGHT, ah, yesternight, betwixt her lips and mine
There fell thy shadow, Cynara! Thy breath was shed
Upon my soul between the kisses and the wine;
And I was desolate and sick of an old passion—
Yea, I was desolate and bowed my head.
I have been faithful to thee, Cynara!—In my fashion.

All night upon mine heart I felt her warm heart beat,
Night-long within mine arms in love and sleep she lay;
Surely the kisses of her bought red mouth were sweet;
But I was desolate and sick of an old passion,
When I woke and found the dawn was gray:
I have been faithful to thee, Cynara!—In my fashion.

I have forgot much, Cynara! Gone with the wind,
Flung roses, roses riotously with the throng,
Dancing, to put thy pale, lost lilies out of mind;
But I was desolate and sick of an old passion—
Yea, all the time, because the dance was long:
I have been faithful to thee, Cynara!—In my fashion.

I cried for madder music and for stronger wine,
But when the feast is finished and the lamps expire,

Then falls thy shadow, Cynara! The night is thine;
And I am desolate and sick of an old passion,
Yea, hungry for the lips of my desire:
I have been faithful to thee, Cynara!—In my fashion.

ERNEST DOWSON.

YOU KISSED ME

You KISSED ME! My head drooped low on your breast
With a feeling of shelter and infinite rest,
While the holy emotions my tongue dared not speak,
Flashed up as in flame, from my heart to my cheek;
Your arms held me fast; oh! your arms were so bold—
Heart beat against heart in their passionate fold.
Your glances seemed drawing my soul through mine eyes,
As the sun draws the mist from the sea to the skies.
Your lips clung to mine till I prayed in my bliss
They might never unclasp from the rapturous kiss.

You kissed me! My heart, my breath and my will
In delirious joy for a moment stood still.
Life had for me then no temptations, no charms,
No visions of rapture outside of your arms;
And were I this instant an angel possessed
Of the peace and the joy that belong to the blest,
I would fling my white robes unrepiningly down,
I would tear from my forehead its beautiful crown,
To nestle once more in that haven of rest—
Your lips upon mine, my head on your breast.

You kissed me! My soul in a bliss so divine
Reeled and swooned like a drunkard when foolish with wine,
And I thought 'twere delicious to die there, if death
Would but come while my lips were yet moist with your breath:
While your arms clasped me round in that blissful embrace,
While your eyes melt in mine could e'en death e'er efface—
Oh, these are the questions I ask day and night:
Must my lips taste no more such exquisite delight?
Would you wish that your breast were my shelter as then?
And if you were here, would you kiss me again?

JOSEPHINE SLOCUM HUNT.

I WANT YOU

I WANT you when the shades of eve are falling
  And purpling shadows drift across the land;
When sleepy birds to loving mates are calling—
  I want the soothing softness of your hand.

I want you when the stars shine up above me,
  And Heaven's flooded with the bright moonlight;
I want you with your arms and lips to love me
  Throughout the wonder watches of the night.

I want you when in dreams I still remember
  The ling'ring of your kiss—for old times' sake—
With all your gentle ways, so sweetly tender,
  I want you in the morning when I wake.

I want you when the day is at its noontime,
  Sun-steeped and quiet, or drenched with sheets of rain;
I want you when the roses bloom in June-time;
  I want you when the violets come again.

I want you when my soul is thrilled with passion;
  I want you when I'm weary and depressed;
I want you when in lazy, slumbrous fashion
  My senses need the haven of your breast.

I want you when through field and wood I'm roaming;
  I want you when I'm standing on the shore;
I want you when the summer birds are homing—
  And when they've flown—I want you more and more.

I want you, dear, through every changing season;
  I want you with a tear or with a smile;
I want you more than any rhyme or reason—
  I want you, want you, want you—all the while.

ARTHUR L. GILLOM.

SONG

A PLACE in thy memory, dearest,
   Is all that I claim,
To pause and look back when thou hearest
   The sound of my name.
Another may woo thee nearer,
Another may win and wear;
I care not, though he be dearer,
If I am remembered there.

Could I be thy true lover, dearest,
   Couldst thou smile on me,
I would be the fondest and nearest
   That ever loved thee.
But a cloud o'er my pathway is glooming
Which never must break upon thine,
And Heaven, which made thee all blooming,
Ne'er made thee to wither on mine.

Remember me not as a lover
   Whose fond hopes are crossed,
Whose bosom can never recover
   The light it has lost;
As the young bride remembers the mother
She loves, yet never may see,
As a sister remembers a brother,
Oh, dearest, remember me.

GERALD GRIFFIN.

THE UNKNOWN

I DO not understand . . .
   They bring so many, many flowers to me—
Rainbows of roses, wreaths from every land;
   And hosts of solemn strangers come to see
My tomb here on these quiet, wooded heights.
   My tomb here seems to be
One of the sights.

The low-voiced men, who speak
    Of me quite fondly, call me "The Unknown";
But now and then at dusk, Madonna-meek,
    Bent, mournful mothers come to me alone
And whisper down—the flowers and grasses through—
    Such names as "Jim" and "John" . . .
I wish they knew.

And once my sweetheart came.
    She did not—nay, of course she could not—know,
But thought of me and crooned to me the name
    She called me by—how many years ago?
A very precious name. Her eyes were wet,
    Yet glowing, flaming so . . .
She won't forget.

E. O. LAUGHLIN.

FORGET THEE?

"FORGET thee?" If to dream by night and muse on thee by day,
If all the worship deep and wild a poet's heart can pay,
If prayers in absence breathed for thee to Heaven's protecting power,
If winged thoughts that flit to thee—a thousand in an hour—
If busy fancy blending thee with all my future lot—
If this thou call'st "forgetting," thou, indeed, shalt be forgot!

"Forget thee?" Bid the forest-birds forget their sweetest tune;
"Forget thee?" Bid the sea forget to swell beneath the moon;
Bid the thirsty flowers forget to drink the eve's refreshing dew;
Thyself forget thine own "dear land," and its "mountains wild and
    blue."
Forget each old familiar face, each long-remember'd spot—
When these things are forgot by thee, then thou shalt be forgot!

Keep, if thou wilt, thy maiden peace, still calm and fancy-free,
For God forbid thy gladsome heart should grow less glad for me;
Yet, while that heart is still unwon, oh! bid not mine to rove,
But let it nurse its humble faith and uncomplaining love;
If these, preserved for patient years, at last avail me not,
Forget me then; but ne'er believe that thou canst be forgot!

JOHN MOULTRIE.

THOU HAST WOUNDED THE SPIRIT THAT LOVED THEE

Thou hast wounded the spirit that loved thee,
  And cherished thine image for years,
Thou hast taught me at last to forget thee,
  In secret, in silence, and tears,
As a young bird when left by its mother,
  Its earliest pinions to try,
Round the nest will still lingering hover,
  Ere its trembling wings to try.

Thus we're taught in this cold world to smother
  Each feeling that once was so dear;
Like that young bird I'll seek to discover
  A home of affection elsewhere.
Though this heart may still cling to thee fondly
  And dream of sweet memories past,
Yet hope, like the rainbow of summer,
  Gives a promise of Lethe at last.

Like the sunbeams that play on the ocean,
  In tremulous touches of light,
Is the heart in its early emotion,
  Illumined with versions as bright.
Yet ofttimes beneath the waves swelling,
  A tempest will suddenly come,
All rudely and wildly dispelling
  The love of the happiest home.

MRS. DAVID PORTER.

FIDELIS

You have taken back the promise
  That you spoke so long ago;
Taken back the heart you gave me—
  I must even let it go.
Where Love once has breathed, Pride dieth;
  So I struggled, but in vain,
First to keep the links together,
  Then to piece the broken chain.

48

But it might not be—so freely
  All your friendship I restore,
And the heart that I had taken
  As my own forevermore.
No shade of reproach shall touch you,
  Dread no more a claim from me—
But I will not have you fancy
  That I count myself as free.

I am bound by the old promise;
  What can break that golden chain?
Not even the words that you have spoken,
  Or the sharpness of my pain:
Do you think, because you fail me
And draw back your hand today,
That from out the heart I gave you
  My strong love can fade away?

It will live. No eyes may see it;
  In my soul it will lie deep,
Hidden from all; but I shall feel it
  Often stirring in its sleep.
So remember that the friendship
  Which you now think poor and vain,
Will endure in hope and patience,
  Till you ask for it again.

Perhaps in some long twilight hour,
  Like those we have known of old,
When past shadows gather round you,
  And your present friends grow cold,
You may stretch your hands out towards me—
Ah! You will—I know not when—
I shall nurse my love and keep it
  Faithfully, for you, till then.

ADELAIDE ANNE PROCTER.

VASES

Two VASES stood on the Shelf of Life
  As Love came by to look,
One was of priceless cloisonné,
The other of solid common clay.
  Which do you think Love took?

He took them both from the Shelf of Life,
　　He took them both with a smile;
He clasped them both with his finger tips,
And touched them both with caressing lips,
　　And held them both for a while.

From tired hands Love let them fall,
　　And never a word was spoken.
One was of priceless cloisonné,
The other of solid common clay.
　　Which do you think was broken?

NAN TERRELL REED.

AND THEN NO MORE

I saw her once, one little while, and then no more:
'Twas Eden's light on earth awhile, and then no more.
Amid the throng she pass'd along the meadow-floor:
Spring seem'd to smile on earth awhile, and then no more;
But whence she came, which way she went, what garb she wore,
I noted not; I gazed awhile, and then no more.

I saw her once, one little while, and then no more:
'Twas Paradise on earth awhile, and then no more:
Ah! what avail my vigils pale, my magic lore?
She shone before mine eyes awhile, and then no more.
The shallop of my peace is wreck'd on Beauty's shore;
Near Hope's fair isle it rode awhile, and then no more.

I saw her once, one little while, and then no more.
Earth looked like heaven a little while, and then no more.
Her presence thrill'd and lighted to its inner core
My desert breast a little while, and then no more.
So may, perchance, a meteor glance at midnight o'er
Some ruin'd pile a little while, and then no more.

I saw her once, one little while, and then no more.
The earth was peri-land awhile, and then no more.
Oh, might I see but once again, as once before,
Through chance or wile, that shape awhile, and then no more!
Death soon would heal my griefs! This heart now sad and sore
Would beat anew a little while, and then no more.

FRIEDRICH RUECKERT.
Translated by James Clarence Mangon.

SONG

How PLEASANT it is that always
There's somebody older than you—
Someone to pet and caress you,
Someone to scold you, too!

Someone to call you a baby,
To laugh at you when you're wise;
Someone to care when you're sorry,
To kiss the tears from your eyes;

When life has begun to be weary,
And youth to melt like the dew,
To know, like the little children
Somebody's older than you.

The path cannot be so lonely,
For someone has trod it before;
The golden gates are the nearer,
That someone stands at the door.

I can think of nothing sadder
Than to feel, when days are few,
There's nobody left to lean on,
Nobody older than you!

The younger ones may be tender
To the feeble steps and slow;
But they can't talk the old times over—
Alas, how should they know!

'Tis a romance to them—a wonder
You were ever a child at play;
But the dear ones waiting in heaven
Know it is all as you say.

I know that the great All-Father
Loves us, and the little ones too;
Keep only childlike-hearted—
Heaven is older than you!

FLORENCE SMITH.

51

AT NIGHTFALL

I NEED so much the quiet of your love
    After the day's loud strife;
I need your calm all other things above
    After the stress of life.

I crave the haven that in your dear heart lies,
    After all toil is done;
I need the starshine of your heavenly eyes,
    After the day's great sun.

                CHARLES HANSON TOWNE.

CREED

I BELIEVE if I should die,
And you should kiss my eyelids when I lie
Cold, dead, and dumb to all the world contains,
The folded orbs would open at thy breath,
And, from its exile in the isles of death,
Life would come gladly back along my veins.

I believe if I were dead,
And you upon my lifeless heart should tread,
Not knowing what the poor clod chanced to be,
It would find sudden pulse beneath the touch
Of him it ever loved in life so much,
And throb again—warm, tender, true to thee.

I believe if on my grave,
Hidden in woody depths or by the wave,
Your eyes should drop some warm tears of regret,
From every salty seed of your dear grief
Some fair, sweet blossom would leap into leaf
To prove death could not make my love forget.

I believe if I should fade
Into those mystic realms where light is made,
And you should long once more my face to see,
I would come forth upon the hills of night
And gather stars, like fagots, till thy sight,
Led by their beacon blaze, fell full on me.

I believe my faith in thee,
Strong as my life, so nobly placed to be,
I would as soon expect to see the sun
Fall like a dead king from his height sublime,
His glory stricken from the throne of time,
As thee unworth the worship thou hast won.

I believe who hath not loved
Hath half the sweetness of his life unproved;
Like one who, with the grape within his grasp,
Drops it with all its crimson juice unpressed,
And all its luscious sweetness left unguessed,
Out from his careless and unheeding clasp.

I believe love, pure and true,
Is to the soul a sweet, immortal dew
That gems life's petals in its hours of dusk.
The waiting angels see and recognize
The rich crown jewel, Love, of Paradise,
When life falls from us like a withered husk.

MARY ASHLEY TOWNSEND.

QUIET WATERS

OUR LIVES float on quiet waters . . .
Down softly flowing streams,
Where silvery willows
Shadow calm waves.
Gentle bird-songs
And murmuring freshets
Leap from the woodland
In snowy circlets.
Green embowers us,
And fragrant mosses,
Spicy odors
That drift in the languid
Swaying breezes . . .

Our lives float on quiet waters . . .
And my Love and I
Wonder at twilight,
When flaming banners

53

Spread in the heavens,
How long this Beauty—
This stately silence . . .
E'er once again we shall drift
On the turbulent, open sea.

BLANCHE SHOEMAKER WAGSTAFF.

LORENA

THE YEARS creep slowly by, Lorena;
   The snow is on the grass again;
The sun's low down the sky, Lorena;
   The frost gleams where the flowers have been
But the heart throbs on as warmly now
   As when the summer days were nigh;
Oh! the sun can never dip so low
   Adown affection's cloudless sky.

A hundred months have passed, Lorena,
   Since last I held that hand in mine,
And felt the pulse beat fast, Lorena,
   Though mine beat faster far than thine.
A hundred months—'twas flowery May,
   When up the hilly slope we climbed,
To watch the dying of the day
   And hear the distant church bells chime.

We loved each other then, Lorena,
   More than we ever dared to tell;
And what we might have been, Lorena,
   Had but our loving prospered well!
But then, 'tis past; the years have gone,
   I'll not call up their shadowy forms;
I'll say to them, "Lost years, sleep on,
   Sleep on, nor heed life's pelting storms."

The story of the past, Lorena,
   Alas! I care not to repeat;
The hopes that could not last, Lorena,
   They lived, but only lived to cheat.

I would not cause e'en one regret
　　To rankle in your bosom now;
"For if we try we may forget,"
　　Were words of thine long years ago.

Yes, these were words of thine, Lorena—
　　They are within my memory yet;
They touched some tender chords, Lorena,
　　Which thrill and tremble with regret.
'Twas not the woman's heart which spoke—
　　Thy heart was always true to me;
A duty stern and piercing broke
　　The tie which linked my soul with thee.

It matters little now, Lorena,
　　The past is in the eternal past;
Our hearts will soon lie low, Lorena,
　　Life's tide is ebbing out so fast.
There is a future, oh, thank God!
　　Of life this is so small a part;
'Tis dust to dust beneath the sod,
　　But there, up there, 'tis heart to heart.

H. D. L. WEBSTER.

GROWING OLD

THE DAYS grow shorter, the nights grow longer;
　　The headstones thicken along the way;
And life grows sadder, but love grows stronger
　　For those who walk with us day by day.

The tear comes quicker, the laugh comes slower;
　　The courage is lesser to do and dare;
And the tide of joy in the heart falls lower,
　　And seldom covers the reefs of care.

But all true things in the world seem truer,
　　And the better things of earth seem best,
And friends are dearer, as friends are fewer,
　　And love is all as our sun dips west.

Then let us clasp hands as we walk together,
  And let us speak softly in low, sweet tone,
For no man knows on the morrow whether
  We two pass on—or but one alone.

ELLA WHEELER WILCOX.

I LOVE YOU

I LOVE your lips when they're wet with wine
  And red with a wild desire;
I love your eyes when the lovelight lies
  Lit with a passionate fire.
I love your arms when the warm white flesh
  Touches mine in a fond embrace;
I love your hair when the strands enmesh
  Your kisses against my face.

Not for me the cold, calm kiss
  Of a virgin's bloodless love;
Not for me the saint's white bliss,
  Nor the heart of a spotless dove.
But give me the love that so freely gives
  And laughs at the whole world's blame,
With your body so young and warm in my arms,
  It sets my poor heart aflame.

So kiss me sweet with your warm wet mouth,
  Still fragrant with ruby wine,
And say with a fervor born of the South
  That your body and soul are mine.
Clasp me close in your warm young arms,
  While the pale stars shine above,
And we'll live our whole young lives away
  In the joys of a living love.

ELLA WHEELER WILCOX.

THE WANT OF YOU

THE WANT of you is like no other thing;
  It smites my soul with sudden sickening;
It binds my being with a wreath of rue—
  This want of you.

56

It flashes on me with the waking sun;
It creeps upon me when the day is done;
It hammers at my heart the long night through—
  This want of you.

It sighs within me with the misting skies;
Oh, all the day within my heart it cries,
Old as your absence, yet each moment new—
  This want of you.

Mad with demand and aching with despair,
It leaps within my heart and you are—where?
God has forgotten, or he never knew—
  This want of you.

IVAN LEONARD WRIGHT.

ADMONITION

No, I AM THROUGH and you can call in vain.
  There is too great a fee for your caress;
Too great a share of heartbreak and of pain
  And all the kindred hurts of loneliness.
What does it mean at best? A fevered hour
  When I forget that you are not for me;
Your charm aglow like some exotic flower
  To rouse again the waves of memory.

No, I am through—the trumpet call of youth
  Must sound in vain—for I have need of rest;
You have no peace to give—no certain truth—
  And I am sick and weary of my quest.

Leave me to books and wine and memories—
  Nothing you have to give can equal these!

KID KAZANOVA (PHILIP STACK).

LOYALTY

He MAY BE six kinds of a liar,
  He may be ten kinds of a fool,
He may be a wicked highflyer
  Beyond any reason or rule;

57

There may be a shadow above him
  Of ruin and woes to impend,
And I may not respect, but I love him,
  Because—well, because he's my friend.

I know he has faults by the billion,
  But his faults are a portion of him;
I know that his record's vermilion,
  And he's far from the sweet Seraphim;
But he's always been square with yours truly,
  Ready to give or to lend,
And if he is wild and unruly,
  I like him—because he's my friend.

I criticize him but I do it
  In just a frank, comradely key,
And back-biting gossips will rue it
  If ever *they* knock him to me!
I never make diagrams of him,
  No maps of his soul have I penned;
I don't analyze—I just love him,
  Because—well, because he's my friend.

BERTON BRALEY.

NEW FRIENDS AND OLD FRIENDS

MAKE new friends, but keep the old;
Those are silver, these are gold.
New-made friendships, like new wine,
Age will mellow and refine.
Friendships that have stood the test—
Time and change—are surely best;
Brow may wrinkle, hair grow gray,
Friendship never knows decay.
For 'mid old friends, tried and true,
Once more we our youth renew.
But old friends, alas! may die,
New friends must their place supply.
Cherish friendship in your breast—
New is good, but old is best;
Make new friends, but keep the old;
Those are silver, these are gold.

JOSEPH PARRY.

OUR OWN

IF I HAD KNOWN in the morning
  How wearily all the day
The words unkind would trouble my mind
  That I said when you went away,
I had been more careful, darling,
  Nor given you needless pain;
But we vex our own with look and tone
  We may never take back again.

For though in the quiet evening
  You may give me the kiss of peace,
Yet it well might be that never for me
  The pain of the heart should cease!
How many go forth at morning
  Who never come home at night!
And hearts have broken for harsh words spoken
  That sorrow can ne'er set right.

We have careful thought for the stranger,
  And smiles for the sometime guest;
But oft for "our own" the bitter tone,
  Though we love our own the best.
Ah! lips with the curve impatient,
  Ah! brow with the shade of scorn,
'Twere a cruel fate, were the night too late
  To undo the work of the morn!

MARGARET E. SANGSTER.

"I HEAR IT SAID"

LAST NIGHT my friend—he says he is my friend—
Came in and questioned me. "I hear it said
You have done this and that. I come to ask
Are these things true?" A glint was in his eye
Of small distrust. His words were crisp and hot.
He measured me with anger, and flung down
A little heap of facts had come to him.
"I hear it said you have done this and that."

Suppose I have? And are you not my friend?
And are you not my friend enough to say,
"If it were true, there would be reason in it.
And if I cannot know the how and why,
Still I can trust you, waiting for a word,
Or for no word, if no word ever come!"

Is friendship just a thing of afternoons,
Of pleasuring one's friend and one's dear self—
Greed for sedate approval of his pace,
Suspicion if he take one little turn
Upon the road, one flight into the air,
And has not sought you for your Yea or Nay!

No. Friendship is not so. I am my own.
And howsoever near my friend may draw
Unto my soul, there is a legend hung
Above a certain straight and narrow way
Says "Dear my friend, ye may not enter here!"

I would the time has come—as it has not—
When men shall rise and say, "He is my friend.
He has done this? And what is that to me!
Think you I have a check upon his head,
Or cast a guiding rein across his neck?
I am his friend. And for that cause I walk
Not overclose beside him, leaving still
Space for his silences, and space for mine."

BARBARA YOUNG.

SWEET PERIL

Alas, how easily things go wrong!
A sigh too much, or a kiss too long,
And there follows a mist and a weeping rain,
And life is never the same again.

Alas, how hardly things go right!
'Tis hard to watch in a summer night,
For the sigh will come, and the kiss will stay,
And the summer night is a wintry day.

And yet how easily things go right,
If the sigh and a kiss of a summer's night
Come deep from the soul in the stronger ray
That is born in the light of the winter's day.

And things can never go badly wrong
If the heart be true and the love be strong,
For the mist, if it comes, and the weeping rain
Will be changed by the love into sunshine again.

GEORGE MACDONALD.

II. INSPIRATION

IF—

If you can keep your head when all about you
 Are losing theirs and blaming it on you;
If you can trust yourself when all men doubt you,
 But make allowance for their doubting too;
If you can wait and not be tired by waiting,
 Or, being lied about, don't deal in lies,
Or, being hated, don't give way to hating,
 And yet don't look too good, nor talk too wise;

If you can dream—and not make dreams your master;
 If you can think—and not make thoughts your aim;
If you can meet with triumph and disaster
 And treat those two impostors just the same;
If you can bear to hear the truth you've spoken
 Twisted by knaves to make a trap for fools,
Or watch the things you gave your life to broken,
 And stoop and build 'em up with wornout tools;

If you can make one heap of all your winnings
 And risk it on one turn of pitch-and-toss,
And lose, and start again at your beginnings
 And never breathe a word about your loss;
If you can force your heart and nerve and sinew
 To serve your turn long after they are gone,
And so hold on when there is nothing in you
 Except the Will which says to them: "Hold on";

If you can talk with crowds and keep your virtue,
 Or walk with kings—nor lose the common touch;
If neither foes nor loving friends can hurt you;
 If all men count with you, but none too much;

If you can fill the unforgiving minute
　　With sixty seconds' worth of distance run—
Yours is the Earth and everything that's in it,
　　And—which is more—you'll be a Man, my son!

RUDYARD KIPLING.

A FAREWELL

MY FAIREST CHILD, I have no song to give you;
　　No lark could pipe to skies so dull and gray;
Yet, ere we part, one lesson I can leave you
　　　　For every day.

Be good, sweet maid, and let who will be clever;
　　Do noble things, not dream them, all day long:
And so make life, death, and that vast forever
　　　　One grand, sweet song.

CHARLES KINGSLEY.

LIFE

LIFE! I know not what thou art,
But know that thou and I must part;
And when, or how, or where we met
I own to me's a secret yet.

Life! we've been long together,
Through pleasant and through cloudy weather;
'Tis hard to part when friends are dear—
Perhaps 'twill cost a sigh, a tear;
　Then steal away, give little warning,
Choose thine own time;
Say not good night—but in some brighter clime
　Bid me good morning.

ANNA LÆTITIA BARBAULD.

THE RIGHT KIND OF PEOPLE

　GONE is the city, gone the day,
　Yet still the story and the meaning stay:

Once where a prophet in the palm shade basked
A traveler chanced at noon to rest his miles.
"What sort of people may they be," he asked,
"In this proud city on the plains o'erspread?"
"Well, friend, what sort of people whence you came?"
"What sort?" the packman scowled; "why, knaves and fools."
"You'll find the people here the same," the wise man said.

Another stranger in the dusk drew near,
And pausing, cried "What sort of people here
In your bright city where yon towers arise?"
"Well, friend, what sort of people whence you came?"
"What sort?" the pilgrim smiled,
"Good, true and wise."
"You'll find the people here the same,"
The wise man said.

EDWIN MARKHAM.

OUTWITTED

HE DREW a circle that shut me out—
Heretic, rebel, a thing to flout.
But Love and I had the wit to win:
We drew a circle that took him in!

EDWIN MARKHAM.

TODAY

To BE alive in such an age!
With every year a lightning page
Turned in the world's great wonder book
Whereon the leaning nations look.
When men speak strong for brotherhood,
For peace and universal good,
When miracles are everywhere,
And every inch of common air
Throbs a tremendous prophecy
Of greater marvels yet to be.
    O thrilling age,
    O willing age!

When steel and stone and rail and rod
Become the avenue of God—
A trump to shout His thunder through
To crown the work that man may do.

To be alive in such an age!
When man, impatient of his cage,
Thrills to the soul's immortal rage
For conquest—reaches goal on goal,
Travels the earth from pole to pole,
Garners the tempests and the tides
And on a Dream Triumphant rides.
When, hid within the lump of clay,
A light more terrible than day
Proclaims the presence of that Force
Which hurls the planets on their course.
    O age with wings
    O age that flings
A challenge to the very sky,
Where endless realms of conquest lie!
When, earth on tiptoe, strives to hear
The message of a sister sphere,
Yearning to reach the cosmic wires
That flash Infinity's desires.

To be alive in such an age!
That blunders forth its discontent
With futile creed and sacrament,
Yet craves to utter God's intent,
Seeing beneath the world's unrest
Creation's huge, untiring quest,
And through Tradition's broken crust
The flame of Truth's triumphant thrust;
Below the seething thought of man
The push of a stupendous Plan.
    O age of strife!
    O age of life!
When Progress rides her chariots high,
And on the borders of the sky
The signals of the century
Proclaims the things that are to be—
The rise of woman to her place,
The coming of a nobler race.

To be alive in such an age—
    To live in it,
      To give to it!
Rise, soul, from thy despairing knees.
What if thy lips have drunk the lees?
Fling forth thy sorrows to the wind
And link thy hope with humankind—
The passion of a larger claim
Will put thy puny grief to shame.
Breathe the world thought, do the world deed,
Think hugely of thy brother's need.
And what thy woe, and what thy weal?
Look to the work the times reveal!
Give thanks with all thy flaming heart—
Crave but to have in it a part.
Give thanks and clasp thy heritage—
To be alive in such an age!

                ANGELA MORGAN.

WHERE THERE'S A WILL THERE'S A WAY

WE HAVE faith in old proverbs full surely,
    For Wisdom has traced what they tell,
And Truth may be drawn up as purely
    From them, as it may from "a well."
Let us question the thinkers and doers,
    And hear what they honestly say;
And you'll find they believe, like bold wooers,
    In "Where there's a will there's a way."

The hills have been high for man's mounting,
    The woods have been dense for his axe,
The stars have been thick for his counting,
    The sands have been wide for his tracks.
The sea has been deep for his diving,
    The poles have been broad for his sway,
But bravely he's proved in his striving,
    That "Where there's a will there's a way."

Have ye vices that ask a destroyer?
    Or passions that need your control?
Let Reason become your employer,
    And your body be ruled by your soul.

Fight on, though ye bleed in the trial,
    Resist with all strength that ye may;
Ye may conquer Sin's host by denial;
    For "Where there's a will there's a way."

Have ye Poverty's pinching to cope with?
    Does Suffering weigh down your might?
Only call up a spirit to hope with,
    And dawn may come out of the night.
Oh! much may be done by defying
    The ghosts of Despair and Dismay;
And much may be gained by relying
    On "Where there's a will there's a way."

Should ye see afar off that worth winning,
    Set out on the journey with trust;
And ne'er heed if your path at beginning
    Should be among brambles and dust.
Though it is but by footsteps ye do it.
    And hardships may hinder and stay,
Walk with faith, and be sure you'll get through it;
    For "Where there's a will there's a way."

ELIZA COOK.

HAPPINESSS

Happinesss is like a crystal,
Fair and exquisite and clear,
Broken in a million pieces,
Shattered, scattered far and near.
Now and then along life's pathway,
Lo! some shining fragments fall;
But there are so many pieces
No one ever finds them all.

You may find a bit of beauty,
Or an honest share of wealth,
While another just beside you
Gathers honor, love or health.
Vain to choose or grasp unduly,
Broken is the perfect ball;
And there are so many pieces
No one ever finds them all.

Yet the wise as on they journey
Treasure every fragment clear,
Fit them as they may together,
Imaging the shattered sphere,
Learning ever to be thankful,
Though their share of it is small;
For it has so many pieces
No one ever finds them all.

PRISCILLA LEONARD.

TADOUSSAC

I'VE SEEN the Thousand Islands
In the beauty of the dawn;
And sailed on Lake Ontario,
When shades of night were drawn;
I've wandered in Toronto;
Climbed the "Mount" at Montreal;
Run the great St. Lawrence rapids,
Where the waters swirl and fall.

I've slept up in the Chateau,
At Quebec; and known the thrill
Of rambling through the "old town"
And the fort upon the hill.
I've felt the sacred beauty
Of the splendor on Sag'nay;
The warmth of homespun blankets
That were made at Murray Bay.

But in my soul's a hunger
Once again for Tadoussac;
The endless fascination
Of its quaintness draws me back.
I hear again the mission bell
That calls the folks to prayer,
And as I walk the city streets
My heart is with them there.

CHARLES BANCROFT.

71

SONNET

To ONE who has been long in city pent,
  'Tis very sweet to look into the fair
  And open face of heaven,—to breathe a prayer
Full in the smile of the blue firmament.
Who is more happy, when, with heart content,
  Fatigued he sinks into some pleasant lair
  Of wavy grass, and reads a debonair
And gentle tale of love and languishment?
  Returning home at evening, with an ear
Catching the notes of Philomel,—an eye
  Watching the sailing cloudlet's bright career,
He mourns that day so soon has glided by:
  E'en like the passage of an angel's tear
That falls through the clear ether silently.

JOHN KEATS.

THE WINNERS

L'Envoi to "The Story of the Gadsbys"

WHAT is the moral? Who rides may read.
When the night is thick and the tracks are blind,
A friend at a pinch is a friend indeed,
But a fool to wait for the laggard behind.
Down to Gehenna or up to the Throne,
He travels the fastest who travels alone.

White hands cling to the tightened rein,
Slipping the spur from the booted heel,
Tenderest voices cry "Turn again,"
Red lips tarnish the scabbarded steel,
High hopes faint on a warm hearth stone—
He travels the fastest who travels alone.

One may fall but he falls by himself—
Falls by himself with himself to blame,
One may attain and to him is the pelf,
Loot of the city in Gold or Fame.
Plunder of earth shall be all his own
Who travels the fastest and travels alone.

Wherefore the more be ye holpen and stayed—
Stayed by a friend in the hour of toil,
Sing the heretical song I have made—
His be the labor and yours be the spoil.
Win by his aid and the aid disown—
He travels the fastest who travels alone!

RUDYARD KIPLING.

INVICTUS

Out of the night that covers me,
   Black as the Pit from pole to pole,
I thank whatever gods may be
   For my unconquerable soul.

In the fell clutch of circumstance
   I have not winced nor cried aloud.
Under the bludgeonings of chance
   My head is bloody, but unbowed.

Beyond this place of wrath and tears
   Looms but the Horror of the shade,
And yet the menace of the years
   Finds and shall find me unafraid.

It matters not how strait the gate,
   How charged with punishments the scroll,
I am the master of my fate:
   I am the captain of my soul.

WILLIAM ERNEST HENLEY.

MY CAPTAIN

Out of the light that dazzles me,
   Bright as the sun from pole to pole,
I thank the God I know to be
   For Christ the conqueror of my soul.

73

Since His the sway of circumstance,
  I would not wince nor cry aloud.
Under that rule which men call chance
  My head with joy is humbly bowed.

Beyond this place of sin and tears
  That life with Him! And His the aid,
Despite the menace of the years,
  Keeps, and shall keep me, unafraid.

I have no fear, though strait the gate,
  He cleared from punishment the scroll.
Christ is the Master of my fate,
  Christ is the Captain of my soul.

DOROTHEA DAY.

"WHERE ARE YOU GOING, GREATHEART?"

Where *are you going, Greatheart,*
With your eager face and your fiery grace?
  Where are you going, Greatheart?

"To fight a fight with all my might,
For Truth and Justice, God and Right,
To grace all Life with His fair Light."
  Then God go with you, Greatheart!

Where are you going, Greatheart?
"To beard the Devil in his den;
To smite him with the strength of ten;
To set at large the souls of men."
  Then God go with you, Greatheart!

*   *   *   *   *   *

Where are you going, Greatheart?
"To cleanse the earth of noisome things;
To draw from life its poison stings;
To give free play to Freedom's wings."
  Then God go with you, Greatheart!

Where are you going, Greatheart?
"To lift Today above the Past;
To make Tomorrow sure and fast;
To nail God's colors to the mast."
  Then God go with you, Greatheart!

74

Where are you going, Greatheart?
"To break down old dividing lines;
To carry out my Lord's designs;
To build again His broken shrines."
   Then God go with you, Greatheart!

Where are you going, Greatheart?
"To set all burdened peoples free;
To win for all God's liberty;
To 'stablish His sweet sovereignty."
   God goeth with you, Greatheart!

JOHN OXENHAM.

THE TORCH

LORD, let me be the torch that springs to light
   And lives its life in one exultant flame,
One leap of living fire against the night,
   Dropping to darkness even as it came.
For I have watched the smouldering of a soul
   Choked in the ashes that itself hath made,
Waiting the slow destruction of the whole,
   And turned from it, bewildered and afraid.

Light me with love—with hate—with all desire
   For that I may not reach, but let me burn
My little moment in pulsating fire
   Ere yet into the darkness I return;
Be it for guard, or menace, peace or sword,
   Make me thy torch to burn out swiftly, Lord.

THEODOSIA GARRISON.

RED GERANIUMS

LIFE did not bring me silken gowns,
   Nor jewels for my hair,
Nor signs of gabled foreign towns
   In distant countries fair,
But I can glimpse, beyond my pane, a green and friendly hill,
And red geraniums aflame upon my window sill.

The brambled cares of everyday,
　The tiny humdrum things,
May bind my feet when they would stray,
　But still my heart has wings
While red geraniums are bloomed against my window glass,
And low above my green-sweet hill the gypsy wind-clouds pass.

And if my dreamings ne'er come true,
　The brightest and the best,
But leave me lone my journey through,
　I'll set my heart at rest,
And thank God for home-sweet things, a green and friendly hill,
And red geraniums aflame upon my window sill.

MARTHA HASKELL CLARK.

THE ROSE STILL GROWS BEYOND THE WALL

NEAR a shady wall a rose once grew,
　Budded and blossomed in God's free light,
Watered and fed by morning dew,
　Shedding its sweetness day and night.

As it grew and blossomed fair and tall,
　Slowly rising to loftier height,
It came to a crevice in the wall,
　Through which there shone a beam of light.

Onward it crept with added strength,
　With never a thought of fear or pride.
It followed the light through the crevice's length
　And unfolded itself on the other side.

The light, the dew, the broadening view
　Were found the same as they were before;
And it lost itself in beauties new,
　Breathing its fragrance more and more.

Shall claim of death cause us to grieve,
　And make our courage faint or fail?
Nay! Let us faith and hope receive:
　The rose still grows beyond the wall.

76

Scattering fragrance far and wide,
   Just as it did in days of yore,
Just as it did on the other side,
   Just as it will for evermore.

                A. L. FRINK.

WHO WALKS WITH BEAUTY

WHO WALKS with Beauty has no need of fear;
The sun and moon and stars keep pace with him;
Invisible hands restore the ruined year,
And time itself grows beautifully dim.
One hill will keep the footprints of the moon
That came and went a hushed and secret hour;
One star at dusk will yield the lasting boon;
Remembered beauty's white immortal flower.

Who takes of Beauty wine and daily bread
Will know no lack when bitter years are lean;
The brimming cup is by, the feast is spread;
The sun and moon and stars his eyes have seen
Are for his hunger and the thirst he slakes:
The wine of Beauty and the bread he breaks.

                DAVID MORTON.

I SHALL NOT PASS THIS WAY AGAIN

THROUGH this toilsome world, alas!
Once and only once I pass;
If a kindness I may show,
If a good deed I may do
To a suffering fellow man,
Let me do it while I can.
No delay, for it is plain
I shall not pass this way again.

              UNKNOWN.

77

A SOUL'S SOLILOQUY

TODAY the journey is ended,
    I have worked out the mandates of fate;
Naked, alone, undefended,
    I knock at the Uttermost Gate.
Behind is life and its longing,
    Its trial, its trouble, its sorrow;
Beyond is the Infinite Morning
    Of a day without a tomorrow.

Go back to dust and decay,
    Body, grown weary and old;
You are worthless to me from today—
    No longer my soul can you hold.
I lay you down gladly forever
    For a life that is better than this;
I go where partings ne'er sever
    You into oblivion's abyss.

Lo, the gate swings wide at my knocking,
    Across endless reaches I see
Lost friends with laughter come flocking
    To give a glad welcome to me.
Farewell, the maze has been threaded,
    This is the ending of strife;
Say not that death should be dreaded—
    'Tis but the beginning of life.

                    WENONAH STEVENS ABBOTT.

HYACINTHS TO FEED THY SOUL

IF OF THY MORTAL GOODS thou art bereft,
And from thy slender store two loaves alone to thee are left,
Sell one, and with the dole
Buy hyacinths to feed thy soul.

*Attributed to the Gulistan of Moslih Eddin Saadi, a Moham-
medan sheik and Persian poet who lived about 1184–1291.*

THE LOOM OF TIME

MAN'S LIFE is laid in the loom of time
  To a pattern he does not see,
While the weavers work and the shuttles fly
  Till the dawn of eternity.

Some shuttles are filled with silver threads
  And some with threads of gold,
While often but the darker hues
  Are all that they may hold.

But the weaver watches with skillful eye
  Each shuttle fly to and fro,
And sees the pattern so deftly wrought
  As the loom moves sure and slow.

God surely planned the pattern:
  Each thread, the dark and fair,
Is chosen by His master skill
  And placed in the web with care.

He only knows its beauty,
  And guides the shuttles which hold
The threads so unattractive,
  As well as the threads of gold.

Not till each loom is silent,
  And the shuttles cease to fly,
Shall God reveal the pattern
  And explain the reason why

The dark threads were as needful
  In the weaver's skillful hand
As the threads of gold and silver
  For the pattern which He planned.

UNKNOWN.

79

PEDRA

It seems no work of man's creative hand,
By labour wrought as wavering fancy plann'd,
But from the rock as if by magic grown,
Eternal, silent, beautiful, alone!
Not virgin-white like the old Doric shrine
Where erst Athena held her rites divine;
Not saintly-grey, like many a minster fane,
That crowns the hill, and consecrates the plain;
But rosy-red as if the blush of dawn
That first beheld them were not yet withdrawn;
The hues of youth upon a brow of woe,
Which man deemed old two thousand years ago.
Match me such marvel save in Eastern clime,
A rose-red city half as old as Time.

JOHN WILLIAM BURGON.

WAITING

Serene I fold my arms and wait,
   Nor care for wind, or tide, or sea:
I rave no more 'gainst time or fate,
   For lo! my own shall come to me.

I stay my haste, I make delays,
   For what avails this eager pace?
I stand amid the eternal ways,
   And what is mine shall know my face.

Asleep, awake, by night or day,
   The friends I seek are seeking me;
No wind can drive my bark astray,
   Nor change the tide of destiny.

What matter if I stand alone?
   I wait with joy the coming years;
My heart shall reap where it has sown,
   And garner up its fruit of tears.

The waters know their own, and draw
   The brook that springs in yonder height;
So flows the good with equal law
   Unto the soul of pure delight.

The floweret nodding in the wind
   Is ready plighted to the bee;
And, maiden, why that look unkind?
   For lo! thy lover seeketh thee.

The stars come nightly to the sky;
   The tidal wave unto the sea;
Nor time, nor space, nor deep, nor high
   Can keep my own away from me.

JOHN BURROUGHS.

OUR HEROES

HERE'S A HAND to the boy who has courage
   To do what he knows to be right;
When he falls in the way of temptation,
   He has a hard battle to fight.
Who strives against self and his comrades
   Will find a most powerful foe.
All honor to him if he conquers.
   A cheer for the boy who says "No!"

There's many a battle fought daily
   The world knows nothing about;
There's many a brave little soldier
   Whose strength puts a legion to rout.
And he who fights sin singlehanded
   Is more of a hero, I say,
Than he who leads soldiers to battle
   And conquers by arms in the fray.

Be steadfast, my boy, when you're tempted,
   To do what you know to be right.
Stand firm by the colors of manhood,
   And you will o'ercome in the fight.

"The right," be your battle cry ever
　　In waging the warfare of life,
And God, who knows who are the heroes,
　　Will give you the strength for the strife.

PHOEBE CARY.

THE REVEL

East India

WE MEET 'neath the sounding rafter,
　　And the walls around are bare;
As they shout back our peals of laughter
　　It seems that the dead are there.
Then stand to your glasses, steady!
　　We drink in our comrades' eyes:
One cup to the dead already—
　　Hurrah for the next that dies!

Not here are the goblets glowing,
　　Not here is the vintage sweet;
'Tis cold as our hearts are growing,
　　And dark as the doom we meet.
But stand to your glasses, steady!
　　And soon shall our pulses rise:
A cup to the dead already—
　　Hurrah for the next that dies!

There's many a hand that's shaking,
　　And many a cheek that's sunk;
But soon, though our hearts are breaking,
　　They'll burn with the wine we've drunk.
Then stand to your glasses, steady!
　　'Tis here the revival lies:
Quaff a cup to the dead already—
　　Hurrah for the next that dies.

Time was when we laughed at others;
　　We thought we were wiser then;
Ha! Ha! Let them think of their mothers,
　　Who hope to see them again.

No! stand to your glasses, steady!
   The thoughtless is here the wise:
One cup to the dead already—
   Hurrah for the next that dies!

Not a sigh for the lot that darkles,
   Not a tear for the friends that sink;
We'll fall, 'midst the wine-cup's sparkles,
   As mute as the wine we drink.
Come, stand to your glasses, steady!
   'Tis this that the respite buys:
A cup to the dead already—
   Hurrah for the next that dies!

There's a mist on the glass congealing,
   'Tis the hurricane's sultry breath;
And thus does the warmth of feeling
   Turn ice in the grasp of Death.
But stand to your glasses, steady!
   For a moment the vapor flies:
Quaff a cup to the dead already—
   Hurrah for the next that dies!

Who dreads to the dust returning?
   Who shrinks from the sable shore,
Where the high and haughty yearning
   Of the soul can sting no more?
No, stand to your glasses, steady!
   The world is a world of lies:
A cup to the dead already—
   And hurrah for the next that dies!

Cut off from the land that bore us,
   Betrayed by the land we find,
When the brightest have gone before us,
   And the dullest are most behind—
Stand, stand to your glasses, steady!
   'Tis all we have left to prize:
One cup to the dead already—
   Hurrah for the next that dies!

BARTHOLOMEW DOWLING.

[*The above poem is supposed to have been written in India while the plague was playing havoc among the British residents and troops there. It has been attributed to Alfred Domett as well as Bartholomew Dowling.*]

HOLD FAST YOUR DREAMS

HOLD FAST your dreams!
Within your heart
Keep one still, secret spot
Where dreams may go,
And, sheltered so,
May thrive and grow
Where doubt and fear are not.
O keep a place apart,
Within your heart,
For little dreams to go!

Think still of lovely things that are not true.
Let wish and magic work at will in you.
Be sometimes blind to sorrow. Make believe!
Forget the calm that lies
In disillusioned eyes.
Though we all know that we must die,
Yet you and I
May walk like gods and be
Even now at home in immortality.

We see so many ugly things—
Deceits and wrongs and quarrelings;
We know, alas! we know
How quickly fade
The color in the west,
The bloom upon the flower,
The bloom upon the breast
And youth's blind hour.
Yet keep within your heart
A place apart
Where little dreams may go,
May thrive and grow.
Hold fast—hold fast your dreams!

LOUISE DRISCOLL.

IMMORTALITY

Two caterpillars crawling on a leaf
By some strange accident in contact came;
Their conversation, passing all belief,
Was that same argument, the very same,
That has been "proed and conned" from man to man,
Yea, ever since this wondrous world began.
   The ugly creatures,
     Deaf and dumb and blind,
   Devoid of features
     That adorn mankind,
Were vain enough, in dull and wordy strife,
To speculate upon a future life.
The first was optimistic, full of hope;
The second, quite dyspeptic, seemed to mope.
Said number one, "I'm sure of our salvation."
Said number two, "I'm sure of our damnation;
Our ugly forms alone would seal our fates
And bar our entrance through the golden gates.
Suppose that death should take us unawares,
How could we climb the golden stairs?
If maidens shun us as they pass us by,
Would angels bid us welcome in the sky?
I wonder what great crimes we have committed,
That leave us so forlorn and so unpitied.
Perhaps we've been ungrateful, unforgiving;
'Tis plain to me that life's not worth the living."
"Come, come, cheer up," the jovial worm replied,
"Let's take a look upon the other side;
Suppose we cannot fly like moths or millers,
Are we to blame for being caterpillars?
Will that same God that doomed us crawl the earth,
A prey to every bird that's given birth,
Forgive our captor as he eats and sings,
And damn poor us because we have not wings?
If we can't skim the air like owl or bat,
A worm will turn 'for a' that.' "
They argued through the summer; autumn nigh,
The ugly things composed themselves to die;
And so, to make their funeral quite complete,
Each wrapped him in his little winding sheet.
The tangled web encompassed them full soon,
Each for his coffin made him a cocoon,

All through the winter's chilling blast they lay
Dead to the world, aye, dead as human clay.
Lo, spring comes forth with all her warmth and love;
She brings sweet justice from the realms above;
She breaks the chrysalis, she resurrects the dead;
Two butterflies ascend encircling her head.
And so this emblem shall forever be
A sign of immortality.

JOSEPH JEFFERSON.

WHO ARE MY PEOPLE?

MY PEOPLE? Who are they?
I went into the church where the congregation
Worshiped my God. Were they my people?
I felt no kinship to them as they knelt there.
My people! Where are they?
I went into the land where I was born,
Where men spoke my language . . .
I was a stranger there.
"My people," my soul cried. "Who are my people?"

Last night in the rain I met an old man
Who spoke a language I do not speak,
Which marked him as one who does not know my God.
With apologetic smile he offered me
The shelter of his patched umbrella.
I met his eyes . . . And then I knew. . . .

ROSA ZAGNONI MARINONI.

THERE IS NO DEATH

THERE IS no death! The stars go down
    To rise upon some other shore,
And bright in heaven's jewelled crown
    They shine forevermore.

There is no death! The forest leaves
    Convert to life the viewless air;
The rocks disorganize to feed
    The hungry moss they bear.

86

There is no death! The dust we tread
   Shall change, beneath the summer showers
To golden grain, or mellowed fruit,
   Or rainbow-tinted flowers.

There is no death! The leaves may fall,
   And flowers may fade and pass away—
They only wait, through wintry hours,
   The warm, sweet breath of May.

There is no death! The choicest gifts
   That heaven hath kindly lent to earth
Are ever first to seek again
   The country of their birth.

And all things that for growth or joy
   Are worthy of our love or care,
Whose loss has left us desolate,
   Are safely garnered there.

Though life become a desert waste,
   We know its fairest, sweetest flowers,
Transplanted into Paradise,
   Adorn immortal bowers.

The voice of birdlike melody
   That we have missed and mourned so long,
Now mingles with the angel choir
   In everlasting song.

There is no death! Although we grieve
   When beautiful, familiar forms
That we have learned to love are torn
   From our embracing arms—

Although with bowed and breaking heart,
   With sable garb and silent tread,
We bear their senseless dust to rest,
   And say that they are "dead,"

They are not dead! They have but passed
   Beyond the mists that blind us here
Into the new and larger life
   Of that serener sphere.

They have but dropped their robe of clay
　　To put their shining raiment on;
They have not wandered far away—
　　They are not "lost" nor "gone."

Though disenthralled and glorified
　　They still are here and love us yet;
The dear ones they have left behind
　　They never can forget.

And sometimes, when our hearts grow faint
　　Amid temptations fierce and deep,
Or when the wildly raging waves
　　Of grief or passion sweep,

We feel upon our fevered brow
　　Their gentle touch, their breath of balm;
Their arms enfold us, and our hearts
　　Grow comforted and calm.

And ever near us, though unseen,
　　The dear, immortal spirits tread—
For all the boundless universe
　　Is Life—there are no dead!

　　　　　　　　　　J. L. MCCREERY.

OPPORTUNITY

THIS I BEHELD, or dreamed it in a dream:
There spread a cloud of dust along a plain;
And underneath the cloud, or in it, raged
A furious battle, and men yelled, and swords
Shocked upon swords and shields. A prince's banner
Wavered, then staggered backward, hemmed by foes.
A craven hung along the battle's edge
And thought, "Had I a sword of keener steel—
That blue blade that the king's son bears—but this
Blunt thing——!" He snapt and flung it from his hand,
And, lowering, crept away and left the field.
Then came the king's son, wounded, sore bestead,
And weaponless, and saw the broken sword,

Hilt-buried in the dry and trodden sand,
And ran and snatched it, and with battle-shout
Lifted afresh, he hewed his enemy down,
And saved a great cause that heroic day.

EDWARD ROWLAND SILL.

IT COULDN'T BE DONE

SOMEBODY SAID that it couldn't be done,
  But he with a chuckle replied
That "maybe it couldn't," but he would be one
  Who wouldn't say so till he'd tried.
So he buckled right in with the trace of a grin
  On his face. If he worried he hid it.
He started to sing as he tackled the thing
  That couldn't be done, and he did it.

Somebody scoffed: "Oh, you'll never do that;
  At least no one ever has done it";
But he took off his coat and he took off his hat,
  And the first thing we knew he'd begun it.
With a lift of his chin and a bit of a grin,
  Without any doubting or quiddit,
He started to sing as he tackled the thing
  That couldn't be done, and he did it.

There are thousands to tell you it cannot be done,
  There are thousands to prophesy failure;
There are thousands to point out to you, one by one,
  The dangers that wait to assail you.
But just buckle in with a bit of a grin,
  Just take off your coat and go to it;
Just start to sing as you tackle the thing
  That "cannot be done," and you'll do it.

EDGAR A. GUEST.

LORD, MAKE A REGULAR MAN OUT OF ME

THIS I WOULD LIKE to be—braver and bolder,
Just a bit wiser because I am older,
Just a bit kinder to those I may meet,
Just a bit manlier taking defeat;
This for the New Year my wish and my plea—
Lord, make a regular man out of me.

This I would like to be—just a bit finer,
More of a smiler and less of a whiner,
Just a bit quicker to stretch out my hand
Helping another who's struggling to stand,
This is my prayer for the New Year to be,
Lord, make a regular man out of me.

This I would like to be—just a bit fairer,
Just a bit better, and just a bit squarer,
Not quite so ready to censure and blame,
Quicker to help every man in the game,
Not quite so eager men's failings to see,
Lord, make a regular man out of me.

This I would like to be—just a bit truer,
Less of the wisher and more of the doer,
Broader and bigger, more willing to give,
Living and helping my neighbor to live!
This for the New Year my prayer and my plea—
Lord, make a regular man out of me.

EDGAR A. GUEST.

A FRIEND'S GREETING

I'D LIKE to be the sort of friend that you have been to me;
I'd like to be the help that you've been always glad to be;
I'd like to mean as much to you each minute of the day
As you have meant, old friend of mine, to me along the way.

I'd like to do the big things and the splendid things for you,
To brush the gray from out your skies and leave them only blue;
I'd like to say the kindly things that I so oft have heard,
And feel that I could rouse your soul the way that mine you've stirred.

I'd like to give you back the joy that you have given me,
Yet that were wishing you a need I hope will never be;
I'd like to make you feel as rich as I, who travel on
Undaunted in the darkest hours with you to lean upon.

I'm wishing at this Christmas time that I could but repay
A portion of the gladness that you've strewn along my way;
And could I have one wish this year, this only would it be:
I'd like to be the sort of friend that you have been to me.

EDGAR A. GUEST.

MYSELF

I HAVE to live with myself, and so
I want to be fit for myself to know,
I want to be able, as days go by,
Always to look myself straight in the eye;
I don't want to stand, with the setting sun,
And hate myself for things I have done.

I don't want to keep on a closet shelf
A lot of secrets about myself,
And fool myself, as I come and go,
Into thinking that nobody else will know
The kind of a man I really am;
I don't want to dress up myself in sham.

I want to go out with my head erect,
I want to deserve all men's respect;
But here in the struggle for fame and pelf
I want to be able to like myself.
I don't want to look at myself and know
That I'm bluster and bluff and empty show.

I can never hide myself from me;
I see what others may never see;
I know what others may never know,
I never can fool myself, and so,
Whatever happens, I want to be
Self-respecting and conscience free.

EDGAR A. GUEST.

TELL HIM SO

IF YOU HEAR a kind word spoken
　　Of some worthy soul you know,
It may fill his heart with sunshine
　　If you only tell him so.

If a deed, however humble,
　　Helps you on your way to go,
Seek the one whose hand has helped **you,**
　　Seek him out and tell him so!

If your heart is touched and tender
　　Toward a sinner, lost and low,
It might help him to do better
　　If you'd only tell him so!

Oh, my sisters, oh, my brothers,
　　As o'er life's rough path you go,
If God's love has saved and kept you,
　　Do not fail to tell men so!

UNKNOWN.

THE MANLY MAN

THE WORLD has room for the manly man, with the spirit of manly cheer;
The world delights in the man who smiles when his eyes keep back the
　　tear;
It loves the man who, when things are wrong, can take his place and
　　stand
With his face to the fight and his eyes to the light, and toil with a will-
　　ing hand;
The manly man is the country's need, the moment's need, forsooth,
With a heart that beats to the pulsing troop of the lilied leagues of
　　truth;
The world is his and it waits for him, and it leaps to hear the ring
Of the blow he strikes and the wheels he turns and hammers he dares
　　to swing;
It likes the forward look on his face, the poise of his noble head,
And the onward lunge of his tireless will and the sweep of his dauntless
　　tread!

Hurrah for the manly man who comes with sunlight on his face,
And the strength to do and the will to dare and the courage to find his
    place!
The world delights in the manly man, and the weak and evil flee
When the manly man goes forth to hold his own on land or sea!

UNKNOWN.

GET A TRANSFER

    IF YOU ARE on the Gloomy Line,
      Get a transfer.
    If you're inclined to fret and pine,
      Get a transfer.
    Get off the track of doubt and gloom,
    Get on the Sunshine Track—there's room—
      Get a transfer.

    If you're on the Worry Train,
      Get a transfer.
    You must not stay there and complain,
      Get a transfer.
    The Cheerful Cars are passing through,
    And there's lots of room for you—
      Get a transfer.

    If you're on the Grouchy Track,
      Get a transfer.
    Just take a Happy Special back,
      Get a transfer.
    Jump on the train and pull the rope,
    That lands you at the station Hope—
      Get a transfer.

UNKNOWN.

IT ISN'T THE CHURCH—IT'S YOU

    IF YOU WANT to have the kind of a church
      Like the kind of a church you like,
    You needn't slip your clothes in a grip
      And start on a long, long hike.

You'll only find what you left behind,
    For there's nothing really new.
It's a knock at yourself when you knock your church;
    It isn't the church—it's *you*.

When everything seems to be going wrong,
    And trouble seems everywhere brewing;
When prayer meeting, Young People's meeting, and **all,**
    Seem simmering slowly—stewing,
Just take a look at yourself and say,
    "What's the use of being blue?"
Are you doing your "bit" to make things "hit"?
    It isn't the church—it's *you*.

It's really strange sometimes, don't you know,
    That things go as well as they do,
When we think of the little—the very small mite—
    We add to the work of the few.
We sit, and stand round, and complain of what's done,
    And do very little but fuss.
Are we bearing our share of the burdens to bear?
    It isn't the church—it's *us*.

So, if you want to have the kind of a church
    Like the kind of a church you like,
Put off your guile, and put on your best smile,
    And hike, my brother, just hike,
To the work in hand that has to be done—
    The work of saving a few.
It isn't the church that is wrong, my boy;
    It isn't the church—it's *you*.

UNKNOWN.

SAY IT NOW

IF YOU HAVE a friend worth loving,
    Love him. Yes, and let him know
That you love him, ere life's evening
    Tinge his brow with sunset glow.
Why should good words ne'er be said
Of a friend—till he is dead?

If you hear a song that thrills you,
   Sung by any child of song,
Praise it. Do not let the singer
   Wait deserved praises long.
Why should one who thrills your heart
Lack the joy you may impart?

If you hear a prayer that moves you
   By its humble, pleading tone,
Join it. Do not let the seeker
   Bow before his God alone.
Why should not your brother share
The strength of "two or three" in prayer?

If you see the hot tears falling
   From a brother's weeping eyes,
Share them. And by kindly sharing
   Own our kinship in the skies.
Why should anyone be glad
When a brother's heart is sad?

If a silvery laugh goes rippling
   Through the sunshine on his face,
Share it. 'Tis the wise man's saying—
   For both grief and joy a place.
There's health and goodness in the mirth
In which an honest laugh has birth.

If your work is made more easy
   By a friendly, helping hand,
Say so. Speak out brave and truly
   Ere the darkness veil the land.
Should a brother workman dear
Falter for a word of cheer?

Scatter thus your seeds of kindness
   All enriching as you go—
Leave them. Trust the Harvest Giver;
   He will make each seed to grow.
So until the happy end
Your life shall never lack a friend.

                        UNKNOWN.

THE QUITTER

It AIN'T THE FAILURES he may meet
    That keeps a man from winnin',
It's the discouragement complete
    That blocks a new beginnin';
You want to quit your habits bad,
    And, when the shadows flittin'
Make life seem worthless an' sad,
    You want to quit your quittin'!

You want to quit a-layin' down
    An' sayin' hope is over,
Because the fields are bare an' brown
    Where once we lived in clover.
When jolted from the water cart
    It's painful to be hittin'
The earth; but make another start.
    Cheer up, an' quit your quittin'!

Although the game seems rather stiff
    Don't be a doleful doubter;
There's always one more innin' if
    You're not a down-and-outer.
But fortune's pretty sure to flee
    From folks content with sittin'
Around an' sayin' life's N. G.
    You've got to quit your quittin'.

                UNKNOWN.

ALWAYS FINISH

IF A TASK is once begun
Never leave it till it's done.
Be the labor great or small,
Do it well or not at all.

                UNKNOWN.

TRY SMILING

WHEN THE WEATHER suits you not,
  Try smiling.
When your coffee isn't hot,
  Try smiling.
When your neighbors don't do right,
Or your relatives all fight,
Sure 'tis hard, but then you might
  Try smiling.

Doesn't change the things, of course—
  Just smiling.
But it cannot make them worse—
  Just smiling.
And it seems to help your case,
Brightens up a gloomy place,
Then, it sort o' rests your face—
  Just smiling.

UNKNOWN.

DO IT NOW!

IF YOU'VE GOT a job to do,
          Do it now!
If it's one you wish were through,
          Do it now!
If you're sure the job's your own,
Do not hem and haw and groan—
          Do it now!
Don't put off a bit of work,
          Do it now!
It doesn't pay to shirk,
          Do it now!
If you want to fill a place
And be useful to the race,
Just get up and take a brace—
          Do it now!
Don't linger by the way,
          Do it now!
You'll lose if you delay,
          Do it now!

If the other fellows wait,
Or postpone until it's late,
You hit up a faster gait—
           Do it now!
         UNKNOWN.

SMILE

LIKE A BREAD without the spreadin',
  Like a puddin' without sauce,
Like a mattress without beddin',
  Like a cart without a hoss,
Like a door without a latchstring,
  Like a fence without a stile,
Like a dry an' barren creek bed—
  Is the face without a smile.

Like a house without a dooryard,
  Like a yard without a flower,
Like a clock without a mainspring,
  That will never tell the hour;
A thing that sort o' makes yo' feel
  A hunger all the while—
Oh, the saddest sight that ever was
  Is a face without a smile!

The face of man was built for smiles,
  An' thereby he is blest
Above the critters of the field,
  The birds an' all the rest;
He's just a little lower
  Than the angels in the skies,
An' the reason is that he can smile;
  Therein his glory lies!

So smile an' don't forgit to smile,
  An' smile, an' smile ag'in;
'Twill help you all along the way,
  An' cheer you mile by mile;
An' so, whatever is your lot,
  Jes' smile, an' smile, an' smile.
         UNKNOWN.

A SMILE

LET OTHERS CHEER the winning man,
There's one I hold worth while;
'Tis he who does the best he can,
Then loses with a smile.
Beaten he is, but not to stay
Down with the rank and file;
That man will win some other day,
Who loses with a smile.

UNKNOWN.

A BAG OF TOOLS

ISN'T IT strange
That princes and kings,
And clowns that caper
In sawdust rings,
And common people
Like you and me
Are builders for eternity?

Each is given a bag of tools,
A shapeless mass,
A book of rules;
And each must make—
Ere life is flown—
A stumbling block
Or a steppingstone.

R. L. SHARPE.

IT'S FINE TODAY

SURE, THIS WORLD is full of trouble—
I ain't said it ain't.
Lord, I've had enough and double
Reason for complaint;

Rain and storm have come to fret me,
　　Skies are often gray;
Thorns and brambles have beset me
　　On the road—but say,
　　　Ain't it fine today?

What's the use of always weepin',
　　Making trouble last?
What's the use of always keepin'
　　Thinkin' of the past?
Each must have his tribulation—
　　Water with his wine;
Life, it ain't no celebration,
　　Trouble?—I've had mine—
　　　But today is fine!

It's today that I am livin',
　　Not a month ago.
Havin'; losin'; takin'; givin';
　　As time wills it so.
Yesterday a cloud of sorrow
　　Fell across the way;
It may rain again tomorrow,
　　It may rain—but say,
　　　Ain't it fine today?

　　　　　　　　DOUGLAS MALLOCH.

OPPORTUNITY

THEY DO ME WRONG who say I come no more
　　When once I knock and fail to find you in,
For every day I stand outside your door
　　And bid you wake, and rise to fight and win.

Wail not for precious chances passed away,
　　Weep not for golden ages on the wane!
Each night I burn the records of the day;
　　At sunrise every soul is born again.

Laugh like a boy at splendors that have sped,
　　To vanished joys be blind and deaf and dumb;
My judgments seal the dead past with its dead,
　　But never bind a moment yet to come.

Tho' deep in mire, wring not your hands and weep;
    I lend my arm to all who say, "I can!"
No shamefaced outcast ever sank so deep
    But yet might rise and be again a man.

Dost thou behold thy lost youth all aghast?
    Dost reel from righteous retribution's blow?
Then turn from blotted archives of the past
    And find the future's pages white as snow.

Art thou a mourner? Rouse thee from thy spell;
    Art thou a sinner? Sins may be forgiven;
Each morning gives thee wings to flee from hell,
    Each night a star to guide thy feet to Heaven.

WALTER MALONE.

THE LAND OF BEGINNING AGAIN

I wish that there were some wonderful place
    Called the Land of Beginning Again,
Where all our mistakes and all our heartaches
    And all of our poor selfish grief
Could be dropped like a shabby old coat at the door,
    And never be put on again.

I wish we could come on it all unaware,
    Like the hunter who finds a lost trail;
And I wish that the one whom our blindness had done
    The greatest injustice of all
Could be at the gates like an old friend that waits
    For the comrade he's gladdest to hail.

We would find all the things we intended to do
    But forgot, and remembered too late,
Little praises unspoken, little promises broken,
    And all of the thousand and one
Little duties neglected that might have perfected
    The day for one less fortunate.

It wouldn't be possible not to be kind
    In the Land of Beginning Again;
And the ones we misjudged and the ones whom we grudged
    Their moments of victory here
Would find in the grasp of our loving handclasp
    More than penitent lips could explain.

For what had been hardest we'd know had been best,
  And what had seemed loss would be gain;
For there isn't a sting that will not take wing
  When we've faced it and laughed it away;
And I think that the laughter is most what we're after
  In the Land of Beginning Again.

So I wish that there were some wonderful place
  Called the Land of Beginning Again,
Where all our mistakes and all our heartaches
  And all of our poor selfish grief
Could be dropped like a shabby old coat at the door,
  And never be put on again.

LOUISA FLETCHER.

BE THE BEST OF WHATEVER YOU ARE

[We all dream of great deeds and high positions, away from the pettiness and humdrum of ordinary life. Yet success is not occupying a lofty place or doing conspicuous work; it is being the best that is in you. Rattling around in too big a job is worse than filling a small one to overflowing. Dream, aspire by all means; but do not ruin the life you must lead by dreaming pipe dreams of the one you would like to lead. Make the most of what you have and are. Perhaps your trivial, immediate task is your one sure way of proving your mettle. Do the thing near at hand, and great things will come to your hand to be done.]

IF YOU CAN'T BE a pine on the top of the hill,
  Be a scrub in the valley—but be
The best little scrub by the side of the rill;
  Be a bush if you can't be a tree.

If you can't be a bush be a bit of the grass,
  And some highway happier make;
If you can't be a muskie then just be a bass—
  But the liveliest bass in the lake!

We can't all be captains, we've got to be crew,
  There's something for all of us here,
There's big work to do, and there's lesser to do,
  And the task you must do is the near.

If you can't be a highway then just be a trail,
    If you can't be the sun be a star;
It isn't by size that you win or you fail—
    Be the best of whatever you are!

DOUGLAS MALLOCH.

THE TOWN OF DON'T-YOU-WORRY

THERE'S A TOWN called Don't-You-Worry,
    On the banks of River Smile;
Where the Cheer-Up and Be-Happy
    Blossom sweetly all the while.
Where the Never-Grumble flower
    Blooms beside the fragrant Try,
And the Ne'er-Give-Up and Patience
    Point their faces to the sky.

In the valley of Contentment,
    In the province of I-Will,
You will find this lovely city,
    At the foot of No-Fret Hill.
There are thoroughfares delightful
    In this very charming town,
And on every hand are shade trees
    Named the Very-Seldom-Frown.

Rustic benches quite enticing
    You'll find scattered here and there;
And to each a vine is clinging
    Called the Frequent-Earnest-Prayer.
Everybody there is happy
    And is singing all the while,
In the town of Don't-You-Worry,
    On the banks of River Smile.

I. J. BARTLETT.

IT ISN'T THE TOWN, IT'S YOU

IF YOU WANT to live in the kind of a town
    That's the kind of a town you like,
You needn't slip your clothes in a grip
    And start on a long, long hike.

You'll find elsewhere what you left behind,
  For there's nothing that's really new.
It's a knock at yourself when you knock your town;
  It isn't your town—it's you.

Real towns are not made by men afraid
  Lest somebody else gets ahead.
When everybody works and nobody shirks
  You can raise a town from the dead.

And if while you make your stake
  Your neighbor can make one, too,
Your town will be what you want to see,
  It isn't your town—it's you.

                                    R. W. GLOVER.

THE TOWN OF NOGOOD

My FRIEND, have you heard of the town of Nogood,
  On the banks of the River Slow,
Where blooms the Waitawhile flower fair,
Where the Sometimeorother scents the air,
  And the soft Goeasies grow?

It lies in the Valley of Whatstheuse,
  In the Province of Letterslide.
That Tiredfeeling is native there,
It's the home of the reckless Idontcare,
  Where the Giveitups abide.

It stands at the bottom of Lazyhill,
  And is easy to reach, I declare;
You've only to fold up your hands and glide
Down the slope of Weakwill's toboggan slide
  To be landed quickly there.

The town is as old as the human race
  And it grows with the flight of years.
It is wrapped in the fog of idlers' dreams,
Its streets are paved with discarded schemes,
  And sprinkled with useless tears.

The Collegebred fool and the Richman's heir
   Are plentiful there, no doubt.
The rest of its crowd are a motley crew,
With every class except one in view—
   The Foolkiller is barred out.

The town of Nogood is all hedged about
   By the mountains of Despair.
No sentinel stands on its gloomy walls,
No trumpet to battle and triumph calls,
   For cowards alone are there.

My friend, from the dead-alive town Nogood
   If you would keep far away,
Just follow your duty through good and ill,
Take this for your motto, "I can, I will,"
   And live up to it each day.

W. E. PENNY.

THE HOUSE BY THE SIDE OF THE ROAD

"He was a friend to man, and lived in a house by the side of the road"—Homer.

THERE ARE HERMIT SOULS that live withdrawn
   In the peace of their self-content;
There are souls, like stars, that dwell apart,
   In a fellowless firmament;
There are pioneer souls that blaze their paths
   Where highways never ran;
But let me live by the side of the road
   And be a friend to man.

Let me live in a house by the side of the road,
   Where the race of men go by—
The men who are good and the men who are bad,
   As good and as bad as I.
I would not sit in the scorner's seat,
   Or hurl the cynic's ban;
Let me live in a house by the side of the road
   And be a friend to man.

I see from my house by the side of the road,
  By the side of the highway of life,
The men who press with the ardor of hope,
  The men who are faint with the strife.
But I turn not away from their smiles nor their tears—
  Both parts of an infinite plan;
Let me live in my house by the side of the road
  And be a friend to man.

I know there are brook-gladdened meadows ahead,
  And mountains of wearisome height,
That the road passes on through the long afternoon
  And stretches away to the night.
But still I rejoice when the travelers rejoice,
  And weep with the strangers that moan,
Nor live in my house by the side of the road
  Like a man who dwells alone.

Let me live in my house by the side of the road
  Where the race of men go by—
They are good, they are bad, they are weak, they are strong,
  Wise, foolish—so am I.
Then why should I sit in the scorner's seat
  Or hurl the cynic's ban?—
Let me live in my house by the side of the road
  And be a friend to man.

SAM WALTER FOSS.

CROWDED WAYS OF LIFE

[Written in reply to *The House by the Side of the Road*,
    by Sam Walter Foss.]

'TIS ONLY A HALF TRUTH the poet has sung
  Of the "house by the side of the way."
Our Master had neither a house nor a home,
  But He walked with the crowd day by day.
And I think, when I read of the poet's desire,
  That a house by the road would be good;
But service is found in its tenderest form
  When we walk with the crowd in the road.

So I say, Let me walk with the men in the road,
   Let me seek out the burdens that crush,
Let me speak a kind word of good cheer to the weak
   Who are falling behind in the rush.
There are wounds to be healed, there are breaks we must mend,
   There's a cup of cold water to give;
And the man in the road by the side of his friend
   Is the man who has learned to live.

Then tell me no more of the house by the road;
   There is only one place I can live—
It's there with the men who are toiling along,
   Who are needing the cheer I can give.
It is pleasant to live in the house by the way
And be a friend, as the poet has said;
But the Master is bidding us: "Bear ye their load,
   For your rest waiteth yonder ahead."

I could not remain in the house by the road
   And watch as the toilers go on,
Their faces beclouded with pain and with sin,
   So burdened their strength nearly gone.
I'll go to their side, I'll speak in good cheer,
   I'll help them to carry their load;
And I'll smile at the man in the house by the way,
As I walk with the crowd in the road.

Out there in the road that goes by the house,
   Where the poet is singing his song,
I'll walk and I'll work 'midst the heat of the day,
   And I'll help falling brothers along—
Too busy to live in the house by the way,
   Too happy for such an abode.
And my heart sings its praise to the Master of all,
   Who is helping me serve in the road.

WALTER S. GRESHAM.

THE COMING AMERICAN

Bring me men to match my mountains,
Bring me men to match my plains,
And new eras in their brains.
Bring me men to match my prairies,

Men to match my inland seas,
Men whose thoughts shall pave a highway
Up to ampler destinies,
Pioneers to cleanse thought's marshlands,
   And to cleanse old error's fen;
Bring me men to match my mountains—
   Bring me men!

Bring me men to match my forests,
Strong to fight the storm and beast,
Branching toward the skyey future,
Rooted on the futile past.
Bring me men to match my valleys,
   Tolerant of rain and snow,
Men within whose fruitful purpose
   Time's consummate blooms shall **grow,**
Men to tame the tigerish instincts
   Of the lair and cave and den,
Cleanse the dragon slime of nature—
   Bring me men!

Bring me men to match my rivers,
   Continent cleansers, flowing free,
Drawn by eternal madness,
   To be mingled with the sea—
Men of oceanic impulse,
   Men whose moral currents sweep
Toward the wide, infolding ocean
   Of an undiscovered deep—
Men who feel the strong pulsation
   Of the central sea, and then
Time their currents by its earth throbs—
   Bring me Men.

SAM WALTER FOSS.

DO IT NOW

IF WITH PLEASURE you are viewing any work a man is doing,
   If you like him or you love him, tell him now;
Don't withhold your approbation till the parson makes oration
   And he lies with snowy lilies on his brow;

No matter how you shout it he won't really care about it;
  He won't know how many teardrops you have shed;
If you think some praise is due him now's the time to slip it to him,
  For he cannot read his tombstone when he's dead.

More than fame and more than money is the comment kind and sunny
  And the hearty, warm approval of a friend.
For it gives to life a savor, and it makes you stronger, braver,
  And it gives you heart and spirit to the end;
If he earns your praise—bestow it; if you like him let him know it;
  Let the words of true encouragement be said;
Do not wait till life is over and he's underneath the clover,
  For he cannot read his tombstone when he's dead.

BERTON BRALEY.

THE THINKER

BACK OF the beating hammer
  By which the steel is wrought,
Back of the workshop's clamor
  The seeker may find the Thought—
The Thought that is ever master
  Of iron and steam and steel,
That rises above disaster
  And tramples it under heel!

The drudge may fret and tinker
  Or labor with lusty blows,
But back of him stands the Thinker,
  The clear-eyed man who knows;
For into each plow or saber,
  Each piece and part and whole,
Must go the Brains of Labor,
  Which gives the work a soul!

Back of the motors humming,
  Back of the bells that sing,
Back of the hammers drumming,
  Back of the cranes that swing,
There is the eye which scans them
  Watching through stress and strain,
There is the Mind which plans them—
  Back of the brawn, the Brain!

Might of the roaring boiler,
    Force of the engine's thrust,
Strength of the sweating toiler—
    Greatly in these we trust.
But back of them stands the Schemer,
    The Thinker who drives things through;
Back of the Job—the Dreamer
    Who's making the dream come true!

BERTON BRALEY.

THEN LAUGH

BUILD FOR YOURSELF a strong box,
    Fashion each part with care;
When it's strong as your hand can make it,
    Put all your troubles there;
Hide there all thought of your failures,
    And each bitter cup that you quaff;
Lock all your heartaches within it,
    Then sit on the lid and laugh.

Tell no one else its contents,
    Never its secrets share;
When you've dropped in your care and worry
    Keep them forever there;
Hide them from sight so completely
    That the world will never dream half;
Fasten the strong box securely—
    Then sit on the lid and laugh.

BERTHA ADAMS BACKUS.

A PRAYER

LORD, LET ME LIVE like a Regular Man,
    With Regular friends and true;
Let me play the game on a Regular plan
    And play it that way all through;

110

Let me win or lose with a Regular smile
   And never be known to whine,
For that is a Regular Fellow's style
   And I want to make it mine!

Oh, give me a Regular chance in life,
   The same as the rest, I pray,
And give me a Regular girl for wife
   To help me along the way;
Let us know the lot of humanity,
   Its regular woes and joys,
And raise a Regular family
   Of Regular girls and boys!

Let me live to a Regular good old age,
   With Regular snow-white hair,
Having done my labor and earned my wage
   And played my game for fair;
And so at last when the people scan
   My face on its peaceful bier,
They'll say, "Well, he was a Regular Man!"
   And drop a Regular tear!

BERTON BRALEY.

AT YOUR SERVICE: THE PANAMA GANG

HERE WE ARE, gentlemen; here's the whole gang of us,
   Pretty near through with the job we are on;
Size up our work—it will give you the hang of us—
   South to Balboa and north to Colon.
Yes, the Canal is our letter of reference;
   Look at Culebra and glance at Gatun;
What can we do for you—got any preference—
   Wireless to Saturn or bridge to the moon?

Don't send us back to a life that is flat again,
   We who have shattered a continent's spine;
Office work—Lord, but we couldn't do that again.
   Haven't you something that's more in our line?
Got any river they say isn't crossable?
   Got any mountains that can't be cut through?
We specialize in the wholly impossible,
   Doing things "nobody ever could do."

Take a good look at the whole husky gang of us,
   Engineers, doctors and steam-shovel men;
Taken together you'll find quite a few of us
   Soon to be ready for trouble again.
Bronzed by the tropical sun that is blistery,
   Chockful of energy, vigor and tang,
Trained by a task that's the biggest in history—
   Who has a job for this Panama Gang?

BERTON BRALEY.

CO–OPERATION

It AIN'T THE GUNS nor armament,
   Nor funds that they can pay,
But the close co-operation,
   That makes them win the day.

It ain't the individual,
   Nor the army as a whole,
But the everlasting teamwork
   Of every bloomin' soul.

J. MASON KNOX.

VITAÏ LAMPADA

There's A BREATHLESS HUSH in the Close to-night—
   Ten to make and the match to win—
A bumping pitch and a blinding light,
   An hour to play and the last man in.
And it's not for the sake of a ribboned coat,
   Or the selfish hope of a season's fame,
But his Captain's hand on his shoulder smote
   "Play up! play up! and play the game!"

The sand of the desert is sodden red,—
   Red with the wreck of a square that broke;—
The Gatling's jammed and the colonel dead,
   And the regiment blind with dust and smoke.

The river of death has brimmed his banks,
   And England's far, and Honor a name,
But the voice of a schoolboy rallies the ranks,
   "Play up! play up! and play the game!"

This is the word that year by year
   While in her place the School is set
Every one of her sons must hear,
   And none that hears it dare forget.
This they all with a joyful mind
   Bear through life like a torch in flame,
And falling fling to the host behind—
   "Play up! play up! and play the game!"

HENRY NEWBOLT.

LIVING

To touch the cup with eager lips and taste, not drain it;
To woo and tempt and court a bliss—and not attain it;
To fondle and caress a joy, yet hold it lightly,
Lest it become necessity and cling too tightly;
To watch the sun set in the west without regretting;
To hail its advent in the east—the night forgetting;
To smother care in happiness and grief in laughter;
To hold the present close—not questioning hereafter;
To have enough to share—to know the joy of giving;
To thrill with all the sweets of life—is living.

UNKNOWN.

DON'T QUIT

When things go wrong, as they sometimes will,
When the road you're trudging seems all up hill,
When the funds are low and the debts are high,
And you want to smile, but you have to sigh,
When care is pressing you down a bit,
Rest, if you must—but don't you quit.

113

Life is queer with its twists and turns,
As everyone of us sometimes learns,
And many a failure turns about
When he might have won had he stuck it out;
Don't give up, though the pace seems slow—
You might succeed with another blow.

Often the goal is nearer than
It seems to a faint and faltering man,
Often the struggler has given up
When he might have captured the victor's cup.
And he learned too late, when the night slipped down,
How close he was to the golden crown.

Success is failure turned inside out—
The silver tint of the clouds of doubt—
And you never can tell how close you are,
It may be near when it seems afar;
So stick to the fight when you're hardest hit—
It's when things seem worst that you mustn't quit.

UNKNOWN.

HOW TO BE HAPPY

ARE YOU ALMOST DISGUSTED with life, little man?
  I'll tell you a wonderful trick
That will bring you contentment, if anything can,
  Do something for somebody, quick!

Are you awfully tired with play, little girl?
  Wearied, discouraged, and sick—
I'll tell you the loveliest game in the world,
  Do something for somebody, quick!

Though it rains, like the rain of the flood, little man,
  And the clouds are forbidding and thick,
You can make the sun shine in your soul, little man,
  Do something for somebody, quick!

Though the stars are like brass overhead, little girl,
  And the walks like a well-heated brick,
And our earthly affairs in a terrible whirl,
  Do something for somebody, quick!

UNKNOWN.

114

THE DAY IS DONE

THE DAY IS DONE, and the darkness
  Falls from the wings of Night,
As a feather is wafted downward
  From an eagle in his flight.

I see the lights of the village
  Gleam through the rain and the mist:
And a feeling of sadness comes o'er me,
  That my soul cannot resist:

A feeling of sadness and longing,
  That is not akin to pain,
And resembles sorrow only
  As the mist resembles the rain.

Come, read to me some poem,
  Some simple and heartfelt lay,
That shall soothe this restless feeling,
  And banish the thoughts of day.

Not from the grand old masters,
  Not from the bards sublime,
Whose distant footsteps echo
  Through the corridors of Time.

For, like strains of martial music,
  Their mighty thoughts suggest
Life's endless toil and endeavor;
  And to-night I long for rest.

Read from some humbler poet,
  Whose songs gush'd from his heart,
As showers from the clouds of summer,
  Or tears from the eyelids start;

Who, through long days of labor,
  And nights devoid of ease,
Still heard in his soul the music
  Of wonderful melodies.

Such songs have power to quiet
  The restless pulse of care,
And come like the benediction
  That follows after prayer.

Then read from the treasured volume
  The poem of thy choice;
And lend to the rhyme of the poet
  The beauty of thy voice.

And the night shall be fill'd with music,
  And the cares that infest the day
Shall fold their tents like the Arabs,
  And as silently steal away.

                    HENRY WADSWORTH LONGFELLOW.

I KNOW SOMETHING GOOD ABOUT YOU

WOULDN'T THIS old world be better
  If the folks we meet would say—
"I know something good about you!"
  And treat us just that way?

Wouldn't it be fine and dandy
  If each handclasp, fond and true,
Carried with it this assurance—
  "I know something good about you!"

Wouldn't life be lots more happy
  If the good that's in us all
Were the only thing about us
  That folks bothered to recall?

Wouldn't life be lots more happy
  If we praised the good we see?
For there's such a lot of goodness
  In the worst of you and me!

Wouldn't it be nice to practise
  That fine way of thinking, too?
You know something good about me,
  I know something good about you?

                    LOUIS C. SHIMON.

116

BORN WITHOUT A CHANCE

THE TIME: *Napoleonic in Europe, Jeffersonian in America.*
THE SCENE: *An outlying border state, sometimes called "the dark and bloody ground."*
THE EXACT DATE: *February 12, 1809.*

A SQUALID VILLAGE set in wintry mud.
A hub-deep oxcart slowly groans and creaks.
A horseman hails and halts. He shifts his cud
And speaks:

Well, did you hear? Tom Lincoln's wife today.
The devil's luck for folk as poor as they!
    Poor Tom! poor Nance!
Poor youngun born without a chance!

"A baby in that Godforsaken den,
That worse than cattle pen!
Well, what are they but cattle? Cattle? Tut!
A critter is beef, hide and tallow, but
Who'd swap one for the critters of that hut?
    White trash! small fry!
Whose only instincts are to multiply!
    They're good at that,
And so, today, God wot! another brat!

"Another squawking, squalling, red-faced good-for-naught
Spilled on the world, heaven only knows for what.
    Better if he were black,
For then he'd have a shirt upon his back,
And something in his belly, as he grows.
More than he's like to have, as I suppose.
    Yet there be those
Who claim 'equality' for this new brat,
    And that damned democrat
Who squats today where Washington once sat,
He'd have it that this Lincoln cub might be
Of even value in the world with you and me!

"Yes, Jefferson, Tom Jefferson, who but he?
Who even hints that black men should be free.
That featherheaded fool would tell you maybe
A president might lie in this new baby!

117

In this new squawker born without a rag
To hide himself! Good God, it makes me gag!
   This human spawn
Born for the world to wipe its feet upon
   A few years hence, but now
More helpless than the litter of a sow,
And—— Oh, well! send the womenfolks to see to Nance.

"Poor little devil! born without a chance!"

EDMUND VANCE COOKE.

HOW DID YOU DIE?

DID YOU TACKLE that trouble that came your way
   With a resolute heart and cheerful?
Or hide your face from the light of day
   With a craven soul and fearful?
Oh, a trouble's a ton, or a trouble's an ounce,
   Or a trouble is what you make it,
And it isn't the fact that you're hurt that counts,
   But only how did you take it?

You are beaten to earth? Well, well, what's that!
   Come up with a smiling face.
It's nothing against you to fall down flat,
   But to lie there—that's disgrace.
The harder you're thrown, why the higher you bounce;
   Be proud of your blackened eye!
It isn't the fact that you're licked that counts;
   It's how did you fight—and why?

And though you be done to the death, what then?
   If you battled the best you could;
If you played your part in the world of men,
   Why, the Critic will call it good.
Death comes with a crawl, or comes with a pounce,
   And whether he's slow or spry,
It isn't the fact that you're dead that counts,
   But only how did you die?

EDMUND VANCE COOKE.

ALL TO MYSELF

ALL TO MYSELF I find the way
Back to each golden yesterday,
Faring in fancy until I stand
Clasping your ready, friendly hand;
The picture seems half true, half dream,
And I keep its color and its gleam
   All to myself.

All to myself I hum again
Fragments of some old-time refrain,
Something that comes at fancy's choice,
And I hear the cadence of your voice:
Sometimes 'tis dim, sometimes 'tis clear,
But I keep the music that I hear
   All to myself.

All to myself I hold and know
All of the days of long ago—
Wonderful days when you and I
Owned all the sunshine in the sky:
The days come back as the old days will,
And I keep their tingle and their thrill
   All to myself.

All to myself! My friend, do you
Count all the memories softly, too?
Summer and Autumn, Winter, Spring,
The hopes we cherish, and everything?
They course my veins as a draft divine,
And I keep them wholly, solely mine—
   All to myself.

All to myself I think of you,
Think of the things we used to do,
Think of the things we used to say,
Think of each happy, bygone day;
Sometimes I sigh and sometimes I smile,
But I keep each olden, golden while
   All to myself.

                WILBUR DICK NESBIT.

WATCH YOURSELF GO BY

JUST STAND ASIDE and watch yourself go by;
Think of yourself as "he" instead of "I."
Note, closely as in other men you note,
The bag-kneed trousers and the seedy coat.
Pick flaws; find fault; forget the man is you,
And strive to make your estimate ring true.
Confront yourself and look you in the eye—
Just stand aside and watch yourself go by.

Interpret all your motives just as though
You looked on one whose aims you did not know.
Let undisguised contempt surge through you when
You see you shirk, O commonest of men!
Despise your cowardice; condemn whate'er
You note of falseness in you anywhere.
Defend not one defect that shames your eye—
Just stand aside and watch yourself go by.

And then, with eyes unveiled to what you loathe,
To sins that with sweet charity you'd clothe,
Back to your self-walled tenement you'll go
With tolerance for all who dwell below.
The faults of others then will dwarf and shrink,
Love's chain grow stronger by one mighty link,
When you, with "he" as substitute for "I,"
Have stood aside and watched yourself go by.

STRICKLAND GILLILAN.

OUT WHERE THE WEST BEGINS

OUT WHERE the handclasp's a little stronger,
Out where the smile dwells a little longer,
   That's where the West begins;
Out where the sun is a little brighter,
Where the snows that fall are a trifle whiter,
Where the bonds of home are a wee bit tighter,—
   That's where the West begins.

Out where the skies are a trifle bluer,
Out where friendship's a little truer,
   That's where the West begins;
Out where a fresher breeze is blowing,
Where there's laughter in every streamlet flowing,
Where there's more of reaping and less of sowing,—
   That's where the West begins.

Out where the world is in the making,
Where fewer hearts in despair are aching,
   That's where the West begins;
Where there's more of singing and less of sighing,
Where there's more of giving and less of buying,
And a man makes friends without half trying—
   That's where the West begins.

                ARTHUR CHAPMAN.

A SONG FROM "SYLVAN"

THE LITTLE CARES that fretted me,
   I lost them yesterday
Among the fields above the sea,
   Among the winds at play;
Among the lowing herds,
   The rustling of the trees,
Among the singing birds,
   The humming of the bees.

The fears of what may come to pass,
   I cast them all away,
Among the clover-scented grass,
   Among the new-mown hay;
Among the husking of the corn,
   Where the drowsy poppies nod,
Where ill thoughts die and good are born,
   Out in the fields with God.

          LOUISE IMOGEN GUINEY.

MY WAGE

I BARGAINED with Life for a penny,
  And Life would pay no more,
However I begged at evening
  When I counted my scanty store;

For Life is a just employer,
  He gives you what you ask,
But once you have set the wages,
  Why, you must bear the task.

I worked for a menial's hire,
  Only to learn, dismayed,
That any wage I had asked of Life,
  Life would have paid.

JESSIE B. RITTENHOUSE.

MY "PATCH OF BLUE"

THERE'S A BIT of sky across the street
Which I have learned to love,
One end of it rests on the house tops high,
The other on the heavens above.
It looks most beautiful at times
And has been such a comfort, too,
That when I look thro' my windowpane
I call it my "Patch of Blue."
When I think of God's great universe
With its vast expanse of sky,
And of those who can roam from sea to sea
Without a thought of why
This wondrous joy is given to them
By a God so kind and true,
I wonder if they are quite as glad
As I, for my "Patch of Blue."

I call it mine: God's gift to me,
From September until June.
It heals my hurt; it warms my heart;
And I'm sure that very soon

The lesson that it teaches me
Will warm me thro' and thro';
For it seems as though God's blessed smile
Shines thro' my "Patch of Blue."

I've seen it when light, fleecy clouds
Went scurrying 'cross its face
And made that tiny bit of sky
Look like a bit of lace.
I've also seen the storm clouds burst,
And winds go rushing thro',
But I always knew that once again
I'd see my "Patch of Blue."

I've watched it when the wintry snows
Had hidden it from sight,
But I have known full well that soon
It would once more be bright.
When sunset drops her curtain down
She turns to golden hue
That little bit of lovely sky
That was my "Patch of Blue."

When I lie upon my bed at night,
With a heart full of pain and fear,
I think of the twinkling stars out there
That shine so bright and clear.
I think of the radiant, glorious moon
Shining the whole night thro',
And I know that the morning sun will bring
Once more my "Patch of Blue."

I've looked across that bit of sky
As the twilight hour drew near,
And thought of one in that "Great Beyond"
Who was to me most dear.
He was such a very little lad,
Only four years old,
When he passed the portals thro'
And he's still waiting for me there
Beyond my "Patch of Blue."

There are other dear ones over there
Whose journey here is o'er.
I shall see them sometime, somewhere,
At rest on the shining shore.

Dear Lord! Please help my life to be
So patient, kind and true
That when at last my race is run
I can cross my "Patch of Blue."

And then one day—when I tried to look
I found I could not see.
In my despair I cried aloud,
"O God—it cannot be
That I must nevermore enjoy
This precious, precious view,
That I must learn to do without
My little 'Patch of Blue.' "

I know not what's in store for me
Of sorrow, joy or pain;
I do not know when I can see
My bit of sky again.
But I'm sure God's love and mercy
Will lead me safely thro',
And in my very heart of hearts
He can put a "Patch of Blue."

Oh! Friend o' mine! Are you shut in?
Does your life seem hard to bear?
Does your heart grow sick with longing
For the joys you once could share?
"I'll go with you," saith the Master,
And his promises are true;
So we're sure that in His blessed arms
We'll find our "Patch of Blue."

MARY NEWLAND CARSON.

DROP A PEBBLE IN THE WATER

DROP A PEBBLE in the water: just a splash, and it is gone;
  But there's half-a-hundred ripples circling on and on and on,
Spreading, spreading from the center, flowing on out to the sea.
  And there is no way of telling where the end is going to be.

Drop a pebble in the water: in a minute you forget,
  But there's little waves a-flowing, and there's ripples circling yet,

And those little waves a-flowing to a great big wave have grown;
You've disturbed a mighty river just by dropping in a stone.

Drop an unkind word, or careless: in a minute it is gone;
    But there's half-a-hundred ripples circling on and on and on.
They keep spreading, spreading, spreading from the center as they go,
    And there is no way to stop them, once you've started them to flow.

Drop an unkind word, or careless: in a minute you forget;
    But there's little waves a-flowing, and there's ripples circling yet,
And perhaps in some sad heart a mighty wave of tears you've stirred,
    And disturbed a life was happy ere you dropped that unkind word.

Drop a word of cheer and kindness: just a flash and it is gone;
    But there's half-a-hundred ripples circling on and on and on,
Bearing hope and joy and comfort on each splashing, dashing wave
    Till you wouldn't believe the volume of the one kind word you gave.

Drop a word of cheer and kindness: in a minute you forget;
    But there's gladness still a-swelling, and there's joy a-circling yet,
And you've rolled a wave of comfort whose sweet music can be heard
    Over miles and miles of water just by dropping one kind word.

                                          JAMES W. FOLEY.

TO THE MEN WHO LOSE

HERE'S TO THE MEN who lose!
What though their work be e'er so nobly planned,
And watched with zealous care,
No glorious halo crowns their efforts grand;
Contempt is failure's share.

Here's to the men who lose!
If triumph's easy smile our struggles greet,
Courage is easy then;
The king is he who, after fierce defeat,
Can up and fight again.

Here's to the men who lose!
The ready plaudits of a fawning world
Ring sweet in victor's ears;
The vanquished's banners never are unfurled;
For them sound no cheers.

Here's to the men who lose!
The touchstone of true worth is not success;
There is a higher test—
Though fate may darkly frown, onward to press,
And bravely do one's best.

Here's to the men who lose!
It is the vanquished's praises that I sing,
And this is the toast I choose:
"A hard-fought failure is a noble thing!
Here's to the men who lose."

GEORGE L. SCARBOROUGH.

TOUCHING SHOULDERS

THERE'S A COMFORTING THOUGHT at the close of the day,
When I'm weary and lonely and sad,
That sort of grips hold of my crusty old heart
And bids it be merry and glad.
It gets in my soul and it drives out the blues,
And finally thrills through and through.
It is just a sweet memory that chants the refrain:
"I'm glad I touch shoulders with you!"

Did you know you were brave, did you know you were strong?
Did you know there was one leaning hard?
Did you know that I waited and listened and prayed,
And was cheered by your simplest word?
Did you know that I longed for that smile on your face,
For the sound of your voice ringing true?
Did you know I grew stronger and better because
I had merely touched shoulders with you?

I am glad that I live, that I battle and strive
For the place that I know I must fill;
I am thankful for sorrows, I'll meet with a grin
What fortune may send, good or ill.
I may not have wealth, I may not be great,
But I know I shall always be true,
For I have in my life that courage you gave
When once I rubbed shoulders with you.

UNKNOWN.

126

BEAUTIFUL THINGS

BEAUTIFUL FACES are those that wear—
It matters little if dark or fair—
Whole-souled honesty printed there.

Beautiful eyes are those that show,
Like crystal panes where hearthfires glow,
Beautiful thoughts that burn below.

Beautiful lips are those whose words
Leap from the heart like songs of birds,
Yet whose utterance prudence girds.

Beautiful hands are those that do
Work that is honest and brave and true,
Moment by moment the long day through.

Beautiful feet are those that go
On kindly ministries to and fro,
Down lowliest ways, if God wills it so.

Beautiful shoulders are those that bear
Ceaseless burdens of homely care
With patient grace and daily prayer.

Beautiful lives are those that bless
Silent rivers of happiness,
Whose hidden fountains but few may guess.

Beautiful twilight at set of sun,
Beautiful goal with race well won,
Beautiful rest with work well done.

Beautiful graves where grasses creep,
Where brown leaves fall, where drifts lie deep
Over worn-out hands—oh! beautiful sleep!

ELLEN P. ALLERTON.

GIVE US MEN!

GIVE US Men!
Men—from every rank,
Fresh and free and frank;
Men of thought and reading,
Men of light and leading,
Men of loyal breeding,
The nation's welfare speeding;
Men of faith and not of fiction,
Men of lofty aim in action;
　Give us Men—I say again,
　　Give us Men!

Give us Men!
Strong and stalwart ones;
Men whom highest hope inspires,
Men whom purest honor fires,
Men who trample self beneath them,
Men who make their country wreathe them
　As her noble sons,
　Worthy of their sires;
Men who never shame their mothers,
Men who never fail their brothers,
True, however false are others:
　Give us Men—I say again,
　　Give us Men!

Give us Men!
Men who, when the tempest gathers,
Grasp the standard of their fathers
　In the thickest fight;
Men who strike for home and altar,
(Let the coward cringe and falter),
　God defend the right!
True as truth the lorn and lonely,
Tender, as the brave are only;
Men who tread where saints have trod,
Men for Country, Home—and God:
　Give us Men! I say again—again—
　　Give us Men!

JOSIAH GILBERT HOLLAND.

EMANCIPATION

I WORK or play, as I think best;
  I fare abroad, or stay at home;
When weary, I sit down and rest;
  I bid one go, another come—
    Because I'm sixty!

When whistles blow with clamorous hue,
  I rouse me not, as I was wont.
I do the things I like to do,
  And leave undone the things I don't—
    Because I'm sixty!

I grow not blind, nor deaf, nor lame,
  I still can dance, and hear, and see,
But love the restful book or game;
  No more the strenuous life for me,
    I quit at sixty!

My toilet is my fondest care,
  The serial story I peruse;
I glory in my silvering hair,
  I love my comfortable shoes—
    I'm glad I'm sixty!

Let youngsters lift the weary load,
  And at the burden tug and strain:
I love the easy, downward road;
  I would not climb life's hill again—
    Glory be! I'm sixty!

UNKNOWN. ATTRIBUTED
TO "MRS. C. B. F."

LIFE'S MIRROR

THERE ARE LOYAL HEARTS, there are spirits brave,
  There are souls that are pure and true;
Then give to the world the best you have,
  And the best will come back to you.

Give love, and love to your life will flow,
  A strength in your utmost need;
Have faith, and a score of hearts will show
  Their faith in your word and deed.

Give truth, and your gift will be paid in kind,
  And honor will honor meet;
And a smile that is sweet will surely find
  A smile that is just as sweet.

Give sorrow and pity to those who mourn;
  You will gather in flowers again
The scattered seeds of your thought outborne,
  Though the sowing seemed but vain.

For life is the mirror of king and slave—
  'Tis just what we are and do;
Then give to the world the best you have,
  And the best will come back to you.

"MADELINE BRIDGES"
(MARY AINGE DE VERE).

THE HUMAN TOUCH

'TIS THE HUMAN TOUCH in this world that counts,
  The touch of your hand and mine,
Which means far more to the fainting heart
  Than shelter and bread and wine;
For shelter is gone when the night is o'er,
  And bread lasts only a day,
But the touch of the hand and the sound of the voice
  Sing on in the soul alway.

SPENCER MICHAEL FREE.

YOUR MISSION

IF YOU CANNOT on the ocean
  Sail among the swiftest fleet,
Rocking on the highest billows,
  Laughing at the storms you meet,

You can stand among the sailors,
  Anchored yet within the bay;
You can lend a hand to help them,
  As they launch their boats away.

If you are too weak to journey
  Up the mountain, steep and high,
You can stand within the valley,
  While the multitude go by.
You can chant in happy measure,
  As they slowly pass along;
Though they may forget the singer,
  They will not forget the song.

If you have not gold and silver
  Ever ready to command,
If you cannot toward the needy
  Reach an ever-open hand,
You can visit the afflicted,
  O'er the erring you can weep;
You can be a true disciple,
  Sitting at the Saviour's feet.

If you cannot in the conflict
  Prove yourself a soldier true,
If where the fire and smoke are thickest
  There's no work for you to do,
When the battle field is silent,
  You can go with a careful tread;
You can bear away the wounded,
  You can cover up the dead.

Do not then stand idly waiting
  For some greater work to do;
Fortune is a lazy goddess,
  She will never come to you.
Go and toil in any vineyard,
  Do not fear to do or dare;
If you want a field of labor,
  You can find it anywhere.

ELLEN M. H. GATES.

MY NEIGHBOR'S ROSES

THE ROSES RED upon my neighbor's vine
Are owned by him, but they are also mine.
His was the cost, and his the labor, too,
But mine as well as his the joy, their loveliness to view.

They bloom for me and are for me as fair
As for the man who gives them all his care.
Thus I am rich, because a good man grew
A rose-clad vine for all his neighbors' view.

I know from this that others plant for me,
And what they own, my joy may also be.
So why be selfish, when so much that's fine
Is grown for you, upon your neighbor's vine.

ABRAHAM L. GRUBER.

GOD, GIVE US MEN!

GOD, GIVE US MEN! A time like this demands
Strong minds, great hearts, true faith and ready hands;
   Men whom the lust of office does not kill;
Men whom the spoils of office cannot buy;
   Men who possess opinions and a will;
Men who have honor; men who will not lie;
Men who can stand before a demagogue
   And damn his treacherous flatteries without winking!
Tall men, sun-crowned, who live above the fog
   In public duty and in private thinking;
For while the rabble, with their thumb-worn creeds,
Their large professions and their little deeds,
Mingle in selfish strife, lo! Freedom weeps,
Wrong rules the land and waiting Justice sleeps.

JOSIAH GILBERT HOLLAND.

THE FIGHTER

I FIGHT a battle every day
   Against discouragement and fear;
Some foe stands always in my way,
   The path ahead is never clear!

I must forever be on guard
  Against the doubts that skulk along;
I get ahead by fighting hard,
  But fighting keeps my spirit strong.

I hear the croakings of Despair,
  The dark predictions of the weak;
I find myself pursued by Care,
  No matter what the end I seek;
My victories are small and few,
  It matters not how hard I strive;
Each day the fight begins anew,
  But fighting keeps my hopes alive.

My dreams are spoiled by circumstance,
  My plans are wrecked by Fate or Luck;
Some hour, perhaps, will bring my chance,
  But that great hour has never struck;
My progress has been slow and hard,
  I've had to climb and crawl and swim,
Fighting for every stubborn yard;
  But I have kept in fighting trim.

I have to fight my doubts away
  And be on guard against my fears;
The feeble croaking of Dismay
  Has been familiar through the years;
My dearest plans keep going wrong,
  Events combine to thwart my will;
But fighting keeps my spirit strong,
  And I am undefeated still!

S. E. KISER.

WHEN I AM OLD

WHEN I AM OLD—and O, how soon
Will life's sweet morning yield to noon,
And noon's broad, fervid, earnest light
Be shaded in the solemn night,
Till, like a story well-nigh told,
Will seem my life—when I am old.

When I am old, this breezy earth
Will lose for me its voice of mirth;
The streams will have an undertone
Of sadness not by right their own;
And Spring's sweet power in vain unfold
In rosy charms—when I am old.

When I am old, I shall not care
To deck with flowers my faded hair;
'Twill be no vain desire of mine
In rich and costly dress to shine;
Bright jewels and the brightest gold
Will charm me naught—when I am old.

When I am old, my friends will be
Old and infirm and bowed like me;
Or else (their bodies 'neath the sod,
Their spirits dwelling safe with God);
The old church bells will long have tolled
Above the rest—when I am old.

When I am old, I'd rather bend
Thus sadly o'er each buried friend
Than see them lose the earnest truth
That marks the friendship of our youth;
'Twill be so sad to have them cold
Or strange to me—when I am old!

When I am old—O! how it seems
Like the wild lunacy of dreams
To picture in prophetic rhyme
That dim, far-distant, shadowy time—
So distant that it seems o'erbold
Even to say, "When I am old."

Ere I am old—that time is now;
For youth sits lightly on my brow;
My limbs are firm, and strong, and free;
Life hath a thousand charms for me—
Charms that will long their influence hold
Within my heart—ere I am old.

Ere I am old, O! let me give
My life to learning how to live;

Then shall I meet, with willing heart,
An early summons to depart.
Or find my lengthened days consoled
By God's sweet peace—when I am old.

CAROLINE ATHERTON BRIGGS MASON.

THE COMMON ROAD

I WANT TO TRAVEL the common road
With the great crowd surging by,
Where there's many a laugh and many a load,
And many a smile and sigh.
I want to be on the common way
With its endless tramping feet,
In the summer bright and winter gray,
In the noonday sun and heat.
In the cool of evening with shadows nigh,
At dawn, when the sun breaks clear,
I want the great crowd passing by,
To ken what they see and hear.
I want to be one of the common herd,
Not live in a sheltered way,
Want to be thrilled, want to be stirred
By the great crowd day by day;
To glimpse the restful valleys deep,
To toil up the rugged hill,
To see the brooks which shyly creep,
To have the torrents thrill.
I want to laugh with the common man
Wherever he chance to be,
I want to aid him when I can
Whenever there's need of me.
I want to lend a helping hand
Over the rough and steep
To a child too young to understand—
To comfort those who weep.
I want to live and work and plan
With the great crowd surging by,
To mingle with the common man,
No better or worse than I.

SILAS H. PERKINS.

BEAUTY AS A SHIELD

I WILL HOLD BEAUTY as a shield against despair.
When my heart faints I will remember sights like these:
Bronze cypresses that framed a sapphire sea,
A desert mesa wrapped in sunset flame,
An airplane that raced the Overland
Above a trail still marked with whitening bones;
A path through a dim forest, hushed and sweet,
Lit by one amber beam that fell aslant;
Foam, silver-laced, along a curving wave;
Sprawled golden hills, with shadows like spilled wine;
Tall office buildings rearing through the night
Sheer walls of alabaster pierced with gold—
And snowflakes falling on a lonely pine.

I will hold beauty as a shield against despair.
When my heart faints I will remember sights like these:
The dawning wonder in a baby's face,
The kindness in a weary wanton's smile,
The gallant challenge of a cripple's grin,
Seeing forever bodies that are straight;
The fighting courage in a mother's eyes
When she waits, braced, to meet birth's gripping pains;
The shy adoring of a boy's first love,
The eager beauty of his first crusade
Against some wrong which he alone can right—
The tolerance that sometimes comes with age.

When my heart faints I will remember sights like these,
Holding their beauty as a shield against despair:
For if I can see glory such as this
With my dim eyes, my undeveloped brain,
And if from other darkened, selfish lives
Such flashes of brave loveliness can come,
Then surely there is something more than this
Sad maze of pain, bewilderment and fear—
And if there's something, I can still hope on.

ELSIE ROBINSON.

[To be accompanied by
Chopin Nocturne Op. 48—No. 1 movement.]

THE BRIDGE BUILDER

AN OLD man, going a lone highway,
Came at the evening, cold and gray,
To a chasm, vast and deep and wide,
Through which was flowing a sullen tide.
The old man crossed in the twilight dim—
That sullen stream had no fears for him;
But he turned, when he reached the other side,
And built a bridge to span the tide.

"Old man," said a fellow pilgrim near,
"You are wasting strength in building here.
Your journey will end with the ending day;
You never again must pass this way.
You have crossed the chasm, deep and wide,
Why build you the bridge at the eventide?"

The builder lifted his old grey head.
"Good friend, in the path I have come," he said,
"There followeth after me today
A youth whose feet must pass this way.
This chasm that has been naught to me
To that fair-haired youth may a pitfall be.
He, too, must cross in the twilight dim;
Good friend, I am building the bridge for *him*."

WILL ALLEN DROMGOOLE.

THE LORD GOD PLANTED A GARDEN

THE Lord God planted a garden
    In the first white days of the world,
And he set there an angel warden
    In a garment of light enfurled.

So near to the peace of Heaven,
    That the hawk might nest with the wren,
For there in the cool of the even'
    God walked with the first of men.

The kiss of the sun for pardon,
    The song of the birds for mirth—
One is nearer God's heart in a garden
    Than anywhere else on earth.

DOROTHY FRANCES GURNEY.

FATE

Two SHALL BE BORN, the whole wide world apart,
And speak in different tongues and have no thought
Each of the other's being, and no heed;
And these, o'er unknown seas, to unknown lands
Shall cross, escaping wreck, defying death;
And all unconsciously shape every act
And bend each wandering step to this one end—
That one day out of darkness they shall meet
And read life's meaning in each other's eyes.

And two shall walk some narrow way of life
So nearly side by side that, should one turn
Ever so little space to left or right,
They needs must stand acknowledged, face to face,
And yet, with wistful eyes that never meet,
And groping hands that never clasp, and lips
Calling in vain to ears that never hear,
They seek each other all their weary days
And die unsatisfied—and this is Fate!

SUSAN MARR SPALDING.

THIS, TOO, SHALL PASS AWAY

WHEN SOME GREAT SORROW, like a mighty river,
  Flows through your life with peace-destroying power,
And dearest things are swept from sight forever,
    Say to your heart each trying hour:
      "This, too, shall pass away."

When ceaseless toil has hushed your song of gladness,
  And you have grown almost too tired to pray,
Let this truth banish from your heart its sadness,
    And ease the burdens of each trying day:
      "This, too, shall pass away."

When fortune smiles, and, full of mirth and pleasure,
  The days are flitting by without a care,
Lest you should rest with only earthly treasure,
    Let these few words their fullest import bear:
      "This, too, shall pass away."

When earnest labor brings you fame and glory,
   And all earth's noblest ones upon you smile,
Remember that life's longest, grandest story
   Fills but a moment in earth's little while:
     "This, too, shall pass away."

LANTA WILSON SMITH.

A VERY MINOR POET SPEAKS

A GLOWWORM in a garden prayed:
"I cannot glow! God, Thou hast made
Me with an ache to glow; Thy stamp
Is on my kin; each has a lamp,
Which, as Thou breathest through the night,
Goes down and up; I have no light.
Unless Thyself within him burn,
How should Thy crawling creature learn
To trace his circle in the sand
Cast rayless from Thy ray-filled hand—
A thing not worth the Maker's mark?
Who builds a temple leaves it dark—
Forgets the candle in the shrine?
God! Set me glowing! Let me shine!"

ISABEL VALLE.

TO KNOW ALL IS TO FORGIVE ALL

IF I KNEW YOU and you knew me—
If both of us could clearly see,
And with an inner sight divine
The meaning of your heart and mine—
I'm sure that we would differ less
And clasp our hands in friendliness;
Our thoughts would pleasantly agree
If I knew you, and you knew me.

If I knew you and you knew me,
As each one knows his own self, we
Could look each other in the face
And see therein a truer grace.

Life has so many hidden woes,
So many thorns for every rose;
The "why" of things our hearts would see,
If I knew you and you knew me.

NIXON WATERMAN.

OPTIMISM

TALK HAPPINESS. The world is sad enough
Without your woes. No path is wholly rough;
Look for the places that are smooth and clear,
And speak of those, to rest the weary ear
Of Earth, so hurt by one continuous strain
Of human discontent and grief and pain.

Talk faith. The world is better off without
Your uttered ignorance and morbid doubt.
If you have faith in God, or man, or self,
Say so. If not, push back upon the shelf
Of silence all your thoughts, till faith shall come;
No one will grieve because your lips are dumb.

Talk health. The dreary, never-changing tale
Of mortal maladies is worn and stale.
You cannot charm, or interest, or please
By harping on that minor chord, disease.
Say you are well, or all is well with you,
And God shall hear your words and make them true.

ELLA WHEELER WILCOX.

PROGRESS

LET THERE BE MANY WINDOWS to your soul,
That all the glory of the universe
May beautify it. Not the narrow pane
Of one poor creed can catch the radiant rays
That shine from countless sources. Tear away
The blinds of superstition; let the light
Pour through fair windows broad as Truth itself
And high as God.

Why should the spirit peer
Through some priest-curtained orifice, and grope
Along dim corridors of doubt, when all
The splendor from unfathomed seas of space
Might bathe it with the golden waves of Love?
Sweep up the débris of decaying faiths;
Sweep down the cobwebs of worn-out beliefs,
And throw your soul wide open to the light
Of Reason and of Knowledge. Tune your ear
To all the wordless music of the stars
And to the voice of Nature, and your heart
Shall turn to truth and goodness as the plant
Turns to the sun. A thousand unseen hands
Reach down to help you to their peace-crowned heights,
And all the forces of the firmament
Shall fortify your strength. Be not afraid
To thrust aside half-truths and grasp the whole.

ELLA WHEELER WILCOX.

THE TWO GLASSES

THERE SAT TWO GLASSES filled to the brim,
On a rich man's table, rim to rim;
One was ruddy and red as blood,
And one as clear as the crystal flood.

Said the glass of wine to the paler brother:
"Let us tell the tales of the past to each other;
I can tell of banquet and revel and mirth,
And the proudest and grandest souls on earth
Fell under my touch as though struck by blight,
Where I was king, for I ruled in might;
From the heads of kings I have torn the crown,
From the heights of fame I have hurled men down:
I have blasted many an honored name;
I have taken virtue and given shame;
I have tempted the youth with a sip, a taste,
That has made his future a barren waste.
Greater, far greater than king am I,
Or than any army beneath the sky.
I have made the arm of the driver fail,
And sent the train from the iron rail;

I have made good ships go down at sea,
And the shrieks of the lost were sweet to me,
For they said, 'Behold how great you be!
Fame, strength, wealth, genius before you fall,
For your might and power are over all.'
Ho! ho! pale brother," laughed the wine,
"Can you boast of deeds as great as mine?"

Said the water glass: "I cannot boast
Of a king dethroned or a murdered host;
But I can tell of a heart once sad,
By my crystal drops made light and glad;
Of thirsts I've quenched, of brows I've laved,
Of hands I have cooled, and souls I have saved;
I have leaped through the valley, dashed down the mountain,
Flowed in the river and played in the fountain,
Slept in the sunshine and dropped from the sky,
And everywhere gladdened the landscape and eye.
I have eased the hot forehead of fever and pain;
I have made the parched meadows grow fertile with grain;
I can tell of the powerful wheel of the mill,
That ground out the flour and turned at my will.
I can tell of manhood debased by you,
That I have lifted and crowned anew.
I cheer, I help, I strengthen and aid;
I gladden the heart of man and maid;
I set the chained wine-captive free;
And all are better for knowing me."

These are the tales they told each other,
The glass of wine and the paler brother,
As they sat together filled to the brim,
On the rich man's table, rim to rim.

ELLA WHEELER WILCOX.

WHATEVER IS—IS BEST

I know, as my life grows older,
    And mine eyes have clearer sight,
That under each rank wrong somewhere
    There lies the root of Right;

That each sorrow has its purpose,
  By the sorrowing oft unguessed;
But as sure as the sun brings morning,
  Whatever is—is best.

I know that each sinful action,
  As sure as the night brings shade,
Is somewhere, sometime punished,
  Tho' the hour be long delayed.
I know that the soul is aided
  Sometimes by the heart's unrest,
And to grow means often to suffer—
  But whatever is—is best.

I know there are no errors,
  In the great Eternal plan,
And all things work together
  For the final good of man.
And I know when my soul speeds onward,
  In its grand Eternal quest,
I shall say as I look back earthward,
  Whatever is—is best.

ELLA WHEELER WILCOX.

WILL

THERE IS NO CHANCE, no destiny, no fate,
  Can circumvent or hinder or control
  The firm resolve of a determined soul.
Gifts count for nothing; will alone is great;
All things give way before it, soon or late.
  What obstacle can stay the mighty force
  Of the sea-seeking river in its course,
Or cause the ascending orb of day to wait?

Each wellborn soul must win what it deserves.
  Let the fool prate of luck. The fortunate
    Is he whose earnest purpose never swerves,
    Whose slightest action or inaction serves
The one great aim. Why, even Death stands still,
And waits an hour sometimes for such a will.

ELLA WHEELER WILCOX.

WORTH WHILE

IT IS EASY ENOUGH to be pleasant,
    When life flows by like a song,
But the man worth while is one who will smile,
    When everything goes dead wrong.
For the test of the heart is trouble,
    And it always comes with the years,
And the smile that is worth the praises of earth
    Is the smile that shines through tears.

It is easy enough to be prudent,
    When nothing tempts you to stray,
When without or within no voice of sin
    Is luring your soul away;
But it's only a negative virtue
    Until it is tried by fire,
And the life that is worth the honor on earth
    Is the one that resists desire.

By the cynic, the sad, the fallen,
    Who had no strength for the strife,
The world's highway is cumbered to-day;
    They make up the sum of life.
But the virtue that conquers passion,
    And the sorrow that hides in a smile,
It is these that are worth the homage on earth
    For we find them but once in a while.

ELLA WHEELER WILCOX.

YOU NEVER CAN TELL

YOU NEVER CAN TELL when you send a word
    Like an arrow shot from a bow
By an archer blind, be it cruel or kind,
    Just where it may chance to go.
It may pierce the breast of your dearest friend,
    Tipped with its poison or balm,
To a stranger's heart in life's great mart
    It may carry its pain or its calm.

You never can tell when you do an act
  Just what the result will be,
But with every deed you are sowing a seed,
  Though the harvest you may not see.
Each kindly act is an acorn dropped
  In God's productive soil;
You may not know, but the tree shall grow
  With shelter for those who toil.

You never can tell what your thoughts will do
  In bringing you hate or love,
For thoughts are things, and their airy wings
  Are swifter than carrier doves.
They follow the law of the universe—
  Each thing must create its kind,
And they speed o'er the track to bring you back
  Whatever went out from your mind.

ELLA WHEELER WILCOX.

THE CRY OF A DREAMER

I AM TIRED of planning and toiling
  In the crowded hives of men;
Heart-weary of building and spoiling,
  And spoiling and building again.
And I long for the dear old river,
  Where I dreamed my youth away;
For a dreamer lives forever,
  And a toiler dies in a day.

I am sick of the showy seeming
  Of a life that is half a lie;
Of the faces lined with scheming
  In the throng that hurries by.
From the sleepless thoughts' endeavour,
  I would go where the children play;
For a dreamer lives forever,
  And a thinker dies in a day.

I can feel no pride, but pity
  For the burdens the rich endure;
There is nothing sweet in the city
  But the patient lives of the poor.

Oh, the little hands too skillful
  And the child mind choked with weeds!
The daughter's heart grown willful,
  And the father's heart that bleeds!

No, no! from the street's rude bustle,
  From trophies of mart and stage,
I would fly to the woods' low rustle
  And the meadows' kindly page.
Let me dream as of old by the river,
  And be loved for the dream alway;
For a dreamer lives forever,
  And a toiler dies in a day.

                              JOHN BOYLE O'REILLY.

III. POEMS THAT TELL A STORY

THE FACE UPON THE FLOOR

'Twas a BALMY SUMMER EVENING, and a goodly crowd was there.
Which well-nigh filled Joe's barroom on the corner of the square,
And as songs and witty stories came through the open door
A vagabond crept slowly in and posed upon the floor.

"Where did it come from?" someone said: "The wind has blown it in."
"What does it want?" another cried. "Some whisky, rum or gin?"
"Here, Toby, seek him, if your stomach's equal to the work—
I wouldn't touch him with a fork, he's as filthy as a Turk."

This badinage the poor wretch took with stoical good grace;
In fact, he smiled as though he thought he'd struck the proper place.
"Come, boys, I know there's kindly hearts among so good a crowd—
To be in such good company would make a deacon proud.

"Give me a drink—that's what I want—I'm out of funds, you know;
When I had cash to treat the gang, this hand was never slow.
What? You laugh as though you thought this pocket never held a sou;
I once was fixed as well, my boys, as anyone of you.

"There, thanks; that's braced me nicely; God bless you one and all;
Next time I pass this good saloon, I'll make another call.
Give you a song? No, I can't do that, my singing days are past;
My voice is cracked, my throat's worn out, and my lungs are going fast.

"Say! Give me another whisky, and I'll tell you what I'll do—
I'll tell you a funny story, and a fact, I promise, too.
That I was ever a decent man not one of you would think;
But I was, some four or five years back. Say, give me another drink.

149

"Fill her up, Joe, I want to put some life into my frame—
Such little drinks, to a bum like me, are miserably tame;
Five fingers—there, that's the scheme—and corking whisky, too.
Well, here's luck, boys; and, landlord, my best regards to you.

"You've treated me pretty kindly, and I'd like to tell you how
I came to be the dirty sot you see before you now.
As I told you, once I was a man, with muscle, frame and health,
And, but for a blunder, ought to have made considerable wealth.

"I was a painter—not one that daubed on bricks and wood
But an artist, and, for my age, was rated pretty good.
I worked hard at my canvas and was bidding fair to rise,
For gradually I saw the star of fame before my eyes.

"I made a picture, perhaps you've seen, 'tis called the 'Chase of Fame,'
It brought me fifteen hundred pounds and added to my name.
And then I met a woman—now comes the funny part—
With eyes that petrified my brain, and sunk into my heart.

"Why don't you laugh? 'Tis funny that the vagabond you see
Could ever love a woman and expect her love for me;
But 'twas so, and for a month or two her smiles were freely given,
And when her loving lips touched mine it carried me to heaven.

"Did you ever see a woman for whom your soul you'd give,
With a form like the Milo Venus, too beautiful to live;
With eyes that would beat the Koh-i-noor, and a wealth of chestnut
     hair?
If so, 'twas she, for there never was another half so fair.

"I was working on a portrait, one afternoon in May,
Of a fair-haired boy, a friend of mine, who lived across the way,
And Madeline admired it, and, much to my surprise,
Said that she'd like to know the man that had such dreamy eyes.

"It didn't take long to know him, and before the month had flown
My friend had stolen my darling, and I was left alone;
And, ere a year of misery had passed above my head,
The jewel I had treasured so had tarnished, and was dead.

"That's why I took to drink, boys. Why, I never saw you smile,
I thought you'd be amused, and laughing all the while.
Why, what's the matter, friend? There's a teardrop in your eye,
Come, laugh, like me; 'tis only babes and women that should cry.

"Say, boys, if you give me just another whisky, I'll be glad,
And I'll draw right here a picture of the face that drove me mad.
Give me that piece of chalk with which you mark the baseball score—
You shall see the lovely Madeline upon the barroom floor."

Another drink, and with chalk in hand the vagabond began
To sketch a face that well might buy the soul of any man.
Then, as he placed another lock upon the shapely head,
With a fearful shriek, he leaped and fell across the picture—dead.

H. ANTOINE D'ARCY.

THE LAST HYMN

THE SABBATH DAY was ending in a village by the sea,
The uttered benediction touched the people tenderly,
And they rose to face the sunset in the glowing, lighted west,
And then hastened to their dwellings for God's blessed boon of rest.

But they looked across the waters, and a storm was raging there;
A fierce spirit moved above them—the wild spirit of the air—
And it lashed, and shook, and tore them till they thundered, groaned
    and boomed,
And, alas! for any vessel in their yawning gulfs entombed.

Very anxious were the people on that rocky coast of Wales,
Lest the dawns of coming morrows should be telling awful tales,
When the sea had spent its passion and should cast upon the shore
Bits of wreck, and swollen victims, as it had done heretofore.

With the rough winds blowing round her a brave woman strained her
    eyes,
As she saw along the billows a large vessel fall and rise.
Oh! it did not need a prophet to tell what the end must be,
For no ship could ride in safety near that shore on such a sea.

Then the pitying people hurried from their homes and thronged the
    beach.
Oh, for power to cross the waters and the perishing to reach!
Helpless hands were wrung in terror, tender hearts grew cold with
    dread,
And the ship urged by the tempest to the fatal rock-shore sped.

"She has parted in the middle! Oh, the half of her goes down!
God have mercy! Is His heaven far to seek for those who drown?"
Lo! when next the white, shocked faces looked with terror on the sea,
Only one last clinging figure on a spar was seen to be.

Nearer to the trembling watchers came the wreck tossed by the wave,
And the man still clung and floated, though no power on earth could
    save.
"Could we send him a short message? Here's a trumpet, shout away!"
'Twas the preacher's hand that took it, and he wondered what to say.

Any memory of his sermon? Firstly? Secondly? Ah, no.
There was but one thing to utter in that awful hour of woe.
So he shouted through the trumpet, "Look to Jesus! Can you hear?"
And "Aye, aye, sir!" rang the answer o'er the waters loud and clear.

Then they listened. "He is singing, 'Jesus, lover of my soul,'"
And the winds brought back the echo, "While the nearer waters roll."
Strange indeed it was to hear him, "Till the storm of life is past,"
Singing bravely o'er the waters. "Oh, receive my soul at last."

He could have no other refuge—"Hangs my helpless soul on thee."
"Leave, oh! leave me not"—— The singer dropped at last into the sea.
And the watchers looking homeward, through their eyes by tears made
    dim,
Said, "He passed to be with Jesus in the singing of that hymn."

MARIANNE FARNINGHAM.

CASABIANCA

[Young Casabianca, a boy about thirteen years old, son of the Admiral of the
Orient, remained at his post (in the Battle of the Nile) after the ship had taken fire
and all the guns had been abandoned, and perished in the explosion of the vessel,
when the flames had reached the powder.]

THE BOY stood on the burning deck,
    Whence all but him had fled;
The flame that lit the battle's wreck
    Shone round him o'er the dead.

Yet beautiful and bright he stood,
　　As born to rule the storm;
A creature of heroic blood,
　　A proud though childlike form.

The flames rolled on; he would not go
　　Without his father's word;
That father, faint in death below,
　　His voice no longer heard.

He called aloud, "Say, Father, say,
　　If yet my task be done!"
He knew not that the chieftain lay
　　Unconscious of his son.

"Speak, Father!" once again he cried,
　　"If I may yet be gone!"
And but the booming shots replied,
　　And fast the flames rolled on.

Upon his brow he felt their breath,
　　And in his waving hair,
And looked from that lone post of death
　　In still yet brave despair;

And shouted but once more aloud,
　　"My father! must I stay?"
While o'er him fast, through sail and shroud,
　　The wreathing fires made way.

They wrapt the ship in splendor wild,
　　They caught the flag on high,
And streamed above the gallant child,
　　Like banners in the sky.

There came a burst of thunder sound;
　　The boy,—Oh! where was *he?*
Ask of the winds, that far around
　　With fragments strewed the sea,—

With shroud and mast and pennon fair,
　　That well had borne their part,—
But the noblest thing that perished there
　　Was that young, faithful heart.

FELICIA HEMANS.

153

ABOU BEN ADHEM

ABOU BEN ADHEM (may his tribe increase!)
Awoke one night from a deep dream of peace,
And saw, within the moonlight in his room,
Making it rich, and like a lily in bloom,
An Angel writing in a book of gold:
Exceeding peace had made Ben Adhem bold,
And to the Presence in the room he said,
"What writest thou?" The Vision raised its head,
And with a look made of all sweet accord
Answered, "The names of those who love the Lord."
"And is mine one?" said Abou. "Nay, not so,"
Replied the Angel. Abou spoke more low,
But cheerily still; and said, "I pray thee, then,
Write me as one that loves his fellow men."

The Angel wrote, and vanished. The next night
It came again with a great wakening light,
And showed the names whom love of God had blessed,
And, lo! Ben Adhem's name led all the rest!

JAMES HENRY LEIGH HUNT.

THE MISTLETOE BOUGH

THE MISTLETOE hung in the castle hall,
The holly branch shone on the old oak wall;
And the baron's retainers were blithe and gay,
And keeping their Christmas holiday.
The baron beheld with a father's pride
His beautiful child, young Lovell's bride;
While she with her bright eyes seemed to be
The star of the goodly company.

"I'm weary of dancing now," she cried;
"Here, tarry a moment—I'll hide, I'll hide!
And, Lovell, be sure thou'rt first to trace
The clew to my secret lurking place."
Away she ran—and her friends began
Each tower to search, and each nook to scan;
And young Lovell cried, "O, where dost thou hide?
I'm lonesome without thee, my own dear bride."

154

They sought her that night, and they sought her next day,
And they sought her in vain while a week passed away;
In the highest, the lowest, the loneliest spot,
Young Lovell sought wildly—but found her not.
And years flew by, and their grief at last
Was told as a sorrowful tale long past;
And when Lovell appeared the children cried,
"See! the old man weeps for his fairy bride."

At length an oak chest, that had long lain hid,
Was found in the castle—they raised the lid,
And a skeleton form lay moldering there
In the bridal wreath of that lady fair!
O, sad was her fate!—in sportive jest
She hid from her lord in the old oak chest.
It closed with a spring!—and, dreadful doom,
The bride lay clasped in her living tomb!

THOMAS HAYNES BAYLY.

MARY, QUEEN OF SCOTS

I LOOKED far back into other years, and lo, in bright array
I saw, as in a dream, the form of ages passed away.
It was a stately convent with its old and lofty walls,
And gardens with their broad green walks, where soft the footstep falls;
And o'er the antique dial stones the creeping shadows passed,
And all around the noonday sun a drowsy radiance cast.
No sound of busy life was heard, save from the cloisters dim
The tinkling of the silver bell, or the sisters' holy hymn.
And there five noble maidens sat beneath the orchard trees,
In that first budding spring of youth, when all its prospects please;
And little recked they, when they sang, or knelt at vesper prayers,
That Scotland knew no prouder names—held none more dear than theirs;
And little even the loveliest thought, before the Virgin's shrine,
Of royal blood and high descent from the ancient Stuart line;
Calmly her happy days flew on, uncounted in their flight,
And as they flew they left behind a long-continuing light.

The scene was changed: it was the court, the gay court of Bourbon,
And 'neath a thousand silver lamps a thousand courtiers throng;

And proudly kindles Henry's eye—well pleased I ween, to see
The land assemble all its wealth of grace and chivalry;
But fairer far than all the rest who bask in fortune's tide,
Effulgent in the light of youth is she, the new-made bride!
The homage of a thousand hearts—the fond, deep love of one—
The hopes that dance around a life whose charms are but begun—
They lighten up her chestnut eye, they mantle o'er her cheek,
They sparkle on her open brow, and high-souled joy bespeak.
Ah, who shall blame, if scarce that day, through all its brilliant hours,
She thought of the quiet convent's calm, its sunshine and its flowers?

The scene was changed: it was a barque that slowly held its way,
And o'er its lee the coast of France in light of evening lay;
And on its deck a lady sat, who gazed with tearful eyes
Upon the fast-receding hills that, dim and distant, rise.
No marvel that the lady wept—there was no land on earth
She loved like that dear land, although she owed it not her birth.
It was her mother's land, the land of childhood and of friends,
It was the land where she had found for all her griefs amends;
The land where her dead husband slept, the land where she had known
The tranquil convent's hushed repose, and the splendors of a throne.
No marvel that the lady wept—it was the land of France,
The chosen home of chivalry, the garden of romance.
The past was bright, like those dear hills so far behind her barque;
The future, like the gathering night, was ominous and dark.
One gaze again—one long, last gaze, "Adieu, fair France, to thee!"
The breeze comes forth—she is alone on the unconscious sea!

The scene was changed: it was an eve of raw and surly mood,
And in a turret chamber high of ancient Holyrood
Sat Mary, listening to the rain and sighing with the winds
That seemed to suit the stormy state of men's uncertain minds.
The touch of care had blanched her cheek, her smile was sadder now,
The weight of royalty had pressed too heavy on her brow;
And traitors to her councils came, and rebels to the field;
The Stuart sceptre well she swayed, but the sword she could not wield.
She thought of all her blighted hopes, the dreams of youth's brief day,
And summoned Rizzio with his lute, and bade the ministrel play
The songs she loved in early years—the songs of gay Navarre,
The songs perchance that erst were sung by gallant Chattilor.

They half beguiled her of her cares, they soothed her into smiles,
They won her thoughts from bigot zeal and fierce domestic broils;
But hark, the tramp of armed men, the Douglas' battle cry!
They come! they come! and lo, the scowl of Ruthven's hollow eye!

The swords are drawn, the daggers gleam, the tears and words are
    vain—
The ruffian steel is in his heart, the faithful Rizzio's slain!
Then Mary Stuart dashed aside the tears that trickling fell:
"Now for my father's arm!" she cried; "my woman's heart farewell!"

The scene was changed: a royal host a royal banner bore,
And the faithful of the land stood round their smiling Queen once
    more;
She stayed her steed upon a hill—she saw them marching by—
She heard their shouts—she read success in every flashing eye.
The tumult of the strife begins—it roars—it dies away;
And Mary's troops and banners now—and courtiers—where are they?
Scattered and strewn, and flying far, defenceless and undone;
Alas! to think what she had lost, and all that guilt had won!
Away! Away! thy noble steed must act no laggard's part;
Yet vain his speed, for thou dost bear the arrow in thy heart!

The scene was changed: it was a lake, with one small lonely isle,
And there, within the prison walls of its baronial pile,
Stern men stood menacing their queen, till she should stoop to sign
The traitorous scroll that snatched the crown from her ancestral line;
"My lords, my lords," the captive said, "were I but once more free,
With ten good knights on yonder shore to aid my cause and me,
This parchment would I scatter wide to every breeze that blows,
And once more reign a Stuart queen o'er my remorseless foes!"
A red spot burned upon her cheek, streamed her rich tresses down,
She wrote the words, she stood erect, a queen without a crown!

The scene was changed: beside the block a sullen headsman stood,
And gleamed the broad axe in his hand, that soon must drip with blood.
With slow and steady step there came a Lady through the hall,
And breathless silence chained the lips and touched the hearts of all.
I knew that queenly form again, though blighted was its bloom;
I saw that grief and decked it out—an offering for the tomb!
I knew that eye, though faint its light, that once so brightly shone;
I knew the voice, though feeble now, that thrilled with every tone;
I knew the ringlets almost grey, once threads of living gold;
I knew that bounding grace of step, that symmetry of mould!

Even now I see her far away in that calm convent aisle,
I hear her chant her vesper hymn, I mark her holy smile;
Even now I see her bursting forth upon the bridal morn,
A new star in the firmament, to light and glory born!

Alas, the change! she placed her foot upon a triple throne,
And on the scaffold now she stands—beside the block—alone!
The little dog that licks her hand the last of all the crowd
Who sunned themselves beneath her glance, and round her footsteps
　　bowed.
Her neck is bared—the blow is struck—the soul is passed away!
The bright—the beautiful—is now a bleeding piece of clay.
The dog is moaning piteously; and, as it gurgles o'er,
Laps the warm blood that trickling runs unheeded to the floor.
The blood of beauty, wealth and power, the heart-blood of a queen,
The noblest of the Stuart race, the fairest earth has seen,
Lapped by a dog! Go think of it, in silence and alone;
Then weigh against a grain of sand the glories of a throne.

HENRY GLASSFORD BELL.

CURFEW MUST NOT RING TONIGHT

SLOWLY ENGLAND'S SUN was setting o'er the hilltops far away,
Filling all the land with beauty at the close of one sad day;
And the last rays kissed the forehead of a man and maiden fair,
He with footsteps slow and weary, she with sunny floating hair;
He with bowed head, sad and thoughtful, she with lips all cold and
　　white,
Struggling to keep back the murmur, "Curfew must not ring tonight!"

"Sexton," Bessie's white lips faltered, pointing to the prison old,
With its turrets tall and gloomy, with its walls, dark, damp and cold—
"I've a lover in the prison, doomed this very night to die
At the ringing of the curfew, and no earthly help is nigh.
Cromwell will not come till sunset"; and her face grew strangely white
As she breathed the husky whisper, "Curfew must not ring tonight!"

"Bessie," calmly spoke the sexton—and his accents pierced her heart
Like the piercing of an arrow, like a deadly poisoned dart—
"Long, long years I've rung the curfew from that gloomy, shadowed
　　tower;
Every evening, just at sunset, it has told the twilight hour;
I have done my duty ever, tried to do it just and right—
Now I'm old I still must do it: Curfew, girl, must ring tonight!"

Wild her eyes and pale her features, stern and white her thoughtful
　　brow,
And within her secret bosom Bessie made a solemn vow.

She had listened while the judges read, without a tear or sigh,
"At the ringing of the curfew, Basil Underwood must die."
And her breath came fast and faster, and her eyes grew large and bright,
As in undertone she murmured, "Curfew must not ring tonight!"

With quick step she bounded forward, sprang within the old church
    door,
Left the old man threading slowly paths he'd often trod before;
Not one moment paused the maiden, but with eye and cheek aglow
Mounted up the gloomy tower, where the bell swung to and fro
As she climbed the dusty ladder, on which fell no ray of light,
Up and up, her white lips saying, "Curfew shall not ring tonight!"

She has reached the topmost ladder, o'er her hangs the great dark bell:
Awful is the gloom beneath her like the pathway down to hell;
Lo, the ponderous tongue is swinging. 'Tis the hour of curfew now,
And the sight has chilled her bosom, stopped her breath and paled her
    brow;
Shall she let it ring? No, never! Flash her eyes with sudden light,
And she springs and grasps it firmly: "Curfew shall not ring tonight!"

Out she swung, far out; the city seemed a speck of light below;
She 'twixt heaven and earth suspended as the bell swung to and fro;
And the sexton at the bell rope, old and deaf, heard not the bell,
But he thought it still was ringing fair young Basil's funeral knell.
Still the maiden clung more firmly, and, with trembling lips and white,
Said, to hush her heart's wild beating, "Curfew shall not ring tonight!"

It was o'er; the bell ceased swaying, and the maiden stepped once more
Firmly on the dark old ladder, where for hundred years before
Human foot had not been planted; but the brave deed she had done
Should be told long ages after—often as the setting sun
Should illume the sky with beauty, aged sires, with heads of white,
Long should tell the little children, "Curfew did not ring that night."

O'er the distant hills came Cromwell; Bessie sees him, and her brow,
Full of hope and full of gladness, has no anxious traces now.
At his feet she tells her story, shows her hands all bruised and torn;
And her face so sweet and pleading, yet with sorrow pale and worn,
Touched his heart with sudden pity—lit his eye with misty light;
"Go, your lover lives!" said Cromwell; "Curfew shall not ring tonight!"

ROSA HARTWICK THORPE.

AUX ITALIENS

AT PARIS it was, at the opera there;—
    And she look'd like a queen in a book that night,
With the wreath of pearl in her raven hair,
    And the brooch on her breast so bright.

Of all the operas that Verdi wrote,
    The best, to my taste, is the Trovatore;
And Mario can soothe, with a tenor note,
    The souls in purgatory.

The moon on the tower slept soft as snow;
    And who was not thrill'd in the strangest way,
As we heard him sing, while the gas burn'd low,
    "Non ti scordar di me"?*

The emperor there, in his box of state,
    Look'd grave, as if he had just then seen
The red flag wave from the city gate,
    Where his eagles in bronze had been.

The empress, too, had a tear in her eye:
    You'd have said that her fancy had gone back again,
For one moment, under the old blue sky,
    To the old glad life in Spain.

Well, there in our front-row box we sat
    Together, my bride betroth'd and I;
My gaze was fixed on my opera hat,
    And hers on the stage hard by.

And both were silent, and both were sad;
    Like a queen she lean'd on her full white arm,
With that regal, indolent air she had,
    So confident of her charm!

I have not a doubt she was thinking then
    Of her former lord, good soul that he was,
Who died the richest and roundest of men,
    The Marquis of Carabas.

*Do not forget me.

160

I hope that, to get to the kingdom of heaven,
   Through a needle's eye he had not to pass;
I wish him well, for the jointure given
   To my lady of Carabas.

Meanwhile, I was thinking of my first love,
   As I had not been thinking of aught for years,
Till over my eyes there began to move
   Something that felt like tears.

I thought of the dress that she wore last time,
   When we stood 'neath the cypress trees together,
In that lost land, in that soft clime,
   In the crimson evening weather;

Of that muslin dress (for the eve was hot),
   And her warm white neck in its golden chain,
And her full, soft hair, just tied in a knot,
   And falling loose again;

And the jasmine flower in her fair young breast,
   (Oh, the faint, sweet smell of that jasmine flower!)
And the one bird singing alone to his nest,
   And the one star over the tower.

I thought of our little quarrels and strife,
   And the letter that brought me back my ring;
And it all seem'd then, in the waste of life,
   Such a very little thing!

For I thought of her grave below the hill,
   Which the sentinel cypress tree stands over,
And I thought, "Were she only living still,
   How I could forgive her, and love her!"

And I swear, as I thought of her thus, in that hour,
   And of how, after all, old things were best,
That I smelt the smell of that jasmine flower
   Which she used to wear in her breast.

It smelt so faint, and it smelt so sweet,
   It made me creep, and it made me cold;
Like the scent that steals from the crumbling sheet
   Where a mummy is half unroll'd.

And I turn'd and look'd: she was sitting there,
  In a dim box over the stage, and drest
In that muslin dress, with that full, soft hair,
  And that jasmine in her breast.

I was here: and she was there:
  And the glittering horseshoe curved between,
From my bride betroth'd, with her raven hair,
  And her sumptuous, scornful mien,

To my early love, with her eyes downcast,
  And over her primrose face the shade.
(In short, from the future back to the past
  There was but a step to be made.)

To my early love from my future bride
  One moment I look'd. Then I stole to the door,
I traversed the passage, and down at her side
  I was sitting, a moment more.

My thinking of her, or the music's strain,
  Or something which never will be exprest,
Had brought her back from the grave again,
  With the jasmine in her breast.

She is not dead, and she is not wed,
  But she loves me now, and she loved me then!
And the very first word that her sweet lips said,
  My heart grew youthful again.

The marchioness there, of Carabas,
  She is wealthy, and young, and handsome still;
And but for her—well, we'll let that pass;
  She may marry whomever she will.

But I will marry my own first love,
  With her primrose face, for old things are best;
And the flower in her bosom, I prize it above
  The brooch in my lady's breast.

The world is filled with folly and sin,
  And love must cling where it can, I say:
For beauty is easy enough to win;
  But one is n't loved every day.

And I think, in the lives of most women and men,
   There's a moment when all would go smooth and even,
If only the dead could find out when
   To come back and be forgiven.

But O, the smell of that jasmine flower!
   And O, that music! and O, the way
That voice rang out from the donjon tower,
   Non ti scordar di me,
   Non ti scordar di me!

ROBERT BULWER-LYTTON.

CHRISTMAS DAY IN THE WORKHOUSE

IT IS CHRISTMAS DAY in the workhouse, and the cold, bare walls are bright
With garlands of green and holly, and the place is a pleasant sight;
For with clean-washed hands and faces in a long and hungry line
The paupers sit at the table, for this is the hour they dine.

And the guardians and their ladies, although the wind is east,
Have come in their furs and wrappers to watch their charges feast;
To smile and be condescending, putting on pauper plates.
To be hosts at the workhouse banquet they've paid for—with the rates.

O, the paupers are meek and lowly with their "Thank'ee kindly, mums!"
So long as they fill their stomachs what matter it whence it comes?
But one of the old men mutters and pushes his plate aside,
"Great God!" he cries, "but it chokes me; for this is the day she died!"

The guardians gazed in horror, the master's face went white;
"Did a pauper refuse their pudding? Could that their ears believe aright?"
Then the ladies clutched their husbands, thinking the man would die,
Struck by a bolt, or something, by the outraged One on high.

But the pauper sat for a moment, then rose 'mid silence grim,
For the others had ceased to chatter and trembled in every limb:
He looked at the guardians' ladies, then, eyeing their lords, he said;
"I eat not the food of villains whose hands are foul and red;

"Whose victims cry for vengeance from their dark, unhallowed graves."
"He's drunk," said the workhouse master, "or else he's mad and raves."
"Not drunk or mad," cried the pauper, "but only a haunted beast,
Who, torn by the hounds and mangled, declines the vulture's feast.

"I care not a curse for the guardians, and I won't be dragged away;
Just let me have the fit out, it's only on Christmas Day
That the black past comes to goad me and prey on my burning brain;
I'll tell you the rest in a whisper—I swear I won't shout again.

"Keep your hands off me, curse you! Hear me right out to the end.
You come here to see how paupers the season of Christmas spend;
You come here to watch us feeding, as they watched the capture beast;
Here's why a penniless pauper spits on your paltry feast.

"Do you think I will take your bounty and let you smile and think
You're doing a noble action with the parish's meat and drink?
Where is my wife, you traitors—the poor old wife you slew?
Yes, by the God above me, my Nance was killed by you.

"Last Winter my wife lay dying, starved in a filthy den.
I had never been to the parish—I came to the parish then;
I swallowed my pride in coming! for ere the ruin came
I held up my head as a trader, and I bore a spotless name.

"I came to the parish, craving bread for a starving wife—
Bread for the woman who'd loved me thro' fifty years of life;
And what do you think they told me, mocking my awful grief,
That the house was open to us, but they wouldn't give out relief.

"I slunk to the filthy alley—'twas a cold, raw Christmas Eve—
And the bakers' shops were open, tempting a man to thieve;
But I clenched my fists together, holding my head awry,
So I came to her empty-handed and mournfully told her why.

"Then I told her the house was open; she had heard of the ways of that
For her bloodless cheeks went crimson, and up in her rags she sat,
Crying, 'Bide the Christmas here, John, we've never had one apart;
I think I can bear the hunger—the other would break my heart.'

"All through that eve I watched her, holding her hand in mine,
Praying the Lord and weeping till my lips were salt as brine;

I asked her once if she hungered, and she answered 'No.'
The moon shone in at the window, set in a wreath of snow.

"Then the room was bathed in glory, and I saw in my darling's eyes
The faraway look of wonder that comes when the spirit flies;
And her lips were parched and parted, and her reason came and went.
For she rav'd of our home in Devon, where our happiest years were
    spent.

"And the accents, long forgotten, came back to the tongue once more.
For she talked like the country lassie I woo'd by the Devon shore;
Then she rose to her feet and trembled, and fell on the rags and
    moaned,
And, 'Give me a crust—I'm famished—for the love of God,' she
    groaned.

'I rushed from the room like a madman and flew to the workhouse
    gate,
Crying, 'Food for a dying woman!' and the answer came, 'Too late;'
They drove me away with curses; then I fought with a dog in the street
And tore from the mongrel's clutches a crust he was trying to eat.

"Back through the filthy byways! Back through the trampled slush!
Up to the crazy garret, wrapped in an awful hush;
My heart sank down at the threshold, and I paused with a sudden thrill,
For there, in the silv'ry moonlight, my Nance lay cold and still.

"Up to the blackened ceiling the sunken eyes were cast—
I knew on those lips, all bloodless, my name had been the last;
She called for her absent husband—O God! Had I known——
Had called in vain, and, in anguish, had died in that den alone.

"Yes, there in a land of plenty, lay a loving woman dead.
Cruelly starved and murdered for a loaf of the parish bread;
At yonder gate, last Christmas, I craved for a human life,
You, who would feed us paupers, what of my murdered wife?

"There, get ye gone to your dinners, don't mind me in the least;
Think of the happy paupers eating your Christmas feast;
And when you recount their blessings in your parochial way,
Say what you did for me, too, only last Christmas Day."

GEORGE R. SIMS.

ANNIE AND WILLIE'S PRAYER

'TWAS THE EVE before Christmas. "Good night," had been said,
And Annie and Willie had crept into bed;
There were tears on their pillows, and tears in their eyes,
And each little bosom was heaving with sighs,
For tonight their stern father's command had been given
That they should retire precisely at seven
Instead of at eight—for they troubled him more
With questions unheard of than ever before:
He had told them he thought this delusion a sin,
No such creature as "Santa Claus" ever had been.
And he hoped, after this, he should never more hear
How he scrambled down chimneys with presents each year.
And this was the reason that two little heads
So restlessly tossed on their soft, downy beds.
Eight, nine, and the clock on the steeple tolled ten,
Not a word had been spoken by either till then,
When Willie's sad face from the blanket did peep,
And whispered, "Dear Annie, is 'ou fast as'eep?"
"Why no, brother Willie," a sweet voice replies,
"I've long tried in vain, but I can't shut my eyes,
For somehow it makes me so sorry because
Dear papa has said there is no 'Santa Claus.'
Now we know there is, and it can't be denied,
For he came every year before mamma died;
But, then, I've been thinking that she used to pray,
And God would hear everything mamma would say,
And maybe she asked him to send Santa Claus here
With that sackful of presents he brought every year."
"Well, why tan't we p'ay dest as mamma did den,
And ask Dod to send him with p'esents aden?"
"I've been thinking so too," and without a word more
Four little bare feet bounded out on the floor,
And four little knees the soft carpet pressed,
And two tiny hands were clasped close to each breast.
"Now, Willie, you know we must firmly believe
That the presents we ask for we're sure to receive;
You must wait very still till I say the 'Amen,'
And by that you will know that your turn has come then."

"Dear Jesus, look down on my brother and me,
And grant us the favor we are asking of thee.
I want a wax dolly, a teaset, and ring,

And an ebony workbox that shuts with a spring.
Bless papa, dear Jesus, and cause him to see
That Santa Claus loves us as much as does he;
Don't let him get fretful and angry again
At dear brother Willie and Annie. Amen."
"Please, Desus, 'et Santa Taus tum down tonight,
And b'ing us some p'esents before it is light;
I want he should div' me a nice 'ittie s'ed,
With bright shinin' 'unners, and all painted red;
A box full of tandy, a book, and a toy,
Amen, and then, Desus, I'll be a dood boy."

Their prayers being ended, they raised up their heads,
With hearts light and cheerful, again sought their beds.
They were lost soon in slumber, both peaceful and deep,
And with fairies in dreamland were roaming in sleep.

Eight, nine, and the little French clock had struck ten,
Ere the father had thought of his children again:
He seems now to hear Annie's half-suppressed sighs,
And to see the big tears stand in Willie's blue eyes.
"I was harsh with my darlings," he mentally said,
"And should not have sent them so early to bed;
But then I was troubled; my feelings found vent,
But of course they've forgotten their troubles ere this,
And that I denied them the thrice-asked-for kiss:
But, just to make sure, I'll go up to their door,
For I never spoke harsh to my darlings before."
So saying, he softly ascended the stairs,
And arrived at the door to hear both of their prayers;
His Annie's "Bless papa" drew forth the big tears,
And Willie's grave promise fell sweet on his ears.
"Strange—strange—I'd forgotten," said he with a sigh,
"How I longed when a child to have Christmas draw nigh."
"I'll atone for my harshness," he inwardly said,
"By answering their prayers ere I sleep in my bed."
Then he turned to the stairs and softly went down,
Threw off velvet slippers and silk dressing gown,
Donned hat, coat, and boots, and was out in the street,
A millionaire facing the cold, driving sleet!
Nor stopped he until he had bought everything
From the box full of candy to the tiny gold ring;
Indeed, he kept adding so much to his store,
That the various presents outnumbered a score.

Then homeward he turned. When his holiday load,
With Aunt Mary's help, in the nursery was stowed.
Miss Dolly was seated beneath a pine tree,
By the side of a table spread out for her tea;
A workbox well fitted in the center was laid,
And on it the ring for which Annie had prayed,
A soldier in uniform stood by a sled
"With bright shining runners, and all painted red."
There were balls, dogs, and horses, books pleasing to see,
And birds of all colors were perched in the tree!
While Santa Claus, laughing, stood up in the top,
As if getting ready more presents to drop.
And as the fond father the picture surveyed,
He thought for his trouble he had amply been paid,
And he said to himself, as he brushed off a tear,
"I'm happier tonight than I've been for a year;
I've enjoyed more pure pleasure than ever before,
What care I if bank stock falls ten per cent more!
Hereafter I'll make it a rule, I believe,
To have Santa Claus visit us each Christmas Eve."
So thinking, he gently extinguished the light,
And, tripping down stairs, retired for the night.

As soon as the beams of the bright morning sun
Put the darkness to flight, and the stars one by one,
Four little blue eyes out of sleep opened wide,
And at the same moment the presents espied;
Then out of their beds they sprang with a bound,
And the very gifts prayed for were all of them found.
They laughed and they cried, in their innocent glee,
And shouted for papa to come quick and see
What presents old Santa Claus brought in the night
(Just the things that they wanted,) and left before light:
"And now," added Annie, in a voice soft and low,
"You'll believe there's a 'Santa Claus', papa, I know";
While dear little Willie climbed up on his knee,
Determined no secret between them should be,
And told in soft whispers how Annie had said
That their dear, blessed mamma, so long ago dead,
Used to kneel down by the side of her chair,
And that God up in heaven had answered her prayer.
"Den we dot up and prayed dust well as we tould,
And Dod answered our prayers: now wasn't He dood?"
"I should say that He was, if He sent you all these,
And knew just what presents my children would please.

168

(Well, well, let him think so, the dear little elf,
'Twould be cruel to tell him I did it myself.")

Blind father! who caused your stern heart to relent,
And the hasty words spoken so soon to repent?
'Twas the Being who bade you steal softly upstairs,
And made you His agent to answer their prayers.

SOPHIA P. SNOW.

HOW HE SAVED ST. MICHAEL'S

So YOU BEG for a story, my darling, my brown-eyed Leopold,
And you, Alice, with face like morning and curling locks of gold;
Then come, if you will, and listen—stand close beside my knee—
To a tale of the Southern city, proud Charleston by the sea.

It was long ago, my children, ere ever the signal gun
That blazed above Fort Sumter had wakened the North as one;
Long ere the wondrous pillar of battle cloud and fire
Had marked where the unchained millions marched on to their hearts'
    desire.

On the roofs and the glittering turrets, that night, as the sun went
    down,
The mellow glow of the twilight shone like a jeweled crown;
And, bathed in the living glory, as the people lifted their eyes,
They saw the pride of the city, the spire of St. Michael's, rise

High over the lesser steeples, tipped with a golden ball
That hung like a radiant planet caught in its earthward fall—
First glimpse of home to the sailor who made the harbor round,
And last slow-fading vision dear to the outward bound.

The gently gathering shadows shut out the waning light,
The children prayed at their bedsides, as you will pray tonight;
The noise of buyer and seller from the busy mart was gone,
And in dreams of a peaceful morrow the city slumbered on.

But another light than sunrise aroused the sleeping street;
For a cry was heard at midnight, and the rush of tramping feet;
Men stared in each other's faces through mingled fire and smoke,
While the frantic bells went clashing, clamorous stroke on stroke.

By the glare of her blazing rooftree the houseless mother fled,
With the babe she pressed to her bosom shrieking in nameless dread,
While the fire king's wild battalions scaled wall and capstone high,
And planted their flaring banners against an inky sky.

For the death that raged behind them, and the crash of ruin loud,
To the great square of the city were driving the surging crowd;
Where yet, firm in all the tumult, unscathed by the fiery flood,
With its heavenward-pointing finger, the Church of St. Michael stood.

But, e'en as they gazed upon it, there rose a sudden wail—
A cry of horror blended with the roaring of the gale,
On whose scorching wings updriven, a single flaming brand
Aloft on the towering steeple clung like a bloody hand.

"Will it fall?" The whisper trembled from a thousand whitening lips;
Far out on the lurid harbor they watched it from the ships—
A baleful gleam that brighter and ever brighter shone,
Like a flickering, trembling will-o'-the-wisp to a steady beacon grown.

"Uncounted gold shall be given to the man whose brave right hand,
For the love of the periled city, plucks down yon burning brand."
So cried the mayor of Charleston, that all the people heard;
But they looked each one at his fellow; and no man spoke a word.

Who is it leans from the belfry, with face upturned to the sky,
Clings to a column and measures the dizzy spire with his eye,
Will he dare it, the hero undaunted, that terrible, sickening height?
Or will the hot blood of his courage freeze in his veins at the sight?

But see! He has stepped on the railing; he climbs with his feet and his
  hands;
And, firm on a narrow projection, with the belfry beneath him, he
  stands;
Now once, and once only, they cheer him—a single tempestuous breath,
And there falls on the multitude gazing a hush like the stillness of
  death.

Slow, steadily mounting, unheeding aught save the goal of the fire,
Still higher and higher, an atom, he moves on the face of the spire.
He stops! Will he fall? Lo! for answer, a gleam like a meteor's track,
And, hurled on the stones of the pavement, the red brand lies shattered
  and black.

Once more the shouts of the people have rent the quivering air:
At the church door Mayor and Council wait with their feet on the stair;

And the eager throng behind them press for a touch of his hand—
The unknown savior, whose daring could compass a deed so grand.

But why does a sudden tremor seize on them while they gaze?
And what meaneth that stifled murmur of wonder and amaze?
He stood in the gate of the temple he had periled his life to save;
And the face of the hero, my children, was the sable face of a slave!

With folded arms he was speaking in tones that were clear, not loud,
And his eyes, ablaze in their sockets, burnt into the eyes of the crowd:
"You may keep your gold; I scorn it! But answer me, ye who can,
If the deed I have done before you be not the deed of a man?"

He stepped but a short space backward; and from all the women and
    men
There were only sobs for answer; and the Mayor called for a pen,
And the great seal of the city, that he might read who ran:
And the slave who saved St. Michael's went out from its door, a man.

MARY A. P. STANSBURY.

THE DOCTOR'S STORY

GOOD FOLKS ever will have their way—
Good folks ever for it must pay.

But we, who are here and everywhere,
The burden of their faults must bear.

We must shoulder others' shame,
Fight their follies, and take their blame:

Purge the body, and humor the mind;
Doctor the eyes when the soul is blind;

Build the column of health erect
On the quicksands of neglect:

Always shouldering others' shame—
Bearing their faults and taking the blame!

Deacon Rogers, he came to me;
"Wife is a-goin' to die," said he.

171

"Doctors great, an' doctors small,
Haven't improved her any at all.

"Physic and blister, powders and pills,
And nothing sure but the doctors' bills!

"Twenty women, with remedies new,
Bother my wife the whole day through.

"Sweet as honey, or bitter as gall—
Poor old woman, she takes 'em all.

"Sour or sweet, whatever they choose;
Poor old woman, she daren't refuse.

"So she pleases whoe'er may call,
An' Death is suited the best of all.

"Physic and blister, powder an' pill—
Bound to conquer, and sure to kill!"

Mrs. Rogers lay in her bed,
Bandaged and blistered from foot to head.

Blistered and bandaged from head to toe,
Mrs. Rogers was very low.

Bottle and saucer, spoon and cup,
On the table stood bravely up;

Physics of high and low degree;
Calomel, catnip, boneset tea;

Everything a body could bear,
Excepting light and water and air.

I opened the blinds; the day was bright,
And God gave Mrs. Rogers some light.

I opened the window; the day was fair,
And God gave Mrs. Rogers some air.

Bottles and blisters, powders and pills,
Catnip, boneset, sirups and squills;

Drugs and medicines, high and low,
I threw them as far as I could throw.

"What are you doing?" my patient cried;
"Frightening Death," I coolly replied.

"You are crazy!" a visitor said:
I flung a bottle at his head.

Deacon Rogers he came to me;
"Wife is a-gettin' her health," said he.

"I really think she will worry through;
She scolds me just as she used to do.

"All the people have poohed an' slurred,
All the neighbors have had their word;

" 'Twere better to perish, some of 'em say,
Than be cured in such an irregular way.'"

"Your wife," said I, "had God's good care,
And His remedies, light and water and air.

"All of the doctors, beyond a doubt,
Couldn't have cured Mrs. Rogers without."

The deacon smiled and bowed his head;
"Then your bill is nothing," he said.

"God's be the glory, as you say!
God bless you, Doctor! Good day! Good day!"

If ever I doctor that woman again,
I'll give her medicine made by men.

WILL M. CARLETON.

OVER THE HILL TO THE POOR-HOUSE

OVER THE HILL to the poor-house I'm trudgin' my weary way—
I, a woman of seventy, and only a trifle gray—
I, who am smart an' chipper, for all the years I've told,
As many another woman that's only half as old.

Over the hill to the poor-house—I can't quite make it clear!
Over the hill to the poor-house—it seems so horrid queer!
Many a step I've taken a-toilin' to and fro,
But this is a sort of journey I never thought to go.

What is the use of heapin' on me a pauper's shame?
Am I lazy or crazy? am I blind or lame?
True, I am not so supple, nor yet so awful stout;
But charity ain't no favor, if one can live without.

I am willin' and anxious an' ready any day
To work for a decent livin', an' pay my honest way;
For I can earn my victuals, an' more too, I'll be bound,
If anybody only is willin' to have me round.

Once I was young an' han'some—I was, upon my soul—
Once my cheeks was roses, my eyes as black as coal;
And I can't remember, in them days, of hearin' people say,
For any kind of a reason, that I was in their way.

'T ain't no use of boastin', or talkin' over free,
But many a house an' home was open then to me;
Many a han'some offer I had from likely men,
And nobody ever hinted that I was a burden then.

And when to John I was married, sure he was good and smart,
But he and all the neighbors would own I done my part;
For life was all before me, an' I was young an' strong,
And I worked the best that I could in tryin' to get along.

And so we worked together: and life was hard, but gay,
With now and then a baby for to cheer us on our way;
Till we had half a dozen, an' all growed clean an' neat,
An' went to school like others, an' had enough to eat.

So we worked for the child'rn, and raised 'em every one;
Worked for 'em summer and winter, just as we ought to 've done;
Only perhaps we humored 'em, which some good folks condemn,
But every couple's child'rn's a heap the best to them.

Strange how much we think of our blessed little ones!—
I'd have died for my daughters, I'd have died for my sons!
And God he made that rule of love; but when we're old and gray,
I've noticed it sometimes somehow fails to work the other way.

Strange, another thing: when our boys an' girls was grown,
And when, exceptin' Charley, they'd left us there alone,
When John he nearer an' nearer come, an' dearer seemed to be,
The Lord of Hosts he come one day an' took him away from me.

Still I was bound to struggle, an' never to cringe or fall—
Still I worked for Charley, for Charley was now my all;
And Charley was pretty good to me, with scarce a word or frown,
Till at last he went a-courtin', and brought a wife from town.

She was somewhat dressy, an' hadn't a pleasant smile—
She was quite conceity, and carried a heap o' style;
But if ever I tried to be friends, I did with her, I know;
But she was hard and proud, an' I couldn't make it go.

She had an edication, an' that was good for her;
But when she twitted me on mine, 't was carryin' things too fur;
An' I told her once, 'fore company (an' it almost made her sick),
That I never swallowed a grammar, or 'et a 'rithmetic.

So 't was only a few days before the thing was done—
They was a family of themselves, and I another one;
And a very little cottage one family will do,
But I never have seen a house that was big enough for two.

An' I never could speak to suit her, never could please her eye,
An' it made me independent, an' then I didn't try;
But I was terribly staggered, an' felt it like a blow,
When Charley turned ag'in me, an' told me I could go.

I went to live with Susan, but Susan's house was small,
And she was always a-hintin' how snug it was for us all;
And what with her husband's sisters, and what with child'rn three,
'T was easy to discover that there wasn't room for me.

An' then I went to Thomas, the oldest son I've got,
For Thomas' buildings'd cover the half of an acre lot;
But all the child'rn was on me—I couldn't stand their sauce—
And Thomas said I needn't think I was comin' there to boss.

An' then I wrote to Rebecca, my girl who lives out West,
And to Isaac, not far from her—some twenty miles at best;
And one of 'em said 't was too warm there for anyone so old,
And t' other had an opinion the climate was too cold.

So they have shirked and slighted me, an' shifted me about—
So they have well-nigh soured me, an' wore my old heart out;
But still I've born up pretty well, an' wasn't much put down,
Till Charley went to the poor-master, an' put me on the town.

Over the hill to the poor-house—my child'rn dear, good-by!
Many a night I've watched you when only God was nigh;
And God 'll judge between us; but I will al'ays pray
That you shall never suffer the half I do today.

WILL M. CARLETON.

OSTLER JOE

I stood at eve, as the sun went down, by a grave where a woman lies,
Who lured men's souls to the shores of sin with the light of her wanton
eyes;
Who sang the song that the Siren sang on the treacherous Lurley height,
Whose face was as fair as a summer day, and whose heart was as black
as night.

Yet a blossom I fain would pluck today from the garden above her
dust—
Not the languorous lily of soulless sin, nor the blood-red rose of lust,
But a pure white blossom of holy love that grew in the one green spot
In the arid desert of Phryne's life, where all was parched and hot.

In the summer, when the meadows were aglow with blue and red,
Joe, the hostler of the "Magpie," and fair Annie Smith were wed.
Plump was Annie, plump and pretty, with cheek as white as snow;
He was anything but handsome, was the "Magpie" hostler, Joe.

But he won the winsome lassie. They'd a cottage and a cow;
And her matronhood sat lightly on the village beauty's brow.
Sped the months and came a baby—such a blue-eyed baby boy;
Joe was working in the stables when they told him of his joy.

He was rubbing down the horses, and he gave them then and there
All a special feed of clover, just in honor of the heir.
It had been his great ambition, and he told the horses so,
That the Fates would send a baby who might bear the name of Joe.

Little Joe the child was christened, and, like babies, grew apace,
He'd his mother's eyes of azure and his father's honest face.
Swift the happy years went over, years of blue and cloudless sky;
Love was lord of that small cottage, and the tempest passed them by.

Passed them by for years, then swiftly burst in fury o'er their home.
Down the lane by Annie's cottage chanced a gentleman to roam;
Thrice he came and saw her sitting by the window with her child,
And he nodded to the baby, and the baby laughed and smiled.

So at last it grew to know him—little Joe was nearly four—
He would call the "pretty gemlum" as he passed the open door;
And one day he ran and caught him, and in child's play pulled him in,
And the baby Joe had prayed for brought about the mother's sin.

'Twas the same old wretched story that for ages bards had sung,
'Twas a woman weak and wanton, and a villain's tempting tongue;
'Twas a picture deftly painted for a silly creature's eyes
Of the Babylonian wonders, and the joy that in them lies.

Annie listened and was tempted—she was tempted and she fell,
As the angel fell from heaven to the blackest depths of hell;
She was promised wealth and splendour, and a life of guilty sloth,
Yellow gold for child and husband—and the woman left them both.

Home one eve came Joe the hostler, with a cheery cry of "Wife,"
Finding that which blurred forever all the story of his life.
She had left a silly letter,—through the cruel scrawl he spelt;
Then he sought his lonely bedroom, joined his horny hands, and knelt.

"Now, O Lord, O God, forgive her, for she ain't to blame," he cried;
"For I owt to seen her trouble, and 'a' gone away and died.
Why, a wench like her—God bless her! 'twasn't likely as her'd rest
With that bonnie head forever on a hostler's rugged breast.

"It was kind o' her to bear me all this long and happy time;
So, for my sake please to bless her, though you count her deed a crime;
If so be I don't pray proper, Lord, forgive me; for you see
I can talk all right to 'osses; but I'm nervouslike with Thee."

Ne'er a line came to the cottage, from the woman who had flown;
Joe, the baby, died that winter, and the man was left alone.

Ne'er a bitter word he uttered, but in silence kissed the rod,
Saving what he told the horses—saving what he told his God.

Far away, in mighty London, rose the woman into fame,
For her beauty won men's homage, and she prospered in her shame.
Quick from lord to lord she flitted, higher still each prize she won,
And her rivals paled beside her, as the stars beside the sun.

Next she trod the stage half naked, and she dragged a temple down
To the level of a market for the women of the town.
And the kisses she had given to poor hostler Joe for naught
With their gold and priceless jewels rich and titled roués bought.

Went the years with flying footsteps while her star was at its height,
Then the darkness came on swiftly, and the gloaming turned to night.
Shattered strength and faded beauty tore the laurels from her brow;
Of the thousands who had worshipped never one came near her now.

Broken down in health and fortune, men forgot her very name,
Till the news that she was dying woke the echoes of her fame;
And the papers, in their gossip, mentioned how an actress lay
Sick to death in humble lodgings, growing weaker every day.

One there was who read the story in a far-off country place,
And that night the dying woman woke and looked upon his face.
Once again the strong arms clasped her that had clasped her years ago,
And the weary head lay pillowed on the breast of hostler Joe.

All the past had he forgiven, all the sorrow and the shame;
He had found her sick and lonely, and his wife he now could claim,
Since the grand folks who had known her, one and all, had slunk away,
He could clasp his long-lost darling, and no man would say him nay.

In his arms death found her lying, in his arms her spirit fled;
And his tears came down in torrents as he knelt beside her dead.
Never once his love had faltered, through her base, unhallowed life,
And the stone above her ashes bears the honored name of wife.

That's the blossom I fain would pluck today, from the garden above
    her dust;
Not the languorous lily of soulless sin, nor the blood-red rose of lust;
But a sweet white blossom of holy love, that grew in the one green spot
In the arid desert of Phryne's life, where all was parched and hot.

GEORGE R. SIMS.

ST. PETER AT THE GATE

[This poem originally appeared in the Brooklyn *Eagle,* under the title of *Thirty Years With a Shrew.* It was founded upon the incidents of a case in the local police court. A woman had her husband haled before a city magistrate for the alleged offenses of cruelty and neglect. The wife was such a garrulous witness against her husband that the judge became wearied with the woman's tongue, and he asked the husband how long he had been married. "Thirty years," replied the defendant, "Well," said the judge, "a man who has lived with this woman for thirty years has had punishment enough. Defendant, you are discharged."]

St. Peter stood guard at the golden gate,
With solemn mien and air sedate,
When up to the top of the golden stair,
A man and a woman ascending there,
Applied for admission. They came and stood
Before St. Peter, so great and good,
In hopes the City of Peace to win,
And asked St. Peter to let them in.

The woman was tall, and lank, and thin,
With a scraggy beardlet upon her chin.
The man was short, and thick, and stout,
His stomach was built so it rounded out;
His face was pleasant, and all the while
He wore a kindly and pleasant smile.
The choirs in the distance the echoes awoke,
And the man kept still while the woman spoke.

"O thou who guards the gate," said she,
"We two came hither, beseeching thee
To let us enter the heavenly land
And play our harps with the angel band.
Of me, St. Peter, there is no doubt.
There is nothing from heaven to bar me out;
I've been to meeting three times a week,
And almost always I'd rise and speak.

"I've told the sinners about the day
When they repent of their evil way;
I've told my neighbors—I've told 'em all—
'Bout Adam and Eve and the Primal Fall;

179

I've shown them what they'd have to do
If they'd pass in with the chosen few;
I've marked their path of duty clear—
Laid out the plan for their whole career.

"I've talked and talked to 'em loud and long
For my lungs are good, and my voice is strong,
So good, St. Peter, you'll clearly see
The gate of heaven is open for me.
But my old man, I regret to say,
Hasn't walked in exactly the narrow way;
He smokes and he swears, and grave faults he's got,
And I don't know whether he'll pass or not.

"He never would pray with an earnest vim,
Or go to revival, or join in a hymn,
So I had to leave him in sorrow there
While I, with the chosen, united in prayer;
He ate what the pantry chanced to afford,
While I, in my purity, sang to the Lord.

"And if cucumbers were all he got
It's a chance if he merited them or not.
But, O St. Peter, I love him so.
To the pleasures of heaven, please let him go.
I've done enough, a saint I've been,
Won't that atone? Can't you let him in?
By my grim gospel I know 'tis so
That the unrepentant must try below.
But isn't there some way you can see
That he may enter, who's dear to me?

"It's narrow gospel by which I pray,
But the chosen expect to find some way
Of coaxing, or fooling, or bribing you
So that their relations can amble through,
And say, St. Peter, it seems to me
The gate isn't kept as it ought to be.
You ought to stand by the opening there,
And never sit down in that easy chair.

"And say, St. Peter, my sight is dimmed,
But I don't like the way your whiskers are trimmed;
They're cut too wide and outward toss;
They'd look better narrow, cut straight across.

Well, we must be going, our crown to win,
So open, St. Peter, and we'll pass in."
St. Peter sat quiet and stroked his staff,
But, in spite of his office, he had to laugh,
Then said with a fiery gleam in his eye,
"Who's tending this gateway, you or I?"
And then he arose in his stature tall,
And pressed a button upon the wall,
And said to an imp, who came all aglow,
"Escort this woman to the regions below."

The man stood still as a piece of stone—
Stood sadly, gloomily, there alone.
A lifelong settled idea he had
That his wife was good and he was bad;
He thought if the woman went down below
That he would certainly have to go;
That if she went to the regions dim
There wasn't a ghost of a chance for him.

Slowly he turned, by habit bent,
To follow wherever the woman went.
St. Peter, standing on duty there,
Observed that the top of his head was bare.
He called the gentleman back and said:
"Friend, how long have you been wed?"
"Thirty years" (with a heavy sigh),
And then he thoughtfully added, "Why?"

St. Peter was silent. With head bent down,
He raised his hand and scratched his crown.
Then, seeming a different thought to take,
Slowly, half to himself, he spake:
"Thirty years with that woman there?
No wonder the man hasn't any hair.
Swearing is wicked; smoking's not good;
He smoked and swore—I should think he would.

"Thirty years with that tongue so sharp?
O Angel Gabriel, give him a harp,
A jeweled harp with a golden string.
Good sir, pass in where the angels sing;
Gabriel, give him a seat alone—
One with a cushion—up near the throne."

Call up some angels to play their best;
Let him enjoy the music—and rest.

"See that on the finest ambrosia he feeds;
He's had about all the hell he needs;
It isn't just hardly the thing to do—
To roast him on earth and the future, too."

They gave him a harp with golden strings,
A glittering robe and a pair of wings,
And he said as he entered the Realms of Day:
"Well, this beats cucumbers, anyway."
And so the Scriptures had come to pass—
"The last shall be first and the first shall be last."

JOSEPH BERT SMILEY.

DOWN AND OUT

So, you've come to the tropics, heard all you had to do
Was sit in the shade of a cocoanut glade while the dollars roll in to you.
They told you that at the bureau? Did you get the statistics all straight?
Well, hear what it did to another kid, before you decide your fate.
You don't go down with a hard, short fall—you just sort of shuffle along
And loosen your load of the moral code, till you can't tell the right
    from the wrong.

I started out to be honest, with everything on the square,
But a man can't fool with the Golden Rule in a crowd that won't play
    fair.
'Twas a case of riding a dirty race, or of being an also-ran,
My only hope was to steal and dope the horse of another man.

I pulled a deal at Guayaquil in an Inca silver mine,
But before they found it was salted ground I was safe in Argentine.
I made short weight on the River Plate, when running a freighter there;
And I cracked a crib on a rich estate without even turning a hair.

But the deal that will everlastingly bar my soul
When it knocks at Heaven's doors,
Was peddling booze to the Santa Cruz, and Winchester forty-fours.
Made unafraid by my kindly aid, the drunk-crazed brutes came down
And left in a shivering, blazing mass a flourishing border town.

I was next in charge of a smuggler's barge off the coast of Yucatan,
But she sank to hell off Cozonel one night in a hurricane.
I got to shore on a broken oar, in the filthy, shrieking dark;
With the other two of the good ship's crew converted into shark.

From a limestone cliff I flagged a skiff with a pair of salt-soaked jeans,
And I worked my way, for I couldn't pay, on a fruiter to New Orleans.
It's kind of a habit, the tropics; it gets you worse than rum;
You'll get away and swear you'll stay, but it calls, and back you come.

Six years went by before I was back on the job,
Running a war in Salvador, with a black-faced, barefooted mob;
I was General Santiago Hicks at the head of a grand revolt,
And my only friend from start to end was a punishing army Colt.
I might have been a president, a prosperous man of means,
But a gunboat came and blocked my game with a hundred and ten
  marines.

So I awoke from my dream, dead broke—drifted from bad to worse:
Sank as low as a man can go who walks with an empty purse.
But stars, they say, appear by day, when you're down in a deep, black
  pit;
My lucky star found me that way, when I was about to quit.

On a fiery hot, flea-ridden cot, I was down with the yellow jack,
Alone in the bush and all but dead, when she found me and nursed me
  back.
She came like the miracle man of old and opened my poor blind eyes,
And upon me shone a bright new dawn as I turned my face to the skies.

There was pride and grace in her brown young face,
For hers was the blood of kings;
In her eyes shone the glory of empires gone,
And the secret of world-old things.

We were spliced in a Yankee meeting house on the land of your Uncle
  Sam,
And I drew my pay from the U. S. A., for I worked at the Gatun Dam.
Then the Devil sent his right-hand man (I might have expected he
  would)
And he took her life with a long, thin knife, because she was straight
  and good.

Within me died hope, honor, pride—all but a primitive will
To hunt him down on his blood-red trail—find him and kill, and kill.

Through logwood swamps and chicle camps I hunted him many a
    moon,
And I found my man in a long pit-pen, by the side of a blue lagoon.

The chase was o'er at the farthest shore—it ended my two years quest;
And I left him there with a vacant stare and a John Crow on his chest.
You see these punctures on my arm? Do you want to know what they
    mean?
Those marks were left by fingers deft of my trained nurse, "Miss Mor-
    phine."

Of course you'll say that's worse than drink; it's possible, too, you're
    right;
At least it drives away the things that come and peer in the night.
There is a homestead down in an old Maine town, with lilacs around
    the gate,
And the Northerners whisper "It might have been," but the truth has
    come too late.

They say they'll give me one month to live—a month or a year is the
    same;
I haven't the heart to play my part to the end of a losing game.
For whenever you play, whatever the way, for stakes that are large or
    small,
The claws of the tropics will gather your pile and the dealer gets it all.

CLARENCE LEONARD HAY

THE BLACKBERRY GIRL

"WHY, PHOEBE, are you come so soon,
    Where are your berries, child?
You cannot, sure, have sold them all,
    You had a basket piled."

"No, Mother, as I climbed the fence,
    The nearest way to town,
My apron caught upon a stake,
    And so I tumbled down.

"I scratched my arm and tore my hair,
    But still did not complain;
And had my blackberries been safe,
    Should not have cared a grain.

"But when I saw them on the ground,
All scattered by my side,
I pick'd my empty basket up,
And down I sat and cried.

"Just then a pretty little miss
Chanced to be walking by;
She stopped, and, looking pitiful,
She begged me not to cry.

" 'Poor little girl, you fell,' said she,
'And must be sadly hurt.'
'Oh no,' I cried, 'but see my fruit
All mixed with sand and dirt!'

" 'Well, do not grieve for that,' she said;
'Go home and get some more.'
'Ah no, for I have stripped the vines;
These were the last they bore.'

"My father, miss, is very poor,
And works in yonder stall;
He has so many little ones,
He cannot clothe us all.

"I always longed to go to church,
But never could I go;
For when I asked him for a gown,
He always answered, No.

"There's not a father in the world
That loves his children more;
'I'd get you one with all my heart,
But, Phoebe, I am poor.'

"But when the blackberries were ripe,
He said to me one day,
'Phoebe, if you will take the time
That's given you to play,

" 'And gather blackberries enough,
And carry them to town,
To buy your bonnet and your shoes,
I'll try to get a gown.'

"O miss, I fairly jumped for joy,
My spirits were so light,
And so when I had leave to play,
I picked with all my might.

"I sold enough to get my shoes
About a week ago,
And these if they had not been spilt,
Would buy a bonnet too.

"But now they are gone, they all are gone,
And I can get no more,
And Sundays I must stay at home
Just as I did before.

"And, Mother, then I cried again
As hard as I could cry;
And, looking up, I saw a tear
Was standing in her eye.

"She caught her bonnet from her head;
'Here, here,' she cried, 'take this!'
'Oh no, indeed—I fear your ma
Would be offended, miss.'

" 'My ma! No, never! She delights
All sorrow to beguile;
And 'tis the sweetest joy she feels
To make the wretched smile.

" 'She taught me when I had enough
To share it with the poor,
And never let a needy child
Go empty from the door.

" 'So take it, for you need not fear
Offending her, you see;
I have another, too, at home,
And one's enough for me.'

"So then I took it—here it is;
For, pray, what could I do?
And, Mother, I shall love that miss
As long as I love you."

NANCY DENNIS SPROAT.

EVEN THIS SHALL PASS AWAY

ONCE IN PERSIA reigned a king,
Who upon his signet ring
Graved a maxim true and wise,
Which, if held before his eyes,
Gave him counsel at a glance
Fit for every change and chance.
Solemn words, and these are they;
"Even this shall pass away."

Trains of camels through the sand
Brought him gems from Samarcand;
Fleets of galleys through the seas
Brought him pearls to match with these;
But he counted not his gain
Treasures of the mine or main;
"What is wealth?" the king would say;
"Even this shall pass away."

'Mid the revels of his court,
At the zenith of his sport,
When the palms of all his guests
Burned with clapping at his jests,
He, amid his figs and wine,
Cried, "O loving friends of mine;
Pleasures come, but not to stay;
'Even this shall pass away.'"

Lady, fairest ever seen,
Was the bride he crowned his queen.
Pillowed on his marriage bed,
Softly to his soul he said:
"Though no bridegroom ever pressed
Fairer bosom to his breast,
Mortal flesh must come to clay—
Even this shall pass away."

Fighting on a furious field,
Once a javelin pierced his shield;
Soldiers, with a loud lament,
Bore him bleeding to his tent.

Groaning from his tortured side,
"Pain is hard to bear," he cried;
"But with patience, day by day,
Even this shall pass away."

Towering in the public square,
Twenty cubits in the air,
Rose his statue, carved in stone.
Then the king, disguised, unknown,
Stood before his sculptured name,
Musing meekly: "What is fame?
Fame is but a slow decay;
Even this shall pass away."

Struck with palsy, sore and old,
Waiting at the Gates of Gold,
Said he with his dying breath,
"Life is done, but what is Death?"
Then, in answer to the king,
Fell a sunbeam on his ring,
Showing by a heavenly ray,
"Even this shall pass away."

THEODORE TILTON.

BEAUTIFUL SNOW

OH! THE SNOW, the beautiful snow,
Filling the sky and the earth below;
Over the house tops, over the street,
Over the heads of the people you meet;
  Dancing,
    Flirting,
      Skimming along,
Beautiful snow! it can do nothing wrong.
Flying to kiss a fair lady's cheek,
Clinging to lips in a frolicsome freak;
Beautiful snow, from the heavens above,
Pure as an angel and fickle as love!

Oh! the snow, the beautiful snow!
How the flakes gather and laugh as they go!

Whirling about in its maddening fun,
It plays in its glee with everyone.
  Chasing,
    Laughing,
      Hurrying by,
It lights up the face and it sparkles the eye;
And even the dogs, with a bark and a bound,
Snap at the crystals that eddy around.
The town is alive, and its heart in a glow,
To welcome the coming of beautiful snow.

How the wild crowd go swaying along,
Hailing each other with humor and song!
How the gay sledges like meteors flash by—
Bright for a moment, then lost to the eye!
  Ringing,
    Swinging,
      Dashing they go
Over the crest of the beautiful snow:
Snow so pure when it falls from the sky,
To be trampled in mud by the crowd rushing by;
To be trampled and tracked by the thousands of feet
Till it blends with the horrible filth in the street.

Once I was pure as the snow—but I fell:
Fell, like the snowflakes, from heaven—to hell;
Fell, to be tramped as the filth of the street;
Fell, to be scoffed, to be spit on, and beat.
  Pleading,
    Cursing,
      Dreading to die,
Selling my soul to whoever would buy,
Dealing in shame for a morsel of bread,
Hating the living and fearing the dead.
Merciful God! have I fallen so low?
And yet I was once like this beautiful snow!

Once I was fair as the beautiful snow,
With an eye like its crystals, a heart like its glow;
Once I was loved for my innocent grace,
Flattered and sought for the charm of my face.
  Father,
    Mother,
      Sisters all,
God, and myself, I have lost by my fall.

The veriest wretch that goes shivering by
Will take a wide sweep, lest I wander too nigh;
For all that is on or about me, I know
There is nothing that's pure but the beautiful snow.

How strange it should be that this beautiful snow
Should fall on a sinner with nowhere to go!
How strange it would be, when the night comes again,
If the snow and the ice struck my desperate brain!
  Fainting,
    Freezing,
      Dying alone,
Too wicked for prayer, too weak for my moan
To be heard in the crash of the crazy town,
Gone mad in its joy at the snow's coming down;
To lie and to die in my terrible woe,
With a bed and a shroud of the beautiful snow!

JAMES W. WATSON.

TWO PICTURES

Two PICTURES hung on the dingy wall
Of a grand old Florentine hall—

One of a child of beauty rare,
With a cherub face and golden hair;
The lovely look of whose radiant eyes
Filled the soul with thoughts of Paradise.

The other was a visage vile
Marked with the lines of lust and guile,
A loathsome being, whose features fell
Brought to the soul weird thoughts of hell.

Side by side in their frames of gold,
Dingy and dusty and cracked and old,
This is the solemn tale they told:

A youthful painter found one day,
In the streets of Rome, a child at play,

And, moved by the beauty it bore,
The heavenly look that its features wore,
On a canvas, radiant and grand,
He painted its face with a master hand.

Year after year on his wall it hung;
'Twas ever joyful and always young—
Driving away all thoughts of gloom
While the painter toiled in his dingy room.

Like an angel of light it met his gaze,
Bringing him dreams of his boyhood days,
Filling his soul with a sense of praise.

His raven ringlets grew thin and gray,
His young ambition all passed away;
Yet he looked for years in many a place,
To find a contrast to that sweet face.

Through haunts of vice in the night he stayed
To find some ruin that crime had made.
At last in a prison cell he caught
A glimpse of the hideous fiend he sought.

On a canvas weird and wild but grand,
He painted the face with a master hand.

His task was done; 'twas a work sublime—
An angel of joy and a fiend of crime—
A lesson of life from the wrecks of time.

O Crime: with ruin thy road is strewn;
The brightest beauty the world has known
Thy power has wasted, till in the mind
No trace of its presence is left behind.

The loathsome wretch in the dungeon low,
With a face of a fiend and a look of woe,
Ruined by revels of crime and sin,
A pitiful wreck of what might have been,
Hated and shunned, and without a home,
Was the *child* that played in the streets of Rome.

UNKNOWN.

STREETS OF BALTIMORE

[The subjoined poem, singularly suggestive in spirit and rhymn of Poe's *The Raven*, appeared anonymously forty years ago—ten years after Poe's death—in a New York newspaper. It purported to have been dictated to a spiritualistic medium by the dead poet, whose untimely death in these same "streets of Baltimore" occurred on October 7, 1849.]

WOMAN WEAK and woman mortal, through the spirit's open portal
I would read the Punic record of mine earthly being o'er—
I would feel that fire returning which within my soul was burning
When my star was quenched in darkness, set to rise on earth no more.
When I sank beneath Life's burdens in the streets of Baltimore.

Ah, those memories sore and saddening! Ah, that night of anguish
    maddening!
When my lone heart suffered shipwreck on a demon-haunted shore—
When the fiends grew wild with laughter, and the silence following
    after
Was more awful and appalling than the cannon's deadly roar—
Than the tramp of mighty armies thro' the streets of Baltimore.

Like a fiery serpent crawling, like a maelstrom madly boiling,
Did this Phlegethon of fury sweep my shuddering spirit o'er,
Rushing onward, blindly reeling—tortured by intensest feeling
Like Prometheus when the vultures to his quivering vitals tore—
Swift I fled from death and darkness thro' the streets of Baltimore.

No one near to save or love me, no kind face to watch above me,
Though I heard the sound of footsteps like the waves upon the shore—
Beating—beating—beating—beating—now advancing—now retreating
With a dull and dreary rhythm, with a long, continuous roar—
Heard the sound of human footsteps in the streets of Baltimore.

There, at length, they found me lying, weak and 'wildered, sick and
    dying,
And my shattered wreck of being to a kindly refuge bore;
But my woe was past enduring, and my soul cast off its mooring,
Crying, as I floated onward, "I am of the earth no more!
I have forfeited Life's blessing in the streets of Baltimore."

Where wast thou, O Power Eternal, when the fiery fiend infernal
Beat me with his burning fasces till I sank to rise no more!
Oh! was all my lifelong error crowded in that night of terror?

Did my sin find expiation which to judgment went before,
Summoned to a dread tribunal in the streets of Baltimore?

Nay, with deep, delirious pleasure I had drained my life's full measure
Till the fatal fiery serpent fed upon my being's core;
Then, with force and fire volcanic, summoning a strength Titanic,
Did I burst the bonds that bound me—battered down my being's
  door—
Fled, and left my shattered dwelling to the dust of Baltimore.

                                                    UNKNOWN.

THE SIEGE OF BELGRADE

[A classic and probably unequaled example of "apt alliteration's artful aid."]

AN AUSTRIAN ARMY, awfully arrayed,
Boldly by battery besieged Belgrade.
Cossack commanders cannonading come,
Dealing destruction's devastating doom.
Every endeavor engineers essay,
For fame, for fortune fighting—furious fray!
Generals 'gainst generals grapple—gracious God!
How honors Heaven heroic hardihood!
Infuriate, indiscriminate in ill,
Kindred kill kinsmen, kinsmen kindred kill.
Labor low levels longest, loftiest lines;
Men march 'mid mounds, 'mid moles, 'mid murderous mines;
Now noxious, noisy numbers nothing, naught
Of outward obstacles, opposing ought;
Poor patriots, partly purchased, partly pressed,
Quite quaking, quickly "Quarter! Quarter!" quest.
Reason returns, religious right redounds,
Suwarrow stops such sanguinary sounds.
Truce to thee, Turkey! Triumph to thy train,
Unwise, unjust, unmerciful Ukraine!
Vanish, vain victory! vanish, victory vain!
Why wish we warfare? Wherefore welcome were
Xerxes, Ximenes, Xanthus, Xavier?
Yield, yield, ye youths! ye yeomen, yield your yell!
Zeus', Zarpater's, Zoroaster's zeal,
Attracting all, arms against acts appeal!

                                 ALARIC ALEXANDER WATTS.

193

THE SHIP THAT NEVER RETURNED

On a summer's day when the sea was rippled
   By a soft and gentle breeze,
A ship set sail for a harbor laden
   To a port beyond the seas.
There were fond farewells and loving signals
   While her form was yet discerned,
But they knew not 'twas a solemn parting,
   For the ship has never returned.

Chorus:

Did she ever return? No, she never returned,
   And her fate is yet unlearned;
And for years and years fond hearts have been waiting
   For the ship that never returned.

Said a feeble youth to his aged mother,
   "I must cross the wide, wide sea,
For they say perchance in a foreign clime
   There is health and strength for me."
'Twas a gleam of hope 'mid a maze of danger,
   And her heart for her youngest yearned,
So she sent him forth with smiles and blessings
   In the ship that never returned.

HENRY C. WORK

PAUL REVERE'S RIDE

Listen, my children, and you shall hear
Of the midnight ride of Paul Revere,
On the eighteenth of April, in Seventy-five;
Hardly a man is now alive
Who remembers that famous day and year.

He said to his friend, "If the British march
By land or sea from the town tonight,
Hang a lantern aloft in the belfry arch
Of the North Church tower as a signal light,—

194

One, if by land, and two, if by sea;
And I on the opposite shore will be,
Ready to ride and spread the alarm
Through every Middlesex village and farm,
For the country folk to be up and to arm."

Then he said, "Good night!" and with muffled oar
Silently rowed to the Charlestown shore,
Just as the moon rose over the bay,
Where swinging wide at her moorings lay
The Somerset, British man-of-war;
A phantom ship, with each mast and spar
Across the moon like a prison bar,
And a huge black hulk, that was magnified
By its own reflection in the tide.

Meanwhile, his friend, through alley and street,
Wanders and watches with eager ears,
Till in the silence around him he hears
The muster of men at the barrack door,
The sound of arms, and the tramp of feet,
And the measured tread of the grenadiers,
Marching down to their boats on the shore.

Then he climbed the tower of the Old North Church,
By the wooden stairs, with stealthy tread,
To the belfry-chamber overhead,
And startled the pigeons from their perch
On the somber rafters, that round him made
Masses and moving shapes of shade,—
By the trembling ladder, steep and tall,
To the highest window in the wall,
Where he paused to listen and look down
A moment on the roofs of the town,
And the moonlight flowing over all.

Beneath, in the churchyard, lay the dead,
In their night-encampment on the hill,
Wrapped in silence so deep and still
That he could hear, like a sentinel's tread,
The watchful night-wind, as it went
Creeping along from tent to tent,
And seeming to whisper, "All is well!"
A moment only he feels the spell

Of the place and the hour, and the secret dread
Of the lonely belfry and the dead;
For suddenly all his thoughts are bent
On a shadowy something far away,
Where the river widens to meet the bay,—
A line of black that bends and floats
On the rising tide, like a bridge of boats.

Meanwhile, impatient to mount and ride,
Booted and spurred, with a heavy stride
On the opposite shore walked Paul Revere.
Now he patted his horse's side,
Now gazed at the landscape far and near,
Then, impetuous, stamped the earth,
And turned and tightened his saddle-girth;
But mostly he watched with eager search
The belfry-tower of the Old North Church,
As it rose above the graves on the hill,
Lonely and spectral and somber and still.
And lo! as he looks, on the belfry's height
A glimmer, and then a gleam of light!
He springs to the saddle, the bridle he turns,
But lingers and gazes, till full on his sight
A second lamp in the belfry burns!

A hurry of hoofs in a village street,
A shape in the moonlight, a bulk in the dark,
And beneath, from the pebbles, in passing, a spark
Struck out by a steed flying fearless and fleet;
That was all! And yet, through the gloom and the light
The fate of a nation was riding that night;
And the spark struck out by that steed in his flight,
Kindled the land into flame with its heat.

He has left the village and mounted the steep,
And beneath him, tranquil and broad and deep,
Is the Mystic, meeting the ocean tides;
And under the alders, that skirt its edge,
Now soft on the sand, now loud on the ledge,
Is heard the tramp of his steed as he rides.

It was twelve by the village clock
When he crossed the bridge into Medford town.
He heard the crowing of the cock,

And the barking of the farmer's dog,
And felt the damp of the river fog,
That rises after the sun goes down.

It was one by the village clock,
When he galloped into Lexington.
He saw the gilded weathercock
Swim in the moonlight as he passed,
And the meeting-house windows, blank and bare,
Gaze at him with a spectral glare,
As if they already stood aghast
At the bloody work they would look upon.

It was two by the village clock,
When he came to the bridge in Concord town.
He heard the bleating of the flock,
And the twitter of birds among the trees,
And felt the breath of the morning breeze
Blowing over the meadows brown.
And one was safe and asleep in his bed
Who at the bridge would be first to fall,
Who that day would be lying dead,
Pierced by a British musket-ball.

You know the rest. In the books you have read,
How the British Regulars fired and fled,—
How the farmers gave them ball for ball,
From behind each fence and farmyard wall,
Chasing the redcoats down the lane,
Then crossing the fields to emerge again
Under the trees at the turn of the road,
And only pausing to fire and load.
So through the night rode Paul Revere;
And so through the night went his cry of alarm
To every Middlesex village and farm,—
A cry of defiance, and not of fear,
A voice in the darkness, a knock at the door,
And a word that shall echo forevermore!
For, borne on the night-wind of the Past,
Through all our history, to the last,
In the hour of darkness and peril and need,
The people will waken and listen to hear
The hurrying hoofbeats of that steed,
And the midnight message of Paul Revere.

HENRY WADSWORTH LONGFELLOW.

MUSIC IN CAMP

TWO ARMIES covered hill and plain,
  Where Rappahannock's waters
Ran deeply crimsoned with the stain
  Of battle's recent slaughters.

The summer clouds lay pitched like tents
  In meads of heavenly azure;
And each dread gun of the elements
  Slept in its high embrasure.

The breeze so softly blew, it made
  No forest leaf to quiver;
And the smoke of the random cannonade
  Rolled slowly from the river.

And now where circling hills looked down
  With cannon grimly planted,
O'er listless camp and silent town
  The golden sunset slanted.

When on the fervid air there came
  A strain now rich now tender;
The music seemed itself aflame
  With day's departing splendor.

A Federal band which eve and morn
  Played measures brave and nimble,
Had just struck up with flute and horn
  And lively clash of cymbal.

Down flocked the soldiers to the banks;
  Till, margined by its pebbles,
One wooded shore was blue with "Yanks,"
  And one was gray with "Rebels."

Then all was still; and then the band,
  With movement light and tricksy,
Made stream and forest, hill and strand
  Reverberate with "Dixie."

The conscious stream, with burnished glow,
    Went proudly o'er its pebbles,
But thrilled throughout its deepest flow
    With yelling of the Rebels.

Again a pause; and then again
    The trumpet pealed sonorous,
And "Yankee Doodle" was the strain
    To which the shore gave chorus.

The laughing ripple shoreward flew
    To kiss the shining pebbles;
Loud shrieked the swarming Boys in Blue
    Defiance to the Rebels.

And yet once more the bugle sang
    Above the stormy riot;
No shout upon the evening rang—
    There reigned a holy quiet.

The sad, slow stream its noiseless flood
    Poured o'er the glistening pebbles;
All silent now the Yankes stood,
    All silent stood the Rebels.

No unresponsive soul had heard
    That plaintive note's appealing,
So deeply "Home, Sweet Home" had stirred
    The hidden founts of feeling.

Or Blue, or Gray, the soldier sees,
    As by the wand of fairy,
The cottage 'neath the live-oak trees,
    The cabin by the prairie.

Tho' cold or warm, his native skies
    Bend in their beauty o'er him;
Seen through the tear-mist in his eyes,
    His loved ones stand before him.

As fades the iris after rain
    In April's tearful weather,
The vision vanished as the strain
    And daylight died together.

But Memory, waked by Music's art,
  Expressed in simple numbers,
Subdued the sternest Yankee's heart,
  Made light the Rebel's slumbers.

And fair the form of Music shines—
  That bright celestial creature—
Who still 'mid War's embattled lines
  Gives this one touch of Nature.

               JOHN R. THOMPSON.

THE HIGH TIDE AT GETTYSBURG

[July 3, 1863]

A CLOUD possessed the hollow field,
The gathering battle's smoky shield:
  Athwart the gloom the lightning flashed,
  And through the cloud some horsemen dashed,
And from the heights the thunder pealed.

Then, at the brief command of Lee,
Moved out that matchless infantry,
  With Picket leading grandly down,
  To rush against the roaring crown
Of those dread heights of destiny.

Far heard above the angry guns,
A cry across the tumult runs:
  The voice that rang through Shiloh's woods,
  And Chickamauga's solitudes:
The fierce South cheering on her sons!

Ah, how the withering tempest blew
Against the front of Pettigrew!
  A Khamsin wind that scorched and singed,
  Like that infernal flame that fringed
The British squares at Waterloo!

A thousand fell where Kemper led;
A thousand died where Garnett bled;
  In blinding flame and strangling smoke,
  The remnant through the batteries broke,
And crossed the works with Armistead.

"Once more in Glory's van with me!"
Virginia cried to Tennessee:
"We two together, come what may,
    Shall stand upon those works today!"
The reddest day in history.

Brave Tennessee! In reckless way
Virginia heard her comrade say:
    "Close round this rent and riddled rag!"
    What time she set her battle flag
Amid the guns of Doubleday.

But who shall break the guards that wait
Before the awful face of Fate?
    The tattered standards of the South
    Were shriveled at the cannon's mouth,
And all her hopes were desolate.

In vain the Tennesseean set
His breast against the bayonet;
    In vain Virginia charged and raged,
    A tigress in her wrath uncaged,
Till all the hill was red and wet!

Above the bayonets, mixed and crossed,
Men saw a gray, gigantic ghost
    Receding through the battle cloud,
    And heard across the tempest loud
The death cry of a nation lost!

The brave went down! Without disgrace
They leaped to Ruin's red embrace;
    They only heard Fame's thunders wake,
    And saw the dazzling sunburst break
In smiles on Glory's bloody face!

They fell, who lifted up a hand
And bade the sun in heaven to stand;
    They smote and fell, who set the bars
    Against the progress of the stars,
And stayed the march of Motherland!

They stood, who saw the future come
On through the fight's delirium;
   They smote and stood, who held the hope
   Of nations on that slippery slope,
Amid the cheers of Christendom!

God lives! He forged the iron will
That clutched and held that trembling hill!
   God lives and reigns! He built and lent
   The heights for Freedom's battlement,
Where floats her flag in triumph still!

Fold up the banners! Smelt the guns!
Love rules. Her gentler purpose runs.
   A mighty mother turns in tears
   The pages of her battle years,
Lamenting all her fallen sons!

                 WILL HENRY THOMPSON.

YUSSOUF

A STRANGER came one night to Yussouf's tent,
Saying, "Behold one outcast and in dread,
Against whose life the bow of power is bent,
Who flies, and hath not where to lay his head;
I come to thee for shelter and for food,
To Yussouf, called through all our tribes 'The Good.'"

"This tent is mine," said Yussouf, "but no more
Than it is God's; come in, and be at peace;
Freely shalt thou partake of all my store
As I of His who buildeth over these
Our tents his glorious roof of night and day,
And at whose door none ever yet heard Nay."

So Yussouf entertained his guest that night,
And, waking him ere day, said: "Here is gold;
My swiftest horse is saddled for thy flight;
Depart before the prying day grow bold."
As one lamp lights another, nor grows less,
So nobleness enkindleth nobleness.

That inward light the stranger's face made grand,
Which shines from all self-conquest; kneeling low,
He bowed his forehead upon Yussouf's hand,
Sobbing: "O Sheik, I cannot leave thee so;
I will repay thee; all this thou hast done
Unto that Ibrahim who slew thy son!"

"Take thrice the gold," said Yussouf, "for with thee
Into the desert, never to return,
My one black thought shall ride away from me;
First-born, for whom by day and night I yearn,
Balanced and just are all of God's decrees;
Thou art avenged, my first-born, sleep in peace!"

JAMES RUSSELL LOWELL.

ANTONY AND CLEOPATRA

I AM DYING, Egypt, dying,
   Ebbs the crimson life-tide fast,
And the dark Plutonian shadows
   Gather on the evening blast;
Let thine arms, O Queen, enfold me,
   Hush thy sobs and bow thine ear;
Listen to the great heart-secrets,
   Thou, and thou alone, must hear.

Though my scarr'd and veteran legions
   Bear their eagles high no more,
And my wreck'd and scatter'd galleys
   Strew dark Actium's fatal shore,
Though no glittering guards surround me,
   Prompt to do their master's will,
I must perish like a Roman,
   Die the great Triumvir still.

Let not Cæsar's servile minions
   Mock the lion thus laid low;
'Twas no foeman's arm that fell'd him,
   'Twas his own that struck the blow;
His who, pillow'd on thy bosom,
   Turn'd aside from glory's ray,
His who, drunk with thy caresses,
   Madly threw a world away.

Should the base plebeian rabble
  Dare assail my name at Rome,
Where my noble spouse, Octavia,
  Weeps within her widow'd home,
Seek her; say the gods bear witness—
  Altars, augurs, circling wings—
That her blood, with mine commingled,
  Yet shall mount the throne of kings.

As for thee, star-eyed Egyptian,
  Glorious sorceress of the Nile,
Light the path to Stygian horrors
  With the splendors of thy smile.
Give the Cæsar crowns and arches,
  Let his brow the laurel twine;
I can scorn the Senate's triumphs,
  Triumphing in love like thine.

I am dying, Egypt, dying;
  Hark! the insulting foeman's cry.
They are coming! quick, my falchion,
  Let me front them ere I die.
Ah! no more amid the battle
  Shall my heart exulting swell;
Isis and Osiris guard thee!
  Cleopatra, Rome, farewell!

             WILLIAM HAINES LYTLE.

CARCASSONNE

"I'M GROWING OLD, I've sixty years;
  I've labored all my life in vain.
In all that time of hopes and fears
  I've failed my dearest wish to gain.
I see full well that here below
  Bliss unalloyed there is for none;
My prayer would else fulfillment know—
  Never have I seen Carcassonne!

"You see the city from the hill,
  It lies beyond the mountains blue;
And yet to reach it one must still
  Five long and weary leagues pursue,

And, to return, as many more.
   Had but the vintage plenteous grown——
But, ah! the grape withheld its store.
   I shall not look on Carcassonne!

"They tell me every day is there
   Not more or less than Sunday gay;
In shining robes and garments fair
   The people walk upon their way.
One gazes there on castle walls
   As grand as those of Babylon;
A bishop and two generals!
   What joy to dwell in Carcassonne!

"The vicar's right: he says that we
   Are ever wayward, weak, and blind;
He tells us in his homily
   Ambition ruins all mankind.
Yet could I there two days have spent,
   While still the autumn sweetly shone,
Ah, me! I might have died content
   When I had looked on Carcassonne.

"Thy pardon, Father, I beseech,
   In this my prayer if I offend;
One something sees beyond his reach
   From childhood to his journey's end.
My wife, our little boy, Aignan,
   Have traveled even to Narbonne;
My grandchild has seen Perpignan;
   And I—have not seen Carcassonne!"

So crooned, one day, close by Limoux,
   A peasant, double-bent with age.
"Rise up, my friend," said I; "with you
   I'll go upon this pilgrimage."
We left, next morning, his abode,
   But (Heaven forgive him!) halfway on
The old man died upon the road—
   He never gazed on Carcassonne.

GUSTAVE NADAUD.

Translated by John R. Thompson

THE VAGABONDS

WE ARE two travelers, Roger and I.
  Roger's my dog—come here, you scamp!
Jump for the gentleman,—mind your eye!
  Over the table,—look out for the lamp!
The rogue is growing a little old;
  Five years we've tramp'd through wind and weather.
And slept out doors when nights were cold,
  And ate and drank—and starved—together.

We've learn'd what comfort is, I tell you!
  A bed on the floor, a bit of rosin,
A fire to thaw our thumbs (poor fellow!
  The paw he holds up there has been frozen),
Plenty of catgut for my fiddle
  (This outdoor business is bad for strings),
Then a few nice buckwheats hot from the griddle,
  And Roger and I set up for kings!

No, thank you, sir,—I never drink;
  Roger and I are exceedingly moral,—
Aren't we, Roger?—see him wink!
  Well, something hot, then, we won't quarrel.
He's thirsty, too—see him nod his head?
  What a pity, sir, that dogs can't talk!
He understands every word that's said,—
  And he knows good milk from water and chalk.

The truth is, sir, now I reflect,
  I've been so sadly given to grog,
I wonder I've not lost the respect
  (Here's to you, sir!) even of my dog.
But he sticks by, through thick and thin;
  And this old coat, with its empty pockets,
And rags that smell of tobacco and gin,
  He'll follow while he has eyes in his sockets.

There isn't another creature living
  Would do it, and prove, through every disaster,
So fond, so faithful, and so forgiving
  To such a miserable, thankless master!

No, sir!—see him wag his tail and grin!
  By George! it makes my old eyes water!
That is, there's something in this gin
  That chokes a fellow. But no matter!

We'll have some music, if you are willing,
  And Roger (hem! what a plague a cough is, sir!)
Shall march a little. Start, you villain!
  Stand straight! 'Bout face! Salute your officer!
Put up that paw! Dress! Take your rifle!
  (Some dogs have arms, you see.) Now hold your
Cap while the gentlemen give a trifle
  To aid a poor old patriot soldier.

March! Halt! Now show how the rebel shakes
  When he stands up to hear his sentence.
Now tell how many drams it takes
  To honor a jolly new acquaintance.
Five yelps, that's five! he's mighty knowing!
  The night's before us, fill the glasses!
Quick, sir! I'm ill,—my brain is going;
  Some brandy,—thank you; there,—it passes!

Why not reform? That's easily said;
  But I've gone through such wretched treatment,
Sometimes forgetting the taste of bread,
  And scarce remembering what meat meant,
That my poor stomach's past reform;
  And there are times when, mad with thinking,
I'd sell out heaven for something warm
  To prop a horrible inward sinking.

Is there a way to forget to think?
  At your age, sir, home, fortune, friends,
A dear girl's love,—but I took to drink,—
  The same old story; you know how it ends.
If you could have seen these classic features,—
  You needn't laugh, sir; they were not then
Such a burning libel on God's creatures;
  I was one of your handsome men!

If you had seen her, so fair and young,
  Whose head was happy on this breast!
If you could have heard the songs I sung
  When the wine went round, you wouldn't have guessed

That ever I, sir, should be straying
  From door to door, with fiddle and dog,
Ragged and penniless, and playing
  To you tonight for a glass of grog!

She's married since,—a parson's wife;
  'T was better for her that we should part,—
Better the soberest, prosiest life
  Than a blasted home and a broken heart.
I have seen her? Once: I was weak and spent
  On the dusty road; a carriage stopped;
But little she dreamed, as on she went,
  Who kissed the coin that her fingers dropped!

You've set me talking, sir; I'm sorry;
  It makes me wild to think of the change!
What do you care for a beggar's story?
  Is it amusing? you find it strange?
I had a mother so proud of me!
  'T was well she died before—— Do you know
If the happy spirits in heaven can see
  The ruin and wretchedness here below?

Another glass, and strong, to deaden
  This pain; then Roger and I will start.
I wonder, has he such a lumpish, leaden,
  Aching thing in place of a heart?
He is sad sometimes, and would weep, if he could,
  No doubt, remembering things that were,—
A virtuous kennel, with plenty of food,
  And himself a sober, respectable cur.

I'm better now; that glass was warming.
  You rascal! limber your lazy feet!
We must be fiddling and performing
  For supper and bed, or starve in the street.
Not a very gay life to lead, you think?
  But soon we shall go where lodgings are free,
And the sleepers need neither victuals nor drink;
  The sooner the better for Roger and me!

JOHN TOWNSEND TROWBRIDGE.

THE RAVEN

ONCE UPON A MIDNIGHT dreary, while I pondered, weak and weary,
Over many a quaint and curious volume of forgotten lore,—
While I nodded, nearly napping, suddenly there came a tapping,
As of some one gently rapping, rapping at my chamber door.
" 'Tis some visitor," I muttered, "tapping at my chamber door;
　　　　Only this, and nothing more."

Ah, distinctly I remember, it was in the bleak December,
And each separate dying ember wrought its ghost upon the floor.
Eagerly I wished the morrow; vainly I had sought to borrow
From my books surcease of sorrow,—sorrow for the lost Lenore,—
For the rare and radiant maiden whom the angels named Lenore,—
　　　　Nameless here forevermore.

And the silken, sad, uncertain rustling of each purple curtain
Thrilled me,—filled me with fantastic terrors never felt before;
So that now, to still the beating of my heart, I stood repeating,
" 'Tis some visitor entreating entrance at my chamber door,—
Some late visitor entreating entrance at my chamber door;
　　　　That it is, and nothing more."

Presently my soul grew stronger; hesitating then no longer,
"Sir," said I, "or madam, truly your forgiveness I implore;
But the fact is, I was napping, and so gently you came rapping,
And so faintly you came tapping, tapping at my chamber door,
That I scarce was sure I heard you."—Here I opened wide the door;
　　　　Darkness there, and nothing more.

Deep into that darkness peering, long I stood there, wondering, fearing,
Doubting, dreaming dreams no mortal ever dared to dream before;
But the silence was unbroken, and the darkness gave no token,
And the only word there spoken was the whispered word "Lenore!"
This I whispered, and an echo murmured back the word "Lenore!"
　　　　Merely this, and nothing more.

Back into the chamber turning, all my soul within me burning,
Soon again I heard a tapping, something louder than before:
"Surely," said I, "surely that is something at my window-lattice;
Let me see then what thereat is, and this mystery explore,—
Let my heart be still a moment, and this mystery explore;—
　　　　'Tis the wind, and nothing more."

Open then I flung the shutter, when, with many a flirt and flutter,
In there stepped a stately raven of the saintly days of yore.
Not the least obeisance made he; not an instant stopped or stayed he;
But, with mien of lord or lady, perched above my chamber door,—
Perched upon a bust of Pallas, just above my chamber door,—
      Perched, and sat, and nothing more.

Then this ebony bird beguiling my sad fancy into smiling,
By the grave and stern decorum of the countenance it wore,
"Though thy crest be shorn and shaven, thou," I said, "art sure no
    craven;
Ghastly, grim, and ancient raven, wandering from the nightly shore,
Tell me what thy lordly name is on the night's Plutonian shore?"
      Quoth the raven, "Nevermore!"

Much I marvelled this ungainly fowl to hear discourse so plainly,
Though its answer little meaning, little relevancy bore;
For we cannot help agreeing that no living human being
Ever yet was blessed with seeing bird above his chamber door,
Bird or beast upon the sculptured bust above his chamber door,
      With such name as "Nevermore!"

But the raven, sitting lonely on the placid bust, spoke only
That one word, as if his soul in that one word he did outpour.
Nothing further then he uttered,—not a feather then he fluttered,—
Till I scarcely more than muttered, "Other friends have flown before,—
On the morrow he will leave me, as my hopes have flown before."
      Then the bird said, "Nevermore!"

Startled at the stillness, broken by reply so aptly spoken,
"Doubtless," said I, "what it utters is its only stock and store,
Caught from some unhappy master, whom unmerciful disaster
Followed fast and followed faster, till his song one burden bore,
Till the dirges of his hope that melancholy burden bore,—
      Of 'Nevermore,—nevermore!'"

But the raven still beguiling all my sad soul into smiling,
Straight I wheeled a cushioned seat in front of bird and bust and door;
Then, upon the velvet sinking, I betook myself to linking
Fancy unto fancy, thinking what this ominous bird of yore—
What this grim, ungainly, ghastly, gaunt, and ominous bird of yore—
      Meant in croaking "Nevermore!"

This I sat engaged in guessing, but no syllable expressing
To the fowl whose fiery eyes now burned into my bosom's core;
This and more I sat divining, with my head at ease reclining
On the cushion's velvet lining that the lamplight gloated o'er,
But whose velvet violet lining, with the lamplight gloating o'er,
        She shall press—ah! nevermore!

Then methought the air grew denser, perfumed from an unseen censer,
Swung by seraphim, whose footfalls tinkled on the tufted floor.
"Wretch," I cried, "thy God hath lent thee,—by these angels he hath
    sent thee
Respite,—respite and nepenthe from the memories of Lenore!
Quaff, O, quaff this kind nepenthe, and forget this lost Lenore!"
        Quoth the raven, "Nevermore!"

"Prophet!" said I, "thing of evil!—prophet still, if bird or devil!
Whether tempter sent, or whether tempest tossed thee here ashore,
Desolate yet all undaunted, on this desert land enchanted,—
On this home by horror haunted,—tell me truly, I implore,—
Is there—is there balm in Gilead?—tell me,—tell me, I implore!"
        Quoth the raven, "Nevermore!"

"Prophet!" said I, "thing of evil!—prophet still, if bird or devil!
By that heaven that bends above us,—by that God we both adore,
Tell this soul with sorrow laden, if, within the distant Aidenn,
It shall clasp a sainted maiden, whom the angels name Lenore,
Clasp a fair and radiant maiden, whom the angels name Lenore!"
        Quoth the raven, "Nevermore!"

"Be that word our sign of parting, bird or fiend!" I shrieked, up-
    starting,—
"Get thee back into the tempest and the night's Plutonian shore!
Leave no black plume as a token of that lie thy soul hath spoken!
Leave my loneliness unbroken!—quit the bust above my door!
Take thy beak from out my heart, and take thy form from off my door!"
        Quoth the raven, "Nevermore!"

And the raven, never flitting, still is sitting, still is sitting
On the pallid bust of Pallas, just above my chamber door;
And his eyes have all the seeming of a demon that is dreaming,
And the lamplight o'er him streaming throws his shadow on the floor;
And my soul from out that shadow that lies floating on the floor
        Shall be lifted—*nevermore!*

                                EDGAR ALLAN POE.

EVOLUTION

WHEN YOU WERE a tadpole and I was a fish
  In the Paleozoic time,
And side by side on the ebbing tide
  We sprawled through the ooze and slime,
Or skittered with many a caudal flip
  Through the depths of the Carbrian fen,
My heart was rife with the joy of life,
  For I loved you even then.

Mindless we lived and mindless we loved
  And mindless at last we died;
And deep in the rift of the Caradoc drift
  We slumbered side by side.
The world turned on in the lathe of time,
  The hot lands heaved amain,
Till we caught our breath from the womb of death
  And crept into light again.

We were amphibians, scaled and tailed,
  And drab as a dead man's hand;
We coiled at ease 'neath the dripping trees
  Or trailed through the mud and sand.
Croaking and blind, with our three-clawed feet
  Writing a language dumb,
With never a spark in the empty dark
  To hint at a life to come.

Yet happy we lived and happy we loved,
  And happy we died once more;
Our forms were rolled in the clinging mold
  Of a Neocomian shore.
The eons came and the eons fled
  And the sleep that wrapped us fast
Was riven away in a newer day
  And the night of death was past.

Then light and swift through the jungle trees
  We swung in our airy flights,
Or breathed in the balms of the fronded palms
  In the hush of the moonless nights;

And, oh! what beautiful years were there
 When our hearts clung each to each;
When life was filled and our senses thrilled
 In the first faint dawn of speech.

Thus life by life and love by love
 We passed through the cycles strange,
And breath by breath and death by death
 We followed the chain of change.
Till there came a time in the law of life
 When over the nursing side
The shadows broke and the soul awoke
 In a strange, dim dream of God.

I was thewed like an Auroch bull
 And tusked like the great cave bear;
And you, my sweet, from head to feet
 Were gowned in your glorious hair.
Deep in the gloom of a fireless cave,
 When the night fell o'er the plain
And the moon hung red o'er the river bed
 We mumbled the bones of the slain.

I flaked a flint to a cutting edge
 And shaped it with brutish craft;
I broke a shank from the woodland lank
 And fitted it, head and haft;
Then I hid me close to the reedy tarn,
 Where the mammoth came to drink;
Through the brawn and bone I drove the stone
 And slew him upon the brink.

Loud I howled through the moonlit wastes,
 Loud answered our kith and kin;
From west and east to the crimson feast
 The clan came tramping in.
O'er joint and gristle and padded hoof
 We fought and clawed and tore,
And cheek by jowl with many a growl
 We talked the marvel o'er.

I carved that fight on a reindeer bone
 With rude and hairy hand;
I pictured his fall on the cavern wall
 That men might understand.

For we lived by blood and the right of might
  Ere human laws were drawn,
And the age of sin did not begin
  Till our brutal tush were gone.

And that was a million years ago
  In a time that no man knows;
Yet here tonight in the mellow light
  We sit at Delmonico's.
Your eyes are deep as the Devon springs,
  Your hair is dark as jet,
Your years are few, your life is new,
  Your soul untried, and yet—

Our trail is on the Kimmeridge clay
  And the scarp of the Purbeck flags;
We have left our bones in the Bagshot stones
  And deep in the Coralline crags;
Our love is old, our lives are old,
  And death shall come amain;
Should it come today, what man may say
  We shall not live again?

God wrought our souls from the Tremadoc beds
  And furnished them wings to fly;
He sowed our spawn in the world's dim dawn,
  And I know that it shall not die,
Though cities have sprung above the graves
  Where the crook-bone men make war
And the oxwain creaks o'er the buried caves
  Where the mummied mammoths are.

Then as we linger at luncheon here
  O'er many a dainty dish,
Let us drink anew to the time when you
  Were a tadpole and I was a fish.

                    LANGDON SMITH.

BETH–GÊLERT

Or, *The Grave of the Greyhound*

THE SPEARMEN heard the bugle sound,
  And cheerily smiled the morn,
And many a brach and many a hound
  Obey'd Llewelyn's horn.

And still he blew a louder blast,
  And gave a lustier cheer:
"Come, Gêlert, come, wert never last
  Llewelyn's horn to hear.

"Oh! where does faithful Gêlert roam,
  The flow'r of all his race?
So true, so brave; a lamb at home,
  A lion in the chase!"

'Twas only at Llewelyn's board
  The faithful Gêlert fed;
He watch'd, he serv'd, he cheer'd his lord,
  And sentinell'd his bed.

In sooth he was a peerless hound,
  The gift of royal John;
But now no Gêlert could be found,
  And all the chase rode on.

And now, as o'er the rocks and dells
  The gallant chidings rise,
All Snowdon's craggy chaos yells
  The many-mingled cries!

That day Llewelyn little loved
  The chase of Hart or Hare,
And scant and small the booty proved,
  For Gêlert was not there.

Unpleased, Llewelyn homeward hied:
  When, near the portal seat,
His truant Gêlert he espied
  Bounding his lord to greet.

But, when he gained his castle door,
   Aghast the chieftain stood:
The hound all o'er was smear'd with gore,
   His lips, his fangs, ran blood.

Llewelyn gazed with fierce surprise:
   Unused such looks to meet,
His fav'rite check'd his joyful guise,
   And crouch'd and lick'd his feet.

Onward in haste Llewelyn pass'd,
   And on went Gêlert too,
And still, where'er his eyes he cast,
   Fresh blood-gouts shock'd his view.

O'erturn'd his infant's bed he found,
   With blood-stain'd covert rent;
And all around, the walls and ground
   With recent blood besprent.

He call'd his child, no voice replied;
   He search'd with terror wild;
Blood, blood he found on ev'ry side;
   But nowhere found his child.

"Hell-hound! my child by thee's devour'd!"
   The frantic father cried;
And to the hilt his vengeful sword
   He plunged in Gêlert's side.

His suppliant looks as prone he fell,
   No pity could impart;
But still his Gêlert's dying yell
   Pass'd heavy o'er his heart.

Aroused by Gêlert's dying yell
   Some slumb'rer waken'd nigh:
What words the parent's joy could tell
   To hear his infant's cry!

Conceal'd beneath a tumbled heap
   His hurried search had miss'd,
All glowing from his rosy sleep,
   The cherub boy he kiss'd.

Nor scath had he, nor harm, nor dread;
  But the same couch beneath
Lay a gaunt wolf, all torn and dead,
  Tremendous still in death.

Ah, what was then Llewelyn's pain!
  For now the truth was clear;
His gallant hound the wolf had slain,
  To save Llewelyn's heir.

Vain, vain was all Llewelyn's woe:
  "Best of thy kind, adieu!
The frantic blow, which laid thee low,
  This heart shall ever rue."

And now a gallant tomb they raise,
  With costly sculpture deckt;
And marbles, storied with his praise,
  Poor Gêlert's bones protect.

There never could the spearman pass,
  Or forester, unmoved;
There oft the tear-besprinkled grass
  Llewelyn's sorrow proved.

And there he hung his sword and spear,
  And there as evening fell,
In Fancy's ear he oft would hear
  Poor Gêlert's dying yell.

And till great Snowdon's rocks grow old,
  And cease the storm to brave,
The consecrated spot shall hold
  The name of "Gêlert's Grave."

                    WILLIAM ROBERT SPENCER.

THE LANDING OF THE PILGRIM FATHERS
IN NEW ENGLAND

THE BREAKING WAVES dashed high
  On a stern and rock-bound coast,
And the woods against a stormy sky
  Their giant branches tossed:

217

And the heavy night hung dark
  The hills and waters o'er,
When a band of exiles moored their bark
  On the wild New England shore.

Not as the conqueror comes,
  They, the true-hearted, came;
Not with the roll of the stirring drums,
  And the trumpet that sings of fame:

Not as the flying come,
  In silence and in fear;
They shook the depths of the desert gloom
  With their hymns of lofty cheer.

Amidst the storm they sang,
  And the stars heard, and the sea;
And the sounding aisles of the dim woods rang
  To the anthem of the free.

The ocean eagle soared
  From his nest by the white wave's foam,
And the rocking pines of the forest roared,—
  This was their welcome home.

There were men with hoary hair
  Amidst that pilgrim-band:
Why had they come to wither there,
  Away from their childhood's land?

There was woman's fearless eye,
  Lit by her deep love's truth;
There was manhood's brow serenely high,
  And the fiery heart of youth.

What sought they thus afar?
  Bright jewels of the mine?
The wealth of seas, the spoils of war?—
  They sought a faith's pure shrine!

Ay, call it holy ground,
  The soil where first they trod;
They have left unstained what there they found,—
  Freedom to worship God.

FELICIA D. HEMANS.

CONCORD HYMN

(Sung at the Completion of the Concord Monument, April 19, 1836.)

By THE RUDE BRIDGE that arched the flood,
    Their flag to April's breeze unfurled,
Here once the embattled farmers stood,
    And fired the shot heard round the world.

The foe long since in silence slept;
    Alike the conqueror silent sleeps;
And Time the ruined bridge has swept
    Down the dark stream which seaward creeps.

On this green bank, by this soft stream,
    We set to-day a votive stone;
That memory may their deed redeem,
    When, like our sires, our sons are gone.

Spirit, that made those heroes dare
    To die, and leave their children free,
Bid Time and Nature gently spare
    The shaft we raise to them and thee.

                RALPH WALDO EMERSON.

MY MADONNA

I HAILED ME a woman from the street,
    Shameless, but oh, so fair!
I bade her sit in the model's seat
    And I painted her sitting there.

I hid all trace of her heart unclean;
    I painted a babe at her breast;
I painted her as she might have been
    If the Worst had been the Best.

She laughed at my picture and went away
    Then came with a knowing nod,
A connoisseur, and I heard him say;
    " 'Tis Mary, the Mother of God."

So I painted a halo round her hair,
  And I sold her and took my fee,
And she hangs in the church of Saint Hilaire,
  Where you and all may see.

ROBERT W. SERVICE.

THE LEGEND OF THE ORGAN–BUILDER

DAY BY DAY the Organ-Builder in his lonely chamber wrought;
Day by day the soft air trembled to the music of his thought,

Till at last the work was ended; and no organ-voice so grand
Ever yet had soared responsive to the master's magic hand.

Ay, so rarely was it builded that whenever groom and bride,
Who in God's sight were well pleasing, in the church stood side by side

Without touch or breath the organ of itself began to play,
And the very airs of heaven through the soft gloom seemed to stray.

He was young, the Organ-Builder, and o'er all the land his fame
Ran with fleet and eager footsteps, like a swiftly rushing flame.

All the maidens heard the story; all the maidens blushed and smiled,
By his youth and wondrous beauty and his great renown beguiled.

So he sought and won the fairest, and the wedding day was set:
Happy day—the brightest jewel in the glad year's coronet!

But when they the portal entered he forgot his lovely bride—
Forgot his love, forgot his God, and his heart swelled high with pride.

"Ah!" thought he; "how great a master am I! When the organ plays,
How the vast cathedral arches will re-echo with my praise!"

Up the aisle the gay procession moved. The altar shone afar,
With every candle gleaming through soft shadows like a star.

But he listened, listened, listened, with no thought of love or prayer,
For the swelling notes of triumph from his organ standing there.

All was silent. Nothing heard he save the priest's low monotone,
And the bride's robe trailing softly o'er the floor of fretted stone.

Then his lips grew white with anger. Surely God was pleased with him
Who had built the wondrous organ for His temple vast and dim!

Whose the fault, then? Hers—the maiden standing meekly at his side!
Flamed his jealous rage, maintaining she was false to him—his bride.

Vain were all her protestations, vain her innocence and truth;
On that very night he left her to her anguish and her ruth.

Far he wandered to a country wherein no man knew his name;
For ten weary years he dwelt there, nursing still his wrath and shame.

Then his haughty heart grew softer, and he thought by night and day
Of the bride he had deserted, till he hardly dared to pray;

Thought of her, a spotless maiden, fair and beautiful and good;
Thought of his relentless anger, that had cursed her womanhood;

Till his yearning grief and penitence at last were all complete,
And he longed, with bitter longing, just to fall down at her feet.

Ah! how throbbed his heart when, after many a weary day and night,
Rose his native towers before him, with the sunset glow alight!

Through the gates into the city, on he pressed with eager tread;
There he met a long procession—mourners following the dead.

"Now, why weep ye so, good people? and whom bury ye today?
Why do yonder sorrowing maidens scatter flowers along the way?

"Has some saint gone up to heaven?" "Yes," they answered, weeping
    sore;
For the Organ-Builder's saintly wife our eyes shall see no more;

"And because her days were given to the service of God's poor,
From his church we mean to bury her. See! yonder is the door."

No one knew him; no one wondered when he cried out, white with
    pain;
No one questioned when, with pallid lips, he poured his tears like rain.

" 'Tis some one whom she has comforted, who mourns with us," they
    said,
As he made his way unchallenged, and bore the coffin's head;

Bore it through the open portal, bore it up the echoing aisle,
Let it down before the altar, where the lights burned clear the while:

When, oh, hark! the wondrous organ of itself began to play
Strains of rare, unearthly sweetness never heard until that day!

All the vaulted arches rang with the music sweet and clear;
All the air was filled with glory, as of angels hovering near;

And ere yet the strain was ended, he who bore the coffin's head,
With the smile of one forgiven, gently sank beside it—dead.

They who raised the body knew him, and they laid him by his bride;
Down the aisle and o'er the threshold they were carried, side by side.

While the organ played a dirge that no man ever heard before,
And then softly sank to silence—silence kept for evermore.

JULIA C. R. DORR.

THE TOUCH OF THE MASTER'S HAND

'TWAS BATTERED and scarred, and the auctioneer
Thought it scarcely worth his while
To waste much time on the old violin,
But held it up with a smile:
"What am I bidden, good folks," he cried,
"Who'll start the bidding for me?"
"A dollar, a dollar"; then, "Two!" "Only two?
Two dollars, and who'll make it three?
Three dollars, once; three dollars, twice;
Going for three——" But no,
From the room, far back, a gray-haired man
Came forward and picked up the bow;
Then, wiping the dust from the old violin,
And tightening the loose strings,
He played a melody pure and sweet
As a caroling angel sings.

The music ceased, and the auctioneer,
With a voice that was quiet and low,
Said: "What am I bid for the old violin?"
And he held it up with the bow.

222

"A thousand dollars, and who'll make it two?
Two thousand! And who'll make it three?
Three thousand, once, three thousand, twice,
And going, and gone," said he.
The people cheered, but some of them cried,
"We do not quite understand
What changed its worth." Swift came the reply:
"The touch of a master's hand."

And many a man with life out of tune,
And battered and scarred with sin,
Is auctioned cheap to the thoughtless crowd,
Much like the old violin.
A "mess of pottage," a glass of wine;
A game—and he travels on.
He is "going" once, and "going" twice,
He's "going" and almost "gone."
But the Master comes, and the foolish crowd
Never can quite understand
The worth of a soul and the change that's wrought
By the touch of the Master's hand.

MYRA BROOKS WELCH.

JOHN MAYNARD

'TWAS ON LAKE ERIE's broad expanse
  One bright midsummer day,
The gallant steamer *Ocean Queen*
  Swept proudly on her way.
Bright faces clustered on the deck
  Or, leaning o'er the side,
Watched carelessly the feathery foam
  That flecked the rippling tide.

Ah, who beneath that cloudless sky,
  That, smiling, bends serene,
Could dream that danger, awful, vast,
  Impended o'er the scene—
Could dream that ere an hour had sped
  That frame of sturdy oak
Would sink beneath the lake's blue waves,
  Blackened with fire and smoke?

A seaman sought the captain's side,
  A moment whispered low;
The captain's swarthy face grew pale;
  He hurried down below.
Alas, too late! Though quick and sharp
  And clear his orders came,
No human efforts could avail
  To quench the insidious flame.

The bad news quickly reached the deck,
  It sped from lip to lip,
And ghastly faces everywhere
  Looked from the doomed ship.
"Is there no hope, no chance of life?"
  A hundred lips implore;
"But one," the captain made reply,
  "To run the ship on shore."

A sailor whose heroic soul
  That hour should yet reveal,
By name John Maynard, Eastern born,
  Stood calmly at the wheel.
"Head her southeast!" the captain shouts
  Above the smothered roar,
"Head her southeast without delay!
  Make for the nearest shore!"

No terror pales the helmsman's cheek,
  Or clouds his dauntless eye,
As, in a sailor's measured tone
  His voice responds "Ay! ay!"
Three hundred souls, the steamer's freight,
  Crowd forward, wild with fear,
While at the stern the dreaded flames
  Above the deck appear.

John Maynard watched the nearing flames,
  But still with steady hand
He grasped the wheel and steadfastly
  He steered the ship to land.
"John Maynard, can you still hold out?"
  He heard the captain cry;
A voice from out the stifling smoke
  Faintly responds, "Ay! ay!"

But half a mile, a hundred hands
   Stretch eagerly to shore;
But half a mile that distance sped,
   Peril shall all be o'er.
But half a mile! Yet stay, the flames
   No longer slowly creep,
But gather round that helmsman bold
   With fierce, impetuous sweep.

"John Maynard!" with an anxious voice
   The captain cries once more,
"Stand by the wheel five minutes yet,
   And we shall reach the shore."
Through flame and smoke that dauntless **heart**
   Responded firmly still,
Unawed, though face to face with death,
   "With God's good help I will!"

The flames approach with giant strides,
   They scorch his hand and brow;
One arm, disabled, seeks his side,
   Ah! he is conquered now.
But no, his teeth are firmly set,
   He crushes down his pain;
His knee upon the stanchion pressed,
   He guides the ship again.

One moment yet! one moment yet!
   Brave heart, thy task is o'er;
The pebbles grate beneath the keel
   The steamer touches shore.
Three hundred grateful voices rise
   In praise to God that he
Hath saved them from the fearful fire,
   And from the engulfing sea.

But where is he, that helmsman bold?
   The captain saw him reel;
His nerveless hands released their task;
   He sank beside the wheel.
The wave received his lifeless corse,
   Blackened with smoke and fire.
God rest him! Never hero had
   A nobler funeral pyre!

               HORATIO ALGER, JR.

225

"GUILTY OR NOT GUILTY?"

SHE STOOD at the bar of justice,
A creature wan and wild,
In form too small for a woman,
In feature too old for a child.
For a look so worn and pathetic
Was stamped on her pale young face,
It seemed long years of suffering
Must have left that silent trace.

"Your name," said the judge, as he eyed her,
With kindly look, yet keen,
"Is——" "Mary Maguire, if you please, sir."
"And your age?" "I am turned fifteen."
"Well, Mary,"—and then from a paper
He slowly and gravely read—
"You are charged here—I am sorry to say it—
With stealing three loaves of bread.

"You look not like an old offender,
And I hope that you can show
The charge to be false. Now, tell me,
Are you guilty of this, or no?"
A passionate burst of weeping
Was at first her sole reply;
But she dried her tears in a moment,
And looked in the judge's eye.

"I will tell you just how it was, sir:
My father and mother are dead,
And my little brothers and sisters
Were hungry, and asked me for bread.
At first I earned it for them,
By working hard all day,
But somehow the times were hard, sir,
And the work all fell away.

"I could get no more employment;
The weather was bitter cold;
The young ones cried and shivered
(Little Johnnie's but four years old);

226

So what was I to do, sir?
I am guilty, but do not condemn;
I took—O! was it stealing?—
The bread to give to them."

Every man in the courtroom—
Graybeard and thoughtless youth—
Knew, as he looked upon her,
That the prisoner spoke the truth.
Out from their pockets came kerchiefs,
Out from their eyes sprung tears,
And out from old, faded wallets
Treasures hoarded for years.

The judge's face was a study,
The strangest you ever saw,
As he cleared his throat and murmured
Something about the law.
For one so learned in such matters,
So wise in dealing with men,
He seemed, on a simple question,
Sorely puzzled just then.

But no one blamed him, or wondered
When at last these words they heard:
"The sentence of this young prisoner
Is for the present deferred."
And no one blamed him or wondered
When he went to her and smiled,
And tenderly led from the courtroom,
Himself, the "guilty" child!

UNKNOWN.

THE MAN ON THE FLYING TRAPEZE

ONCE I WAS happy, but now I'm forlorn,
Like an old coat, all tattered and torn,
Left in this wide world to fret and to mourn,
Betrayed by a wife in her teens.
Oh, the girl that I loved she was handsome,
I tried all I knew her to please,
But I could not please one quarter as well
As the man on the flying trapeze.

Chorus:

He would fly through the air
With the greatest of ease,
This daring young man
On the flying trapeze;
His movements were graceful,
All girls he could please,
And my love he purloined away.

Her father and mother were both on my side,
And very hard tried to make her my bride.
Her father he sighed, and her mother she cried
To see her throw herself away.
'Twas all no avail, she'd go there every night
And throw him bouquets on the stage,
Which caused him to meet her; how he ran me down
To tell you would take a whole page.

One night I as usual called at her dear home,
Found there her father and mother alone.
I asked for my love, and soon they made known
To my horror that she'd run away.
She packed up her goods and eloped in the night
With him with the greatest of ease;
From three stories high he had lowered her down
To the ground on his flying trapeze.

Some months after this, I chanced in a hall,
Was greatly surprised to see on the wall
A bill in red letters that did my heart gall,
That she was appearing with him.
He taught her gymnastics and dressed her in tights
To help him to live at his ease,
And made her assume a masculine name,
And now she goes on the trapeze.

Chorus:

She floats through the air
With the greatest of ease,
You'd think her a man
On the flying trapeze.
She does all the work
While he takes his ease,
And that's what became of my love.

UNKNOWN.

THE HELL-BOUND TRAIN

A Texas cowboy lay down on a barroom floor,
Having drunk so much he could drink no more;
So he fell asleep with a troubled brain
To dream that he rode on a hell-bound train.

The engine with murderous blood was damp
And was brilliantly lit with a brimstone lamp;
An imp, for fuel, was shoveling bones,
While the furnace rang with a thousand groans.

The boiler was filled with lager beer
And the devil himself was the engineer;
The passengers were a most motley crew—
Church member, atheist, Gentile, and Jew,

Rich men in broadcloth, beggars in rags,
Handsome young ladies, and withered old hags,
Yellow and black men, red, brown, and white,
All chained together—O God, what a sight!

While the train rushed on at an awful pace—
The sulphurous fumes scorched their hands and face;
Wider and wider the country grew,
As faster and faster the engine flew.

Louder and louder the thunder crashed
And brighter and brighter the lightning flashed;
Hotter and hotter the air became
Till the clothes were burned from each quivering frame.

And out of the distance there arose a yell,
"Ha, ha," said the devil, "we're nearing hell!"
Then oh, how the passengers all shrieked with pain
And begged the devil to stop the train.

But he capered about and danced for glee,
And laughed and joked at their misery.
"My faithful friends, you have done the work
And the devil never can a payday shirk.

"You've bullied the weak, you've robbed the poor,
The starving brother you've turned from the door;

You've laid up gold where the canker rust,
And have given free vent to your beastly lust.

"You've justice scorned, and corruption sown,
And trampled the laws of nature down.
You have drunk, rioted, cheated, plundered, and lied,
And mocked at God in your hell-born pride.

"You have paid full fare, so I'll carry you through,
For it's only right you should have your due.
Why, the laborer always expects his hire,
So I'll land you safe in the lake of fire,

"Where your flesh will waste in the flames that roar,
And my imps torment you forevermore."
Then the cowboy awoke with an anguished cry,
His clothes wet with sweat and his hair standing high.

Then he prayed as he never had prayed till that hour
To be saved from his sin and the demon's power;
And his prayers and his vows were not in vain,
For he never rode the hell-bound train.

UNKNOWN.

THE *JULIE PLANTE*

ON WAN DARK NIGHT on Lac St. Pierre
De wind, she blow, blow, blow,
An' de crew of de wood-scow *Julie Plante*
Got scairt and run below.

For de wind she blow lak hurricane;
Bianby she blow some more,
An' de scow bust up on Lac St. Pierre
Wan arpent from de shore.

De captain walk on de fronte deck,
An' walk on the hin' deck too.
He call de crew from up de hole;
He call de cook also.

De cook she's name was Rosie,
She come from Montreal,
Was chambermaid on lumber barge
On de Grande Lachine Canal.

De wind she blow for nor'east west,
De south wind she blow too.
Rosie cry, "Non, cher Captain;
Mon cher, what shall I do?"

Den de captain throw the big ankerre,
But still de skow she dreeft;
De crew he can't pass on de shore
Becos he lose heesself.

De night was dark lak wan black cat,
De wave run high and fast
When de captain tak de Rosie girl
An' tie her to de mast.

Den he also tak de life preserve
An' jump off on de lac,
An' say, "Good-bye, my Rosie dear,
I go drown for your sak."

Next morning very early
Bout half-past two, three, four,
De captain, scow and poor Rosie
Was corpses on de shore.

For de wind she blow lak hurricane,
Bianby she blow some more,
An' de scow bust up on Lac St. Pierre,
Wan arpent from de shore.

Now all good wood-scow sailorman
Tak warning from dat storm,
An' go an' marry some nice French girl
An' live on wan beeg farm.

De wind can blow lak hurricane,
An' spose she blow some more,
You can't get drown on Lac St. Pierre
So long you stay on shore.

WILLIAM HENRY DRUMMOND.

231

LORD LOVEL

Lord Lovel he stood at his castle-gate
  Combing his milk-white steed;
When up came Lady Nancy Belle,
  To wish her lover good speed, speed,
  To wish her lover good speed.

"Where are you going, Lord Lovel?" she said,
  "Oh! where are you going?" said she;
"I'm going, my Lady Nancy Belle,
  Strange countries for to see, to see,
  Strange countries for to see."

"When will you be back, Lord Lovel?" she said;
  "Oh! when will you come back?" said she;
"In a year or two—or three, at the most,
  I'll return to my fair Nancy-cy,
  I'll return to my fair Nancy."

But he had not been gone a year and a day,
  Strange countries for to see,
When languishing thoughts came into his head,
  Lady Nancy Belle he would go see, see,
  Lady Nancy Belle he would go see.

So he rode and he rode on his milk-white steed,
  Till he came to London town,
And there he heard St. Pancras' bells,
  And the people all mourning, round, round,
  And the people all mourning round.

"Oh! what is the matter?" Lord Lovel he said,
  "Oh! what is the matter?" said he;
"A lord's lady is dead," a woman replied,
  "And some call her Lady Nancy-cy,
  And some call her Lady Nancy."

So he order'd the grave to be open'd wide,
  And the shroud he turnèd down,
And there he kiss'd her clay-cold lips,
  Till the tears came trickling down, down,
  Till the tears came trickling down.

Lady Nancy she died as it might be to-day,
  Lord Lovel he died as to-morrow;
Lady Nancy she died out of pure, pure grief,
  Lord Lovel he died out of sorrow, sorrow,
  Lord Lovel he died out of sorrow.

Lady Nancy was laid in St. Pancras' church,
  Lord Lovel was laid in the choir;
And out of her bosom there grew a red rose,
  And out of her lover's a brier, brier,
  And out of her lover's a brier.

They grew, and they grew, to the church-steeple top,
  And then they could grow no higher:
So there they entwined in a true-lover's knot,
  For all lovers true to admire-mire,
  For all lovers true to admire.

UNKNOWN.

THE LOVING BALLAD OF LORD BATEMAN

Lord Bateman was a noble lord,
A noble lord he was of high degree;
And he determined to go abroad,
Some foreign countries for to see.

He sailed east and he sailed west,
Until he came to Sentipee,
Where he was taken and bound in irons
Until his life was quite wearee;

And in this prison there grew a tree,
And there it grew so stout and strong;
They took and chained him round his middle,
Until his life was nearly gone.

Now this Turk he had an only daughter,
As fair as my two eyes did see;
She stole the keys of her father's prison,
And said Lord Bateman she would go see.

233

"Lord Bateman, have you got houses and land,
And doth Northumberland belong to thee?
What wilt thou give to the fair young lady
Who out of prison sets you free?"

"Oh yes, I have houses and land,
And half Northumberland belongs to me;
I'll give it all to the fair young lady
Who out of prison sets me free."

Then she took him to her father's cellar,
And gave to him the very best wine,
And every health she drank unto him,
She said: "Lord Bateman, I wish you were mine!"

Then they made a vow for seven long years,
That for seven long years they would keep it strong,
That he would marry no other woman,
And she would marry no other man.

Then she took him to her father's harbor
And gave to him a ship of fame;
"Farewell, farewell, farewell, Lord Bateman!
I fear I ne'er shall see you again!"

When seven long years had passed and gone,
And fourteen days well known to me,
She packed up all her gay gold clothing,
And said Lord Bateman she would go see.

And when she reached Lord Bateman's castle,
She boldly there did ring the bell.
"Who's there? Who's there?" cried the proud young porter,
"Who's there? Who's there? Come, quickly tell!"

"And what is this? Lord Bateman's castle?
And is his lordship here within?"
"Oh yes, oh yes!" cried the proud young porter,
"He's just now taking his fair bride in."

"Go, bid him send me a slice of bread
And eke a bottle of his very best wine,
And not forget the fair young lady
Who did release him from close confine."

And away and away sped this proud young porter,
And away and away and away flew he,
Until he reached Lord Bateman's chamber,
He then fell on his bended knee.

"What news, what news, my proud young porter,
What news, what news can you tell to me?"
"Oh, there is one of the fairest ladies
That ever my two eyes did see!

"She had diamond rings on every finger,
And on one she has got three,
And enough gay gold about her clothing
That would buy all Northumberlee!

"She bids you send her a slice of bread
And a bottle of your very best wine,
And not forget the fair young lady
Who did release you when in close confine."

Then Lord Bateman he flew in a passion,
And he split his sword in splinters three.
"I'll roam no more in foreign countries,
Now my Sophia's crossed the sea!"

Then up spoke the young bride's mother,
Who'd never been known to speak so free:
"You'll not forget my only daughter,
If a Sophia's crossed the sea!"

"I'll own I've made your daughter a bride,
But she's none the better, nor the worse for me.
She came to me in a horse and saddle,
She may go back in her coach and three!"

Then Lord Bateman fixed another wedding,
And with his heart so full of glee
He roamed no more in foreign countries,
Now his Sophia'd crossed the sea.

UNKNOWN.

DERELICT

"FIFTEEN MEN on the Dead Man's Chest—
  Yo-ho-ho and a bottle of rum!
Drink and the devil had done for the rest—
  Yo-ho-ho and a bottle of rum!"
The mate was fixed by the bos'n's pike,
The bos'n brained with a marlinspike,
And Cookey's throat was marked belike
      It had been gripped
        By fingers ten;
      And there they lay,
        All good dead men,
Like break-o'-day in a boozing-ken—
  Yo-ho-ho and a bottle of rum!

Fifteen men of a whole ship's list—
  Yo-ho-ho and a bottle of rum!
Dead and bedamned and the rest gone whist!—
  Yo-ho-ho and a bottle of rum!
The skipper lay with his nob in gore
Where the scullion's ax his cheek had shore—
And the scullion he was stabbed times four.
      And there they lay,
        And the soggy skies
      Dripped all day long
        In upstaring eyes—
At murk sunset and at foul sunrise—
  Yo-ho-ho and a bottle of rum!

Fifteen men of 'em stiff and stark—
  Yo-ho-ho and a bottle of rum!
Ten of the crew had the Murder mark—
  Yo-ho-ho and a bottle of rum!
'Twas a cutlass swipe, or an ounce of lead,
Or a yawing hole in a battered head—
And the scuppers glut with a rotting red.
      And there they lay—
        Aye, damn my eyes!—
      All lookouts clapped
        On paradise—
All souls bound just contrariwise—
  Yo-ho-ho and a bottle of rum!

Fifteen men of 'em good and true—
   Yo-ho-ho and a bottle of rum!
Every man jack could ha' sailed with Old Pew—
   Yo-ho-ho and a bottle of rum!
There was chest on chest full of Spanish gold,
With a ton of plate in the middle hold,
And the cabins riot of stuff untold.
      And they lay there,
        That had took the plum,
      With sightless glare
        And their eyes struck dumb,
While we shared all by the rule of thumb—
   Yo-ho-ho and a bottle of rum!

More was seen through the sternlight screen—
   Yo-ho-ho and a bottle of rum!
Chartings ondoubt where a woman had been!—
   Yo-ho-ho and a bottle of rum!
A flimsy shift on a bunker cot,
With a thin dirk slot through the bosom spot
And the lace stiff-dry in a purplish blot.
      Or was she wench . . .
        Or some shuddering maid . . . ?
      That dared the knife—
        And that took the blade!
By God! she was stuff for a plucky jade—
   Yo-ho-ho and a bottle of rum!

Fifteen men on the Dead Man's Chest—
   Yo-ho-ho and a bottle of rum!
Drink and the devil had done for the rest—
   Yo-ho-ho and a bottle of rum!
We wrapped 'em all in a mains'l tight,
With twice ten turns of a hawser's bight,
And we heaved 'em over and out of sight—
      With a yo-heave-ho!
        And a fare-you-well!
      And a sullen plunge
        In the sullen swell,
Ten fathoms deep on the road to hell!
   Yo-ho-ho and a bottle of rum!

                    YOUNG E. ALLISON.

THE MILLS OF THE GODS

HE WAS the slave of Ambition
And he vowed to the Gods above
To sell his soul to perdition
For Fortune, Fame, and Love.
"Three Wishes," he cried,
And the Devil replied:
"Fortune is a fickle one,
Often wooed but seldom won,
Ever changing like the sun;
Still, I think it can be done.
You have a friend, a rich one too;
Kill him! His wealth is willed to you."
Ambition fled. He paused awhile,
But, daunted by the Devil's smile,
He killed his friend to gain his aim,
Then bowed his head in grief and shame;
But the Devil cried, "It's all in the game.
You wanted Fortune, Love, and Fame,
And so, I came.
Three wishes through your life shall run,
Behold, I've given you Number One."

And the Gods on high, with a watchful eye,
Looked down on the ways of man,
With their hopes and fears through the weary years
Since the days of the world began.
And the man, he prayed, for the soul betrayed
Had breathed a parting call:
"Though the Mills of the Gods grind slowly,
Yet they grind exceeding small."

Urged by the spur of Ambition,
With the Devil still as his guide,
He now sought social position,
For wealth had brought him pride.
"Bring Fame," cried the man,
So the Devil began:
"Fame is but an accident,
Often sought but seldom sent,
Still, I think we're on the scent.

238

You know a genius gone insane;
Go steal the product of his brain.
The man obeyed, then cried, "Begone!
From crime to crime you lead me on,
To kill a friend whose smile was glad,
To rob a genius driven mad
Through want. Oh God! Am I that bad?"
But the Devil cried, "What luck you've had!
You're famous, lad!
Three wishes run your whole life through,
Behold, I've given you Number Two."
And the Gods looked down with an angry frown
Till Satan fled their scorn.
For the Devil may play with the common clay,
But genius is heaven-born.
And the man grew bold with his Fame and Gold,
And cried, "Well, after all,
The Mills of the Gods grind slowly,
If they ever grind at all."

Men, good or bad, are but human,
And he, like the rest, wanted love.
So the Devil soon brought him the woman
As fair as an angel above.
"I love you," he cried,
But the woman replied,
"Love is such an empty word,
Fancy fleeting like a bird,
You have Wealth and Fame, I've heard—
Those are things to be preferred."
He gave her both. The wealth she spent,
And then betrayed him, so Fame went.
But Love came not, in his despair;
She only smiled and left him there,
And he called her "The Woman Who Didn't Care,"
But the Devil cried, "You've had your share,
The game ends there.
Two of your wishes came through me,
But the Mighty Gods keep Number Three."

And the Gods grew stern as the Mills they turned,
That grind before they kill,
Till, staggering blind, with wandering mind,
And the glare of an imbecile,

From day to day he begs his way,
And whines his piteous call,
"The Mills of the Gods grind slowly,
Yet they grind exceeding small."

UNKNOWN.

THE OWL AND THE FOX

THERE WAS an old Fox
That lived under the rocks
At the foot of a huge old tree;
And of all the foxes
That ever did live
There was none so bad as he.
His step was soft,
With his padded feet,
But his claws were sharp beneath;
And sharp were his eyes,
And sharp were his ears,
And sharp were his terrible teeth.

And the dreariest place
You ever did see,
Was this old Fox's den;
It was strewn with the down
Of the tender Chick,
And the quills of the mother hen,
Where he dragged them in
This dismal den
And piled their bones together,
And killed them dead,
And sucked their blood,
And ate their flesh,
And picked their bones,
And warmed his bed with the feathers.

But while the old Fox
Lived under the rocks,
As wicked as he could be,
An Owl built his nest
In a very large hole
That was up in the top of the tree.

This Owl was named Hooty,
And often at night,
When loudly the night wind blew,
He waked the old Fox
In his hole in the rocks,
With his Whit-too-whit-too-whoo-o-o.
Then the Owl would laugh
At the top of the tree
To hear him wake and growl,
For he hated the Fox
That lived down in the rocks;
And the Fox he hated the Owl.

Now the Owl had a little son,
Billy by name,
And a beautiful Owlet was he;
His eyes were as big
As the lamps of a gig,
And his Bill was a wonder to see.
He never cried
When his head was combed,
Nor screamed when they wiped his nose,
Or washed his face,
And got soap in his eyes,
And he never tore his clothes.

When Hooty was going
He said to his son,
"Now, Bill, I command and beseech you,
Don't leave the nest,
'Tis my earnest request,
For the old Fox may catch you and eat you;
He is watching below
To catch you, I know,
So don't try to fly till I teach you."

And poor little Billy
Was so very silly,
He climbed out on the bough;
And the old Fox laughed
With a "Ha, ha, ha!"
And thought he had got him now.

At last he heard a flapping of wings,
    And Hooty lit on a tree,
    And his screams were wild
    When he sought for his child,
And Billy, nowhere was he;
    So he cast him down in his empty nest,
And covered his face with his wing,
    And big sobs came from his speckled breast,
And he cried like anything;
    And he screamed so loud
    In his wrath and woe,
That he shook the huge old tree:
    And the old Fox heard
    As he lay below,
    And not a sign of sorrow did show,
But laughed a "he-he-he!"

    The old Owl stopped crying,
    And wiped his eyes.
And shook his fist at the Fox:
    And said, "You villain.
    You stole my child,
And carried him under the rocks;
    You've eaten my Billy,
    My pretty first-born,
Without an equal for beauty;
    But I'll tell Jack,
    With his hounds and his horn,
As sure as my name is Hooty.
    And the bow-wow dogs,
    And the toot-toot horns,
And the galloping horse and Jack,
    Shall race you, and chase you,
    Wherever they trace you,
And thunder along your track.
And I will think of my Billy, that's dead,
    As I flap along on the trail,
To see the dogs bite off your cruel head,
    And Jack ride away with your tail."

So in the morning
        Out came Jack
With his spurs on his heels
        And his whip to crack;

242

And he saddled his horse,
  And called to his pack,
And started off on the Fox's track.
Away he went
  With the clattering sound
Of the swift-footed horse
 On the frosty ground,
And the horns that rang
  With a merry sound,
And the deepmouthed bay
  Of the rapid hound.
With a toot-e-ty too, and a toot-e-ty too,
They made such a noise as on they flew,
That the old Fox didn't know what to do.
For the Fox he listened
  And heard them come,
And dropped the duck
  He was carrying home,
And ran through the wood
  As fast as he could,
And made for the den
  That he started from.

The Fox went skimming
  Along the ground,
But nearer he heard
  The bay of the hound,
And on he went
  Like the rustling wind—
But the dogs came closer and closer behind,
Till his legs were tired,
  And his feet were sore,
And he found he couldn't
 Run any more.
Then he crept in a hole
 That he chanced to see,
Down at the foot of a hollow tree;
 But just as he thought
  He had ended the chase,
 And was safe from the dogs
  In his hiding place,
He heard old Hooty as down he flew
And lit on the tree with a whit-too-whoo-o-o.
  And the dogs came barking,
   Glad to see

That the Fox was hid
    In the hollow tree.
For there the Fox was crouching beneath,
Arching his back,
    And showing his teeth.

And his eyes were like sparks
Shining back in the dark,
His tongue hanging out
    And gasping for breath,
And froth on his lips,
    But game to the death.
And he fought and fought
    The dogs till he died;
He bit Growler's foot
    And cut Tray's side;
They tore him in pieces—
    No mercy he begs,
But some of the dogs
    Limped home on three legs;
And Jack came and cut
    Off his long gray tail,
And carried it home to hang on a nail;
For that was the Fox, so Jack would tell,
That ran so far and fought so well;
    And the Owl looked down
        From the branch overhead,
Where the lifeless, tailless Fox lay dead,
And laughed aloud, as away he flew,
A Whit-too-who—A whit-too-who-o-o-o.

UNKNOWN.

THE FIRST SNOWFALL

The snow had begun in the gloaming,
    And busily all the night
Had been heaping field and highway
    With a silence deep and white.

Every pine and fir and hemlock
    Wore ermine too dear for an earl,
And the poorest twig on the elm-tree
    Was ridged inch deep with pearl.

From sheds new-roofed with Carrara
    Came Chanticleer's muffled crow,
The stiff rails were softened to swan's-down,
    And still fluttered down the snow.

I stood and watched by the window
    The noiseless work of the sky,
And the sudden flurries of snow-birds,
    Like brown leaves whirling by.

I thought of a mound in sweet Auburn
    Where a little headstone stood;
How the flakes were folding it gently,
    As did robins the babes in the wood.

Up spoke our own little Mabel,
    Saying, "Father, who makes it snow?"
And I told of the good All-father
    Who cares for us here below.

Again I looked at the snow-fall,
    And thought of the leaden sky
That arched o'er our first great sorrow,
    When that mound was heaped so high.

I remembered the gradual patience
    That fell from that cloud-like snow,
Flake by flake, healing and hiding
    The scar of our deep-plunged woe.

And again to the child I whispered,
    "The snow that husheth all,
Darling, the merciful Father
    Alone can make it fall!"

Then, with eyes that saw not, I kissed her;
    And she, kissing back, could not know
That *my* kiss was given to her sister,
    Folded close under deepening snow.

JAMES RUSSELL LOWELL.

KATIE LEE AND WILLIE GREY

Two BROWN HEADS with tossing curls,
Red lips shutting over pearls,
Bare feet, white and wet with dew,
Two eyes black, and two eyes blue;
Little girl and boy were they,
Katie Lee and Willie Grey.

They were standing where a brook,
Bending like a shepherd's crook,
Flashed its silver, and thick ranks
Of willow fringed its mossy banks;
Half in thought, and half in play,
Katie Lee and Willie Grey.

They had cheeks like cherries red;
He was taller—'most a head;
She, with arms like wreaths of snow,
Swung a basket to and fro
As she loitered, half in play,
Chattering to Willie Grey.

"Pretty Katie," Willie said—
And there came a dash of red
Through the brownness of his cheek—
"Boys are strong and girls are weak,
And I'll carry, so I will,
Katie's basket up the hill."

Katie answered with a laugh,
"You shall carry only half;"
And then, tossing back her curls,
"Boys are weak as well as girls."
Do you think that Katie guessed
Half the wisdom she expressed?

Men are only boys grown tall;
Hearts don't change much, after all;
And when, long years from that day,
Katie Lee and Willie Grey
Stood again beside the brook,
Bending like a shepherd's crook,

Is it strange that Willie said,
While again a dash of red
Crossed the brownness of his cheek,
"I am strong and you are weak;
Life is but a slippery steep,
Hung with shadows cold and deep.

"Will you trust me, Katie dear—
Walk beside me without fear?
May I carry, if I will,
All your burdens up the hill?"
And she answered, with a laugh,
"No, but you may carry half."

Close beside the little brook
Bending like a shepherd's crook,
Washing with its silver hands
Late and early at the sands,
Is a cottage, where to-day
Katie lives with Willie Grey.

In a porch she sits, and lo!
Swings a basket to and fro,
Vastly different from the one
That she swung in years agone.
This is long and deep and wide,
And has—rockers at the side.

ATTRIBUTED BOTH TO
JOSIE R. HUNT AND TO J. H. PIXLEY.

GIVE ME THREE GRAINS OF CORN, MOTHER

GIVE ME three grains of corn, Mother,
　　Only three grains of corn;
It will keep the little life I have
　　Till the coming of the morn.
I am dying of hunger and cold, Mother,
　　Dying of hunger and cold;
And half the agony of such a death
　　My lips have never told.

It has gnawed like a wolf at my heart, Mother,
   A wolf that is fierce for blood;
All the livelong day, and the night beside,
   Gnawing for lack of food.
I dreamed of bread in my sleep, Mother,
   And the sight was heaven to see;
I awoke with an eager, famishing lip,
   But you had no bread for me.

How could I look to you, Mother,
   How could I look to you
For bread to give to your starving boy,
   When you were starving too?
For I read the famine in your cheek,
   And in your eyes so wild,
And I felt it in your bony hand,
   As you laid it on your child.

The Queen has lands and gold, Mother,
   The Queen has lands and gold,
While you are forced to your empty breast
   A skeleton babe to hold—
A babe that is dying of want, Mother,
   As I am dying now,
With a ghastly look in its sunken eye,
   And famine upon its brow.

What has poor Ireland done, Mother,
   What has poor Ireland done,
That the world looks on, and sees us starve,
   Perishing one by one?
Do the men of England care not, Mother,
   The great men and the high,
For the suffering sons of Erin's Isle,
   Whether they live or die?

There is many a brave heart here, Mother,
   Dying of want and cold,
While only across the Channel, Mother,
   Are many that roll in gold;
There are rich and proud men there, Mother,
   With wondrous wealth to view,
And the bread they fling to their dogs tonight
   Would give life to me and you.

Come nearer to my side, Mother,
  Come nearer to my side,
And hold me fondly, as you held
  My father when he died;
Quick, for I cannot see you, Mother,
  My breath is almost gone;
Mother! dear Mother! ere I die,
  Give me three grains of corn.

AMELIA BLANDFORD EDWARDS.

YOUNG CHARLOTTIE

YOUNG CHARLOTTIE lived by a mountain side in a wild and lonely spot—
There was no village for miles around except her father's cot;
And yet on many a wintry night young boys would gather there—
Her father kept a social board, and she was very fair.

One New Year's Eve as the sun went down she cast a wistful eye
Out from the windowpane as a merry sleigh went by.
At a village fifteen miles away was to be a ball that night;
Although the air was piercing cold her heart was merry and light.

At last her laughing eye lit up as a well-known voice she heard,
And, dashing in front of the door, her lover's sleigh appeared.
"O Daughter, dear," her mother said, "this blanket round you fold;
'Tis such a dreadful night abroad and you will catch your death of cold."

"Oh no, oh no!" young Charlottie cried, as she laughed like a gipsy
    queen,
"To ride in blankets muffled up, I never would be seen.
My silken coat is quite enough, you know it is lined throughout,
And there is my silken scarf to wrap my head and neck about."

Her bonnet and her gloves were on, she jumped into the sleigh,
And swiftly slid down the mountain side and over the hills away.
All muffled up so silent, five miles at last were past,
When Charlie with few but shivering words the silence broke at last.

"Such a dreadful night I never saw, my reins I can scarcely hold."
Young Charlottie then feebly said, "I am exceedingly cold."
He cracked his whip and urged his speed much faster than before,
While at least five other miles in silence had passed o'er.

Spoke Charles, "How fast the freezing ice is gathering on my brow!
Young Charlottie then feebly said, "I'm growing warmer now."
So on they sped through the frosty air and the glittering, cold starlight
Until at last the village lights and the ballroom came in sight.

They reached the door and Charles sprang out and reached his hands to
  her.
"Why sit you there like a monument that has no power to stir?"
He called her once, he called her twice, she answered not a word;
And then he called her once again but still she never stirred.

He took her hand in his; 'twas cold and hard as any stone.
He tore the mantle from her face while cold stars on it shone.
Then quickly to the lighted hall her lifeless form he bore;
Young Charlottie's eyes were closed forever, her voice was heard no
  more.

And there he sat down by her side while bitter tears did flow,
And cried, "My own, my charming bride, you never more shall know."
He twined his arms around her neck and kissed her marble brow,
And his thoughts flew back to where she said, "I'm growing warmer
  now."

He took her back into the sleigh and quickly hurried home;
When he arrived at her father's door, oh, how her friends did mourn—
They mourned the loss of a daughter dear, while Charles wept over the
  gloom,
Till at last he died with the bitter grief—now they both lie in one tomb.

WILLIAM LORENZO CARTER.

THE MORNIN'S MORNIN'

THIS IS THE TALE that Cassidy told
In his halls a-sheen with purple and gold;
Told as he sprawled in an easy chair,
Chewing cigars at a dollar a pair;
Told with a sigh, and perchance a tear,
As the rough soul showed through the cracked veneer;
Told as he gazed on the walls near by,
Where a Greuze and a Millet were hung on high,
With a rude little print in a frame between—
A picture of Shanahan's ould shebeen.

I'm drinkin' me mornin's mornin'—but it doesn't taste th' same,
Tho' the glass is iv finest crystal, an' th' liquor slips down like crame,
An' me Cockney footman brings it on a soort of a silver plate—
Sherry an' bitters it is, whiskey is out iv date.
In me bran-new brownstone mansion—Fift' Av'noo over th' way—
The cathaydral round th' corner, an' the Lord Archbishop to tay.
Sure I ought to be sthiff wid grandeur, but me tastes are mighty mean,
An' I'd rather a mornin's mornin' at Shanahan's ould shebeen.

Oh, well do I mind th' shanty—th' rocks an' th' field beyant,
The dirt floor yellow wid sawdust, an' th' walls on a three-inch slant;
There's a twelve-story flat on the site now—'twas meself that builded
    the same,
An' they called it the Mont-morincy, tho' I wanted th' good ould name.
Me dinner pail under me oxther before th' whistle blew,
I'd banish the drames from me eyelids wid a noggin or maybe two;
An' oh, 'twas th' illigant whiskey—its like I have never seen
Since I went for me mornin's mornin' to Shanahan's ould shebeen.

I disremember th' makers—I couldn't tell you the brand,
But it smiled like the golden sunlight, an' it looked an' tasted gr-rand.
When me throat was caked wid mortar an' me head was cracked wid a
    blast,
One drink o' Shanahan's dewdrops an' all me troubles was past.
That's why, as I squat on th' cushins, wid divil a hap'orth to do,
In a mornin' coat wid velvit, an' a champagne lunch at two,
Th' memory comes like a banshee, meself an' me wealth between,
An' I long for a mornin's mornin' in Shanahan's ould shebeen.

A mornin' coat lined wid velvit—an' me ould coat used to do
Alike for mornin' an' evenin', (an' sometimes I slep' in it, too!)
An' 'twas divil a sup iv sherry that Shanahan kept—no fear.
If you can't afford good whiskey he'd take you on trust fer beer.
Th' dacintist gang I knew there—McCarthy, (Sinathor since,)
An' Murphy that mixed the morthar, (sure the Pope has made him a
    prince).
You should see 'em, avic, o' Sundays, wid faces scraped an' clean,
When th' boss stood a mornin's mornin' round Shanahan's ould she-
    been.

Whist! here comes His Grace's carriage, 'twill be lunch time by and by,
An' I dasn't drink another—though me throat is powerful dry;
For I've got to meet th' Archbishop—I'm a laborer now no more,
But ohone, those were fine times then, lad, an' to talk o' 'em makes me
    sore.

An' whisper—there's times, I tell you, when I'd swap this easy chair,
An' the velvit coat an' the footman, wid his Sassenach nose in the air,
An' the' Lord Archbishop himself, too, for a drink o' the days that ha'
    been,
For the taste o' a mornin's mornin' in Shanahan's ould shebeen!

GERALD BRENNAN

THE AFRICAN CHIEF

CHAINED IN THE MARKET-PLACE he stood,
    A man of giant frame,
Amid the gathering multitude
    That shrunk to hear his name—
All stern of look and strong of limb,
    His dark eye on the ground;
And silently they gazed on him
    As on a lion bound.

Vainly, but well, that chief had fought;
    He was a captive now,
Yet pride, that fortune humbles not,
    Was written on his brow.
The scars his dark, broad bosom wore
    Showed warrior true and brave;
A prince among his tribe before,
    He could not be a slave.

Then to his conqueror he spake:
    "My brother is a king;
Undo this necklace from my neck,
    And take this bracelet ring,
And send me where my brother reigns,
    And I will fill thy hands
With store of ivory from the plains,
    And gold-dust from the sands."

"Not for thy ivory, nor thy gold
    Will I unbind thy chain;
That bloody hand shall never hold
    The battle-spear again.

A price thy nation never gave
   Shall yet be paid for thee;
For thou shalt be the Christian's slave,
   In lands beyond the sea."

Then wept the warrior chief, and bade
   To shred his locks away;
And one by one, each heavy braid
   Before the victor lay.
Thick were the platted locks, and long,
   And closely hidden there
Shone many a wedge of gold among
   The dark and crispèd hair.

"Look, feast thy greedy eye with gold
   Long kept for sorest need:
Take it—thou askest sums untold—
   And say that I am freed.
Take it—my wife, the long, long day,
   Weeps by the cocoa-tree,
And my young children leave their play,
   And ask in vain for me."

"I take thy gold, but I have made
   Thy fetters fast and strong,
And ween that by the cocoa-shade
   Thy wife will wait thee long."
Strong was the agony that shook
   The captive's frame to hear,
And the proud meaning of his look
   Was changed to mortal fear.

His heart was broken—crazed his brain;
   At once his eye grew wild;
He struggled fiercely with his chain,
   Whispered, and wept, and smiled;
Yet wore not long those fatal bands,
   And once, at shut of day,
They drew him forth upon the sands,
   The foul hyena's prey.

          WILLIAM CULLEN BRYANT.

THE DESTRUCTION OF SENNACHERIB

THE ASSYRIAN came down like the wolf on the fold,
And his cohorts were gleaming in purple and gold;
And the sheen of their spears was like stars on the sea,
When the blue wave rolls nightly on deep Galilee.

Like the leaves of the forest when summer is green,
That host with their banners at sunset were seen;
Like the leaves of the forest when autumn hath blown,
That host on the morrow lay wither'd and strown.

For the Angel of Death spread his wings on the blast,
And breathed in the face of the foe as he pass'd;
And the eyes of the sleepers wax'd deadly and chill,
And their hearts but once heaved, and for ever grew still!

And there lay the steed with his nostril all wide,
But through it there roll'd not the breath of his pride;
And the foam of his gasping lay white on the turf,
And cold as the spray of the rock-beating surf.

And there lay the rider distorted and pale,
With the dew on his brow and the rust on his mail;
And the tents were all silent, the banners alone,
The lances unlifted, the trumpet unblown.

And the widows of Ashur are loud in their wail;
And the idols are broke in the temple of Baal;
And the might of the Gentile, unsmote by the sword,
Hath melted like snow in the glance of the Lord!

LORD BYRON.

THE GRAY SWAN

"OH TELL ME, sailor, tell me true,
    Is my little lad, my Elihu,
A-sailing with your ship?"
The sailor's eyes were dim with dew,—
    "Your little lad, your Elihu?"
He said with trembling lip,—
    "What little lad? what ship?"

254

"What little lad! as if there could be
  Another such an one as he!
What little lad, do you say?
Why, Elihu, that took to the sea
  The moment I put him off my knee!
It was just the other day
  The *Gray Swan* sailed away.

"The other day?" The sailor's eyes
  Stood open with a great surprise.
"The other day? The *Swan?*"
His heart began in his throat to rise,—
  "Ay, ay sir, here in the cupboard lies
The jacket he had on."
  "And so your lad is gone?

"But, my good mother, do you know
  All this was twenty years ago?
I stood on the *Gray Swan's* deck,
And to that lad I saw you throw,
  Taking it off, as it might be, so!
The handkerchief from your neck."
  "Ay, and he'll bring it back!"

"And did the little lawless lad
  That has made you sick and made you sad,
Sail with the *Gray Swan's* crew?"
"Lawless! the man is going mad—
  The best boy mother ever had,—
Be sure he sailed with the crew!
  What would you have him do?"

"And he has never written line,
  Nor sent you word, nor made you sign
To say he was alive?"
"Hold! if 'twas wrong, the wrong is mine,
  Besides, he may be in the brine,
And could he write from the grave?
  Tut, man! what would you have?"

"Gone twenty years,—a long, long cruise,
  'Twas wicked thus your love to abuse,
But if the lad still live
And come back home, think you you can
  Forgive him?" "Miserable man,

You're mad as the sea—you rave—
  What have I to forgive?"

The sailor twitched his shirt so blue,
  And from within his bosom drew
The handkerchief. She was wild.
"My God! my Father! is it true?
  My little lad, my Elihu!
My blessed boy, my child!
  My dead, my living child!"

ALICE CARY.

THE SAILOR'S GRAVE

OUR BARK was out—far, far from land,
When the fairest of our gallant band
Grew sadly pale, and waned away
Like the twilight of an autumn day.
We watched him through long hours of pain;
But our cares were lost, our hopes were vain;
Death brought for him no coward alarm,
For he smiled as he died on a messmate's arm.

He had no costly winding sheet,
But we placed a round shot at his feet;
And he slept in his hammock as safe and sound
As a king in his lawn shroud, marble-bound.
We proudly decked his funeral vest
With the English flag upon his breast:
We gave him that as the badge of the brave,
And then he was fit for his sailor's grave.

Our voices broke—our hearts turned weak—
Hot tears were seen on the brownest cheek—
And a quiver played on the lips of pride,
As we lowered him down the ship's dark side.
A plunge—a splash—and our task was o'er;
The billows rolled as they rolled before;
But many a rude prayer hallowed the wave
That closed above the sailor's grave.

ELIZA COOK.

LASCA

I WANT free life and I want fresh air;
And I sigh for the canter after the cattle,
The crack of the whips like shots in a battle,
The medley of horns and hoofs and heads
That wars and wrangles and scatters and spreads:
The green beneath and the blue above,
And dash and danger, and life and love.

And Lasca!

Lasca used to ride
On a mouse-gray mustang close to my side,
With blue serape and bright-belled spur;
I laughed with joy as I looked at her!
Little knew she of books or of creeds;
An Ave Maria sufficed her needs;
Little she cared, save to be by my side,
To ride with me, and ever to ride,
From San Saba's shore to Lavaca's tide.
She was as bold as the billows that beat,
She was as wild as the breezes that blow;
From her little head to her little feet
She was swayed in her suppleness to and fro
By each gust of passion; a sapling pine,
That grows on the edge of a Kansas bluff,
And wars with the wind when the weather is rough,
Is like this Lasca, this love of mine.
She would hunger that I might eat,
Would take the bitter and leave me the sweet;
But once, when I made her jealous for fun,
At something I'd whispered, or looked, or done,
One Sunday, in San Antonio,
To a glorious girl on the Alamo,
She drew from her garter a dear little dagger,
And—sting of a wasp!—it made me stagger!
An inch to the left, or an inch to the right,
And I shouldn't be maundering here tonight;
But she sobbed, and, sobbing, so swiftly bound
Her torn reboso about the wound,
That I quite forgave her. Scratches don't count
      In Texas, down by the Rio Grande.

Her eye was brown—a deep, deep brown;
Her hair was darker than her eye;
And something in her smile and frown,
Curled crimson lip and instep high,
Showed that there ran in each blue vein,
Mixed with the milder Aztec strain,
The vigorous vintage of Old Spain.
She was alive in every limb
With feeling, to the finger tips;
And when the sun is like a fire,
And sky one shining, soft sapphire,
One does not drink in little sips.

The air was heavy, the night was hot,
I sat by her side, and forgot—forgot;
Forgot the herd that were taking their rest,
Forgot that the air was close opprest,
That the Texas norther comes sudden and soon,
In the dead of night or the blaze of noon;
That once let the herd at its breath take fright,
Nothing on earth can stop the flight;
And woe to the rider, and woe to the steed,
Who falls in front of their mad stampede!

Was that thunder? I grasped the cord
Of my swift mustang without a word.
I sprang to the saddle, and she clung behind.
Away! on a hot chase down the wind!
But never was fox hunt half so hard,
And never was steed so little spared.
For we rode for our lives. You shall hear how we fared
     In Texas, down by the Rio Grande.

The mustang flew, and we urged him on;
There was one chance left, and you have but one;
Halt, jump to ground, and shoot your horse;
Crouch under his carcass, and take your chance;
And, if the steers in their frantic course
Don't batter you both to pieces at once,
You may thank your star; if not, good-by
To the quickening kiss and the long-drawn sigh,
And the open air and the open sky,
     In Texas, down by the Rio Grande!

The cattle gained on us, and, just as I felt
For my old six-shooter behind in my belt,
Down came the mustang, and down came we,
Clinging together, and—what was the rest—
A body that spread itself on my breast.
Two arms that shielded my dizzy head,
Two lips that hard on my lips were prest;
Then came thunder in my ears,
As over us surged the sea of steers,
Blows that beat blood into my eyes,
And when I could rise—
Lasca was dead!

I gouged out a grave a few feet deep,
And there in Earth's arms I laid her to sleep;
And there she is lying, and no one knows,
And the summer shines and the winter snows;
For many a day the flowers have spread
A pall of petals over her head;
And the little gray hawk hangs aloft in the air,
And the sly coyote trots here and there,
And the black snake glides and glitters and slides
Into a rift in a cottonwood tree;
And the buzzard sails on,
And comes and is gone,
Stately and still like a ship at sea;
And I wonder why I do not care
For the things that are like the things that were.
Does half my heart lie buried there
        In Texas, down by the Rio Grande.

                  FRANK DESPREZ.

THE BANK THIEF

'TWAS A BUSY DAY in the courtroom, and a curious crowd was there
In the prison dock an old tramp stood, alone in his despair.
The judge in silence looked at him, "I pity you," said he;
"The charge is not a serious one, and I may set you free."
"Now don't you pity me, Judge, nor say that I am free—
A prison cell is my future home so keep your sympathy;
But let me tell the story, how my brother Tom and I
Together climbed ambitious heights in manhood side by side.

Tom was a lawyer of some renown, and rising in the ranks,
While I for brain and skill was made cashier in a bank.
And so we trod the beaten path and brighter grew each day;
But one, alas, was doomed to fall dishonored by the way.
It was not Tom, but I who fell, the devil gained his own;
I robbed the bank one evil night, and stole away unknown.
'Mid foreign scenes I tried to drown the specter of my crime.
A coward's refuge there I sought, women, cards and wine.
And Tom was faithful through it all, and loved me just the same,
And labored years in vain to lift the stigma from my name.
He knew that somewhere in the world, a fugitive I roamed,
And nobly bore the taunts of shame and paid my debts at home.
The fatal gift of theft is gold, for which men madly crave;
A sequel, too, goes with the gift, which leads down to the grave.
I've stemmed the tide of human woe, by God and man disowned,
A shadow in the dark of night, unpitied and unknown.
Look at me now, and study well this wretched thing called man,
That once with peace of mind was blest, till treachery began
To tempt my soul with pleasures vain and point to life's highway,
When glittering sin allures the weak and poisons with its rays.
I've seen the world, the maddening throng, the cup filled to the brim,
And in the lurid glow I sunk to misery and sin.
The gates of hell are opened full and I have ceased to strive;
The bank thief stands before you now, a wrecked, a worthless life."
It was the oft-told story of temptation's crooked sway;
But see, the judge is rising, what means that pallid face?
Can one so great and learned as he so feel a tramp's disgrace?
A cry is heard that startles all, the thief falls to the floor—
The judge is kneeling at his side, a prey to bitter pain:
"Oh God! 'tis cruel fate's decree, thus we should meet again!"
On life's highway they met at last, brothers, Jack and Tom,
As judge and culprit at the bar, where crime is frowned upon.
They grew to manhood just and true, but one fell by the way,
And God alone will know his sin upon the judgment day.

J. R. FARRELL

SHE IS MORE TO BE PITIED THAN CENSURED

AT THE OLD CONCERT HALL on the Bowery
Round the table were seated one night
A crowd of young fellows carousing;
With them life seemed cheerful and bright.

At the very next table was seated
A girl who had fallen to shame.
All the young fellows jeered at her weakness
Till they heard an old woman exclaim:

Chorus:

She is more to be pitied than censured,
She is more to be helped than despised,
She is only a lassie who ventured
On life's stormy path ill-advised.
Do not scorn her with words fierce and bitter,
Do not laugh at her shame and downfall;
For a moment just stop and consider
That a man was the cause of it all.

There's an old-fashioned church round the corner,
Where the neighbors all gathered one day
While the parson was preaching a sermon
O'er a soul that had just passed away.
'Twas the same wayward girl from the Bow'ry,
Who a life of adventure had led—
Did the clergyman jeer at her downfall?
No—he asked for God's mercy and said:

WILLIAM B. GRAY.

THE WEDDING GIFT

IN THE GARRET under the sloping eaves
   Stood Grandmother Granger's old hair trunk,
With battered bureaus and broken chairs,
   And a spinning wheel and similar junk.
The hirsute cover was worn in spots;
   'Twas once the hide of a brindle cow,
That grazed of yore in the meadows green
   Where Harlem flats are towering now.

I used to climb the garret stairs
   On a rainy day and lift the lid
And loose the fragrance of olden times
   That under the faded finery hid—

Damask roses and lavender,
　Delicate odors, fine and faint,
Clinging still to the crumpled folds
　Of silks and muslins and challies quaint.

Fans and slippers and veils were there,
　Beads of amber and yellow lace,
Coral earrings and Paisley shawls,
　And the big pink bonnet that framed her face
With its golden curls and soft blue eyes,
　And the dimpled chin and the laughing lip,
When Grandfather Granger took his bride
　And the smart new trunk on a wedding trip.

It was the soul of a garden old,
　Dreaming under the stars, I freed.
Jasmine, lilies, and rosemary,
　Stately marigolds gone to seed.
Thyme and pansy and mignonette,
　Sage and balsam and love-in-a-mist,
Where Grandfather Granger, a bold young blade,
　Scaled the walls to the secret tryst.

To the creak and sway of a four-horse stage
　He kissed her hand in its silken mitt,
And her girlish cheek that was like a rose
　As her blissful blushes mantled it.
The honeymoon never waned, they say—
　The pair were lovers through all the years,
Gray-haired sweethearts, tender and true,
　Sharing life with its smiles and tears.

The flowery frocks and the ancient trunk,
　And Grandmother Granger, too, are dust,
But something precious and sweet and rare
　Survives the havoc of moth and rust;
Love with the wings of bright romance,
　And the eyes of youth that are always gay—
Grandmother Granger's wedding gift
　To every girl on her marriage day.

MINNA IRVING.

262

SOMEBODY'S DARLING

INTO A WARD of the whitewashed walls
Where the dead and the dying lay—
Wounded by bayonets, shells, and balls—
Somebody's darling was borne one day.
Somebody's darling! so young and so brave,
Wearing still on his pale, sweet face—
Soon to be hid by the dust of the grave—
The lingering light of his boyhood's grace.

Matted and damp are the curls of gold,
Kissing the snow of that fair young brow;
Pale are the lips of delicate mould—
Somebody's darling is dying now.
Back from the beautiful blue-veined face
Brush every wandering, silken thread;
Cross his hands as a sign of grace—
Somebody's darling is still and dead!

Kiss him once for Somebody's sake;
Murmur a prayer, soft and low;
One bright curl from the cluster take—
They were Somebody's pride, you know.
Somebody's hand hath rested there;
Was it a mother's, soft and white?
And have the lips of a sister fair
Been baptized in those waves of light?

God knows best. He was Somebody's love!
Somebody's heart enshrined him here;
Somebody wafted his name above,
Night and morn, on the wings of prayer.
Somebody wept when he marched away,
Looking so handsome, brave, and grand;
Somebody's kiss on his forehead lay;
Somebody clung to his parting hand.

Somebody's watching and waiting for him,
Yearning to hold him again to her heart;
There he lies—with the blue eyes dim,
And smiling, childlike lips apart.

Tenderly bury the fair young dead,
Pausing to drop on his grave a tear;
Carve on the wooden slab at his head,
"Somebody's darling lies buried here!"

MARIE RAVENAL DE LACOSTE.

WOULD I BE SHRIVED?

(François Villon, being about to die, a worthy friar would fain have shrived him, and did earnestly exhort that he should confess him at this time of those acts of his life which he did regret. Villon bade him return yet again, that he might have time to think of his sins. Upon the good father's return, Villon was dead; but by his side were the following verses, his last, wherein he set forth things which he did regret. Whereat the friar was sore grieved, and hid them away among the manuscripts of his abbey, showing them to no man; yet they were found in somewise. The name of the friar and the very place where stood the abbey are forgot; but the verses have endured unto this day.)

I, FRANÇOIS VILLON, ta'en at last
    To this rude bed where all must lie,
Fain would forget the turbid past
    And lay me down in peace to die.
"Would I be shrived?" Ah, can I tell?
    My sins but trifles seem to be,
Nor worth the dignity of hell;
    If not, then ill avails to me
        To name them one and all—and yet—
        There be some things which I regret!

The sack of abbeys, many a brawl,
    A score of knife thrusts in the dark,
Forced oft, by Fate, against the wall,
    And years in donjons, cold and stark—
These crimes and pains seem far away
    Now that I come at length to die;
'Tis idle for the past to pray,
    'Tis hopeless for the past to sigh:
        These are a troubled dream—and yet—
        For them I have but scant regret!

The toil my mother lived to know,
    What years I lay in gyves for debt;
A pretty song heard long ago:
    Where, I know not; when, I forget;

The crust I once kept for my own
   (Though all too scant for my poor use.)
The friend I left to die alone,
   (Pardie! the watchman pressed us close!)
     Trifles against my crimes to set!
     Yet these are all which I regret.

Captains and cutthroats, not a few,
   And maidens fair of many a clime
Have named me friend in the wild past
   When as we wallowed in the slime;
Gamblers and rogues and clever thieves,
   And unfrocked priests, a sorry crew,
(How stubbornly the memory cleaves
   To all who have befriended you!)
     I drain a cup to them—and yet—
     'Tis not for such I feel regret!

My floundered horse, who died for me
   (Nor whip nor spur was his, I ween!)
That day the hangman looked to see
   Poor Villon earth and sky between!
A mongrel cur who shared my lot
   Three bitter winters on the Ile:
He held the rabble off, God wot,
   One time I cheated in the deal;
'Twas but an instant, while I fled
   Down a vile alley, known to me—
Back in the tavern he lay dead;
     The gamblers raged—but I went free!
     Humble, poor brutes at best; and yet—
     They are the friends whom I regret!

And eke the lilies were a-blow
   Through all the sunny fields of France;
I marked one whiter than the snow
   And would have gathered it, perchance,
Had not some trifle, I forget,
   (A bishop's loot, a cask of wine
Filched from some carbet—a bet—)
   Distracted this wild head of mine.
     A childish fancy this, and yet—
     It is a thing that I regret!

Again I rode through Picardy
 What time the vine was in the bud;
A little maiden smiled on me,
 I might have kissed her, and I would!
I've known a thousand maidens since,
 And many have been kind to me—
I've never seen one quite so fair
 As she, that day in Picardy.
  Ashes of roses these—and yet—
  They are the things which I regret!

One perfect lily grew for me,
 And blossomed on another's breast;
Others have clasped the little hands
 Whose rosy palms I might have pressed;
So, as I die, my wasted youth
 Mocks my dim eye and failing breath:—
Still, I have lived! and having lived
 That much is mine. I mock at Death!
  I should confess, you say? But yet—
  For life alone I have regret.

 Envoy:

O bubbles of the vanished wine
 To which my lips were never set!
O lips that dimpled close to mine,
 Whose ruddy warmth I never met!
  Father, but trifles these, and yet—
  They are the things which I regret!

        JOHN D. SWAIN

BACK TO GRIGGSBY'S STATION

PAP'S GOT HIS PATENT right, and rich as all creation;
 But where's the peace and comfort that we all had had before?
Let's go a-visitin' back to Griggsby's Station—
 Back where we used to be so happy and so pore!

The likes of us a-livin' here! It's jest a mortal pity
 To see us in this great big house with carpets on the stairs
And the pump right in the kitchen! And the city, city, city!
 And nothin' but the city around us everywhere.

         266

Climb clean above the roof and look out from the steeple,
  And never see a robin, nor a beech nor elm tree!
Right there in earshot of at least a thousand people,
  And none that neighbors with us, or we want to go and see.

Let's go a-visitin' back to Griggsby's Station—
  Back where the latch string's a-hangin' from the door,
And every neighbor around the place as dear as a relation—
  Back where we used to be so happy and so pore!

I want to see the Wiggenses, the whole kit and bilin',
  A-driven' up from Shaller Ford to stay the Sunday thru;
And I want to see them hitchin' at their son-in-law's and pilin'
  Out there at Liza Ellen's like they ust to do!

I want to see the piece-quilts the Jones girls is making';
  And I want to pester Laura 'bout their freckled hired hand,
And joke her 'bout the widower she came pert nigh a-takin',
  Till her pap got his pension 'lowed in time to save his land

Let's go a-visitin' back to Griggsby's Station,
  Back where there's nothin' to aggrivate us any more,
Shet away safe about the whole location—
  Back where we used to be so happy and so pore!

I want to see Mirandy and help her with her sewin',
  And hear her talk so lovin' of her man that's dead and gone,
And stand up with Emanuel and to show how he's a-growin',
  And smile as I have seen her 'fore she put her mounin' on.

What's in all this grand life and high situation,
  And nary a pink nor hollyhawk bloomin' at the door?
Let's go a-visitin' back to Griggsby's Station—
  Back where we ust to be so happy and so pore!

                                        JAMES WHITCOMB RILEY

OUT THERE SOMEWHERE

As I WAS HIKING past the woods, the cool and sleepy summer woods,
  I saw a guy a-talking to the sunshine in the air;
Thinks I, he's going to have a fit—I'll stick around and watch a bit;
  But he paid no attention, hardly knowing I was there.

He must have been a college guy, for he was talking big and high—
    The trees were standing all around as silent as a church;
A little closer I saw he was manufacturing poetry,
    Just like a Mocker sitting on a pussy-willow perch.

I squatted down and rolled a smoke and listened to each word he spoke;
    He never stumbled, reared or broke; he never missed a word,
And though he was a Bo like me, he'd been a gent once, I could see;
    I ain't much strong on poetry, but this is what I heard:

"We'll dance a merry saraband from here to drowsy Samarcand;
    Along the sea, across the land, the birds are flying South,
And you, my sweet Penelope, out there somewhere you wait for me,
    With buds of roses in your hair and kisses on your mouth.

"The mountains are all hid in mist; the valley is like amethyst;
    The poplar leaves they turn and twist; oh, silver, silver green!
Out there somewhere along the sea a ship is waiting patiently,
    While up the beach the bubbles slip with white afloat between.

"The tide-hounds race far up the shore—the hunt is on! The breakers
      roar,
    (Her spars are tipped with gold and o'er her deck the spray is flung);
The buoys that rollick in the bay, they nod the way, they nod the way!
    The hunt is up! I am the prey! The hunter's bow is strung!"

"Out there somewhere,"—says I to me. "By gosh! I guess that's poetry!
    Out there somewhere—Penelope, with kisses on her mouth!"
And then, thinks I, "O college guy, your talk it gets me in the eye,
    The North *is* creeping in the air; the birds *are* flying South,"

And yet, the sun was shining down, a-blazing on the little town,
    A mile or so 'way down the track a-dancing in the sun.
But somehow, as I waited there, there came a shiver in the air;
    "The birds are flying South," says he. "The winter has begun."

Says I, "Then let's be on the float; you certainly have got my goat;
    You make me hungry in my throat for seeing things that's new.
Out there somewhere we'll ride the range a-looking for the new and
      strange,
    My feet are tired and need a change. Come on! It's up to you!"

"There ain't no sweet Penelope somewhere that's longing much for me,
    But I can smell the blundering sea and hear the rigging hum;
And I can hear the whispering lips that fly before the outbound ships,
    And I can hear the breakers on the sand a-booming, 'Come!' "

And then that slim, poetic guy, he turned and looked me in the eye:
  ". . . It's overland and overland and overseas to—where?"
"Most anywhere that isn't here," I says. His face went kind of queer:
  "The place we're in is always *here*. The other place is *there*."

He smiled, though, as my eye caught his. "Then what a lot of *there*
    there is
  To go and see and go and see and go and see some more."
He did a fancy step or two. Says he, "I think I'll go with you."
  . . . Two moons, and we were baking in the straits at Singapore.

Around the world and back again; we saw it all, the mist and rain
  In England and the dry old plain from Needles to Berdoo.
We kept a-rambling all the time. I rustled grub, he rustled rhyme—
  Blind-baggage, hoof it, ride or climb—we always put it through.

Just for a con I'd like to know (yes, he crossed over long ago;
  And he was *right,* believe me, Bo!) if somewhere in the South,
Down where the clouds lie on the sea, he found his sweet Penelope,
  With buds of roses in her hair and kisses on her mouth.

                          HENRY HERBERT KNIBBS.

THE ENCHANTED SHIRT

Fytte the First: wherein it shall be shown how the Truth is too
mighty a Drug for such as be of feeble temper.

> THE KING was sick. His cheek was red
>   And his eye was clear and bright;
> He ate and drank with a kingly zest,
>   And peacefully snored at night.

> But he said he was sick, and a king should know,
>   And doctors came by the score.
> They did not cure him. He cut off their heads
>   And sent to the schools for more.

> At last two famous doctors came,
>   And one was as poor as a rat,—
> He had passed his life in studious toil,
>   And never found time to grow fat.

The other had never looked in a book;
   His patients gave him no trouble,—
If they recovered they paid him well,
   If they died their heirs paid double.

Together they looked at the royal tongue,
   As the King on his couch reclined;
In succession they thumped his august chest,
   But no trace of disease could find.

The old sage said, "You're as sound as a nut."
   "Hang him up," roared the King in a gale,—
In a ten-knot gale of royal rage;
   The other leech grew a shade pale,

But he pensively rubbed his sagacious nose,
   And thus his prescription ran,—
The King will be well, if he sleeps one night
   In the Shirt of a Happy Man.

Fytte the Second: tells of the search for the Shirt and how it was nigh found but was not, for reasons which are said or sung.

Wide o'er the realm the couriers rode,
   And fast their horses ran,
And many they saw, and to many they spoke,
   But they found no Happy Man.

They found poor men who would fain be rich,
   And rich who thought they were poor;
And men who twisted their waists in stays,
   And women that shortthose wore.

They saw two men by the roadside sit,
   And both bemoaned their lot;
For one had buried his wife, he said,
   And the other one had not.

At last as they came to a village gate,—
   A beggar lay whistling there;
He whistled and sang and laughed and rolled
   On the grass in the soft June air.

The weary couriers paused and looked
   At the scamp so blithe and gay;

270

And one of them said, "Heaven save you, friend!
   You seem to be happy to-day."

"O yes, fair sirs," the rascal laughed
   And his voice rang free and glad;
"An idle man has so much to do
   That he never has time to be sad."

"This is our man," the courier said;
   "Our luck has led us aright.
"I will give you a hundred ducats, friend,
   For the loan of your shirt to-night."

The merry blackguard lay back on the grass,
   And laughed till his face was black;
"I would do it, God wot," and he roared with the fun,
   "But I haven't a shirt to my back."

Fytte the Third: shewing how His Majesty the King came at last
to sleep in a Happy Man his Shirt.

Each day to the King the reports came in
   Of his unsuccessful spies,
And the sad panorama of human woes
   Passed daily under his eyes.

And he grew ashamed of his useless life,
   And his maladies hatched in gloom;
He opened his windows and let the air
   Of the free heaven into his room.

And out he went in the world and toiled
   In his own appointed way;
And the people blessed him, the land was glad,
   And the King was well and gay.

JOHN HAY.

THE GREEN EYE OF THE YELLOW GOD

THERE'S A ONE-EYED yellow idol to the north of Khatmandu,
There's a little marble cross below the town;
There's a broken-hearted woman tends the grave of Mad Carew,
And the Yellow God forever gazes down.

He was known as "Mad Carew" by the subs of Khatmandu,
He was better than they felt inclined to tell;
But for all his foolish pranks, he was worshiped in the ranks,
And the Colonel's daughter smiled on him as well.

He had loved her all along, with the passion of the strong,
The fact that she loved him was plain to all.
She was nearly twenty-one and arrangements had begun
To celebrate her birthday with a ball.

He wrote to ask what present she would like from Mad Carew;
They met next day, as he dismissed a squad;
And jestingly she told him then that nothing else would do
But the green eye of the little Yellow God.

On the night before the dance Mad Carew seemed in a trance,
And they chaffed him as they puffed at their cigars;
But for once he failed to smile, and he sat alone awhile,
Then went out into the night beneath the stars.

He returned before the dawn, with his shirt and tunic torn,
And a gash across his temples dripping red;
He was patched up right away, and he slept all through the day,
And the Colonel's daughter watched beside his bed.

He woke at last and asked if they could send his tunic through;
She brought it, and he thanked her with a nod;
He bade her search the pocket, saying, "That's from Mad Carew,"
And she found the little green eye of the god.

She upbraided poor Carew in the way that women do,
Though both her eyes were strangely hot and wet;
But she wouldn't take the stone, and Carew was left alone
With the jewel that he'd chanced his life to get.

When the ball was at its height, on that still and tropic night,
She thought of him, and hastened to his room;
As she crossed the barrack square she could hear the dreamy air
Of a waltz tune softly stealing thro' the gloom.

His door was open wide, with silver moonlight shining through,
The place was wet and slipp'ry where she trod;
An ugly knife lay buried in the heart of Mad Carew,
'Twas the "Vengeance of the Little Yellow God."

There's a one-eyed yellow idol to the north of Khatmandu,
There's a little marble cross below the town;
There's a broken-hearted woman tends the grave of Mad Carew,
And the Yellow God forever gazes down.

J. MILTON HAYES

A FENCE OR AN AMBULANCE

'TWAS A DANGEROUS CLIFF, as they freely confessed,
Though to walk near its crest was so pleasant;
But over its terrible edge there had slipped
A duke and full many a peasant.
So the people said something would have to be done,
But their projects did not at all tally;
Some said, "Put a fence around the edge of the cliff,"
Some, "An ambulance down in the valley."

But the cry for the ambulance carried the day,
For it spread through the neighboring city;
A fence may be useful or not, it is true,
But each heart became brimful of pity
For those who slipped over that dangerous cliff;
And the dwellers in highway and alley
Gave pounds or gave pence, not to put up a fence,
But an ambulance down in the valley.

"For the cliff is all right, if you're careful," they said,
"And, if folks even slip and are dropping,
It isn't the slipping that hurts them so much,
As the shock down below when they're stopping."
So day after day, as these mishaps occurred,
Quick forth would these rescuers sally
To pick up the victims who fell off the cliff,
With their ambulance down in the valley.

Then an old sage remarked: "It's a marvel to me
That people give far more attention
To repairing results than to stopping the cause,
When they'd much better aim at prevention.
Let us stop at its source all this mischief," cried he,
"Come, neighbors and friends, let us rally;
If the cliff we will fence we might almost dispense
With the ambulance down in the valley."

273

"Oh, he's a fanatic," the others rejoined,
"Dispense with the ambulance? Never!
He'd dispense with all charities, too, if he could;
No! No! We'll support them forever.
Aren't we picking up folks just as fast as they fall?
And shall this man dictate to us? Shall he?
Why should people of sense stop to put up a fence,
While the ambulance works in the valley?"

But a sensible few, who are practical too,
Will not bear with such nonsense much longer;
They believe that prevention is better than cure,
And their party will soon be the stronger.
Encourage them then, with your purse, voice, and pen,
And while other philanthropists dally,
They will scorn all pretense and put up a stout fence
On the cliff that hangs over the valley.

Better guide well the young than reclaim them when old,
For the voice of true wisdom is calling,
"To rescue the fallen is good, but 'tis best
To prevent other people from falling."
Better close up the source of temptation and crime
Than deliver from dungeon or galley;
Better put a strong fence round the top of the cliff
Than an ambulance down in the valley.

JOSEPH MALINS.

KENTUCKY BELLE

SUMMER OF 'SIXTY-THREE, sir, and Conrad was gone away—
Gone to the county town, sir, to sell our first load of hay.
We lived in the log house yonder, poor as ever you've seen;
Roschen there was a baby, and I was only nineteen.

Conrad, he took the oxen, but he left Kentucky Belle;
How much we thought of Kentuck, I couldn't begin to tell—
Came from the Bluegrass country; my father gave her to me
When I rode north with Conrad, away from the Tennessee.

Conrad lived in Ohio—a German he is, you know—
The house stood in broad cornfields, stretching on, row after row;

The old folks made me welcome; they were kind as kind could be;
But I kept longing, longing, for the hills of the Tennessee.

O, for a sight of water, the shadowed slope of a hill!
Clouds that hang on the summit, a wind that never is still!
But the level land went stretching away to meet the sky—
Never a rise, from north to south, to rest the weary eye!

From east to west, no river to shine out under the moon,
Nothing to make a shadow in the yellow afternoon;
Only the breathless sunshine, as I looked out, all forlorn,
Only the "rustle, rustle," as I walked among the corn.

When I fell sick with pining we didn't wait any more,
But moved away from the cornlands out to this river shore—
The Tuscarawas it's called, sir—off there's a hill, you see—
And now I've grown to like it next best to the Tennessee.

I was at work that morning. Someone came riding like mad
Over the bridge and up the road—Farmer Rouf's little lad.
Bareback he rode; he had no hat; he hardly stopped to say,
"Morgan's men are coming, Fraü, they're galloping on this way.

"I'm sent to warn the neighbors. He isn't a mile behind;
He sweeps up all the horses—every horse that he can find;
Morgan, Morgan the raider, and Morgan's terrible men,
With bowie knives and pistols, are galloping up the glen."

The lad rode down the valley, and I stood still at the door—
The baby laughed and prattled, playing with spools on the floor;
Kentuck was out in the pasture; Conrad, my man, was gone;
Near, near Morgan's men were galloping, galloping on!

Sudden I picked up baby and ran to the pasture bar:
"Kentuck!" I called; "Kentucky!" She knew me ever so far!
I led her down the gully that turns off there to the right,
And tied her to the bushes; her head was just out of sight.

As I ran back to the log house at once there came a sound—
The ring of hoofs, galloping hoofs, trembling over the ground,
Coming into the turnpike out from the White-Woman Glen—
Morgan, Morgan the raider, and Morgan's terrible men.

As near they drew and nearer my heart beat fast in alarm;
But still I stood in the doorway, with baby on my arm.

They came; they passed; with spur and whip in haste they sped along;
Morgan, Morgan the raider, and his band six hundred strong.

Weary they looked and jaded, riding through night and through day;
Pushing on east to the river, many long miles away,
To the border strip where Virginia runs up into the west,
And for the Upper Ohio before they could stop to rest.

On like the wind they hurried, and Morgan rode in advance;
Bright were his eyes like live coals, as he gave me a sideways glance;
And I was just breathing freely, after my choking pain,
When the last one of the troopers suddenly drew his rein.

Frightened I was to death, sir; I scarce dared look in his face,
As he asked for a drink of water and glanced around the place;
I gave him a cup, and he smiled—'twas only a boy, you see,
Faint and worn, with dim blue eyes; and he'd sailed on the Tennessee.

Only sixteen he was, sir—a fond mother's only son—
Off and away with Morgan before his life had begun!
The damp drops stood on his temples; drawn was the boyish mouth;
And I thought me of the mother waiting down in the South!

O, pluck was he to the backbone and clear grit through and through;
Boasted and bragged like a trooper; but the big words wouldn't do;
The boy was dying, sir, dying, as plain as plain could be,
Worn out by his ride with Morgan up from the Tennessee.

But, when I told the laddie that I too was from the South,
Water came in his dim eyes and quivers around his mouth.
"Do you know the Bluegrass country?" he wistful began to say,
Then swayed like a willow sapling and fainted dead away.

I had him into the log house, and worked and brought him to;
I fed him and coaxed him, as I thought his mother'd do;
And, when the lad got better, and the noise in his head was gone,
Morgan's men were miles away, galloping, galloping on.

"O, I must go," he muttered; "I must be up and away!
Morgan, Morgan is waiting for me! O, what will Morgan say?"
But I heard a sound of tramping and kept him back from the door—
The ringing sound of horses' hoofs that I had heard before.

And on, on came the soldiers—the Michigan cavalry—
And fast they rode, and black they looked galloping rapidly;

They had followed hard on Morgan's track; they had followed day and
  night;
But of Morgan and Morgan's raiders they had never caught a sight.

And rich Ohio sat startled through all those summer days,
For strange, wild men were galloping over her broad highways;
Now here, now there, now seen, now gone, now north, now east, now
  west,
Through river valleys and corn-land farms, sweeping away her best.

A bold ride and a long ride! But they were taken at last.
They almost reached the river by galloping hard and fast;
But the boys in blue were upon them ere ever they gained the ford,
And Morgan, Morgan the raider, laid down his terrible sword.

Well, I kept the boy till evening—kept him against his will—
But he was too weak to follow, and sat there pale and still;
When it was cool and dusky—you'll wonder to hear me tell—
But I stole down to that gully and brought up Kentucky Belle.

I kissed the star on her forehead—my pretty, gentle lass—
But I knew that she'd be happy back in the old Bluegrass;
A suit of clothes of Conrad's, with all the money I had,
And Kentuck, pretty Kentuck, I gave to the worn-out lad.

I guided him to the southward as well as I knew how;
The boy rode off with many thanks, and many a backward bow;
And then the glow it faded, and my heart began to swell,
As down the glen away she went, my lost Kentucky Belle!

When Conrad came in the evening the moon was shining high;
Baby and I were both crying—I couldn't tell him why—
But a battered suit of rebel gray was hanging on the wall,
And a thin old horse with drooping head stood in Kentucky's stall.

Well, he was kind, and never once said a hard word to me;
He knew I couldn't help it—'twas all for the Tennessee;
But, after the war was over, just think what came to pass—
A letter, sir; and the two were safe back in the old Bluegrass.

The lad had got across the border, riding Kentucky Belle;
And Kentuck she was thriving, and fat, and hearty, and well;
He cared for her, and kept her, nor touched her with whip or spur:
Ah! we've had many horses, but never a horse like her!

CONSTANCE FENIMORE WOOLSON.

THE BALLAD OF YUKON JAKE

Begging Robert W. Service's Pardon

OH THE NORTH COUNTREE is a hard countree
That mothers a bloody brood;
And its icy arms hold hidden charms
For the greedy, the sinful and lewd.
And strong men rust, from the gold and the lust
That sears the Northland soul,
But the wickedest born, from the Pole to the Horn,
Is the Hermit of Shark-Tooth Shoal.

Now Jacob Kaime was the Hermit's name
In the days of his pious youth,
Ere he cast a smirch on the Baptist Church
By betraying a girl named Ruth.
But now men quake at "Yukon Jake,"
The Hermit of Shark-Tooth Shoal,
For that is the name that Jacob Kaime
Is known by from Nome to the Pole.
He was just a boy and the parson's joy
(Ere he fell for the gold and the muck),
And had learned to pray, with the hogs and the hay
On a farm near Keokuk.
But a Service tale of illicit kale,
And whisky and women wild,
Drained the morals clean as a soup tureen
From this poor but honest child.
He longed for the bite of a Yukon night
And the Northern Light's weird flicker,
Or a game of stud in the frozen mud,
And the taste of raw red licker.
He wanted to mush along in the slush,
With a team of husky hounds,
And to fire his gat at a beaver hat
And knock it out of bounds.

So he left his home for the hell-town Nome,
On Alaska's ice-ribbed shores,
And he learned to curse and to drink, and worse,
Till the rum dripped from his pores,

When the boys on a spree were drinking it free
In a Malamute saloon
And Dan Megrew and his dangerous crew
Shot craps with the piebald coon;
When the Kid on his stool banged away like a fool
At a jag-time melody,
And the barkeep vowed, to the hard-boiled crowd,
That he'd cree-mate Sam McGee—

Then Jacob Kaime, who had taken the name
Of Yukon Jake, the Killer,
Would rake the dive with his forty-five
Till the atmosphere grew chiller.
With a sharp command he'd make 'em stand
And deliver their hard-earned dust,
Then drink the bar dry of rum and rye,
As a Klondike bully must.
Without coming to blows he would tweak the nose
Of Dangerous Dan Megrew,
And, becoming bolder, throw over his shoulder
The lady that's known as Lou.

Oh, tough as a steak was Yukon Jake—
Hard-boiled as a picnic egg.
He washed his shirt in the Klondike dirt,
And drank his rum by the keg.
In fear of their lives (or because of their wives)
He was shunned by the best of his pals,
An outcast he, from the comradery
Of all but wild animals.
So he bought him the whole of Shark-Tooth Shoal,
A reef in the Bering Sea,
And he lived by himself on a sea lion's shelf
In lonely iniquity.

But, miles away, in Keokuk, Ia.,
Did a ruined maiden fight
To remove the smirch from the Baptist Church
By bringing the heathen Light;
And the Elders declared that all would be spared
If she carried the holy words
From her Keokuk home to the hell-town Nome
To save those sinful birds.

So, two weeks later, she took a freighter,
For the gold-cursed land near the Pole,
But Heaven ain't made for a lass that's betrayed—
She was wrecked on Shark-Tooth Shoal!
All hands were tossed in the Sea, and lost—
All but the maiden Ruth,
Who swam to the edge of the sea lion's ledge
Where abode the love of her youth.
He was hunting a seal for his evening meal
(He handled a mean harpoon)
When he saw at his feet, not something to eat,
But a girl in a frozen swoon,
Whom he dragged to his lair by her dripping hair,
And he rubbed her knees with gin.
To his great surprise, she opened her eyes
And revealed—his Original Sin!

His eight-months beard grew stiff and weird,
And it felt like a chestnut burr,
And he swore by his gizzard, and the Arctic blizzard
That he'd do right by her.
But the cold sweat froze on the end of her nose
Till it gleamed like a Tecla pearl,
While her bright hair fell, like a flame from hell,
Down the back of the grateful girl.
But a hopeless rake was Yukon Jake,
The Hermit of Shark-Tooth Shoal!
And the dizzy maid he rebetrayed
And wrecked her immortal soul! . . .
Then he rowed her ashore, with a broken oar,
And he sold her to Dan Megrew
For a husky dog and some hot eggnog,
As rascals are wont to do.
Now ruthless Ruth is a maid uncouth
With scarlet cheeks and lips,
And she sings rough songs to the drunken throngs
That come from the sealing ships.
For a rouge-stained kiss from this infamous miss
They will give a seal's sleek fur,
Or perhaps a sable, if they are able;
It's much the same to her.

Oh, the North Countree is a rough countree,
That mothers a bloody brood;

280

And its icy arms hold hidden charms
For the greedy, the sinful and lewd.
And strong men rust, from the gold and the lust
That sears the Northland soul,
But the wickedest born from the Pole to the Horn
Was the Hermit of Shark-Tooth Shoal!

EDWARD E. PARAMORE, JR.

From *Tom Masson's Annual for 1923* copyrighted by Doubleday, Doran & Company, Inc.

ABDULLAH BULBUL AMIR,
OR,
IVAN PETROFSKY SKOVAR

THE sons of the Prophet are valiant and bold,
  And quite unaccustomed to fear;
And the bravest of all was a man, so I'm told,
  Called Abdullah Bulbul Amir.

When they wanted a man to encourage the van,
  Or harass the foe from the rear,
Storm fort or redoubt, they were sure to call out
  For Abdullah Bulbul Amir.

There are heroes in plenty, and well known to fame,
  In the legions that fight for the Czar;
But none of such fame as the man by the name
  Of Ivan Petrofsky Skovar.

He could imitate Irving, tell fortunes by cards,
  And play on the Spanish guitar;
In fact, quite the cream of the Muscovite guards,
  Was Ivan Petrofsky Skovar.

One day this bold Muscovite shouldered his gun,
  Put on his most cynical sneer,
And was walking downtown when he happened to run
  Into Abdullah Bulbul Amir.

"Young man," said Bulbul, "is existence so dull
  That you're anxious to end your career?
Then, infidel, know you have trod on the toe
  Of Abdullah Bulbul Amir.

"So take your last look at the sea, sky and brook,
    Make your latest report on the war;
For I mean to imply that you are going to die,
    O Ivan Petrofsky Skovar."

So this fierce man he took his trusty chibouk,
    And murmuring, "Allah Aklar!"
With murder intent he most savagely went
    For Ivan Petrofsky Skovar.

The Sultan rose up, the disturbance to quell,
    Likewise, give the victor a cheer.
He arrived just in time to bid hasty farewell
    To Abdullah Bulbul Amir.

A loud-sounding splash from the Danube was heard
    Resounding o'er meadows afar;
It came from the sack fitting close to the back
    Of Ivan Petrofsky Skovar.

There lieth a stone where the Danube doth roll,
    And on it in characters queer
Are "Stranger, when passing by, pray for the soul
    Of Abdullah Bulbul Amir."

A Muscovite maiden her vigil doth keep
    By the light of the pale northern star,
And the name she repeats every night in her sleep
    Is Ivan Petrofsky Skovar.

UNKNOWN.

CASEY AT THE BAT

IT LOOKED extremely rocky for the Boston nine that day;
The score stood two to four, with but an inning left to play.
So, when Cooney died at second, and Burrows did the same,
A pallor wreathed the features of the patrons of the game.

A straggling few got up to go, leaving there the rest,
With that hope which springs eternal within the human breast.
For they thought: "If only Casey could get a whack at that,"
They'd put even money now, with Casey at the bat.

But Flynn preceded Casey, and likewise so did Blake,
And the former was a pudd'n, and the latter was a fake.
So on that stricken multitude a deathlike silence sat;
For there seemed but little chance of Casey's getting to the bat.

But Flynn let drive a "single," to the wonderment of all.
And the much-despised Blakey "tore the cover off the ball."
And when the dust had lifted, and they saw what had occurred,
There was Blakey safe at second, and Flynn a-huggin' third.

Then from the gladdened multitude went up a joyous yell—
It rumbled in the mountaintops, it rattled in the dell;
It struck upon the hillside and rebounded on the flat;
For Casey, mighty Casey, was advancing to the bat.

There was ease in Casey's manner as he stepped into his place,
There was pride in Casey's bearing and a smile on Casey's face;
And when responding to the cheers he lightly doffed his hat,
No stranger in the crowd could doubt 'twas Casey at the bat.

Ten thousand eyes were on him as he rubbed his hands with dirt,
Five thousand tongues applauded when he wiped them on his shirt;
Then when the writhing pitcher ground the ball into his hip,
Defiance glanced in Casey's eye, a sneer curled Casey's lip.

And now the leather-covered sphere came hurtling through the air,
And Casey stood a-watching it in haughty grandeur there.
Close by the sturdy batsman the ball unheeded sped;
"That ain't my style," said Casey. "Strike one," the umpire said.

From the benches, black with people, there went up a muffled roar,
Like the beating of the storm waves on the stern and distant shore.
"Kill him! kill the umpire!" shouted someone on the stand;
And it's likely they'd have killed him had not Casey raised his hand.

With a smile of Christian charity great Casey's visage shone;
He stilled the rising tumult, he made the game go on;
He signaled to the pitcher, and once more the spheroid flew;
But Casey still ignored it, and the umpire said, "Strike two."

"Fraud!" cried the maddened thousands, and the echo answered
    "Fraud!"
But one scornful look from Casey and the audience was awed;
They saw his face grow stern and cold, they saw his muscles strain,
And they knew that Casey wouldn't let the ball go by again.

The sneer is gone from Casey's lips, his teeth are clenched in hate,
He pounds with cruel vengeance his bat upon the plate;
And now the pitcher holds the ball, and now he lets it go,
And now the air is shattered by the force of Casey's blow.

Oh, somewhere in this favored land the sun is shining bright,
The band is playing somewhere, and somewhere hearts are light;
And somewhere men are laughing, and somewhere children shout,
But there is no joy in Boston: Mighty Casey has struck out.

ERNEST LAWRENCE THAYER.

CASEY'S REVENGE

Being a Reply to the Famous Baseball Classic, "CASEY AT THE BAT."

THERE WERE saddened hearts in Mudville for a week or even more;
There were muttered oaths and curses—every fan in town was sore.
"Just think," said one, "how soft it looked with Casey at the bat!
And then to think he'd go and spring a bush-league trick like that."

All his past fame was forgotten; he was now a hopeless "shine,"
They called him "Strike-out Casey" from the mayor down the line,
And as he came to bat each day his bosom heaved a sigh,
While a look of hopeless fury shone in mighty Casey's eye.

The lane is long, someone has said, that never turns again,
And Fate, though fickle, often gives another chance to men.
And Casey smiled—his rugged face no longer wore a frown;
The pitcher who had started all the trouble came to town.

All Mudville had assembled; ten thousand fans had come
To see the twirler who had put big Casey on the bum;
And when he stepped into the box the multitude went wild.
He doffed his cap in proud disdain—but Casey only smiled.

"Play ball!" the umpire's voice rang out, and then the game began;
But in that throng of thousands there was not a single fan
Who thought that Mudville had a chance; and with the setting sun
Their hopes sank low—the rival team was leading "four to one."

The last half of the ninth came round, with no change in the score;
But when the first man up hit safe the crowd began to roar.
The din increased, the echo of ten thousand shouts was heard
When the pitcher hit the second and gave "four balls" to the third.

Three men on base—nobody out—three runs to tie the game!
A triple meant the highest niche in Mudville's hall of fame;
But here the rally ended and the gloom was deep as night
When the fourth one "fouled to catcher" and the fifth "flew out to
    right."

A dismal groan in chorus came—a scowl was on each face—
When Casey walked up, bat in hand, and slowly took his place;
His bloodshot eyes in fury gleamed; his teeth were clinched in hate;
He gave his cap a vicious hook and pounded on the plate.

But fame is fleeting as the wind, and glory fades away;
There were no wild and woolly cheers, no glad acclaim this day.
They hissed and groaned and hooted as they clamored, "Strike him
    out!"
But Casey gave no outward sign that he had heard this shout.

The pitcher smiled and cut one loose; across the plate it spread;
Another hiss, another groan. "Strike one!" the umpire said.
Zip! Like a shot, the second curve broke just below his knee—
"Strike two!" the umpire roared aloud; but Casey made no plea.

No roasting for the umpire now—his was an easy lot;
But here the pitcher whirled again—was that a rifle shot?
A whack! a crack! and out through space the leather pellet flew,
A blot against the distant sky, a speck against the blue.

Above the fence in center field, in rapid whirling flight,
The sphere sailed on; the blot grew dim and then was lost to sight.
Ten thousand hats were thrown in air, ten thousand threw a fit,
But no one ever found the ball that mighty Casey hit!

Oh, somewhere in this favored land dark clouds may hide the sun,
And somewhere bands no longer play and children have no fun;
And somewhere over blighted lives there hangs a heavy pall;
But Mudville hearts are happy now—for Casey hit the ball!

JAMES WILSON

CASEY—TWENTY YEARS LATER

THE BUGVILLE TEAM was surely up against a rocky game;
The chances were they'd win defeat and undying fame;
Three men were hurt and two were benched; the score stood six to
    four.
They had to make three hard-earned runs in just two innings more.

"It can't be done," the captain said, a pallor on his face;
"I've got two pitchers in the field, a mutt on second base;
And should another man get spiked or crippled in some way,
The team would sure be down and out, with eight men left to play.

"We're up against it anyhow as far as I can see;
My boys ain't hitting like they should and that's what worries me;
The luck is with the other side, no pennant will we win;
It's mighty tough, but we must take our medicine and grin."

The eighth round opened; one, two, three; the enemy went down;
The Bugville boys went out the same, the captain wore a frown;
The first half of the ninth came round, two men had been called out,
When Bugsville's catcher broke a thumb and could not go that route.

A deathly silence settled o'er the crowd assembled there.
Defeat would be allotted them; they felt it in the air;
With only eight men in the field 'twould be a gruesome fray,—
Small wonder that the captain cursed the day he learned to play.

"Lend me a man to finish with," he begged the other team;
"Lend you a man?" the foe replied; "My boy, you're in a dream;
We want to win the pennant, too—that's what we're doing here.
There's only one thing you can do—call for a volunteer."

The captain stood and pondered in a listless sort of way;
He never was a quitter and would not be today!
"Is there within the grandstand here"—his voice rang loud and clear—
"A man who has the sporting blood to be a volunteer?"

Again that awful silence settled o'er the multitude;
Was there a man among them with such recklessness imbued?
The captain stood with cap in hand, while hopeless was his glance,
And then a short and stocky man cried out, "I'll take a chance."

Into the field he bounded with a step both firm and light;
"Give me the mask and mitt," he said; "let's finish up the fight.
The game is now beyond recall; I'll last at least a round;
Although I'm ancient you will find me muscular and sound."

His hair was sprinkled here and there with little streaks of gray;
Around his eyes and on his brow a bunch of wrinkles lay.
The captain smiled despairingly and slowly turned away.
"Why, he's all right," one rooter yelled. Another, "Let him play."

"All right, go on," the captain sighed; the stranger turned around,
Took off his coat and collar, too, and threw them on the ground.
The humor of the situation seemed to hit them all,
And as he donned the mask and mitt, the umpire called, "Play ball!"

Three balls the pitcher at him hurled, three balls of lightning speed;
The stranger caught them all with ease and did not seem to heed.
Each ball had been pronounced a strike, the side had been put out,
And as he walked in towards the bench, he heard the rooters shout.

One Bugville boy went out on strikes, and one was killed at first;
The captain saw his awkward pose, and gnashed his teeth and cursed.
The third man smashed a double and the fourth man swatted clear,
Then, in a thunder of applause, up came the volunteer.

His feet were planted in the earth, he swung a warlike club;
The captain saw his awkward pose and softly whispered, "Dub!"
The pitcher looked at him and grinned, then heaved a mighty ball;
The echo of that fearful swat still lingers with us all.

High, fast and far that spheroid flew; it sailed and sailed away;
It ne'er was found, so it's supposed it still floats on today.
Three runs came in, the pennant would be Bugville's for a year;
The fans and players gathered round to cheer the volunteer.

"What is your name," the captain asked? "Tell us your name," cried all,
As down his cheeks great tears were seen to run and fall.
For one brief moment he was still, then murmured soft and low:
"I'm mighty Casey who struck out just twenty years ago."

S. P. MCDONALD.

287

GRANDMOTHER'S OLD ARMCHAIR

MY GRANDMOTHER, she, at the age of eighty-three,
   One day in May was taken ill and died;
And after she was dead the will of course was read
   By a lawyer as we all stood side by side.
To my brother, it was found, she had left a hundred pound,
   The same unto my sister, I declare;
But when it came to me the lawyer said, "I see
   She has left to you her old armchair."

    Chorus:

   How they tittered, how they chaffed,
   How my brother and sister laughed,
   When they heard the lawyer declare
   Granny'd only left to me her old armchair.

I thought it hardly fair, still I said I did not care,
   And in the evening took the chair away.
My brother at me laughed, the lawyer at me chaffed,
   And said, "It will come useful, John, some day
When you settle down in life,
Find some girl to be your wife,
   You'll find it very handy, I declare;
On a cold and frosty night,
When the fire is burning bright,
   You can sit in your old armchair."

What the lawyer said was true,
For in a year or two,
   Strange to say, I settled down in married life.
I first a girl did court and then the ring I bought,
   Took her to the church, and then she was my wife.
Now the dear girl and me
Are happy as can be,
   And when my work is over, I declare,
I ne'er abroad would roam,
But each night I'd stay at home,
   And be seated in my old armchair.

One night the chair fell down.
When I picked it up I found

The seat had fallen out upon the floor,
And there before my eyes
I saw to my surprise,
    A lot of notes, ten thousand pounds or more.
When my brother heard of this,
The poor fellow, I confess,
    Went nearly wild with rage and tore his hair.
But I only laughed at him,
And I said unto him: "Jim,
    Don't you wish you had the old armchair?"

No more they tittered, no more they chaffed,
No more my brother and my sister laughed,
When they heard the lawyer declare
Granny'd only left to me her old armchair.

UNKNOWN.

GRANDFATHER'S CLOCK

My grandfather's clock was too large for the shelf,
    So it stood ninety years on the floor;
It was taller by half than the old man himself,
    Though it weighed not a pennyweight more.
It was bought on the morn of the day that he was born
    And was always his treasure and pride,
But it stopped short—never to go again—
    When the old man died.

    Ninety years without slumbering—
        Tick, tick, tick, tick.
    His life seconds numbering—
        Tick, tick, tick, tick.
    It stopped short—never to go again—
        When the old man died.

In watching its pendulum swing to and fro
    Many hours had he spent while a boy;
And in childhood and manhood the clock seemed to know
    And to share both his grief and his joy,
For it struck twenty-four when he entered the door
    With a blooming and beautiful bride,
But it stopped short—never to go again—
    When the old man died.

My grandfather said of those he could hire,
   Not a servant so faithful he found,
For it wasted no time and had but one desire—
   At the close of each week to be wound.
And it kept in its place—not a frown upon its face,
   And its hands never hung by its side;
But it stopped short—never to go again—
   When the old man died.

It rang an alarm in the dead of night—
   An alarm that for years had been dumb.
And we knew that his spirit was pluming for flight,
   That his hour for departure had come.
Still the clock kept the time with a soft and muffled chime
   As we silently stood by his side;
But it stopped short—never to go again—
   When the old man died.

HENRY CLAY WORK.

THE FOX WENT OUT ONE FROSTY NIGHT

THE FOX went out one frosty night
And begged for the moon to give him light,
He had so many miles to walk that night,
Before he'd reach his den, oh.

   Chorus:

Den oh, den oh,
Before he reached his den.

The fox caught the gray goose by the neck,
And flung her right across his back
The black duck shouts out, "Quack, quack, quack,
The fox is off to his den, oh."

Mrs. Slipper Slapper jumped out of bed,
Out of the window popped her head;
"John! John! John! the gray goose is gone,
Andthe fox is off to his den, oh."

John went up to the top of the hill
And blew a blast, both loud and shrill,
The fox said, "That's pretty music still—
I'd rather be in my den, oh."

The fox took it home to his hungry wife,
Who made good use of the carving knife.
"Never ate a better goose in all my life!"
And the young ones picked the bones, oh.

UNKNOWN.

IV. FAITH AND REVERENCE

RECESSIONAL

God of our fathers, known of old—
  Lord of our far-flung battle line—
Beneath Whose awful hand we hold
  Dominion over palm and pine—
Lord God of Hosts, be with us yet,
  Lest we forget—lest we forget!

The tumult and the shouting dies;
  The captains and the kings depart:
Still stands Thine ancient Sacrifice,
  An humble and a contrite heart.
Lord God of Hosts, be with us yet,
  Lest we forget—lest we forget!

Far-called, our navies melt away;
  On dune and headland sinks the fire:
Lo, all our pomp of yesterday
  Is one with Nineveh and Tyre!
Judge of the Nations, spare us yet,
  Lest we forget—lest we forget!

If, drunk with sight of power, we loose
  Wild tongues that have not Thee in awe—
Such boasting as the Gentiles use
  Or lesser breeds without the Law—
Lord God of Hosts, be with us yet,
  Lest we forget—lest we forget!

For heathen heart that puts her trust
   In reeking tube and iron shard—
All valiant dust that builds on dust,
   And guarding, calls not Thee to guard—
For frantic boast and foolish word,
   Thy mercy on Thy people, Lord!
Amen.

RUDYARD KIPLING.

HOW THE GREAT GUEST CAME

BEFORE THE CATHEDRAL in grandeur rose
At Ingelburg where the Danube goes;
Before its forest of silver spires
Went airily up to the clouds and fires;
Before the oak had ready a beam,
While yet the arch was stone and dream—
There where the altar was later laid,
Conrad, the cobbler, plied his trade.

*   *   *

It happened one day at the year's white end—
Two neighbors called on their old-time friend;
And they found the shop, so meager and mean,
Made gay with a hundred boughs of green.
Conrad was stitching with face ashine,
But suddenly stopped as he twitched a twine:
"Old friends, good news! At dawn today,
As the cocks were scaring the night away,
The Lord appeared in a dream to me,
And said, 'I am coming your Guest to be!'
So I've been busy with feet astir,
Strewing the floor with branches of fir.
The wall is washed and the shelf is shined,
And over the rafter the holly twined.
He comes today, and the table is spread
With milk and honey and wheaten bread."

His friends went home; and his face grew still
As he watched for the shadow across the sill.
He lived all the moments o'er and o'er,
When the Lord should enter the lowly door—

296

The knock, the call, the latch pulled up,
The lighted face, the offered cup.
He would wash the feet where the spikes had been,
He would kiss the hands where the nails went in,
And then at the last would sit with Him
And break the bread as the day grew dim.

While the cobbler mused there passed his pane
A beggar drenched by the driving rain.
He called him in from the stony street
And gave him shoes for his bruisèd feet.
The beggar went and there came a crone,
Her face with wrinkles of sorrow sown.
A bundle of fagots bowed her back,
And she was spent with the wrench and rack.
He gave her his loaf and steadied her load
As she took her way on the weary road.
Then to his door came a little child,
Lost and afraid in the world so wild,
In the big, dark world. Catching it up,
He gave it the milk in the waiting cup,
And led it home to its mother's arms,
Out of the reach of the world's alarms.

The day went down in the crimson west
And with it the hope of the blessed Guest,
And Conrad sighed as the world turned gray:
"Why is it, Lord, that your feet delay?
Did You forget that this was the day?"
Then soft in the silence a Voice he heard:
"Lift up your heart, for I kept my word.
Three times I came to your friendly door;
Three times my shadow was on your floor.
I was the beggar with bruisèd feet;
I was the woman you gave to eat;
I was the child on the homeless street!"

EDWIN MARKHAM.

MY EVENING PRAYER

IF I HAVE WOUNDED any soul to-day,
If I have caused one foot to go astray,
If I have walked in my own wilful way—
    Good Lord, forgive!

If I have uttered idle words or vain,
If I have turned aside from want or pain,
Lest I myself should suffer through the strain—
    Good Lord, forgive!

If I have craved for joys that are not mine,
If I have let my wayward heart repine,
Dwelling on things of earth, not things divine—
    Good Lord, forgive!

If I have been perverse, or hard, or cold,
If I have longed for shelter in Thy fold,
When Thou hast given me some part to hold—
    Good Lord, forgive.

Forgive the sins I have confessed to Thee,
Forgive the secret sins I do not see,
That which I know not, Father, teach Thou me—
    Help me to live.

                CHARLES H. GABRIEL.

A PRAYER FOR EVERY DAY

MAKE ME too brave to lie or be unkind.
Make me too understanding, too, to mind
The little hurts companions give, and friends,
The careless hurts that no one quite intends.
Make me too thoughtful to hurt others so.
Help me to know
The inmost hearts of those for whom I care,
Their secret wishes, all the loads they bear,
That I may add my courage to their own.
May I make lonely folks feel less alone,
And happy ones a little happier yet.
May I forget
What ought to be forgotten; and recall
Unfailing, all
That ought to be recalled, each kindly thing,
Forgetting what might sting.
To all upon my way,
Day after day,
Let me be joy, be hope! Let my life sing!

                MARY CAROLYN DAVIES.

A CREED

THERE IS A DESTINY that makes us brothers;
  None goes his way alone:
All that we send into the lives of others
  Comes back into our own.

I care not what his temples or his creeds,
  One thing holds firm and fast—
That into his fateful heap of days and deeds
  The soul of man is cast.

EDWIN MARKHAM.

SOMETIME

SOMETIME, when all life's lessons have been learned,
  And sun and stars forevermore have set,
The things which our weak judgments here have spurned,
  The things o'er which we grieved with lashes wet,
Will flash before us out of life's dark night,
  As stars shine most in deeper tints of blue;
And we shall see how all God's plans are right,
  And how what seemed reproof was love most true.

And we shall see how, while we frown and sigh,
  God's plans go on as best for you and me;
How, when we called, He heeded not our cry,
  Because His wisdom to the end could see.
And e'en as prudent parents disallow
  Too much of sweet to craving babyhood,
So God, perhaps, is keeping from us now
  Life's sweetest things, because it seemeth good.

And if, sometimes, commingled with life's wine,
  We find the wormwood, and rebel and shrink,
Be sure a wiser hand than yours or mine
  Pours out the potion for our lips to drink;
And if some friend you love is lying low,
  Where human kisses cannot reach his face,
Oh, do not blame the loving Father so,
  But wear your sorrow with obedient grace!

And you shall shortly know that lengthened breath
  Is not the sweetest gift God sends His friend,
And that, sometimes, the sable pall of death
  Conceals the fairest boon His love can send;
If we could push ajar the gates of life,
  And stand within, and all God's workings see,
We could interpret all this doubt and strife,
  And for each mystery could find a key.

But not today. Then be content, poor heart;
  God's plans, like lilies pure and white, unfold;
We must not tear the close-shut leaves apart,—
  Time will reveal the chalices of gold.
And if, through patient toil, we reach the land
  Where tired feet, with sandals loosed, may rest,
When we shall clearly see and understand,
  I think that we will say, "God knew the best!"

MAY RILEY SMITH.

IF WE KNEW

IF WE KNEW the woe and heartache
  Waiting for us down the road,
If our lips could taste the wormwood,
  If our backs could feel the load,
Would we waste the day in wishing
  For a time that ne'er can be?
Would we wait in such impatience
  For our ships to come from sea?

If we knew the baby fingers
  Pressed against the windowpane
Would be cold and stiff tomorrow—
  Never trouble us again—
Would the bright eyes of our darling
  Catch the frown upon our brow?
Would the print of rosy fingers
  Vex us then as they do now?

Ah! these little ice-cold fingers—
  How they point our memories back
To the hasty words and actions
  Strewn along our backward track!

How these little hands remind us,
　　As in snowy grace they lie,
Not to scatter thorns—but roses—
　　For our reaping by and by.

Strange we never prize the music
　　Till the sweet-voiced bird has flown;
Strange that we should slight the violets
　　Till the lovely flowers are gone;
Strange that summer skies and sunshine
　　Never seem one half so fair
As when winter's snowy pinions
　　Shake their white down in the air!

Lips from which the seal of silence
　　None but God can roll away,
Never blossomed in such beauty
　　As adorns the mouth today;
And sweet words that freight our memory
　　With their beautiful perfume,
Come to us in sweeter accents
　　Through the portals of the tomb.

Let us gather up the sunbeams
　　Lying all around our path;
Let us keep the wheat and roses,
　　Casting out the thorns and chaff;
Let us find our sweetest comfort
　　In the blessings of today,
With a patient hand removing
　　All the briars from the way.

　　　　　　　　　　MAY RILEY SMITH.

BE STRONG!

BE STRONG!
We are not here to play, to dream, to drift;
We have hard work to do and loads to lift;
Shun not the struggle—face it; 'tis God's gift.

Be strong!
Say not, "The days are evil. Who's to blame?"
And fold the hands and acquiesce—oh, shame!
Stand up, speak out, and bravely, in God's name.

Be strong!
It matters not how deep intrenched the wrong,
How hard the battle goes, the day how long;
Faint not—fight on! Tomorrow comes the song.

MALTBIE DAVENPORT BABCOCK.

EACH IN HIS OWN TONGUE

A FIRE MIST and a planet—
 A crystal and a cell,—
A jellyfish and a saurian,
 And caves where the cave men dwell;
Then a sense of law and beauty,
 And a face turned from the clod—
Some call it Evolution,
 And others call it God.

A haze on the far horizon,
 The infinite, tender sky,
The ripe, rich tint of the cornfields,
 And the wild geese sailing high;
And all over upland and lowland
 The charm of the goldenrod—
Some of us call it Autumn,
 And others call it God.

Like tides on a crescent sea beach,
 When the moon is new and thin,
Into our hearts high yearnings
 Come welling and surging in—
Come from the mystic ocean,
 Whose rim no foot has trod—
Some of us call it Longing,
 And others call it God.

A picket frozen on duty,
 A mother starved for her brood,
Socrates drinking the hemlock,
 And Jesus on the rood;
And millions who, humble and nameless,
 The straight, hard pathway plod—
Some call it Consecration,
 And others call it God.

WILLIAM HERBERT CARRUTH.

302

SONG OF HOPE

CHILDREN of yesterday,
  Heirs of tomorrow,
What are you weaving?
  Labor and sorrow?
Look to your looms again.
  Faster and faster
Fly the great shuttles
  Prepared by the Master;
Life's in the loom,
  Room for it—
    Room!

Children of yesterday,
  Heirs of tomorrow,
Lighten the labor
  And sweeten the sorrow.
Now, while the shuttles fly
  Faster and faster,
Up and be at it,
  At work with the Master;
He stands at your loom,
  Room for Him—
    Room!

Children of yesterday,
  Heirs of tomorrow,
Look at your fabric
  Of labor and sorrow.
Seamy and dark
  With despair and disaster,
Turn it, and—lo,
  The design of the Master!
The Lord's at the loom;
  Room for Him—
    Room!

MARY ARTEMISIA LATHBURY.

MIZPAH

Go THOU thy way, and I go mine,
    Apart, yet not afar;
Only a thin veil hangs between
    The pathways where we are.
And "God keep watch 'tween thee and me";
    This is my prayer;
He looks thy way, He looketh mine,
    And keeps us near.

I know not where thy road may lie,
    Or which way mine will be;
If mine will lead thro' parching sands
    And thine beside the sea;
Yet God keeps watch 'tween thee and me,
    So never fear;
He holds thy hands, He claspeth mine,
    And keeps us near.

Should wealth and fame perchance be thine,
    And my lot lowly be,
Or you be sad and sorrowful,
    And glory be for me,
Yet God keep watch 'tween thee and me;
    Both be His care;
One arm round thee and one round me
    Will keep us near.

I sigh sometimes to see thy face,
    But since this may not be,
I'll leave thee to the care of Him
    Who cares for thee and me.
"I'll keep you both beneath my wings,"
    This comforts, dear;
One wing o'er thee and one o'er me,
    Will keep us near.

And though our paths be separate,
    And thy way is not mine,
Yet coming to the Mercy seat,
    My soul will meet with thine.

And "God keep watch 'tween thee and me,"
    I'll whisper there.
He blesseth thee, He blesseth me,
    And we are near.

                    JULIA A. BAKER.

IS IT TRUE?

Is it true, O Christ in Heaven,
    That the highest suffer most?
That the strongest wander furthest,
    And more helplessly are lost?
That the mark of rank in nature
    Is capacity for pain?
And the anguish of the singer
    Makes the sweetness of the strain?

Is it true, O Christ in Heaven,
    That whichever way we go
Walls of darkness must surround us,
    Things we would but cannot know?
That the infinite must bound us
    Like a temple veil unrent,
Whilst the finite ever wearies,
    So that none's therein content?

Is it true, O Christ in Heaven,
    That the fullness yet to come
Is so glorious and so perfect
    That to know would strike us dumb?
That if ever for a moment
    We could pierce beyond the sky
With these poor dim eyes of mortals,
    We should just see God and die?

                    SARAH WILLIAMS.

305

THE COMING OF HIS FEET

IN THE CRIMSON of the morning, in the whiteness of the noon,
  In the amber glory of the day's retreat,
In the midnight, robed in darkness, or the gleaming of the moon,
  I listen to the coming of His feet.

I heard His weary footsteps on the sands of Galilee,
  On the Temple's marble pavement, on the street,
Worn with weight of sorrow, faltering up the slopes of Calvary,
  The sorrow of the coming of His feet.

Down the minster aisles of splendor, from betwixt the cherubim,
  Through the wondering throng, with motion strong and fleet,
Sounds His victor tread approaching, with a music far and dim—
  The music of the coming of His feet.

Sandaled not with sheen of silver, girded not with woven gold,
  Weighted not with shimmering gems and odors sweet,
But white-winged and shod with glory in the Tabor light of old—
  The glory of the coming of His feet.

He is coming, O my spirit, with His everlasting peace,
  With His blessedness immortal and complete;
He is coming, O my spirit, and His coming brings release—
  I listen for the coming of His feet.

LYMAN W. ALLEN.

A PRAYER

LET ME DO my work each day;
  And if the darkened hours of despair overcome me,
May I not forget the strength that comforted me
In the desolation of other times.
May I still remember the bright hours that found me
Walking over the silent hills of my childhood,
Or dreaming on the margin of the quiet river,
When a light glowed within me,
And I promised my early God to have courage
Amid the tempests of the changing years.
Spare me from bitterness
And from the sharp passions of unguarded moments.

May I not forget that poverty and riches are of the spirit.
Though the world know me not,
May my thoughts and actions be such
As shall keep me friendly with myself.
Lift my eyes from the earth,
And let me not forget the uses of the stars.
Forbid that I should judge others,
Lest I condemn myself.
Let me not follow the clamor of the world,
But walk calmly in my path.
Give me a few friends who will love me for what I am;
And keep ever burning before my vagrant steps
The kindly light of hope.
And though age and infirmity overtake me,
And I come not within sight of the castle of my dreams,
Teach me still to be thankful for life,
And for time's olden memories that are good and sweet;
And may the evening's twilight find me gentle still.

MAX EHRMANN.

BUILDING FOR ETERNITY

WE ARE BUILDING in sorrow or joy
A temple the world may not see,
Which time cannot mar nor destroy;
We build for eternity.

Chorus:
We are building ev'ry day,
A temple the world may not see;
Building, building ev'ry day,
Building for eternity.

Ev'ry thought that we've ever had
Its own little place has filled;
Ev'ry deed we have done, good or bad,
Is a stone in the temple we build.

Ev'ry word that so lightly falls,
Giving some heart joy or pain,
Will shine in our temple walls,
Or ever its beauty stain.

Are you building for God alone—
Are you building in faith and love
A temple the Father will own
In the city of light above?

N. B. SARGENT.

THE WATERED LILIES

THE MASTER stood in His garden,
    Among the lilies fair,
Which His own right hand had planted,
    And trained with tend'rest care.

He looked at their snowy blossoms,
    And marked with observant eye
That the flowers were sadly drooping,
    For their leaves were parched and dry.

"My lilies need to be watered,"
    The Heavenly Master said;
"Wherein shall I draw it for them,
    And raise each drooping head?"

Close to his feet on the pathway,
    Empty, and frail, and small,
An earthen vessel was lying,
    Which seemed no use at all;

But the Master saw, and raised it
    From the dust in which it lay,
And smiled, as He gently whispered,
    "This shall do My work today:

"It is but an *earthen* vessel,
    But it lay so close to Me;
It is small, but it is empty—
    That is all it needs to be."

So to the fountain He took it,
    And filled it full to the brim;
How glad was the earthen vessel
    To be of some use to Him!

He poured forth the living water
   Over His lilies fair,
Until the vessel was empty,
   And again He filled it there.

He watered the drooping lilies
   Until they revived again;
And the Master saw with pleasure
   That His labor had not been vain.

His own hand had drawn the water
   Which refreshed the thirsty flowers;
But He used the earthen vessel
   To convey the living showers.

And to itself it whispered,
   As He laid it aside once more,
"Still will I lie in His pathway,
   Just where I did before.

"Close would I keep to the Master,
   Empty would I remain,
And perhaps some day He may use me
   To water His flowers again."

UNKNOWN.

AN ANCIENT PRAYER

GIVE ME a good digestion, Lord, and also something to digest;
Give me a healthy body, Lord, and sense to keep it at its best.
Give me a healthy mind, good Lord, to keep the good and pure in sight,
Which, seeing sin, is not appalled, but finds a way to set it right.

Give me a mind that is not bound, that does not whimper, whine or
   sigh.
Don't let me worry overmuch about the fussy thing called I.
Give me a sense of humor, Lord; give me the grace to see a joke,
To get some happiness from life and pass it on to other folk.

THOMAS H. B. WEBB.

THE ANVIL—GOD'S WORD

LAST EVE I passed beside a blacksmith's door,
    And heard the anvil ring the vesper chime;
Then, looking in, I saw upon the floor
    Old hammers, worn with beating years of time.

"How many anvils have you had," said I,
    "To wear and batter all these hammers so?"
"Just one," said he, and then, with twinkling eye,
    "The anvil wears the hammers out, you know."

And so, thought I, the anvil of God's Word,
    For ages skeptic blows have beat upon;
Yet, though the noise of falling blows was heard,
    The anvil is unharmed—the hammers gone.

UNKNOWN.

THE CROSS WAS HIS OWN

THEY BORROWED a bed to lay His head
    When Christ the Lord came down;
They borrowed the ass in the mountain pass
    For Him to ride to town;
But the crown that He wore and the Cross that He bore
    Were His own—
    The Cross was His own.

He borrowed the bread when the crowd He fed
    On the grassy mountain side,
He borrowed the dish of broken fish
    With which He satisfied.
But the crown that He wore and the Cross that He bore
    Were His own—
    The Cross was His own.

He borrowed the ship in which to sit
    To teach the multitude;
He borrowed a nest in which to rest—
    He had never a home so rude;
But the crown that He wore and the Cross that He bore
    Were His own—
    The Cross was His own.

He borrowed a room on His way to the tomb
　The Passover Lamb to eat;
They borrowed a cave for Him a grave,
　They borrowed a winding sheet.
But the crown that He wore and the Cross that He bore
　Were His own—
　The Cross was His own.

UNKNOWN.

HOW FAR IS IT CALLED TO THE GRAVE?

How FAR is it called to the grave?
The child looked up from its play.
The grave? I have not heard of the grave.
It must be far away.

How far is it called to the grave?
The lover looked up with a smile.
How far? From the golden land of love
It must be many a mile.

He could not see that his darling
With the bridal flowers in her hair,
As he gave her the wedding token,
Was almost there.

How far is it called to the grave?
The mother looked up with a tear,
The rose in her cheek grew pale and white,
Her heart stood still with fear.

How far? O 'tis close to the hearthstone;
Alas for the baby feet,
The little bare feet that all unled,
Are going with step so fleet,
And they are almost there.

How far is it called to the grave?
It is only a life, dear friend,
And the longest life is short at last,
And soon our lives must end.

But there is One who arose from the grave,
Who ascended triumphant on high,
With our trust in Him, we'll know no sting,
Though low in the grave we lie,
And we're almost there.

UNKNOWN.

LAURELS AND IMMORTELLES

HE HAS SOLVED it—Life's wonderful problem,
 The deepest, the strongest, the last;
And into the school of the angels
 With the answer forever has passed.

How strange that, in spite of our questions,
 He maketh no answer, nor tells
Why so soon were earth's honoring laurels
 Displaced by God's own immortelles.

How strange he should sleep so profoundly,
 So young, so unworn by the strife!
While beside him, brimful of Hope's nectar,
 Untouched stands the goblet of life.

Men slumber like that when the evening
 Of a long, weary day droppeth down;
But he wrought so well that the morning
 Brought for him the rest and the crown.

'Tis idle to talk of the future
 And the rare "might have been," 'mid our tears;
God knew all about it, yet took him
 Away from the oncoming years.

God knew all about it—how noble,
 How gentle he was, and how brave,
How brilliant his possible future—
 Yet put him to sleep in the grave.

God knows all about those who loved him,
 How bitter the trial must be;
And right through it all God is loving,
 And knows so much better than we.

So, right in the darkness, be trustful;
  One day you shall sing, "It is well."
God took from his young brow earth's laurels
  And crowned him with death's immortelles.

UNKNOWN.

POOR LIL' BRACK SHEEP

POOR LIL' BRACK SHEEP dat stray'd away,
  Done los' in de win' and rain,
An' de Shepherd He say, "O hirelin',
  Go fin' my sheep again."
An' de hirelin' frowns, "O Shepherd,
  Dat sheep am brack an' bad."
But de Shepherd He smile like de lil' brack sheep
  Is de onliest lamb he had,
  Is de onliest lamb he had.

An' he say, "O hirelin', hasten!
  For de win' an' de rain am col',
And dat lil' brack sheep am lonesome
  Out dere so far from de fol'."
An' de hirelin' frown, "O Shepherd,
  Dat sheep am ol' an' gray."
But de Shepherd He smile like de lil' brack sheep
  Wuz fair as de break ob day,
  Wuz fair as de break ob day.

An He say, "O hirelin', hasten!
  Lo, here is de ninety an' nine,
But dere way off from de sheep fol'
  Is dat lil' brack sheep ob mine."
An' de hirelin' frown, "O Shepherd,
  De rest ob de sheep am here."
But de Shepherd He smile like de lil' brack sheep
  He hol' it de mostes' dear,
  He hol' it de mostes' dear.

An' de Shepherd go out in de darkness,
  Where de night was col' an' bleak,
An' de lil brack sheep He fin' it,
  An' lay it agains' His cheek.

An' de hirelin' frown, "O Shepherd,
  Don't bring dat sheep to me."
But de Shepherd He smile, an' He hol' it close,
  An' de lil' brack sheep—is me!
  An' de lil' brack sheep—is me!

ETHEL M. C. BRAZELTON.

THERE IS NO DEATH

THERE IS A PLAN far greater than the plan you know;
There is a landscape broader than the one you see.
There is a haven where storm-tossed souls may go—
You call it death—we, immortality.

You call it death—this seeming endless sleep;
We call it birth—the soul at last set free.
'Tis hampered not by time or space—you weep.
Why weep at death? 'Tis immortality.

Farewell, dear voyageur—'twill not be long.
Your work is done—now may peace rest with thee.
Your kindly thoughts and deeds—they will live on.
This is not death—'tis immortality.

Farewell, dear voyageur—the river winds and turns;
The cadence of your song wafts near to me,
And now you know the thing that all men learn:
There is no death—there's immortality.

UNKNOWN.

THE WEAVER

A WEAVER sat by the side of his loom
  A-flinging the shuttle fast,
And a thread that would last till the hour of doom
  Was added at every cast.

His warp had been by the angels spun
  And his weft was bright and new,
Like thread that the morning uprays from the sun,
  All jeweled over with dew.

And fresh-lipped, bright-eyed, beautiful flowers
  In the rich, soft web were bedded;
And blithe to the weaver sped onward the hours,
  Not yet were Time's feet leaded.

But something there came slow stealing by,
  And a shade on the fabric fell;
And I saw that the shuttle less blithely did fly;
  For thought has a wearisome spell.

And the thread that next o'er the warp was lain
  Was of a melancholy gray;
And anon I marked there a teardrop's stain
  Where the flowers had fallen away.

But still the weaver kept weaving on,
  Though the fabric all was gray.
And the flowers, and the buds, and the leaves were gone,
  And the gold threads cankered lay.

And dark, and still darker, and darker grew
  Each newly woven thread,
And some were of a death-mocking hue,
  And some of a bloody red.

And things all strange were woven in,
  Sighs, down-crushed hopes and fears;
And the web was broken and poor and thin,
  And it dripped with living tears.

And the weaver fain would have flung it aside,
  But he knew it would be a sin;
So in light and in gloom the shuttle he plied,
  A-weaving those life cords in.

And as he wove, and weeping, still wove,
  A tempter stole him nigh;
And with glowing words to win him strove,
  But the weaver turned his eye—

He upward turned his eye to Heaven,
  And still wove on—on—on!
Till the last, last cord from his heart was riven,
  And the tissue strange was done.

Then he threw it about his shoulders bowed,
  And about his grizzled head,
And, gathering close the folds of his shroud,
  Laid him down among the dead.

And after, I saw in a robe of light
  The weaver in the sky;
And angel's wings were not more bright,
  And the stars grew pale, it nigh.

And I saw 'mid the folds all the iris-hued flowers,
  That beneath his touch had sprung,
More beautiful far than these stray ones of ours,
  Which the angels have to us flung.

And wherever a tear had fallen down
  Gleamed out a diamond rare,
And jewels befitting a monarch's crown
  Were footprints left by care.

And wherever had swept the breath of a sigh
  Was left a rich perfume,
And with light from the fountain of bliss in the sky
  Shone the labor of sorrow and gloom.

And then I prayed: "When my work is done,
  And the silver cord is riven,
May the stain of sorrow the deepest one,
  That I bear with me to Heaven."

                              FANNY FORRESTER.

WHERE, OH WHERE ARE THE HEBREW CHILDREN?

Where, oh where, are the Hebrew children,
Where, oh where, are the Hebrew children,
Who were cast in the furnace of fire?
  Safe now in the Promised Land.

Chorus:

By and by we'll go home to meet them,
By and by we'll go home to meet them,
By and by we'll go home to meet them
  Way o'er the Promised Land.

316

Where, oh where, is the good Elijah,
Where, oh where, is the good Elijah,
Who went up in a chariot of fire?
    Safe now in the Promised Land.

Where, oh where, is the prophet Daniel,
Where, oh where, is the prophet Daniel,
Who was cast in the den of lions?
    Safe now in the Promised Land.

Where, oh where, is the weeping Mary,
Where, oh where, is the weeping Mary,
Who was first at the tomb of Jesus?
    Safe now in the Promised Land.

Where, oh where, is the martyred Stephen,
Where, oh where, is the martyred Stephen,
Who was stoned for his love of Jesus?
    Safe now in the Promised Land.

Where, oh where, is the Blessed Jesus,
Where, oh where, is the Blessed Jesus,
Who was pierced on the mount of Calvary?
    Safe now in the Promised Land.

                      UNKNOWN.

AN ODE

THE SPACIOUS FIRMAMENT on high,
With all the blue ethereal sky,
And spangled heavens, a shining frame,
Their great Original proclaim.
The unwearied sun from day to day
Does his Creator's power display,
And publishes to every land
The work of an almighty Hand.

Soon as the evening shades prevail,
The moon takes up the wondrous tale,
And nightly, to the listening earth,
Repeats the story of her birth;

Whilst all the stars that round her burn,
And all the planets in their turn,
Confirm the tidings as they roll,
And spread the truth from pole to pole.

What though in solemn silence all
Move round the dark terrestrial ball?
What though nor real voice nor sound
Amid their radiant orbs be found?
In reason's ear they all rejoice,
And utter forth a glorious voice,
Forever singing as they shine,
"The Hand that made us is divine!"

JOSEPH ADDISON.

THE BURIAL OF MOSES

"And they buried him in a valley in the land of Moab, over against Beth-peor;
but no man knoweth of his sepulcher unto this day."

By NEBO's lonely mountain,
    On this side Jordan's wave,
In a vale in the land of Moab
    There lies a lonely grave;
And no man knows that sepulcher,
    And no man saw it e'er;
For the angels of God upturn'd the sod
    And laid the dead man there.

That was the grandest funeral
    That ever pass'd on earth;
But no man heard the trampling,
    Or saw the train go forth:
Noiselessly as the daylight
    Comes when the night is done,
And the crimson streak on ocean's cheek
    Grows into the great sun.

Noiselessly as the spring-time
    Her crown of verdure weaves,
And all the trees on all the hills
    Open their thousand leaves;

318

So without sound of music,
   Or voice of them that wept,
Silently down from the mountain's crown
   The great procession swept.

Perchance the bald old eagle
   On gray Beth-peor's height,
Out of his lonely eyrie
   Look'd on the wondrous sight;
Perchance the lion stalking,
   Still shuns that hallowed spot;
For beast and bird have seen and heard
   That which man knoweth not.

But, when the warrior dieth,
   His comrades in the war,
With arms reversed and muffled drums,
   Follow his funeral car;
They show the banners taken,
   They tell his battles won,
And after him lead his masterless steed,
   While peals the minute-gun.

Amid the noblest of the land
   We lay the sage to rest,
And give the bard an honor'd place,
   With costly marble drest,
In the great minster transept
   Where lights like glories fall,
And the sweet choir sings, and the organ rings
   Along the emblazoned wall.

This was the truest warrior
   That ever buckled sword;
This the most gifted poet
   That ever breathed a word;
And never earth's philosopher
   Traced, with his golden pen,
On the deathless page, truths half so sage
   As he wrote down for men.

And had he not high honor?—
   The hillside for a pall!
To lie in state, while angels wait,
   With stars for tapers tall,

And the dark rock-pines like tossing plumes,
    Over his bier to wave,
And God's own hand, in that lonely land,
    To lay him in the grave!—

In that strange grave without a name,
    Whence his uncoffin'd clay
Shall break again—O wondrous thought!—
    Before the judgment day,
And stand, with glory wrapped around,
    On the hills he never trod,
And speak of the strife that won our life
    With the incarnate Son of God.

O lonely grave in Moab's land!
    O dark Beth-peor's hill!
Speak to these curious hearts of ours,
    And teach them to be still.
God hath His mysteries of grace,
    Ways that we cannot tell,
He hides them deep, like the hidden sleep
    Of him He loved so well.

CECIL FRANCES ALEXANDER.

THE HIDDEN LINE

[The Destiny of Men]

THERE IS A TIME, we know not when,
    A point we know not where,
That marks the destiny of men
    To glory or despair.

There is a line by us unseen,
    That crosses every path;
The hidden boundary between
    God's patience and his wrath.

To pass that limit is to die,
    To die as if by stealth;
It does not quench the beaming eye,
    Or pale the glow of health.

The conscience may be still at ease,
    The spirits light and gay;
That which is pleasing still may please,
    And care be thrust away.

But on that forehead God has set
    Indelibly a mark,
Unseen by man, for man as yet
    Is blind and in the dark.

And yet the doomed man's path below
    May bloom as Eden bloomed;
He did not, does not, will not know,
    Or feel that he is doomed.

He knows, he feels that all is well,
    And every fear is calmed;
He lives, he dies, he wakes in hell,
    Not only doomed, but damned.

Oh! where is that mysterious bourne
    By which our path is crossed;
Beyond which, God himself hath sworn,
    That he who goes is lost.

How far may we go on in sin?
    How long will God forbear?
Where does hope end, and where begin
    The confines of despair?

An answer from the skies is sent;
    "Ye that from God depart,
While it called to-day, repent,
    And harden not your heart."

DR. J. ADDISON ALEXANDER.

WHAT I LIVE FOR

I LIVE for those who love me,
    Whose hearts are kind and true;
For the Heaven that smiles above me,
    And awaits my spirit too;

For all human ties that bind me,
For the task by God assigned me,
For the bright hopes yet to find me,
   And the good that I can do.

I live to learn their story
   Who suffered for my sake;
To emulate their glory,
   And follow in their wake;
Bards, patriots, martyrs, sages,
The heroic of all ages,
Whose deeds crowd History's pages,
   And Time's great volume make.

I live to hold communion
   With all that is divine,
To feel there is a union
   'Twixt Nature's heart and mine;
To profit by affliction,
Reap truth from fields of fiction,
Grow wiser from conviction,
   And fulfil God's grand design.

I live to hail that season
   By gifted ones foretold,
When men shall live by reason,
   And not alone by gold;
When man to man united,
And every wrong thing righted,
The whole world shall be lighted
   As Eden was of old.

I live for those who love me,
   For those who know me true,
For the Heaven that smiles above me,
   And awaits my spirit too;
For the cause that lacks assistance,
For the wrong that needs resistance,
For the future in the distance,
   And the good that I can do.

GEORGE LINNAEUS BANKS.

DEATH

I AM a stranger in the land
  Where my forefathers trod;
A stranger I unto each heart,
  But not unto my God!

I pass along the crowded streets,
  Unrecognized my name;
This thought will come amid regrets—
  My God is still the same!

I seek with joy my childhood's home,
  But strangers claim the sod;
Not knowing where my kindred roam,
  Still present is my God!

They tell me that my friends all sleep
  Beneath the valley clod;
Oh, is not faith submissive sweet!
  I have no friend save God!

UNKNOWN. ORIGINALLY
SIGNED "BEATRICE."

O GOD, THE ROCK OF AGES

O GOD, the Rock of Ages,
  Who evermore hast been,
What time the tempest rages,
  Our dwelling-place serene:
Before Thy first creations,
  O Lord, the same as now,
To endless generations,
  The Everlasting Thou!

Our years are like the shadows
  On sunny hills that lie,
Or grasses in the meadows
  That blossom but to die:

323

A sleep, a dream, a story,
    By strangers quickly told,
An unremaining glory
    Of things that soon are old.

O Thou who canst not slumber,
    Whose light grows never pale,
Teach us aright to number
    Our years before they fail!
On us Thy mercy lighten,
    On us Thy goodness rest,
And let Thy Spirit brighten
    The hearts Thyself hast blessed!

EDWARD H. BICKERSTETH.

NOT UNDERSTOOD

NOT UNDERSTOOD. We move along asunder;
    Our paths grow wider as the seasons creep
Along the years; we marvel and we wonder
    Why life is life. And then we fall asleep—
        Not understood.

Not understood.   We gather false impressions,
    And hug them closer as the years go by,
Till virtues often seem to us transgressions;
    And thus men rise and fall, and live and die—
        Not understood.

Not understood. Poor souls with stunted vision
    Oft measure giants by their narrow gauge;
The poisoned shafts of falsehood and derision
    Are oft impelled 'gainst those who mould the age—
        Not understood.

Not understanding. The secret springs of action
    Which lie beneath the surface and the show
Are disregarded; with self-satisfaction
    We judge our neighbor, and they often go—
        Not understood.

324

Not understood. How trifles often change us!
  The thoughtless sentence or the fancied slight
Destroys long years of friendship, and estrange us,
  And on our souls there falls a freezing blight—
        Not understood.

Not understood. How many breasts are aching
  For lack of sympathy! Ah, day to day
How many cheerless, lonely hearts are breaking!
  How many noble spirits pass away—
        Not understood.

O God! that men would see a little clearer,
  Or judge less harshly where they cannot see;
O God! that men would draw a little nearer
  To one another; they'd be nearer Thee—
        And understood.

THOMAS BRACKEN.

PRAY WITHOUT CEASING

UNANSWERED YET the prayer your lips have pleaded
  In agony of heart these many years?
Does faith begin to fail, is hope declining,
  And think you all in vain those falling tears?
Say not the Father has not heard your prayer;
You shall have your desire, sometime, somewhere.

Unanswered yet? tho' when you first presented
  This one petition at the Father's throne,
It seemed you could not wait the time of asking,
  So anxious was your heart to have it done;
If years have passed since then, do not despair,
For God will answer you sometime, somewhere.

Unanswered yet? But you are not unheeded;
  The promises of God forever stand;
To Him our days and years alike are equal;
  Have faith in God! It is your Lord's command.
Hold on to Jacob's angel, and your prayer
Shall bring a blessing down sometime, somewhere.

Unanswered yet? Nay, do not say unanswered,
  Perhaps your part is not yet wholly done,
The work began when first your prayer was uttered,
  And God will finish what He has begun.
Keep incense burning at the shrine of prayer,
And glory shall descend sometime, somewhere.

Unanswered yet? Faith cannot be unanswered;
  Her feet are firmly planted on the Rock;
Amid the wildest storms she stands undaunted,
  Nor quails before the loudest thunder shock.
She knows Omnipotence has heard her prayer,
And cries, "It shall be done sometime, somewhere."

OPHELIA GUYON BROWNING.

THE LAST REVIEW

TWENTY-ONE MILES of boys in blue,
Sixty abreast in the last review—
How grandly the columns stretch away
In the cloudless light of this sweet May day.
Onward in rank and file they come,
To the cheering beat of the victors' drum.

Wearied and scarred and worn they be,
But a *prouder* host you never will see—
Their faded banners, riddled with ball,
But floating triumphantly after all.
Never again in the world's sunlight,
Shall the nations look on a grander sight.

No more, till the Christian army stand,
Whose warriors shall gather from every land,
For a *last* review on the other shore,
Their *life-long* battles and marches o'er,
Will a marshaled host like this appear,
Crowned with the glory that victors wear.

Let the heads of the nation bow as they pass,
And scatter with flowers the dewy grass;

As their gleaming weapons flash in the sun,
Remember the deeds of valor done.
How that solid column of human breasts
Was bared to the storm for the nation's rest.

Then beat the drum for the last reveille,
The echoes of strife are growing still;
With a conquering tread the heroes come,
Back to the dear delights of home.

But alas, the army of countless dead—
We shall list in vain for their coming tread;
Full forty miles of our noble braves,
Sixty abreast, are in their graves.
As your cheers ring out for the living host,
Remember the heroes loved and lost.

And think of the maimed and the wasted band,
Seeking the homes of this stricken land,
For whom the brightness of life is o'er,
Whose feet are nearing the other shore;
Remnants of manhood, *once so* strong,
These cannot march in the gala throng.

Then hail, all hail to the boys in blue,
Gathered today for a last review,
Marching with floating banners back:
Scatter with flowers their joyous track.
Their brows perchance are dark with scars,
And their worn feet seamed with crimson bars,
But *kings and victors* we crown today,
The war-scarred host on their homeward way.

And I wonder, if down from the sweet repose
Which the soul of the martyred hero knows,
The commander in chief looks down and sees
Those banners float in the earthly breeze,
And if in the calm of that world of bliss,
His spirit would thrill at a scene like this.

EMILY J. BUGBEE.

327

THE WEAVER

CEASELESSLY the weaver, Time,
　　Sitting at his mystic loom,
Keeps his arrowy shuttle flying;
Every thread anears our dying—
　　And, with melancholy chime,
Very low and sad withal,
Sings his solemn madrigal
　　As he weaves our web of doom.

"Mortals!" thus he, weaving, sings,
　　"Bright or dark the web shall be,
As ye will it; all the tissues
Blending in harmonious issues,
　　Or discordant colorings;
Time the shuttle drives; but you
Give to every thread its hue,
　　And elect your destiny.

"God bestowed the shining warp,
　　Fill it with as bright a woof;
And the whole shall glow divinely,
As if wrought by angels finely,
　　To the music of the harp,
And the blended colors be
Like perfected harmony,
　　Keeping evil things aloof.

"Envy, malice, pride, and hate—
　　Foulest progeny of sin—
Let not these the weft entangle,
With their blind and furious wrangle,
　　Marring your diviner fate;
But with love and deeds of good
Be the web throughout endued,
　　And the perfect ye shall win."

Thus he singeth very low,
　　Sitting at his mystic loom;
And his shuttle still is flying—
Thread by thread anears our dying,
　　Grows our shroud by every throw;

328

And the hues of woe or heaven
To each thread by us are given,
   As he weaves our web of doom.
                    WILLIAM H. BURLEIGH.

HALLOWED GROUND

WHAT'S HALLOWED GROUND? Has earth a clod
Its Maker meant not should be trod
By man, the image of his God,
   Erect and free,
Unscourged by Superstition's rod
   To bow the knee?

That's hallowed ground, where, mourned and missed,
The lips repose our love has kissed;
But where's their memory's mansion? Is't
   Yon churchyard's bowers?
No! in ourselves their souls exist,
   A part of ours.

A kiss can consecrate the ground
Where mated hearts are mutual bound:
The spot where love's first links were wound,
   That ne'er are riven,
Is hallowed down to earth's profound,
   And up to heaven!

For time makes all but true love old;
The burning thoughts that then were told
Run molten still in memory's mould,
   And will not cool
Until the heart itself be cold
   In Lethe's pool.

What hollows ground where heroes sleep?
'Tis not the sculptured piles you heap!
In dews that heavens far distant weep
   Their turf may bloom;
Or Genii twine beneath the deep
   Their coral tomb.

329

But strew his ashes to the wind
Whose sword or voice has served mankind;
And is he dead, whose glorious mind
　　Lifts thine on high?
To live in hearts we leave behind
　　Is not to die.

Is't death to fall for Freedom's right?
He's dead alone that lacks her light!
And murder sullies in heaven's sight
　　The sword he draws:
What can alone ennoble fight?
　　A noble cause!

Give that—and welcome War to brace
Her drums, and rend heaven's reeking space!
The colors planted face to face,
　　The charging cheer,
Thou Death's pale horse lead on the chase,
　　Shall still be dear.

And place our trophies where men kneel
To Heaven!—but Heaven rebukes my zeal!
The cause of Truth and human weal,
　　O God above!
Transfer it from the sword's appeal
　　To Peace and Love.

Peace, Love! the cherubim, that join
Their spread wings o'er Devotion's shrine—
Prayers sound in vain, and temples shine,
　　Where they are not;
The heart alone can make divine
　　Religion's spot.

To incantations dost thou trust,
And pompous rites in domes august?
See mouldering stones and metal's rust
　　Belie the vaunt,
That man can bless one pile of dust
　　With chime or chant.

The ticking wood-worm mocks thee, man!
Thy temples,—creeds themselves grow wan!

But there's a dome of nobler span,
  A temple given
Thy faith, that bigots dare not ban—
  Its space is heaven!

Its roof, star-pictured Nature's ceiling,
Where, trancing the rapt spirit's feeling,
And God himself to man revealing,
  The harmonious spheres
Make music, though unheard their pealing
  By mortal ears.

Fair stars! are not your beings pure?
Can sin, can death, your worlds obscure?
Else why so swell the thoughts at your
  Aspect above?
Ye must be heavens that make us sure
  Of heavenly love!

And in your harmony sublime
I read the doom of distant time;
That man's regenerate soul from crime
  Shall yet be drawn,
And reason on his mortal clime
  Immortal dawn.

What's hallowed ground? 'Tis what gives birth
To sacred thoughts in souls of worth!
Peace! Independence! Truth! go forth
  Earth's compass round;
And your high priesthood shall make earth
  All hallowed ground.

THOMAS CAMPBELL.

THE CHILD ON THE JUDGMENT SEAT

Where hast been toiling all day, sweetheart,
  That thy brow is burdened and sad?
The Master's work may make weary feet,
  But it leaves the spirit glad.

331

Was thy garden nipped with the midnight frost,
  Or scorched with the midday glare?
Were thy vines laid low, or thy lilies crushed,
  That thy face is so full of care?

"No pleasant garden toils were mine!
  I have sat on the judgment seat,
Where the Master sits at eve, and calls
  The children around his feet."

How camest thou on the judgment seat,
  Sweetheart? Who set thee there?
'Tis a lonely and lofty seat for thee,
  And well might fill thee with care.

"I climbed on the judgment seat myself;
  I have sat there alone all day;
For it grieved me to see the children around
  Idling their life away.

"They wasted the Master's precious seed,
  They wasted the precious hours;
They trained not the vines, nor gathered the fruits,
  And they trampled the sweet, meek flowers."

And what hast thou done in the judgment seat,
  Sweetheart? What didst thou there?
Would the idlers heed thy childish voice?
  Did the garden mend by thy care?

"Nay, that grieved me more! I called and I cried,
  But they left me there forlorn;
My voice was weak, and they heeded not,
  Or they laughed my words to scorn."

Ah, the judgment seat was not for thee!
  The servants were not thine!
And the Eyes which adjudge the praise and the blame,
  See further than thine or mine.

The Voice that shall sound there at eve, sweetheart,
  Will not raise its tones to be heard:
It will hush the earth, and hush the hearts,
  And none will resist its word.

"Should I see the Master's treasures lost,
 The stores that should feed his poor,
And not lift my voice, be it weak as it may,
 And not be grieved sore?"

Wait till the evening falls, sweetheart,
 Wait till the evening falls;
The Master is near, and knoweth all:
 Wait till the Master calls.

But how fared thy garden plot, sweetheart,
 Whilst thou sat's on the judgment seat?
Who watered thy roses, and trained thy vines,
 And kept them from careless feet?

"Nay, that is saddest of all to me!
 That is saddest of all!
My vines are trailing, my roses are parched,
 My lilies droop and fall."

Go back to thy garden plot, sweetheart,
 Go back till the evening falls;
And bind thy lilies, and train thy vines,
 Till for thee the Master calls.

Go make thy garden fair as thou canst—
 Thou workest never alone;
Perchance he whose plot is next to thine
 Will see it, and mend his own.

And the next may copy his, sweetheart,
 Till all grows fair and sweet;
And, when the Master comes at eve,
 Happy faces his coming will greet.

Then shall thy joy be full, sweetheart,
 In the garden so fair to see,
In the Master's words of praise for all,
 In a look of his own for thee.

ELIZABETH RUNDLE CHARLES.

THE TAPESTRY WEAVER

LET US TAKE to our heart a lesson, no braver lesson can be,
From the ways of the tapestry weavers, on the other side of the sea.
Above their head the pattern hangs, they study it with care,
And as to and fro the shuttle leaps their eyes are fastened there.
They tell this curious thing besides, of the patient, plodding weaver;
He works on the wrong side evermore, but works for the right side
    ever.
It is only when the weaving stops, and the web is loosed and turned,
That he sees his real handiwork, that his marvelous skill is learned.
Ah, the sight of its delicate beauty! It pays him for all its cost.
No rarer, daintier work than his was ever done by the frost!
Then the Master bringeth him golden hire and giveth him praise as
    well,
And how happy the heart of the weaver is, no tongue but his can tell.

The years of man are the looms of God, let down from the place of the
    sun,
Wherein we all are weaving, till the mystic web is done,
Weaving blindly but weaving surely, each for himself his fate;
We may not see how the right side looks, we can only weave and wait.
But, looking above for the pattern, no weaver hath need to fear;
Only let him look clear into Heaven—the perfect Pattern is there.
If he keeps the face of the Saviour forever and always in sight,
His toil shall be sweeter than honey, and his weaving is sure to be right.
And when his task is ended, and the web is turned and shown,
He shall hear the voice of the Master; it shall say to him, "Well done!"
And the white-winged angels of heaven, to bear him thence shall come
    down,
And God shall give him gold for his hire—not coin, but a crown!

ANSON G. CHESTER.

NO SECTS IN HEAVEN

TALKING OF SECTS quite late one eve,
What one and another of saints believe,
That night I stood in a troubled dream
By the side of a darkly flowing stream.

And a "churchman" down to the river came,
When I heard a strange voice call his name,—

"Good Father, stop; when you cross this tide
You must leave your robes on the other side."

But the aged father did not mind,
And his long gown floated out behind
As down to the stream his way he took,
His hands firm hold of a gilt-edged book.

"I'm bound for heaven, and when I'm there
I shall want my book of Common Prayer;
And though I put on a starry crown,
I should feel quite lost without my gown."

Then he fixed his eye on the shining track,
But his gown was heavy and held him back,
And the poor old father tried in vain.
A single step in the flood to gain.

I saw him again on the other side,
But his silk gown floated on the tide,
And no one asked in that blissful spot
If he belonged to "the church" or not.

Then down to the river a Quaker strayed;
His dress of a sober hue was made;
"My hat and coat must be all of gray,
I cannot go any other way."

Then he buttoned his coat straight up to his chin,
And staidly, solemnly, waded in,
And his broad-brimmed hat he pulled down tight
Over his forehead, so cold and white.

But a strong wind carried away his hat,
And he sighed a few moments over that;
And then, as he gazed to the farther shore,
The coat slipped off and was seen no more.

Poor, dying Quaker, thy suit of gray
Is quietly sailing—away—away;
But thou'lt go to heaven, as straight as an arrow,
Whether thy brim be broad or narrow.

Next came Dr. Watts with a bundle of psalms
Tied nicely up in his aged arms,

335

And hymns as many, a very wise thing,
That the people in heaven, "all round," might sing.

But I thought that he heaved an anxious sigh
As he saw that the river ran broad and high,
And looked rather surprised, as one by one,
The psalms and hymns in the wave went down.

And after him, with his MSS.,
Came Wesley, the pattern of godliness,
But he cried, "Dear me, what shall I do?
The water has soaked them through and through."

And there, on the river, far and wide,
Away they went on the swollen tide;
And the saint, astonished, passed through alone,
Without his manuscripts, up to the throne.

Then gravely walking, two saints by name,
Down to the stream together came;
But, as they stopped at the river's brink,
I saw one saint from the other shrink.

"Sprinkled or plunged—may I ask you, friend,
How you attained to life's great end?"
"*Thus,* with a few drops on my brow";
"But I have been *dipped,* as you'll see me now.

"And I really think it will hardly do,
As I'm 'close communion,' to cross with you:
You're bound, I know, to the realms of bliss,
But you must go that way, and I'll go this."

And straightway plunging with all his might,
Away to the left—his friend to the right,
Apart they went from this world of sin;
But how did the brethren "enter in"?

And now where the river was rolling on,
A Presbyterian church went down;
Of women, there seemed an innumerable throng,
But the men I could count as they passed along.

And concerning the road they could never agree,
The *old* or the *new* way, which it could be,

Nor ever a moment pause to think
That both would lead to the river's brink.
And a sound of murmuring long and loud
Came ever up from the moving crowd—
"You're in the old way and I'm in the new,
That is the false, and this is the true";
Or, "I'm in the old way, and you're in the new
That is the false, and *this* is the true."

But the brethren only seemed to speak;
Modest the sisters walked, and meek;
And if ever one of them chanced to say
What troubles she met with on the way,
How she longed to pass to the other side,
Nor feared to cross over the swelling tide,
A voice arose from the brethren then,—
"Let no one speak but the 'holy men,'
For have ye not heard the words of Paul?
'Oh let the women keep silence all.'"

I watched them long in my curious dream,
Till they stood by the border of the stream;
Then, just as I thought, the two ways met,
But all the brethren were talking yet,
And would talk on, till the heaving tide
Carried them over, side by side;
Side by side, for the way was one,
The toilsome journey of life was done,
And priest and Quaker, and all who died
Came out alike on the other side;
No forms or crosses or books had they,
No gowns of silk or suits of gray,
No creeds to guide them, or MSS.,
For all had put on "Christ's righteousness."

ELIZABETH H. JOCELYN CLEAVELAND.

THE PRESENT AGE

WE ARE LIVING, we are dwelling,
    In a grand and awful time,
In an age on ages telling
    To be living is sublime.

Hark! the waking up of nations,
  Gog and Magog to the fray.
Hark! what soundeth is creation
  Groaning for its latter day.

Will ye play then, will ye dally
  With your music and your wine?
Up! it is Jehovah's rally!
  God's own arm hath need of thine.
Hark! the onset! will ye fold your
  Faith-clad arms in lazy lock?
Up, oh up, thou drowsy soldier!
  Worlds are charging to the shock.

Worlds are charging—heaven beholding;
  Thou hast but an hour to fight;
Now the blazoned cross unfolding,
  On—right onward for the right.
On! let all the soul within you
  For the truth's sake go abroad!
Strike! let every nerve and sinew
  Tell on ages—tell for God.

                    ARTHUR CLEVELAND COXE.

THROUGH THE YEAR

GOD BE WITH YOU in the Springtime
  When the violets unfold,
And the butterups and cowslips
  Fill the fields with yellow gold;
In the time of apple blossoms,
  When the happy bluebirds sing,
Filling all the world with gladness—
  God be with you in the Spring!

God be with you in the Summer,
  When the sweet June roses blow,
When the bobolinks are laughing
  And the brooks with music flow;
When the fields are white with daisies
  And the days are glad and long—
God be with you in the Summer,
  Filling all your world with song.

God be with you in the Autumn,
   When the birds and flowers have fled,
And along the woodland pathways
   Leaves are falling, gold and red;
When the Summer lies behind you,
   In the evening of the year—
God be with you in the Autumn,
   Then to fill your heart with cheer.

God be with you in the Winter,
   When the snow lies deep and white,
When the sleeping fields are silent
   And the stars gleam cold and bright.
When the hand and heart are tired
   With life's long and weary quest—
God be with you in the Winter,
   Just to guide you into rest.

JULIAN S. CUTLER.

THE PREACHER'S MISTAKE

THE PARISH PRIEST
Of austerity,
Climbed up in a high church steeple
To be nearer God,
So that he might hand
His word down to His people.

When the sun was high,
When the sun was low,
The good man sat unheeding
Sublunary things.
From transcendency
Was he forever reading.

And now and again
When he heard the creak
Of the weather vane a-turning,
He closed his eyes
And said, "Of a truth
From God I now am learning."

339

And in sermon script
He daily wrote
What he thought was sent from heaven,
And he dropped this down
On his people's heads
Two times one day in seven.

In his age God said,
"Come down and die!"
And he cried out from the steeple,
"Where art thou, Lord?"
And the Lord replied,
"Down here among my people."

WILLIAM CROSWELL DOANE.

LIFE SCULPTURE

CHISEL IN HAND stood a sculptor boy
   With his marble block before him,
And his eyes lit up with a smile of joy,
   As an angel dream passed o'er him.

He carved the dream on that shapeless stone,
   With many a sharp incision;
With Heaven's own light the sculptor shone—
   He'd caught that angel vision.

Children of life are we, as we stand
   With our lives uncarved before us,
Waiting the hour when, at God's command,
   Our life dream shall pass o'er us.

If we carve it then on the yielding stone,
   With many a sharp incision,
It's heavenly beauty shall be our own,
   Our lives that angel vision.

WILLIAM CROSWELL DOANE.

THE CHEMISTRY OF CHARACTER

JOHN AND PETER and Robert and Paul,
  God in His wisdom created them all.
John was a statesman and Peter a slave,
  Robert a preacher and Paul was a knave.
Evil or good as the case might be,
  White or colored or bond or free,
John and Peter and Robert and Paul—
  God in His wisdom created them all.

Out of earth's elements mingled with flame,
  Out of life's compounds of glory and shame,
Fashioned and shaped by no will of their own,
  And helplessly into life's history thrown;
Born by the law that compels men to be
  Born to conditions they could not foresee,
John and Peter and Robert and Paul—
  God in His wisdom created them all.

John was the head and the heart of his state,
  Was trusted and honored, was noble and great;
Peter was made 'neath life's burdens to groan,
  And never once dreamed that his soul was his own.
Robert great glory and honor received
  For zealously preaching what no one believed,
While Paul of the pleasures of sin took his fill,
  And gave up his life to the service of ill.

It chanced that these men in passing away
  From earth and its conflicts, all died the same day.
John was mourned through the length and breadth of the land;
  Peter fell 'neath the lash of a merciless hand.
Robert died with the praise of the Lord on his tongue,
  While Paul was convicted of murder and hung.
John and Peter and Robert and Paul—
  God in His wisdom created them all.

Men said of the statesman, how noble and brave,
  But of Peter, alas, he was only a slave;
Of Robert, 'tis well with his soul, it is well,
  While Paul they consigned to the torments of hell.

Born by one law through all nature the same.
  What made them differ, and who was to blame?
John and Peter and Robert and Paul—
  God in His wisdom created them all.

Out in the region of infinite light,
  Where the soul of the black man is pure as the white,
Out where the spirit, through sorrow made wise,
  No longer resorts to deception and lies,
Out where the flesh can no longer control
  The freedom and faith of the God-given soul—
Who shall determine what change shall befall
  John and Peter and Robert and Paul?

John may in goodness and wisdom increase,
  Peter rejoice in infinite peace;
Robert may learn that the truths of the Lord
  Are more in the spirit and less in the word;
And Paul may be blessed with a holier birth
  Than the passions of men had allowed him on earth.
John and Peter and Robert and Paul—
  God in His wisdom created them all.

ELIZABETH DORNEY.

THE CHRISTIAN'S "GOOD-NIGHT"

SLEEP ON, beloved, sleep, and take thy rest;
Lay down thy head upon thy Saviour's breast;
We love thee well, but Jesus loves thee best—
Good-night! Good-night! Good-night!

Calm is thy slumber as an infant's sleep,
But thou shalt wake no more to toil and weep;
Thine is a perfect rest, secure and deep—
Good-night! Good-night! Good-night!

Until the shadows from this earth are cast;
Until He gathers in His sheaves at last;
Until the twilight gloom be overpast—
Good-night! Good-night! Good-night!

Until the Easter glory lights the skies;
Until the dead in Jesus shall arise,
And He shall come, but not in lowly guise—
Good-night! Good-night! Good-night!

Until made beautiful by Love Divine,
Thou, in the likeness of thy Lord shalt shine,
And He shall bring that golden crown of thine—
Good-night! Good-night! Good-night!

Only "Good-night," beloved—not "Farewell!"
A little while, and all His saints shall dwell
In hallowed union, indivisible—
Good-night! Good-night! Good-night!

Until we meet again before His throne,
Clothed in the spotless robe He gives His own;
Until we know even as we are known—
Good-night! Good-night! Good-night!

SARAH DOUDNEY.

THE WATER MILL

LISTEN to the water mill,
  Through the livelong day;
How the clicking of the wheel
  Wears the hours away.
Languidly the autumn wind
  Stirs the withered leaves;
On the field the reapers sing,
  Binding up the sheaves;
And a proverb haunts my mind,
  And as a spell is cast,
"The mill will never grind
  With the water that has passed."

Autumn winds revive no more
  Leaves strewn o'er earth and main.
The sickle never more shall reap
  The yellow, garnered grain;

And the rippling stream flows on
  Tranquil, deep and still,
Never gliding back again
  To the water mill.
Truly speaks the proverb old,
  With a meaning vast:
"The mill will never grind
  With the water that has passed."

Take the lesson to thyself,
  Loving heart and true;
Golden years are fleeting by,
  Youth is passing, too.
Learn to make the most of life,
  Lose no happy day!
Time will ne'er return again—
  Sweet chances thrown away.
Leave no tender word unsaid,
  But love while love shall last:
"The mill will never grind
  With the water that has passed."

Work, while yet the sun does shine,
  Men of strength and will!
Never does the streamlet glide
  Useless by the mill.
Wait not till tomorrow's sun
  Beams brightly on thy way;
All that thou canst call thine own
  Lies in this word: "Today!"
Power, intellect and health
  Will not always last:
"The mill will never grind
  With the water that has passed."

O, the wasted hours of life
  That have swiftly drifted by!
O, the good we might have done!
  Gone, lost without a sigh!
Love that we might once have saved
  By a single kindly word;
Thoughts conceived, but ne'er expressed,
  Perishing unpenned, unheard!

Take the proverb to thy soul!
　　Take, and clasp it fast:
"The mill will never grind
　　With the water that has passed."

O, love thy God and fellow man,
　　Thyself consider last;
For come it will when thou must scan
　　Dark errors of the past.
And when the fight of life is o'er
　　And earth recedes from view.
And heaven in all its glory shines.
　　'Midst the good, the pure, the true,
Then you will see more clearly
　　The proverb, deep and vast:
"The mill will never grind
　　With the water that has passed."

SARAH DOUDNEY.

THE CHURCH WALKING WITH THE WORLD

THE CHURCH AND THE WORLD walked far apart
　　On the changing shores of time,
The World was singing a giddy song,
　　And the Church a hymn sublime.
"Come, give me your hand," said the merry World,
　　"And walk with me this way!"
But the good Church hid her snowy hands
　　And solemnly answered "Nay,
I will not give you my hand at all,
　　And I will not walk with you;
Your way is the way that leads to death;
　　Your words are all untrue."

"Nay, walk with me but a little space,"
　　Said the World with a kindly air;
"The road I walk is a pleasant road,
　　And the sun shines always there;
Your path is thorny and rough and rude,
　　But mine is broad and plain;
My way is paved with flowers and dews,
　　And yours with tears and pain;

345

The sky to me is always blue,
  No want, no toil I know;
The sky above you is always dark,
  Your lot is a lot of woe;
There's room enough for you and me
  To travel side by side."

Half shyly the Church approached the World
  And gave him her hand of snow;
And the old World grasped it and walked along,
  Saying, in accents low,
"Your dress is too simple to please my taste;
  I will give you pearls to wear,
Rich velvets and silks for your graceful form,
  And diamonds to deck your hair."
The Church looked down at her plain white robes,
  And then at the dazzling World,
And blushed as she saw his handsome lip
  With a smile contemptuous curled.
"I will change my dress for a costlier one,"
  Said the Church, with a smile of grace;
Then her pure white garments drifted away,
  And the World gave, in their place,
Beautiful satins and shining silks,
  Roses and gems and costly pearls;
While over her forehead her bright hair fell
  Crisped in a thousand curls.

"Your house is too plain," said the proud old World,
  "I'll build you one like mine;
With walls of marble and towers of gold,
  And furniture ever so fine."
So he built her a costly and beautiful house;
  Most splendid it was to behold;
Her sons and her beautiful daughters dwelt there
  Gleaming in purple and gold;
Rich fairs and shows in the halls were held,
  And the World and his children were there.
Laughter and music and feasts were heard
  In the place that was meant for prayer.
There were cushioned seats for the rich and the gay,
  To sit in their pomp and pride;
But the poor who were clad in shabby array,
  Sat meekly down outside.

"You give too much to the poor," said the World.
  "Far more than you ought to do;
If they are in need of shelter and food,
  Why need it trouble you?
Go, take your money and buy rich robes,
  Buy horses and carriages fine;
Buy pearls and jewels and dainty food,
  Buy the rarest and costliest wine;
My children, they dote on all these things,
  And if you their love would win
You must do as they do, and walk in the ways
  That they are walking in."

So the poor were turned from her door in scorn,
  And she heard not the orphan's cry;
But she drew her beautiful robes aside,
  As the widows went weeping by.

Then the sons of the World and the Sons of the Church
  Walked closely hand and heart,
And only the Master, who knoweth all,
  Could tell the two apart.
Then the Church sat down at her ease, and said,
  "I am rich and my goods increase;
I have need of nothing, or aught to do,
  But to laugh, and dance, and feast."
The sly World heard, and he laughed in his sleeve,
  And mockingly said, aside—
"The Church is fallen, the beautiful Church;
  And her shame is her boast and her pride."

The angel drew near to the mercy seat,
  And whispered in sighs her name;
Then the loud anthems of rapture were hushed,
  And heads were covered with shame;
And a voice was heard at last by the Church
  From Him who sat on the throne,
"I know thy works, and how thou hast said,
  'I am rich, and hast not known
That thou art naked, poor and blind,
  And wretched before my face;'
Therefore from my presence cast I thee out,
  And blot thy name from its place."

MATILDA C. EDWARDS.

347

NOW THE LABORER'S TASK IS O'ER

Now THE LABORER'S TASK is o'er;
  Now the battle day is past;
Now upon the farther shore
  Lands the voyager at last.
Father, in Thy gracious keeping
Leave we now Thy servant sleeping.

There the tears of earth are dried;
  There its hidden things are clear;
There the work of life is tried
  By a juster judge than here.
Father, in Thy gracious keeping
Leave we now Thy servant sleeping.

There the penitents that turn
  To the cross their dying eyes,
All the love of Jesus learn
  At His feet in Paradise.
Father, in Thy gracious keeping
Leave we now Thy servant sleeping.

There no more the powers of hell
  Can prevail to mar their peace;
Christ the Lord shall guard them well,
  He who died for their release.
Father, in Thy gracious keeping
Leave we now Thy servant sleeping.

"Earth to earth, and dust to dust,"
  Calmly now the words we say;
Left behind, we wait in trust
  For the resurrection day.
Father, in Thy gracious keeping
Leave we now Thy servant sleeping.

JOHN LODGE ELLERTON.

WHEN WILT THOU SAVE THE PEOPLE?

WHEN WILT THOU save the people?
    O God of mercy, when?
Not kings and lords, but nations!
    Not thrones and crowns, but men!
Flowers of Thy heart, O God, are they;
Let them not pass, like weeds, away,
Their heritage, a sunless day.
    God, save the people.

Shall crime bring crime forever,
    Strength aiding still the strong?
Is it Thy will, O Father,
    That man shall toil for wrong?
No, say Thy mountains; No, Thy skies;
Man's clouded sun shall brightly rise,
And songs ascend, instead of sighs.
    God, save the people!

When wilt Thou save the people?
    O God of mercy, when?
The people, Lord, the people,
    Not thrones and crowns, but men!
God, save the people, Thine they are,
Thy children as Thine angels fair.
From vice, oppression, and despair,
    God, save the people!

                    EBENEZER ELLIOTT.

MY CHURCH

MY CHURCH has but one temple,
    Wide as the world is wide,
Set with a million stars,
    Where a million hearts abide.

My church has no creed to bar
    A single brother man
But says, "Come thou and worship"
    To every one who can.

349

My church has no roof nor walls,
　　Nor floors save the beautiful sod—
For fear, I would seem to limit
　　The love of the illimitable God.

UNKNOWN. SIGNED E. O. G.

AT THE PLACE OF THE SEA

Exodus 14

HAVE YOU COME to the Red Sea place in your life,
　　Where, in spite of all you can do,
There is no way out, there is no way back,
　　There is no other way but through?
Then wait on the Lord, with a trust serene,
　　Till the night of your fear is gone;
He will send the winds, He will heap the floods,
　　When He says to your soul, "Go on!"

And His hand shall lead you through, clear through,
　　Ere the watery walls roll down;
No wave can touch you, no foe can smite,
　　No mightiest sea can drown.
The tossing billows may rear their crests,
　　Their foam at your feet may break,
But over their bed you shall walk dry-shod
　　In the path that your Lord shall make.

In the morning watch, 'neath the lifted cloud,
　　You shall see but the Lord alone,
When He leads you forth from the place of the sea,
　　To a land that you have not known;
And your fears shall pass as your foes have passed,
　　You shall no more be afraid;
You shall sing His praise in a better place,
　　In a place that His hand hath made.

ANNIE JOHNSON FLINT.

A HUNDRED YEARS FROM NOW

THE SURGING SEA of human life forever onward rolls,
And bears to the eternal shore its daily freight of souls;
Though bravely sails our bark today, pale Death sits at the prow,
And few shall know we ever lived a hundred years from now.

O mighty human brotherhood! Why fiercely war and strive,
While God's great world has ample space for everything alive?
Broad fields uncultured and unclaimed are waiting for the plow
Of progress that shall make them bloom a hundred years from now

Why should we try so earnestly in life's short, narrow span,
On golden stairs to climb so high above our brother man?
Why blindly at an earthly shrine in slavish homage bow?
Our gold will rust, ourselves be dust, a hundred years from now.

Why prize so much the world's applause? Why dread so much its
blame?
A fleeting echo is its voice of censure or of fame;
The praise that thrills the heart, the scorn that dyes with shame the
brow,
Will be as long-forgotten dreams a hundred years from now.

O patient hearts, that meekly bear your weary load of wrong!
O earnest hearts, that bravely dare, and striving, grow more strong!
Press on till perfect peace is won; you'll never dream of how
You struggled o'er life's thorny road a hundred years from now.

Grand, lofty souls, who live and toil that freedom, right and truth
Alone may rule the universe, for you is endless youth.
When 'mid the blest with God you rest, the grateful land shall bow
Above your clay in reverent love a hundred years from now.

Earth's empires rise and fall. Time! like breakers on thy shore
They rush upon thy rocks of doom, go down, and are no more.
The starry wilderness of worlds that gem night's radiant brow
Will light the skies for other eyes a hundred years from now.

Our Father, to whose sleepless eye the past and future stand
An open page, like babes we cling to Thy protecting hand;
Change, sorrow, death, are naught to us, if we may safely bow
Beneath the shadow of Thy throne a hundred years from now.

MARY A. FORD.

IN A HUNDRED YEARS

It will be all the same in a hundred years—
What a spell-word to conjure up smiles and tears!
How oft do I muse, 'mid the thoughtless and gay,
On the marvelous truth that these words convey!

351

And can it be so? Must the valiant and free
Hold their tenure of life on this frail decree?
Are the trophies they've reared and the glories they've won
Only castles of frost-work confronting the sun?
And must all that's as joyous and brilliant to view
As a midsummer dream be as perishing too?
Then have pity, ye proud ones; be gentle, ye great.
O remember how mercy beseemeth your state;
For the rust that consumeth the sword of the brave,
Eats, too, at the chain of the manacled slave;
And the conqueror's frowns and his victim's tears
Will be all the same in a hundred years.

How dark are your fortunes, ye sons of the soil,
Whose heirloom is sorrow, whose birthright is toil!
Yet envy not those who have glory and gold
By the sweat of the poor and the blood of the bold:
For 'tis coming—howe'er they may flaunt in their pride—
The day when they'll molder to dust by your side.
For Time, as he speeds on invisible wings,
Disenamels and withers earth's costliest things.
And the knight's white plume, and the shepherd's crook,
And the minstrel's pipe, and the scholar's book,
And the emperor's crown, and his Cossacks' spears,
Will be dust alike in a hundred years.

Then what meaneth the chase after phantom joys,
And the breaking of human hearts for toys,
And the veteran's pride in his crafty schemes,
And the passion of youth for its darling dreams,
And the aiming at ends we never can span,
And the deadly aversion of man for man?
To what end is this conflict of hopes and fears,
If 'tis all the same in a hundred years?

Ah, 'tis not the same in a hundred years,
How clear soever that motto appears;
For know ye not that beyond the grave,
Far, far beyond where the cedars wave
On the Syrian mountains, and where the stars
Come glittering forth in their golden cars,
There bloometh a land of perennial bliss,
Where we smile to think of the tears in this?
And the pilgrim reaching that radiant shore
Hath the thought of death in his heart no more.

But layeth his staff and sandals down
For the victor's wreath and the angel's crown:
And the mother meets in that tranquil sphere
The delightful child she had wept for here:
And the warrior's sword, who protects the right,
Is bejeweled with stars of undying light;
And we quaff of the same immortal cup,
While the orphan smiles, and the slave looks up.
Then be glad, my heart, and forget thy tears;
For 'tis NOT the same in a hundred years!

ATTRIBUTED TO ELIZABETH DOTEN.

EVENING CONTEMPLATION.

SOFTLY now the light of day
Fades upon my sight away;
Free from care, from labor free,
Lord, I would commune with Thee.

Thou, whose all-pervading eye
  Naught escapes, without, within!
Pardon each infirmity,
  Open fault, and secret sin.

Soon for me the light of day
Shall for ever pass away;
Then, from sin and sorrow free,
Take me, Lord, to dwell with Thee.

Thou who, sinless, yet hast known
  All of man's infirmity!
Then, from Thine eternal throne,
  Jesus, look with pitying eye.

GEORGE WASHINGTON DOANE.

CHRIST AND THE LITTLE ONES

"THE MASTER has come over Jordan,"
  Said Hannah the mother one day;
"He is healing the people who throng Him,
  With a touch of His finger, they say.

353

"And now I shall carry the children,
  Little Rachel and Samuel and John,
I shall carry the baby Esther,
  For the Lord to look upon."

The father looked at her kindly,
  But he shook his head and smiled:
"Now who but a doting mother
  Would think of a thing so wild?

"If the children were tortured by demons,
  Or dying of fever, 'twere well;
Or had they the taint of the leper,
  Like many in Israel."

"Nay, do not hinder me, Nathan,
  I feel such a burden of care;
If I carry it to the Master,
  Perhaps I shall leave it there.

"If He lay His hand on the children,
  My heart will be lighter, I know,
For a blessing for ever and ever
  Will follow them as they go."

So over the hills of Judah,
  Along by the vine rows green,
With Esther asleep on her bosom,
  And Rachel her brothers between;

'Mid the people who hung on His teaching,
  Or waited His touch and His word,
Through the row of proud Pharisees listening
  She pressed to the feet of the Lord.

"Now why shouldst thou hinder the Master,"
  Said Peter, "with children like these?
Seest not how from morning to evening
  He teacheth and healeth disease?"

Then Christ said, "Forbid not the children,
  Permit them to come unto me!"
And He took in His arms little Esther,
  And Rachel He sat on His knee:

354

And the heavy heart of the mother
   Was lifted all earth care above,
As He laid His hand on the brothers,
   And blest them with holiest love;

As He said of the babes in His bosom,
   "Of such are the kingdom of Heaven"—
And strength for all duty and trial
   That hour to her spirit were given.

JULIA GILL.

THE ALOE PLANT

HAVE YOU HEARD the tale of the aloe plant,
   Away in the sunny clime?
By humble growth of a hundred years
   It reaches its blooming time;
And then a wondrous bud at its crown
   Breaks into a thousand flowers;
This floral queen in its blooming seen
   Is the pride of the tropical bowers;
But the plant to the flower is a sacrifice,
For it blooms but once, and in blooming dies.

Have you heard the tale of the pelican,
   The Arab's Gomel el Bahr,
That dwells in the African solitudes
   Where the birds that live lonely are?
Have you heard how it loves its tender young,
   And cares and toils for their good?
It brings them water from fountains afar
   And fishes the seas for their food.
In famine it feeds them what love can devise—
The blood of its bosom—and, feeding them, dies.

Have you heard the tale they tell of the swan,
   The snow-white bird of the lake?
It noiselessly floats on the silvery wave,
   It silently sits in the brake;
For it saves its song till the end of life,
   And then, in the soft, still even,
'Mid the golden light of the setting sun
   It sings as it soars into heaven,

355

And the blessed notes fall back from the skies—
'Tis its only song, for in singing it dies.

You have heard the tales. Shall I tell you one,
    A greater and better than all?
Have you heard of Him whom the Heavens adore,
    Before whom the hosts of them fall?
How He left the choirs and anthems above
    For earth in its wailings and woes,
And suffered the shame and pain of the cross
    To die for the life of His foes.
His death is our life, His loss is our gain—
The joy for the tear—the peace for the pain.

DR. HENRY HARBAUGH.

BATTLE-HYMN OF THE REPUBLIC

MINE EYES have seen the glory of the coming of the Lord:
He is trampling out the vintage where the grapes of wrath are stored;
He hath loosed the fateful lightning of his terrible swift sword:
    His truth is marching on.

I have seen him in the watch-fires of a hundred circling camps;
They have builded him an altar in the evening dews and damps;
I can read his righteous sentence by the dim and flaring lamps:
    His day is marching on.

I have read a fiery gospel, writ in burnished rows of steel:
"As ye deal with my contemners, so with you my grace shall deal;
Let the Hero, born of woman, crush the serpent with his heel,
    Since God is marching on."

He has sounded forth the trumpet that shall never call retreat;
He is sifting out the hearts of men before his judgment-seat:
O, be swift, my soul, to answer him! be jubilant, my feet!
    Our God is marching on.

In the beauty of the lilies Christ was born across the sea,
With a glory in his bosom that transfigures you and me;
As he died to make men holy, let us die to make men free,
    While God is marching on.

JULIA WARD HOWE.

[A sixth stanza, as follows, was written by the author, but is seldom quoted.]

He is coming like the glory of the morning on the wave,
He is wisdom to the mighty, he is honor to the brave,
So the world shall be his footstool, and the soul of wrong his slave.
Our God is marching on!

ONLY WAITING

ONLY WAITING till the shadows
Are a little longer grown;
Only waiting till the glimmer
Of the day's last beam is flown;
Till the night of earth is faded
From this heart once full of day,
Till the dawn of Heaven is breaking
Through the twilight soft and gray.

Only waiting till the reapers
Have the last sheaf gathered home,
For the summer time hath faded
And the autumn winds are come.
Quickly, reapers, gather quickly
The last ripe hours of my heart,
For the bloom of life is withered,
And I hasten to depart.

Only waiting till the angels
Open wide the mystic gate,
At whose feet I long have lingered,
Weary, poor and desolate.
Even now I hear their footsteps
And their voices far away;
If they call me I am waiting,
Only waiting to obey.

Only waiting till the shadows
Are a little longer grown;
Only waiting till the glimmer
Of the day's last beam is flown;
Then from out the folded darkness
Holy, deathless stars shall rise,
By whose light my soul will gladly
Wing her passage to the skies.

MRS. FRANCES LAUGHTON MACE

HOW FAR TO BETHLEHEM?

"How FAR is it to Bethlehem Town?"
Just over Jerusalem hills adown,
Past lovely Rachel's white-domed tomb—
Sweet shrine of motherhood's young doom.

"It isn't far to Bethlehem Town—
Just over the dusty roads adown,
Past Wise Men's well, still offering
Cool draughts from welcome wayside spring;
Past shepherds with their flutes of reed
That charm the woolly sheep they lead;
Past boys with kites on hilltops flying,
And soon you're there where Bethlehem's lying.
Sunned white and sweet on olived slopes,
Gold-lighted still with Judah's hopes.

"And so we find the Shepherd's field
And plain that gave rich Boaz yield,
And look where Herod's villa stood.
We thrill that earthly parenthood
Could foster Christ who was all-good;
And thrill that Bethlehem Town to-day
Looks down on Christmas homes that pray.

"It isn't far to Bethlehem Town!
It's anywhere that Christ comes down
And finds in people's friendly face
A welcome and abiding place.
The road to Bethlehem runs right through
The homes of folks like me and you."

MADELEINE SWEENY MILLER.

AD COELUM

AT THE MUEZZIN'S CALL for prayer,
The kneeling faithful thronged the square,
And on Pushkara's lofty height
The dark priest chanted Brahma's might.
Amid a monastery's weeds
An old Franciscan told his beads,

While to the synagogue there came
A Jew, to praise Jehovah's name.
The one great God looked down and smiled
And counted each his loving child;
For Turk and Brahmin, monk and Jew
Had reached Him through the gods they knew.

HARRY ROMAINE.

UP-HILL

DOES THE ROAD wind up-hill all the way?
   Yes, to the very end.
Will the day's journey take the whole long day?
   From morn to night, my friend.

But is there for the night a resting-place?
   A roof for when the slow dark hours begin.
May not the darkness hide it from my face?
   You cannot miss that inn.

Shall I meet other wayfarers at night?
   Those who have gone before.
Then must I knock, or call when just in sight?
   They will not keep you standing at that door.

Shall I find comfort, travel-sore and weak?
   Of labour you shall find the sum.
Will there be beds for me and all who seek?
   Yea, beds for all who come.

CHRISTINA GEORGINA ROSSETTI.

YOUR CHURCH AND MINE

You GO to your church, and I'll go to mine,
But let's walk along together;
Our Father has built them side by side,
So let's walk along together.
The road is rough and the way is long,
But we'll help each other over;
You go to your church and I'll go to mine,
But let's walk along together.

You go to your church, and I'll go to mine,
But let's walk along together;
Our heavenly Father is the same,
So let's walk along together.
The chimes of your church ring loud and clear,
They chime with the chimes of my church;
You go to your church, and I'll go to mine,
But let's walk along together.

You go to your church, and I'll go to mine,
But let's walk along together;
Our heavenly Father loves us all,
So let's walk along together.
The Lord will be at my church today,
But He'll be at your church also;
You go to your church, and I'll go to mine,
But let's walk along together.

PHILLIPS H. LORD.

THE SIN OF OMISSION

It isn't the thing you do, dear,
It's the thing you leave undone
That gives you a bit of a heartache
At setting of the sun.
The tender word forgotten,
The letter you did not write,
The flowers you did not send, dear,
Are your haunting ghosts at night.

The stone you might have lifted
Out of a brother's way;
The bit of heartsome counsel
You were hurried too much to say;
The loving touch of the hand, dear,
The gentle, winning tone
Which you had no time nor thought for
With troubles enough of your own.

Those little acts of kindness
So easily out of mind,
Those chances to be angels
Which we poor mortals find—

They come in night and silence,
　　Each sad, reproachful wraith,
When hope is faint and flagging,
　　And a chill has fallen on faith.

For life is all too short, dear,
　　And sorrow is all too great,
To suffer our slow compassion
　　That tarries until too late;
And it isn't the thing you do, dear,
　　It's the thing you leave undone
Which gives you a bit of a heartache
　　At the setting of the sun.

MARGARET E. SANGSTER.

THE HANDWRITING ON THE WALL

AT THE FEAST of Belshazzar and a thousand of his lords,
While they drank from golden vessels, as the Book of Truth records,
In the night as they reveled in the royal palace hall,
They were seized with consternation—'twas the Hand upon the wall!

See the brave captive, Daniel, as he stood before the throng,
And rebuked the haughty monarch for his mighty deeds of wrong;
As he read out the writing—'twas the doom of one and all,
For the kingdom now was finished—said the Hand upon the wall!

See the faith, zeal and courage, that would dare to do the right,
Which the spirit gave to Daniel—this the secret of his might;
In his home in Judea, or a captive in the hall,
He understood the writing of his God upon the wall!

So our deeds are recorded—there's a Hand that's writing now:
Sinner, give your heart to Jesus, to His royal mandates bow;
For the day is approaching—it must come to one and all,
When the sinner's condemnation will be written on the wall!

Chorus:

'Tis the Hand of God on the wall! 'Tis the Hand of God on the wall!
Shall the record be "Found wanting!" or shall it be "Found trusting"
　　While the Hand is writing on the wall?

KNOWLES SHAW.

361

CONSCIENCE

I SAT ALONE with my conscience
  In a place where time had ceased,
And we talked of my former living
  In the land where the years increased;
And I felt I should have to answer
  The question it put to me,
And to face the answer and questions
  Through all eternity.

The ghosts of forgotten actions
  Came floating before my sight,
And things that I thought were dead things
  Were alive with terrible might.
And the vision of all my past life
  Was an awful thing to face,
Alone with my conscience sitting
  In that solemnly silent place.

And I thought of a faraway warning,
  Of a sorrow that was to be mine,
In a land that was then the future,
  But now is the present time.
And I thought of my former thinking
  Of the judgment day to be;
But sitting alone with my conscience
  Seemed judgment enough for me.

And I wondered if there was a future
  To this land beyond the grave;
But no one gave me an answer,
  And no one came to save.
Then I felt that the future was present,
  And the present would never go by,
For it was but the thought of my past life
  Growing into eternity.

Then I woke from my timely dreaming,
  And the vision passed away,
And I knew that the far-off seeming
  Was a warning of yesterday;

And I pray that I may not forget it,
  In this land before the grave,
That I may not cry in the future
  And no one come to save.

And so I have learned a lesson
  Which I ought to have known before,
And which, though I learned it dreaming,
  I hope to forget no more.
So I sit alone with my conscience
  In the place where the years increase,
And I try to remember the future
  In the land where time will cease.

And I know of the future Judgment,
  How dreadful soe'er it be,
That to sit alone with my conscience
  Will be judgment enough for me.

CHARLES WILLIAM STUBBS.

ROSES IN DECEMBER

GOD GAVE His children memory
That in life's garden there might be
June roses in December.
But sin the Father's goodness scorns,
And weaves of them a crown of thorns,
That wounds when they remember.

Sharp, stabbing points of vain regret
Around my soul forever set,
Turn June into December.
Ah, Christ, Who wore my crown of thorns,
Have mercy on the heart that mourns,
Forgive, when I remember.

REV. G. ANKETALL STUDDERT-KENNEDY

THE KNEELING CAMEL

THE CAMEL at the close of day
  Kneels down upon the sandy plain
To have his burden lifted off
  And rest again.

363

My soul, thou too shouldst to thy knees
  When daylight draweth to a close,
And let thy Master lift thy load,
  And grant repose.

Else how canst thou tomorrow meet,
  With all tomorrow's work to do,
If thou thy burden all the night
  Dost carry through?

The camel kneels at break of day
  To have his guide replace his load,
Then rises up anew to take
  The desert road.

So thou shouldst kneel at morning dawn
  That God may give thy daily care,
Assured that He no load too great
  Will make thee bear.

                    ANNA TEMPLE WHITNEY.

THE WINDS OF FATE

[This poem was written by Mrs. Wilcox on the steamer *Richard Peck* between New Haven and New York, following her husband's observation that one ship went west and another east in the same wind.]

ONE SHIP drives east and another drives west
  With the selfsame winds that blow.
    'Tis the set of the sails
    And not the gales
  Which tells us the way to go.

Like the winds of the sea are the ways of fate,
  As we voyage along through life:
    'Tis the set of a soul
    That decides its goal,
  And not the calm or the strife.

                    ELLA WHEELER WILCOX.

ENVOY TO THE TOILING OF FELIX

The legend of Felix is ended, the toiling of Felix is done;
The Master has paid him his wages, the goal of his journey is won;
He rests, but he never is idle; a thousand years pass like a day,
In the glad surprise of Paradise where work is sweeter than play.

Yet often the King of that country comes out from his tireless host,
And walks in this world of the weary as if He loved it the most;
For here in the dusty confusion, with eyes that are heavy and dim,
He meets again the labouring men who are looking and longing for
  Him.

He cancels the curse of Eden, and brings them a blessing instead:
Blessed are they that labour, for Jesus partakes of their bread.
He puts His hand to their burdens, He enters their homes at night:
Who does his best shall have as a guest the Master of life and light.

And courage will come with His presence, and patience return at His
  touch,
And manifold sins be forgiven to those who love Him much;
The cries of envy and anger will change to the songs of cheer,
The toiling age will forget its rage when the Prince of Peace draws
  near.

This is the gospel of labour, ring it, ye bells of the kirk!
The Lord of Love came down from above, to live with the men who
  work.
This is the rose that He planted, here in the the thorn-curst soil:
Heaven is blest with perfect rest, but the blessing of Earth is toil.

HENRY VAN DYKE

V. HOME AND MOTHER

HOME, SWEET HOME

'MID PLEASURES and palaces though we may roam,
Be it ever so humble, there's no place like home;
A charm from the sky seems to hallow us there,
Which, seek through the world, is ne'er met with elsewhere.
   Home, home, sweet, sweet home!
There's no place like home, oh, there's no place like home!

An exile from home, splendor dazzles in vain;
Oh, give me my lowly thatched cottage again!
The birds singing gayly, that came at my call—
Give me them—and the peace of mind, dearer than all!
   Home, home, sweet, sweet home!
There's no place like home, oh, there's no place like home!

I gaze on the moon as I tread the drear wild,
And feel that my mother now thinks of her child,
As she looks on that moon from our own cottage door
Thro' the woodbine, whose fragrance shall cheer me no more.
   Home, home, sweet, sweet home!
There's no place like home, oh, there's no place like home!

How sweet 'tis to sit 'neath a fond father's smile,
And the caress of a mother to soothe and beguile!
Let others delight 'mid new pleasure to roam,
But give me, oh, give me, the pleasures of home,
   Home, home, sweet, sweet home!
There's no place like home, oh, there's no place like home!

To thee I'll return, overburdened with care;
The heart's dearest solace will smile on me there;
No more from that cottage again will I roam;
Be it ever so humble, there's no place like home.
   Home, home, sweet, sweet home!
There's no place like home, oh, there's no place like home!

JOHN HOWARD PAYNE.

LIKE MOTHER, LIKE SON

Do YOU KNOW that your soul is of my soul such a part,
That you seem to be fibre and core of my heart?
None other can pain me as you, dear, can do,
None other can please me or praise me as you.

Remember the world will be quick with its blame
If shadow or stain ever darken your name.
"Like mother, like son" is a saying so true
The world will judge largely the "mother" by you.

Be yours then the task, if task it shall be,
To force the proud world to do homage to me.
Be sure it will say, when its verdict you've won,
"She reaped as she sowed. Lo! this is her son."

MARGARET JOHNSTON GRAFFLIN.

MY MOTHER

WHO FED ME from her gentle breast
And hushed me in her arms to rest,
And on my cheek sweet kisses prest?
   My mother.

When sleep forsook my open eye,
Who was it sung sweet lullaby
And rocked me that I should not cry?
   My mother.

Who sat and watched my infant head
When sleeping in my cradle bed,
And tears of sweet affection shed?
   My mother.

When pain and sickness made me cry,
Who gazed upon my heavy eye
And wept, for fear that I should die?
      My mother.

Who ran to help me when I fell
And would some pretty story tell,
Or kiss the part to make it well?
      My mother.

Who taught my infant lips to pray,
To love God's holy word and day,
And walk in wisdom's pleasant way?
      My mother.

And can I ever cease to be
Affectionate and kind to thee
Who wast so very kind to me,—
      My mother.

Oh no, the thought I cannot bear;
And if God please my life to spare
I hope I shall reward thy care,
      My mother.

When thou art feeble, old and gray,
My healthy arm shall be thy stay,
And I will soothe thy pains away,
      My mother.

And when I see thee hang thy head,
'Twill be my turn to watch thy bed,
And tears of sweet affection shed,—
      My mother.

                  JANE TAYLOR.

ROCK ME TO SLEEP

BACKWARD, turn backward, O time, in your flight,
Make me a child again just for to-night!
Mother, come back from the echoless shore,
Take me again to your heart as of yore;

371

Kiss from my forehead the furrows of care,
Smooth the few silver threads out of my hair;
Over my slumbers your loving watch keep;—
Rock me to sleep, Mother—rock me to sleep!

Backward, flow backward, oh, tide of the years!
I am so weary of toil and of tears—
Toil without recompense, tears all in vain—
Take them, and give me my childhood again!
I have grown weary of dust and decay—
Weary of flinging my soul-wealth away;
Weary of sowing for others to reap;—
Rock me to sleep, Mother—rock me to sleep!

Tired of the hollow, the base, the untrue,
Mother, O Mother, my heart calls for you!
Many a summer the grass has grown green,
Blossomed and faded, our faces between:
Yet, with strong yearning and passionate pain,
Long I to-night for your presence again.
Come from the silence so long and so deep;—
Rock me to sleep, Mother—rock me to sleep!

Over my heart, in the days that are flown,
No love like mother-love ever has shone;
No other worship abides and endures—
Faithful, unselfish, and patient like yours:
None like a mother can charm away pain
From the sick soul and the world-weary brain.
Slumber's soft calms o'er my heavy lids creep;—
Rock me to sleep, Mother—rock me to sleep!

Come, let your brown hair, just lighted with gold,
Fall on your shoulders again as of old;
Let it drop over my forehead to-night,
Shading my faint eyes away from the light;
For with its sunny-edged shadows once more
Haply will throng the sweet visions of yore;
Lovingly, softly, its bright billows sweep:—
Rock me to sleep, Mother—rock me to sleep!

Mother, dear Mother, the years have been long
Since I last listened your lullaby song:
Sing, then, and unto my soul it shall seem
Womanhood's years have been only a dream.

Clasped to your heart in a loving embrace,
With your light lashes just sweeping my face,
Never hereafter to wake or to weep;—
Rock me to sleep, Mother—rock me to sleep!

ELIZABETH AKERS ALLEN.

CALL ME NOT BACK FROM THE ECHOLESS SHORE

[In reply to *Rock Me to Sleep.*]

WHY IS YOUR FOREHEAD deep-furrowed with care?
What has so soon mingled frost in your hair?
Why are you sorrowful? Why do you weep?
And why do you ask me to "rock you to sleep"?
Could you but see through this world's vale of tears,
Light would your sorrows be, harmless your fears;
All that seems darkness to you would be light,
All would be sunshine, where now is but night.

Follow me, cheerfully, pray do not weep;
In spirit I'll soothe you, and "rock you to sleep,"
Why would you backward with time again turn?
Why do you still for your childhood's day yearn?
Weary one, why through the past again roam,
While, in the future, the path leads you home?
Oh, dearest child! dry those tears, weep no more,
Call me not back from the echoless shore;
In spirit I'll soothe you and "rock you to sleep."

UNKNOWN.

SOMEBODY'S MOTHER

THE WOMAN was old and ragged and gray
And bent with the chill of the Winter's day.

The street was wet with a recent snow
And the woman's feet were aged and slow.

She stood at the crossing and waited long,
Alone, uncared for, amid the throng

Of human beings who passed her by
Nor heeded the glance of her anxious eye.

Down the street, with laughter and shout,
Glad in the freedom of "school let out,"

Came the boys like a flock of sheep,
Hailing the snow piled white and deep.

Past the woman so old and gray
Hastened the children on their way.

Nor offered a helping hand to her—
So meek, so timid, afraid to stir

Lest the carriage wheels or the horses' feet
Should crowd her down in the slippery street.

At last came one of the merry troop,
The gayest laddie of all the group;

He paused beside her and whispered low,
"I'll help you cross, if you wish to go."

Her aged hand on his strong young arm
She placed, and so, without hurt or harm,

He guided the trembling feet along,
Proud that his own were firm and strong.

Then back again to his friends he went,
His young heart happy and well content.

"She's somebody's mother, boys, you know,
For all she's aged and poor and slow,

"And I hope some fellow will lend a hand
To help my mother, you understand,

"If ever she's poor and old and gray,
When her own dear boy is far away."

And "somebody's mother" bowed low her head
In her home that night, and the prayer she said

Was, "God be kind to the noble boy,
Who is somebody's son, and pride and joy!"

MARY DOW BRINE.

HOME

It takes a heap o' livin' in a house t' make it home,
A heap o' sun an' shadder, an' ye sometimes have t' roam
Afore ye really 'preciate the things ye lef' behind,
An' hunger fer 'em somehow, with 'em allus on yer mind.
It don't make any differunce how rich ye get t' be,
How much yer chairs an' tables cost, how great yer luxury;
It ain't home t' ye, though it be the palace of a king,
Until somehow yer soul is sort o' wrapped round everything.

Home ain't a place that gold can buy or get up in a minute;
Afore it's home there's got t' be a heap o' livin' in it;
Within the walls there's got t' be some babies born, and then
Right there ye've got t' bring 'em up t' women good, an' men;
And gradjerly, as time goes on, ye find ye wouldn't part
With anything they ever used—they've grown into yer heart:
The old high chairs, the playthings, too, the little shoes they wore
Ye hoard; an' if ye could ye'd keep the thumb-marks on the door.

Ye've got t' weep t' make it home, ye've got t' sit an' sigh
An' watch beside a loved one's bed, an' know that Death is nigh;
An' in the stillness o' the night t' see Death's angel come,
An' close the eyes o' her that smiled, an' leave her sweet voice dumb.
For these are scenes that grip the heart, an' when yer tears are dried,
Ye find the home is dearer than it was, an' sanctified;
An' tuggin' at ye always are the pleasant memories
O' her that was an' is no more—ye can't escape from these.

Ye've got to sing an' dance fer years, ye've got t' romp an' play,
An' learn t' love the things ye have by usin' 'em each day;
Even the roses round the porch must blossom year by year
Afore they 'come a part o' ye, suggestin' someone dear
Who used t' love 'em long ago, and trained 'em just t' run
The way they do, so's they would get the early mornin' sun;
Ye've got to love each brick an' stone from cellar up t' dome:
It takes a heap o' livin' in a house t' make it home.

EDGAR A. GUEST.

375

THE READING MOTHER

I HAD A MOTHER who read to me
Sagas of pirates who scoured the sea,
Cutlasses clenched in their yellow teeth,
"Blackbirds" stowed in the hold beneath

I had a Mother who read me lays
Of ancient and gallant and golden days;
Stories of Marmion and Ivanhoe,
Which every boy has a right to know.

I had a Mother who read me tales
Of Gêlert the hound of the hills of Wales,
True to his trust till his tragic death,
Faithfulness blent with his final breath.

I had a Mother who read me the things
That wholesome life to the boy heart brings—
Stories that stir with an upward touch,
Oh, that each mother of boys were such!

You may have tangible wealth untold;
Caskets of jewels and coffers of gold.
Richer than I you can never be—
I had a Mother who read to me.

STRICKLAND GILLILAN.

THE BLUE BOWL

Reward

ALL DAY I did the little things,
The little things that do not show;
I brought the kindling for the fire
I set the candles in a row,
I filled a bowl with marigolds,
The shallow bowl you love the best—
And made the house a pleasant place
Where weariness might take its rest.

376

The hours sped on, my eager feet
Could not keep pace with my desire.
So much to do, so little time!
I could not let my body tire;
Yet, when the coming of the night
Blotted the garden from my sight,
And on the narrow, graveled walks
Between the guarding flower stalks
I heard your step: I was not through
With services I meant for you.

You came into the quiet room
That glowed enchanted with the bloom
Of yellow flame. I saw your face,
Illumined by the firelit space,
Slowly grow still and comforted—
"It's good to be at home," you said.

BLANCHE BANE KUDER.

MY MOTHER'S GARDEN

HER HEART is like her garden,
Old-fashioned, quaint and sweet,
With here a wealth of blossoms,
And there a still retreat.
Sweet violets are hiding,
We know as we pass by,
And lilies, pure as angel thoughts,
Are opening somewhere nigh.

Forget-me-nots there linger,
To full perfection brought,
And there bloom purple pansies
In many a tender thought.
There love's own roses blossom,
As from enchanted ground,
And lavish perfume exquisite
The whole glad year around.

And in that quiet garden—
The garden of her heart—
Songbirds are always singing
Their songs of cheer apart.

And from it floats forever,
O'ercoming sin and strife,
Sweet as the breath of roses blown,
The fragrance of her life.

ALICE E. ALLEN.

A PRAYER FOR A LITTLE HOME

God send us a little home,
To come back to, when we roam.

Low walls and fluted tiles,
Wide windows, a view for miles.

Red firelight and deep chairs,
Small white beds upstairs—

Great talk in little nooks,
Dim colors, rows of books.

One picture on each wall,
Not many things at all.

God send us a little ground,
Tall trees stand round.

Homely flowers in brown sod,
Overhead, thy stars, O God.

God bless thee, when winds blow,
Our home, and all we know.

FLORENCE BONE.

MOTHERHOOD

Mary, the Christ long slain, passed silently,
Following the children joyously astir
Under the cedrus and the olive tree,
Pausing to let their laughter float to her—
Each voice an echo of a voice more dear,
She saw a little Christ in every face.

Then came another woman gliding near
To watch the tender life which filled the place.
And Mary sought the woman's hand, and spoke:
"I know thee not, yet know thy memory tossed
With all a thousand dreams their eyes evoke
Who bring to thee a child beloved and lost.

"I, too, have rocked my Little One.
And He was fair!
Oh, fairer than the fairest sun,
And, like its rays through amber spun,
His sun-bright hair.
Still I can see it shine and shine."
"Even so," the woman said, "was mine."

"His ways were ever darling ways"—
And Mary smiled—
"So soft, so clinging! Glad relays
Of love were all His precious days.
My Little Child!
My vanished star! My music fled!"
"Even so was mine," the woman said.

And Mary whispered: "Tell me, thou,
Of thine." And she:
"Oh, mine was rosy as a bough
Blooming with roses, sent, somehow,
To bloom for me!
His balmy fingers left a thrill
Deep in my breast that warms me still."

Then she gazed down some wilder, darker hour,
And said—when Mary questioned, knowing not:
"Who art thou, mother of so sweet a flower?"—
"I am the mother of Iscariot."

AGNES LEE.

IF I ONLY WAS THE FELLOW

WHILE WALKING down a crowded
    City street the other day,
I heard a little urchin
    To a comrade turn and say,

"Say, Chimmey, lemme tell youse,
  I'd be happy as a clam
If I only was de feller dat
  Me mudder t'inks I am.

"She t'inks I am a wonder,
  An' she knows her little lad
Could never mix wit' nuttin'
  Dat was ugly, mean or bad.
Oh, lot o' times I sit and t'ink
  How nice, 'twould be, gee whiz!
If a feller was de feller
  Dat his mudder t'inks he is."

My friends, be yours a life of toil
  Or undiluted joy,
You can learn a wholesome lesson
  From that small, untutored boy.
Don't aim to be an earthly saint,
  With eyes fixed on a star:
Just try to be the fellow that
  Your mother thinks you are.

WILL S. ADKIN.

HOME IS WHERE THERE IS ONE TO LOVE US

HOME's not merely four square walls,
Though with pictures hung and gilded;
Home is where Affection calls—
Filled with shrines the Hearth had builded!
Home! Go watch the faithful dove,
Sailing 'neath the heaven above us.
Home is where there's one to love!
Home is where there's one to love us.

Home's not merely roof and room,
It needs something to endear it;
Home is where the heart can bloom,
Where there's some kind lip to cheer it!
What is home with none to meet,
None to welcome, none to greet us?
Home is sweet, and only sweet,
Where there's one we love to meet us!

CHARLES SWAIN.

A WONDERFUL MOTHER

God made a wonderful mother,
A mother who never grows old;
He made her smile of the sunshine,
And He molded her heart of pure gold;
In her eyes He placed bright shining stars,
In her cheeks, fair roses you see;
God made a wonderful mother,
And He gave that dear mother to me.

PAT O'REILLY.

NOBODY KNOWS BUT MOTHER

How MANY BUTTONS are missing today?
  Nobody knows but Mother.
How many playthings are strewn in her way?
  Nobody knows but Mother.
How many thimbles and spools has she missed?
How many burns on each fat little fist?
How many bumps to be cuddled and kissed?
  Nobody knows but Mother.

How many hats has she hunted today?
  Nobody knows but Mother.
Carelessly hiding themselves in the hay—
  Nobody knows but Mother.
How many handkerchiefs wilfully strayed?
How many ribbons for each little maid?
How for her care can a mother be paid?
  Nobody knows but Mother.

How many muddy shoes all in a row?
  Nobody knows but Mother.
How many stockings to darn, do you know?
  Nobody knows but Mother.

How many little torn aprons to mend?
How many hours of toil must she spend?
What is the time when her day's work shall end?
  Nobody knows but Mother.

How many lunches for Tommy and Sam?
  Nobody knows but Mother.
Cookies and apples and blackberry jam—
  Nobody knows but Mother.
Nourishing dainties for every "sweet tooth,"
Toddling Dottie or dignified Ruth—
How much love sweetens the labor, forsooth?
  Nobody knows but Mother.

How many cares does a mother's heart know?
  Nobody knows but Mother.
How many joys from her mother love flow?
  Nobody knows but Mother.
How many prayers for each little white bed?
How many tears for her babes has she shed?
How many kisses for each curly head?
  Nobody knows but Mother.

MARY MORRISON.

VI. CHILDHOOD AND YOUTH

THE OLD OAKEN BUCKET

How DEAR to my heart are the scenes of my childhood,
  When fond recollection presents them to view!
The orchard, the meadow, the deep tangled wildwood,
  And every loved spot which my infancy knew,
The wide-spreading pond and the mill that stood by it,
  The bridge and the rock where the cataract fell;
The cot of my father, the dairy house nigh it,
  And e'en the rude bucket that hung in the well.

That moss-covered bucket I hailed as a treasure,
  For often at noon, when returned from the field,
I found it the source of an exquisite pleasure,
  The purest and sweetest that nature can yield.
How ardent I seized it, with hands that were glowing,
  And quick to the white-pebbled bottom it fell.
Then soon, with the emblem of truth overflowing,
  And dripping with coolness, it rose from the well.

How sweet from the green, mossy brim to receive it,
  As, poised on the curb, it inclined to my lips!
Not a full, blushing goblet could tempt me to leave it,
  Tho' filled with the nectar that Jupiter sips.
And now, far removed from the loved habitation,
  The tear of regret will intrusively swell,
As fancy reverts to my father's plantation,
  And sighs for the bucket that hung in the well.

SAMUEL WOODWORTH.

THE OLD OAKEN BUCKET

(As censored by the Board of Health)

WITH WHAT ANGUISH of mind I remember my childhood,
    Recalled in the light of knowledge since gained,
The malarious farm, the wet, fungus-grown wildwood,
    The chills then contracted that since have remained;
The scum-covered duck-pond, the pigsty close by it,
    The ditch where the sour-smelling house drainage fell,
The damp, shaded dwelling, the foul barnyard nigh it—
    But worse than all else was that terrible well,
And the old oaken bucket, the mold-crusted bucket,
    The moss-covered bucket that hung in the well.

Just think of it! Moss on the vessel that lifted
    The water I drank in the days called to mind,
Ere I knew what professors and scientists gifted
    In the waters of wells by analysis find;
The rotting wood-fiber, the oxide of iron,
    The algae, the frog of unusual size,
The water as clear as the verses of Byron,
    Are things I remember with tears in my eyes.

Oh, had I but realized in time to avoid them
    The dangers that lurked in that pestilent draft,
I'd have tested for organic germs and destroyed them
    With potassic permanganate ere I had quaffed.
Or perchance I'd have boiled it, and afterward strained it
    Through filters of charcoal and gravel combined;
Or, after distilling, condensed and regained it
    In potable form with its filth left behind.

How little I knew of the enteric fever
    Which lurked in the water I ventured to drink;
But since I've become a devoted believer
    In the teachings of science, I shudder to think.
And now, far removed from the scenes I'm describing,
    The story of warning to others I tell,
As memory reverts to my youthful imbibing
    And I gag at the thought of that horrible well,
And the old oaken bucket, the fungus-grown bucket—
    In fact, the slop bucket—that hung in the well.

UNKNOWN.

A DUTCH LULLABY

WYNKEN, Blynken, and Nod one night
  Sailed off in a wooden shoe—
Sailed on a river of misty light
  Into a sea of dew.
"Where are you going, and what do you wish?"
  The old moon asked the three.
"We have come to fish for the herring-fish
  That live in this beautiful sea;
  Nets of silver and gold have we,"
        Said Wynken,
        Blynken,
        And Nod.

The old moon laughed and sung a song
  As they rocked in the wooden shoe,
And the wind that sped them all night long
  Ruffled the waves of dew;
The little stars were the herring-fish
  That lived in the beautiful sea;
"Now cast your nets wherever you wish,
  But never afeard are we"—
So cried the stars to the fishermen three,
        Wynken,
        Blynken,
        And Nod.

All night long their nets they threw
  For the fish in the twinkling foam,
Then down from the sky came the wooden shoe,
  Bringing the fishermen home.
'T was all so pretty a sail, it seemed
  As if it could not be;
And some folks thought 't was a dream they'd dreamed
  Of sailing that beautiful sea.
  But I shall name you the fishermen three:
        Wynken,
        Blynken,
        And Nod.

Wynken and Blynken are two little eyes,
  And Nod is a little head,
And the wooden shoe that sailed the skies
  Is a wee one's trundle-bed;

So shut your eyes while mother sings
  Of the wonderful sights that be,
And you shall see the beautiful things
  As you rock in the misty sea
  Where the old shoe rocked the fishermen three—
      Wynken,
      Blynken,
      And Nod.

                        EUGENE FIELD.

THE ORGANIST

I WONDER how the organist
  Can do so many things;
He's getting ready long before
  The choir stands up and sings;
He's pressing buttons, pushing stops,
  He's pulling here and there,
And testing all the working parts
  While listening to the prayer.

He runs a mighty big machine,
  It's full of funny things;
A mass of boxes, pipes and tubes
  And sticks and slats and strings;
There's little whistles for a cent
  In rows and rows and rows;
I'll bet there's twenty miles of tubes
  As large as garden hose.

There's scores as large as stovepipes and
  There's lots so big and wide
That several little boys I know
  Could play around inside.
From little bits of piccolos
  That hardly make a toot
There's every size up to the great
  Big elevator chute.

The organist knows every one
  And how they ought to go;
He makes them rumble like a storm,
  Or plays them sweet and low;

At times you think them very near;
  At times they're soaring high,
Like angel voices, singing far
  Off, somewhere in the sky.

For he can take this structure, that's
  As big as any house,
And make it squeak as softly as
  A tiny little mouse;
And then he'll jerk out something with
  A movement of the hand,
And make you think you're listening to
  A military band.

He plays it with his fingers and
  He plays it with his toes,
And if he really wanted to
  He'd play it with his nose;
He's sliding up and down the bench,
  He's working with his knees;
He's dancing round with both his feet
  As lively as you please.

I always like to take a seat
  Where I can see him go;
He's better than a sermon, and
  He does me good, I know;
I like the life and movement and
  I like to hear him play;
He is the most exciting thing
  In town on Sabbath day.

GEORGE W. STEVENS.

TRAGEDY

I ALWAYS WANTED a red balloon,
It only cost a dime,
But Ma said it was risky,
They broke so quickly,
And beside, she didn't have time;
And even if she did, she didn't
Think they were worth a dime.

We lived on a farm, and I only went
To one circus and fair,
And all the balloons I ever saw
Were there.
There were yellow ones and blue ones,
But the kind I liked the best
Were red, and I don't see why
She couldn't have stopped and said
That maybe I could have one—
But she didn't—I suppose that now
You can buy them anywheres,
And that they still sell red ones
At circuses and fairs.
I got a little money saved;
I got a lot of time,
I got no one to tell me how to spend my dime;
Plenty of balloons—but somehow
There's something died inside of me,
And I don't want one—now.

JILL SPARGUR.

FROM MY ARM-CHAIR

[To the Children of Cambridge who presented to me on my seventy-second birthday, February 27, 1879, this chair made from the wood of the village black-smith's chestnut tree.]

Am I a king, that I should call my own
    This splendid ebon throne?
Or by what reason, or what right divine,
    Can I proclaim it mine?

Only, perhaps, by right divine of song
    It may to me belong;
Only because the spreading chestnut tree
    Of old was sung by me.

Well I remember it in all its prime,
    When in the summer-time
The affluent foliage of its branches made
    A cavern of cool shade.

There, by the blacksmith's forge, beside the street,
    Its blossoms white and sweet,

Enticed the bees, until it seemed alive,
 And murmured like a hive.

And when the winds of autumn, with a shout,
 Tossed its great arms about,
The shining chestnuts, bursting from the sheath,
 Dropped to the ground beneath.

And now some fragments of its branches bare,
 Shaped as a stately chair,
Have by my hearthstone found a home at last,
 And whisper of the past.

The Danish king could not in all his pride
 Repel the ocean tide,
But, seated in this chair, I can in rhyme
 Roll back the tide of Time.

I see again, as one in vision sees,
 The blossoms and the bees,
And hear the children's voices shout and call,
 And the brown chestnuts fall.

I see the smithy with its fires aglow,
 I hear the bellows blow,
And the shrill hammers on the anvil beat
 The iron white with heat!

And thus, dear children, have ye made for me
 This day a jubilee,
And to my more than threescore years and ten
 Brought back my youth again.

The heart hath its own memory, like the mind,
 And in it are enshrined
The precious keepsakes, into which is wrought
 The giver's loving thought.

Only your love and your remembrance could
 Give life to this dead wood,
And make these branches, leafless now so long,
 Blossom again in song.

HENRY WADSWORTH LONGFELLOW.

Mr. Longfellow had this poem printed, and was accustomed to giving a copy to each child who visited him and sat in the chair.

TWO TEMPLES

A Builder builded a temple,
He wrought it with grace and skill;
Pillars and groins and arches
All fashioned to work his will.
Men said, as they saw its beauty,
"It shall never know decay;
Great is thy skill, O Builder!
Thy fame shall endure for aye."

A Mother builded a temple
With loving and infinite care,
Planning each arch with patience,
Laying each stone with prayer.
None praised her unceasing efforts,
None knew of her wondrous plan,
For the temple the Mother builded
Was unseen by the eyes of man.

Gone is the Builder's temple,
Crumpled into the dust;
Low lies each stately pillar,
Food for consuming rust.
But the temple the Mother builded
Will last while the ages roll,
For that beautiful unseen temple
Was a child's immortal soul.

HATTIE VOSE HALL.

AN ORDER FOR A PICTURE

O good painter, tell me true,
Has your hand the cunning to draw
Shapes of things that you never saw?
Ay? Well, here is an order for you.
Woods and cornfield a little brown,—
The picture must not be overbright—
Yet all in the golden and gracious light
Of a cloud, when the summer sun is down.

392

Alway and alway, night and morn,
Woods upon woods, with fields of corn
Lying between them, not quite sere,
And not in the full, thick, leafy bloom
When the wind can hardly find breathing-room
Under their tassels,—cattle near,
Biting shorter the short green grass,
And a hedge of sumac and sassafras,
With bluebirds twittering all around,—
Ah, good painter, you can't paint sound!

These and the house where I was born,
Low and little, and black and old,
With children, as many as it can hold,
All at the windows, open wide,—
Heads and shoulders clear outside,
And fair young faces all a-blush.
Perhaps you may have seen, some day,
Roses crowding the selfsame way,
Out of a wilding wayside bush.
Listen closer. When you have done
With woods and cornfields and grazing herds,
A lady, the loveliest ever the sun
Looked down upon you must paint for me;
O, if I only could make you see
The clear blue eyes, the tender smile,
The sovereign sweetness, the gentle grace,
The woman's soul, and the angel's face
That are beaming on me all the while,
I need not speak these foolish words:
Yet one word tells you all I would say,—
She is my mother. You will agree
That all the rest may be thrown away.

Two little urchins at her knee
You must paint, sir: one like me,—
The other with a clearer brow,
And the light of his adventurous eyes
Flashing with boldest enterprise:
At ten years old he went to sea,—
God knoweth if he be living now,—
He sailed in the good ship *Commodore,*
Nobody ever crossed her track
To bring us news, and she never came back.
Ah, it is twenty long years and more

Since that old ship went out of the bay
With my greathearted brother on her deck;
I watched him till he shrank to a speck,
And his face was toward me all the way.
Bright his hair was, a golden brown,
The time we stood at our mother's knee;
That beauteous head, if it did go down,
Carried sunshine into the sea.

Out in the fields, one summer night,
We were together, half afraid
Of the corn-leaves rustling, and of the shade
Of the high hills stretching so still and far,—
Loitering till after the little light
Of the candle shone through the open door,
And over the haystack's pointed top,
All of a tremble, and ready to drop,
The first half-hour, the great yellow star,
That we, with staring, ignorant eyes,
Had often and often watched to see
Propped and held in its place in the skies
By the fork of a tall red mulberry tree,
Which close in the edge of our flax-field grew,—
Dead at the top,—just one branch full
Of leaves, notched round, and lined with wool
From which it tenderly shook the dew
Over our heads when we came to play
In its hand's breadth of shadow, day after day.
Afraid to go home, sir; for one of us bore
A nest full of speckled and thin-shelled eggs;—
The other, a bird, held fast by the legs,
Not so big as a straw of wheat;
The berries we gave her she wouldn't eat,
But cried and cried, till we held her bill,
So slim and shining, to keep her still.

At last, we stood at our mother's knee,
Do you think, sir, if you try,
You can paint the look of a lie?
If you can, pray have the grace
To put it solely in the face
Of the urchin that is likest me;
I think 'twas solely mine, indeed:
But that's no matter, paint it so;
The eyes of our mother—take good heed—

394

Looking not into the nest full of eggs,
Nor the fluttering bird, held so fast by the legs,
But straight through our faces down to our lies,
And O, with such injured, reproachful surprise!
I felt my heart bleed when that glance went, as though
A sharp blade struck through it. You, sir, know
That you on the canvas are to repeat
Things that are fairest, things most sweet,—
The mother,—the lads, with their bird, at her knee;
But O, that look of reproachful woe!
High as the heavens your name I'll shout,
If you paint me the picture, and leave that out.

ALICE CARY.

SUPPOSE

Suppose, my little lady,
    Your doll should break her head;
Could you make it whole by crying
    Till your eyes and nose were red?
And wouldn't it be pleasanter
    To treat it as a joke,
And say you're glad 'twas dolly's
    And not your own that broke?

Suppose you're dressed for walking,
    And the rain comes pouring down;
Will it clear off any sooner
    Because you scold and frown?
And wouldn't it be nicer
    For you to smile than pout,
And so make sunshine in the house
    When there is none without?

Suppose your task, my little man,
    Is very hard to get;
Will it make it any easier
    For you to sit and fret?
And wouldn't it be wiser,
    Than waiting like a dunce,
To go to work in earnest
    And learn the thing at once?

Suppose that some boys have a horse,
   And some a coach and pair;
Will it tire you less while walking
   To say, "It isn't fair"?
And wouldn't it be nobler
   To keep your temper sweet,
And in your heart be thankful
   You can walk upon your feet?

Suppose the world don't please you.
   Nor the way some people do;
Do you think the whole creation
   Will be altered just for you?
And isn't it, my boy or girl,
   The wisest, bravest plan,
Whatever comes, or doesn't come,
   To do the best you can?

PHOEBE CARY.

WHICH SHALL IT BE?

"WHICH SHALL IT BE? Which shall it be?"
I look'd at John—John look'd at me
(Dear, patient John, who loves me yet
As well as though my locks were jet);
And when I found that I must speak,
My voice seem'd strangely low and weak:
"Tell me again what Robert said."
And then I, listening, bent my head.
"This is his letter: 'I will give
A house and land while you shall live,
If, in return, from out your seven,
One child to me for aye is given.'"
I look'd at John's old garments worn,
I thought of all that John had borne
Of poverty and work and care,
Which I, though willing, could not share;
I thought of seven mouths to feed,
Of seven little children's need,
And then of this. "Come, John," said I,
"We'll choose among them as they lie
Asleep;" so, walking hand in hand,

Dear John and I survey'd our band.
First to the cradle lightly stepp'd,
Where the new nameless baby slept.
"Shall it be Baby?" whispered John.
I took his hand, and hurried on
To Lily's crib. Her sleeping grasp
Held her old doll within its clasp;
Her dark curls lay like gold alight,
A glory 'gainst the pillow white.
Softly her father stoop'd to lay
His rough hand down in loving way,
When dream or whisper made her stir,
Then huskily said John, "Not her, not her!"
We stopp'd beside the trundle bed,
And one long ray of lamplight shed
Athwart the boyish faces there,
In sleep so pitiful and fair;
I saw on Jamie's rough, red cheek
A tear undried. Ere John could speak,
"He's but a baby, too," said I,
And kiss'd him as we hurried by.
Pale, patient Robbie's angel face
Still in his sleep bore suffering's trace.
"No, for a thousand crowns, not him!"
We whisper'd, while our eyes were dim.
Poor Dick! bad Dick! our wayward son,
Turbulent, reckless, idle one—
Could he be spared? Nay; He who gave
Bids us befriend him to his grave;
Only a mother's heart can be
Patient enough for such as he;
"And so," said John, "I would not dare
To send him from her bedside prayer."
Then stole we softly up above
And knelt by Mary, child of love.
"Perhaps for her 'twould better be,"
I said to John. Quite silently
He lifted up a curl astray
Across her cheek in wilful way,
And shook his head: "Nay, love; not thee,"
The while my heart beat audibly.
Only one more, our eldest lad,
Trusty and truthful, good and glad—
So like his father. "No, John, no—
I cannot, will not, let him go."

397

And so we wrote, in courteous way,
We could not give one child away;
And afterward toil lighter seem'd,
Thinking of that of which we dream'd,
Happy in truth that not one face
We miss'd from its accustom'd place;
Thankful to work for all the seven,
Trusting the rest to One in heaven.

ETHEL LYNN BEERS.

TO A CHILD WHO INQUIRES

How DID YOU COME to me, my sweet?
  From the land that no man knows?
Did Mr. Stork bring you here on his wings?
  Were you born in the heart of a rose?

Did an angel fly with you down from the sky?
  Were you found in a gooseberry patch?
Did a fairy bring you from fairyland
  To my door—that was left on a latch?

No—my darling was born of a wonderful love,
  A love that was Daddy's and mine.
A love that was human, but deep and profound,
  A love that was almost divine.

Do you remember, sweetheart, when we went to the zoo,
  And we saw the big bear with a grouch?
And the tigers and lions, and that tall kangaroo
  That carried her babe in a pouch?

Do you remember I told you she kept them there safe
  From the cold and the wind, till they grew
Big enough to take care of themselves? And, dear heart,
  That's just how I first cared for you.

I carried you under my heart, my sweet,
  And I sheltered you safe from alarms;
Then one wonderful day the dear God looked down,
  And I snuggled you tight in my arms.

OLGA PETROVA.

398

LULLABY TOWN

THERE'S A QUAINT little place they call Lullaby Town—
It's just back of those hills where the sunsets go down.
Its streets are of silver, its buildings of gold,
And its palaces dazzling things to behold;
There are dozens of spires, housing musical chimes;
Its people are folk from the Nursery Rimes,
And at night it's alight, like a garden of gleams,
With fairies, who bring the most wonderful dreams.

The Sandman is Mayor, and he rules like a King.
The climate's so balmy that, always, it's spring,
And it's never too cold, and it's never too hot,
And I'm told that there's nowhere a prettier spot;
All in and about it are giant old trees,
Filled with radiant birds that will sing when you please;
But the strange thing about it—this secret, pray, keep—
Is, it never awakes till the world is asleep.

So when night settles down, all its lights snap aglow,
And its streets fill with people who dance to and fro.
Mother Goose, Old King Cole and his fiddlers three,
Miss Muffet, Jack Sprat and his wife, scamper free,
With a whole host of others, a boisterous crew,
Not forgetting the Old Lady Who Lived in a Shoe
And her troublesome brood who, with brownie and sprite,
Go trooping the streets, a bewildering sight.

There's a peddler who carries, strapped high on his back,
A bundle. Now, guess what he has in that pack.
There's a crowd all about him a-buying his wares,
And they're grabbing his goods up in threes and in pairs.
No, he's not peddling jams nor delectable creams.
Would you know what he's selling? Just wonderful dreams!

There are dreams for a penny and dreams that cost two;
And there's no two alike, and they're sure to come true;
And the buyers fare off with a toss of the head,
And they visit the Sandman, then hie them to bed;
For there's nothing to do in this land of Bo-Peep,
But to frolic and sing and then go off to sleep!

JOHN IRVING DILLER.

THERE WAS A LITTLE GIRL

THERE WAS a little girl, she had a little curl
  Right in the middle of her forehead;
And when she was good, she was very, very good,
  And when she was bad, she was horrid.

HENRY WADSWORTH LONGFELLOW.

THE BOY RECITER

YOU'D SCARCE EXPECT one of my age
To speak in public on the stage,
And if I chance to fall below
Demosthenes or Cicero,
Don't view me with a critic's eye,
But pass my imperfections by.
Large streams from little fountains flow,
Tall oaks from little acorns grow;
And though now I am small and young,
Of judgment weak and feeble tongue,
Yet all great, learned men, like me
Once learned to read their ABC.
But why may not Columbia's soil
Rear men as great as Britain's Isle,
Exceed what Greece and Rome have done
Or any land beneath the sun?
Mayn't Massachusetts boast as great
As any other sister state?
Or where's the town, go far or near,
That does not find a rival here?
Or where's the boy but three feet high
Who's made improvement more than I?
These thoughts inspire my youthful mind
To be the greatest of mankind:
Great, not like Caesar, stained with blood,
But only great as I am good.

DAVID EVERETT.

400

THE CHILD'S FIRST GRIEF

OH, CALL my brother back to me,
    I cannot play alone;
The Summer comes, with flower and bee,
    Where is my brother gone?

The flowers run wild, the flowers we sowed,
    Around our garden tree;
Our vine is drooping with its load—
    Oh, call him back to me.

*

He wouldn't hear thy voice, fair child,
    He may not come to thee;
His face that once like summer smiled,
    On earth no more thou'lt see.

A rose's brief, bright life of joy,
    Such unto him was given.
Go, thou must play alone, my boy,
    Thy brother is in Heaven.

*

And has he left his birds and flowers?
    And must I call in vain?
And through the long, long summer hours
    Will he not come again?

And by the brook, and in the glade,
    Are all our wanderings o'er?
Oh, while my brother with me played,
    Would I had loved him more.

                    FELICIA D. HEMANS.

WHERE SHALL THE BABY'S DIMPLE BE?

OVER THE CRADLE the mother hung,
    Softly crooning a slumber song;
And these were the simple words she sung
    All the evening long:

"Cheek or chin, or knuckle or knee,
Where shall the baby's dimple be?
Where shall the angel's finger rest
When he comes down to the baby's nest?
Where shall the angel's touch remain
When he awakens my babe again?"

Still as she bent and sang so low,
    A murmur into her music broke;
And she paused to hear, for she could but know
    The baby's angel spoke:

"Cheek or chin, or knuckle or knee,
Where shall the baby's dimple be?
Where shall my finger fall and rest
When I come down to the baby's nest?
Where shall my finger's touch remain
When I awaken your babe again?"

Silent the mother sat, and dwelt
    Long in the sweet delay of choice;
And then by her baby's side she knelt,
    And sang with pleasant voice:

"Not on the limb, O angel dear!
For the charm with its youth will disappear;
Not on the cheek shall the dimple be,
For the harboring smile will fade and flee;
But touch thou the chin with an impress deep,
And my baby the angel's seal shall keep."

                              JOSIAH G. HOLLAND.

I REMEMBER, I REMEMBER

I REMEMBER, I remember,
    The house where I was born,
The little window where the sun
    Came peeping in at morn:
He never came a wink too soon,
    Nor brought too long a day;
But now, I often wish the night
    Had borne my breath away.

I remember, I remember,
　The roses, red and white;
The violets and the lily-cups,
　Those flowers made of light!
The lilacs where the robin built,
　And where my brother set
The laburnum on his birthday,—
　The tree is living yet!

I remember, I remember,
　Where I was used to swing;
And thought the air must rush as fresh
　To swallows on the wing:
My spirit flew in feathers then,
　That is so heavy now,
And summer pools could hardly cool
　The fever on my brow!

I remember, I remember,
　The fir trees dark and high;
I used to think their slender tops
　Were close against the sky:
It was a childish ignorance,
　But now 'tis little joy
To know I'm farther off from heaven
　Than when I was a boy.

　　　　　　　　　　THOMAS HOOD.

SEVEN TIMES ONE

THERE'S NO DEW left on the daisies and clover,
　There's no rain left in heaven.
I've said my "seven times" over and over,—
　Seven times one are seven.

I am old,—so old I can write a letter;
　My birthday lessons are done.
The lambs play always,—they know no better;
　They are only one times one.

O Moon! in the night I have seen you sailing
　And shining so round and low.
You were bright—ah, bright—but your light is failing;
　You are nothing now but a bow.

403

You Moon! have you done something wrong in heaven,
   That God has hidden your face?
I hope, if you have, you will soon be forgiven,
   And shine again in your place.

O velvet Bee! you're a dusty fellow,—
   You've powdered your legs with gold.
O brave marsh Mary-buds, rich and yellow,
   Give me your money to hold!

O Columbine! open your folded wrapper,
   Where two twin turtle-doves dwell!
O Cuckoo-pint! tell me the purple clapper
   That hangs in your clear green bell!

And show me your nest, with the young ones in it,—
   I will not steal them away;
I am old! you may trust me, linnet, linnet!
   I am seven times one to-day.

JEAN INGELOW.

SERMON IN A STOCKING

THE SUPPER is over, the hearth is swept,
   And in the wood-fire's glow,
The children cluster to hear a tale
   Of the time so long ago.

When Grandmamma's hair was golden brown
   And the warm blood came and went
O'er the face that could scarce have been sweeter then
   Than now, in its rich content.

The face is wrinkled and careworn now,
   And the golden hair is gray,
But the light that shone in the young girl's eyes
   Has never gone away.

And her needles catch the firelight
   As in and out they go,
With the clicking music that Grandma loves,
   Shaping the stocking toe.

And the waking children love it, too,
  For they know the stocking song
Brings many a tale to Grandma's mind
  Which they shall hear ere long.

But it brings no story of olden times
  To Grandma's heart to-night;
Only a ditty, quaint and short,
  Is sung by the needles bright.

"Life is a stocking," Grandma says,
  "And yours is just begun;
And I am knitting the toe of mine,
  And my work is almost done.

"With merry hearts we begin to knit,
  And the ribbing is almost play;
Some are gay colors and some are white,
  And some are ashen gray;

"But most are made of many a hue,
  With many a stitch set wrong,
And many a row to be sadly ripped
  Ere the whole is fair and strong.

"There are long plain spaces, without a break,
  That in youth are hard to bear,
And many a weary tear is dropped
  As we fashion the heel with care.

"But the saddest, happiest time is that
  We court and yet we shun,
When our Heavenly Father breaks the thread
  And says that our work is done."

The children came to say good-night,
  With tears in their bright young eyes,
While in Grandma's lap, with a broken thread,
  The finished stocking lies.

                              ELLEN A. JEWETT.

DAY DREAMS, OR TEN YEARS OLD

I MEASURED myself by the wall in the garden;
The hollyhocks blossomed far over my head.
Oh, when I can touch with the tips of my fingers
The highest green bud, with its lining of red,

I shall not be a child any more, but a woman.
Dear hollyhock blossoms, how glad I shall be!
I wish they would hurry—the years that are coming,
And bring the bright days that I dream of to me!

Oh, when I am grown, I shall know all my lessons,
There's so much to learn when one's only just ten!—
I shall be very rich, very handsome, and stately,
And good, too,—of course,—'twill be easier then!

There'll be many to love me, and nothing to vex me,
No knots in my sewing; no crusts to my bread.
My days will go by like the days in a story,
The sweetest and gladdest that ever was read.

And then I shall come out some day to the garden
(For this little corner must always be mine);
I shall wear a white gown all embroidered with silver,
That trails in the grass with a rustle and shine.

And, meeting some child here at play in the sunshine,
With gracious hands laid on her head, I shall say,
"I measured myself by these hollyhock blossoms
When I was no taller than you, dear, one day!"

She will smile in my face as I stoop low to kiss her,
And—— Hark! they are calling me in to my tea!
O blossoms, I wish that the slow years would hurry!
When, when will they bring all I dream of to me?

MARGARET JOHNSON.

HOW BIG WAS ALEXANDER?

Son.

How BIG was Alexander, Pa,
  That people call him great?
Was he like old Goliath tall,
  His spear a hundredweight?
Was he so large that he could stand
  Like some tall steeple high,
And while his feet were on the ground,
  His hands could touch the sky?

Father.

O no, my child: about as large
  As I or uncle James.
'Twas not his stature made him great
  But greatness of his name.

Son.

His name so great? I know 'tis long,
  But easy quite to spell;
And more than half a year ago
  I knew it very well.

Father.

I mean, my child, his actions were
  So great he got a name
That everybody speaks with praise,
  That tells about his fame.

Son.

Well, what great actions did he do?
  I want to know it all.

Father.

Why, he it was that conquered Tyre,
  And leveled down her wall
And thousands of her people slew,
  And then to Persia went,
And fire and sword on every side
  Through many a region sent.
A hundred conquered cities shone
  With midnight burnings red;
And strewed o'er many a battleground
  A thousand soldiers bled.

Son.

Did killing people make him great?
  Then why was Abdel Young,
Who killed his neighbor training day,
  Put into jail and hung?
I never heard them call him great.

Father.

Why, no, 'twas not in war;
  And him that kills a single man
His neighbors all abhor.

Son.

Well, then, if I should kill a man,
  I'd kill a hundred more;
I should be great and not get hung,
  Like Abdel Young, before.

Father.

Not so, my child, 'twill never do;
  The Gospel bids be kind.

Son.

Then they that kill and they that praise,
  The Gospel do not mind.

Father.

You know, my child, the Bible says
  That you must always do
To other people as you wish
  To have them do to you.

Son.

But, Pa, did Alexander wish
  That some strong man would come
And burn his house and kill him too,
  And do as he had done?
Did everybody call him great,
  For killing people so?
Well, now, what right had he to kill,
  I should be glad to know.
If one should burn the buildings here,
  And kill the folks within,
Would anybody call him great
  For such a wicked thing?

REV. ELIJAH JONES.

408

WHERE DID YOU COME FROM?

WHERE DID YOU come from, Baby dear?
Out of the everywhere into here.

Where did get your eyes so blue?
Out of the sky as I came through.

What makes the light in them sparkle and spin?
Some of the starry spikes left in.

Where did you get that little tear?
I found it waiting when I got here.

What makes your forehead so smooth and high?
A soft hand stroked it as I went by.

What makes your cheek like a warm white rose?
I saw something better than anyone knows.

Whence that three-corner'd smile of bliss?
Three angels gave me at once a kiss.

Where did you get this pearly ear?
God spoke, and it came out to hear.

Where did you get those arms and hands?
Love made itself into hooks and bands.

Feet, whence did you come, you darling things?
From the same box as the cherubs' wings.

How did they all come just to be you?
God thought of me, and so I grew.

But how did you come to us, you dear?
God thought of you, and so I am here.

GEORGE MACDONALD.

A VISIT FROM ST. NICHOLAS

'Twas the night before Christmas, when all through the house
Not a creature was stirring, not even a mouse;
The stockings were hung by the chimney with care,
In hopes that St. Nicholas soon would be there;
The children were nestled all snug in their beds,
While visions of sugar-plums danced in their heads;
And mamma in her kerchief, and I in my cap,
Had just settled our brains for a long winter's nap,—
When out on the lawn there arose such a clatter,
I sprang from my bed to see what was the matter.
Away to the window I flew like a flash,
Tore open the shutters and threw up the sash.
The moon on the breast of the new-fallen snow
Gave a lustre of midday to objects below;
When what to my wondering eyes should appear,
But a miniature sleigh and eight tiny reindeer,
With a little old driver, so lively and quick
I knew in a moment it must be St. Nick.
More rapid than eagles his coursers they came,
And he whistled and shouted, and called them by name:
"Now, Dasher! now, Dancer! now, Prancer and Vixen!
On, Comet! on, Cupid! on, Donder and Blitzen!
To the top of the porch, to the top of the wall!
Now dash away, dash away, dash away all!"
As dry leaves that before the wild hurricane fly,
When they meet with an obstacle, mount to the sky,
So up to the house-top the coursers they flew,
With the sleigh full of toys,—and St. Nicholas too.
And then in a twinkling I heard on the roof
The prancing and pawing of each little hoof.
As I drew in my head, and was turning around,
Down the chimney St. Nicholas came with a bound.
He was dressed all in fur from his head to his foot,
And his clothes were all tarnished with ashes and soot;
A bundle of toys he had flung on his back,
And he looked like a pedlar just opening his pack.
His eyes, how they twinkled! his dimples, how merry!
His cheeks were like roses, his nose like a cherry;
His droll little mouth was drawn up like a bow,
And the beard on his chin was as white as the snow.
The stump of a pipe he held tight in his teeth,
And the smoke it encircled his head like a wreath.

He had a broad face and a little round belly
That shook, when he laughed, like a bowl full of jelly.
He was chubby and plump,—a right jolly old elf;
And I laughed, when I saw him, in spite of myself.
A wink of his eye and a twist of his head
Soon gave me to know I had nothing to dread.
He spoke not a word, but went straight to his work,
And filled all the stockings; then turned with a jerk,
And laying his finger aside of his nose,
And giving a nod, up the chimney he rose.
He sprang to his sleigh, to his team gave a whistle,
And away they all flew like the down of a thistle;
But I heard him exclaim, ere he drove out of sight,
"Happy Christmas to all, and to all a good-night!"

CLEMENT CLARKE MOORE.

WOODMAN, SPARE THAT TREE

Woodman, spare that tree!
　Touch not a single bough!
In youth it sheltered me,
　And I'll protect it now.
'Twas my forefather's hand
　That placed it near his cot;
There, woodman, let it stand,
　Thy axe shall harm it not!

That old familiar tree,
　Whose glory and renown
Are spread o'er land and sea,
　And wouldst thou hew it down?
Woodman, forbear thy stroke!
　Cut not its earth-bound ties;
O, spare that aged oak,
　Now towering to the skies!

When but an idle boy
　I sought its grateful shade;
In all their gushing joy
　Here too my sisters played.

411

My mother kissed me here;
  My father pressed my hand—
Forgive this foolish tear,
  But let that old oak stand!

My heart-strings round thee cling,
  Close as thy bark, old friend!
Here shall the wild-bird sing,
  And still thy branches bend.
Old tree! the storm still brave!
  And, woodman, leave the spot;
While I've a hand to save,
  Thy axe shall hurt it not.

GEORGE PERKINS MORRIS.

MY MOTHER'S PRAYER

As I WANDERED round the homestead,
  Many a dear, familiar spot
Brought within my recollection
  Scenes I'd seemingly forgot.
There the orchard meadow yonder,
  Here the deep, old-fashioned well,
With its old moss-covered bucket,
  Sent a thrill no tongue can tell.

Though the house was held by strangers,
  All remained the same within,
Just as when a child I rambled
  Up and down and out and in.
To the garret dark, ascending,
  Once a source of childish dread,
Peering through the misty cobwebs,
  Lo, I saw my trundle bed.

Quick, I drew it from the rubbish,
  Covered o'er with dust so long,
When, behold, I heard, in fancy,
  Strains of one familiar song,
Often sung by my dear mother
  To me in that trundle bed:
"Hush, my dear, lie still and slumber,
  Holy angels guard thy bed."

As I listened to the music,
  Stealing on in gentle strain,
I am carried back to childhood,
  I am now a child again.
'Tis the hour of my retiring,
  At the dusky eventide,
Near my trundle bed I'm kneeling,
  As of yore, by Mother's side.

Hands are on my head so loving,
  As they were in childhood's days;
I with weary tones am trying
  To repeat the words she says.
'Tis a prayer in language simple
  As a mother's lips can frame,
"Father, Thou who art in Heaven,
  Hallowed ever be Thy name."

Prayer is over, to my pillow,
  With a good-night kiss, I creep,
Scarcely waking while I whisper,
  "Now I lay me down to sleep."
Then my mother over me bending,
  Prays in earnest words but mild,
"Hear my prayer, O Heavenly Father,
  Bless, O bless, my precious child."

Yet I am but only dreaming,
  Ne'er I'll be a child again,
Many years has that dear mother
  In the quiet churchyard lain.
But the memory of her counsels
  O'er my path a light has spread,
Daily calling me to heaven,
  Even from my trundle bed.

                    T. C. O'KANE.

MAKING A MAN

HURRY THE BABY as fast as you can,
Hurry him, worry him, make him a man.
Off with his baby clothes, get him in pants,
Feed him on brain foods and make him advance.

413

Hustle him, soon as he's able to walk,
Into a grammar school; cram him with talk.
Fill his poor head full of figures and facts,
Keep on a-jamming them in till it cracks.
Once boys grew up at a rational rate,
Now we develop a man while you wait,
Rush him through college, compel him to grab
Of every known subject a dip and a dab.
Get him in business and after the cash,
All by the time he can grow a mustache.
Let him forget he was ever a boy,
Make gold his god and its jingle his joy.
Keep him a-hustling and clear out of breath,
Until he wins—nervous prostration and death.

NIXON WATERMAN.

WE ARE SEVEN

A SIMPLE child,
That lightly draws its breath,
And feels its life in every limb,
What should it know of death?

I met a little cottage girl:
She was eight years old, she said;
Her hair was thick with many a curl
That clustered round her head.

She had a rustic, woodland air,
And she was wildly clad;
Her eyes were fair, and very fair:—
Her beauty made me glad.

"Sisters and brothers, little maid,
How many may you be?"
"How many? Seven in all," she said,
And wondering looked at me.

"And where are they? I pray you tell."
She answered, "Seven are we;
And two of us at Conway dwell,
And two are gone to sea;

414

"Two of us in the churchyard lie,
　My sister and my brother;
And in the churchyard cottage I
　Dwell near them with my mother."

"You say that two at Conway dwell,
　And two are gone to sea,
Yet ye are seven! I pray you tell,
　Sweet maid, how this may be?"

Then did the little maid reply:
　"Seven boys and girls are we;
Two of us in the churchyard lie,
　Beneath the churchyard tree."

"You run about, my little maid,
　Your limbs they are alive;
If two are in the churchyard laid,
　Then ye are only five."

"Their graves are green, they may be seen,"
　The little maid replied,
"Twelve steps or more from my mother's door,
　And they are side by side.

"My stockings there I often knit,
　My kerchief there I hem;
And there upon the ground I sit—
　I sit and sing to them.

"And often after sunset, sir,
　When it is light and fair,
I take my little porringer,
　And eat my supper there.

"The first that died was little Jane;
　In bed she moaning lay,
Till God released her of her pain;
　And then she went away.

"So in the churchyard she was laid;
　And when the grass was dry,
Together round her grave we play'd,
　My brother John and I.

"And when the ground was white with snow,
   And I could run and slide,
My brother John was forced to go,
   And he lies by her side."

"How many are you, then," said I,
   "If they two are in Heaven?"
The little maiden did reply,
   "Oh, master, we are seven!"

'But they are dead—those two are dead,
   Their spirits are in Heaven!"
'Twas throwing words away, for still
The little maid would have her will,
   And said, "Nay, we are seven!"

WILLIAM WORDSWORTH.

IN SCHOOL-DAYS

STILL SITS the school-house by the road,
   A ragged beggar sunning;
Around it still the sumachs grow,
   And blackberry-vines are running.

Within, the master's desk is seen,
   Deep scarred by raps official;
The warping floor, the battered seats,
   The jack-knife's carved initial;

The charcoal frescoes on its wall;
   Its door's worn sill, betraying
The feet that, creeping slow to school,
   Went storming out to playing!

Long years ago a winter sun
   Shone over it at setting;
Lit up its western window-panes,
   And low eaves' icy fretting.

It touched the tangled golden curls,
   And brown eyes full of grieving,
Of one who still her steps delay
   When all the school were leaving.

For near her stood the little boy
    Her childish favor singled;
His cap pulled low upon a face
    Where pride and shame were mingled.

Pushing with restless feet the snow
    To right and left, he lingered;—
As restlessly her tiny hands
    The blue-checked apron fingered.

He saw her lift her eyes; he felt
    The soft hand's light caressing,
And heard the tremble of her voice,
    As if a fault confessing.

"I'm sorry that I spelt the word:
    I hate to go above you,
Because,"—the brown eyes lower fell,—
    "Because, you see, I love you!"

Still memory to a gray-haired man
    That sweet child-face is showing.
Dear girl! the grasses on her grave
    Have forty years been growing!

He lives to learn, in life's hard school,
    How few who pass above him
Lament their triumph and his loss,
    Like her,—because they love him.

JOHN GREENLEAF WHITTIER.

VII. PATRIOTISM AND WAR

THE STAR-SPANGLED BANNER

Oh, say, can you see, by the dawn's early light,
　　What so proudly we hailed at the twilight's last gleaming,
Whose broad stripes and bright stars through the perilous fight,
　　O'er the ramparts we watched were so gallantly streaming?
And the rockets' red glare, the bombs bursting in air,
Gave proof thro' the night that our flag was still there.
Oh, say, does that star-spangled banner yet wave
O'er the land of the free, and the home of the brave!

On the shore, dimly seen thro' the mists of the deep,
　　Where the foe's haughty host in dread silence reposes,
What is that which the breeze o'er the towering steep,
　　As it fitfully blows, half conceals, half discloses?
Now it catches the gleam of the morning's first beam,
In full glory reflected, now shines on the stream.
'Tis the star-spangled banner; oh, long may it wave
O'er the land of the free, and the home of the brave!

And where is that band who so vauntingly swore
　　That the havoc of war and the battle's confusion
A home and a country should leave us no more?
　　Their blood has washed out their foul footsteps' pollution.
No refuge could save the hireling and slave
From the terror of flight, or the gloom of the grave:
And the star-spangled banner in triumph doth wave
O'er the land of the free, and the home of the brave!

Oh, thus be it ever when freemen shall stand
　　Between their loved homes and the war's desolation;
Blest with victory and peace, may the heaven-rescued land
　　Praise the power that hath made and preserved us a nation!
Then conquer we must, when our cause it is just,
And this be our motto: "In God is our trust!"
And the star-spangled banner in triumph doth wave,
O'er the land of the free, and the home of the brave!

FRANCIS SCOTT KEY.

AMERICA THE BEAUTIFUL

O BEAUTIFUL for spacious skies,
   For amber waves of grain,
For purple mountain majesties
   Above the fruited plain!
America! America!
   God shed His grace on thee
And crown thy good with brotherhood
   From sea to shining sea!

O beautiful for pilgrim feet,
   Whose stern, impassioned stress
A thoroughfare for freedom beat
   Across the wilderness!
America! America!
   God mend thine every flaw,
Confirm thy soul in self-control,
   Thy liberty in law!

O beautiful for heroes proved
   In liberating strife,
Who more than self their country loved,
   And mercy more than life!
America! America!
   May God thy gold refine,
Till all success be nobleness
   And every gain divine!

O beautiful for patriot dream
   That sees beyond the years
Thine alabaster cities gleam
   Undimmed by human tears!
America! America!
   God shed His grace on thee,
And crown thy good with brotherhood
   From sea to shining sea!

KATHARINE LEE BATES.

BREATHES THERE THE MAN

From *"The Lay of the Last Minstrel,"* CANTO VI.

BREATHES there the man with soul so dead
Who never to himself hath said,
   This is my own, my native land!
Whose heart hath ne'er within him burned,
As home his footsteps he hath turned
   From wandering on a foreign strand?
If such there breathe, go, mark him well;
For him no minstrel raptures swell;
High though his titles, proud his name,
Boundless his wealth as wish can claim,
Despite those titles, power, and pelf,
The wretch, concentred all in self,
Living, shall forfeit fair renown,
And, doubly dying, shall go down
To the vile dust from whence he sprung,
Unwept, unhonored, and unsung.

                     SIR WALTER SCOTT.

I HAVE A RENDEZVOUS WITH DEATH

I HAVE A RENDEZVOUS with Death
At some disputed barricade,
When Spring comes back with rustling shade
And apple blossoms fill the air—
I have a rendezvous with Death
When Spring brings back blue days and fair.

It may be he shall take my hand,
And lead me into his dark land,
And close my eyes and quench my breath—
It may be I shall pass him still.
I have a rendezvous with Death
On some scarred slope of battered hill,
When Spring comes round again this year
And the first meadow flowers appear.

God knows 'twere better to be deep
Pillowed in silk and scented down,
Where Love throbs out in blissful sleep,
Pulse nigh to puise, and breath to breath,
Where hushed awakenings are dear . . .
But I've a rendezvous with Death
At midnight in some flaming town,
When Spring trips north again this year;
And I to my pledged word am true,
I shall not fail that rendezvous.

ALAN SEEGER.

AMERICA FOR ME

TIS FINE to see the Old World, and travel up and down
Among the famous palaces and cities of renown,
To admire the crumbly castles and the statues of the kings,—
But now I think I've had enough of antiquated things.

So it's home again, and home again, America for me!
My heart is turning home again, and there I long to be
In the land of youth and freedom beyond the ocean bars,
Where the air is full of sunlight and the flag is full of stars.

Oh, London is a man's town, there's power in the air;
And Paris is a woman's town, with flowers in her hair;
And it's sweet to dream in Venice, and it's great to study Rome,
But when it comes to living, there is no place like home.

I like the German fir-woods, in green battalions drilled;
I like the gardens of Versailles with flashing fountains filled;
But, oh, to take your hand, my dear, and ramble for a day
In the friendly western woodland where Nature has her way!

I know that Europe's wonderful, yet something seems to lack!
The Past is too much with her, and the people looking back.
But the glory of the Present is to make the Future free,—
We love our land for what she is and what she is to be.

Oh, it's home again, and home again, America for me!
I want a ship that's westward bound to plough the rolling sea,
To the blessed Land of Room Enough beyond the ocean bars,
Where the air is full of sunlight and the flag is full of stars.

HENRY VAN DYKE.

BOOTS

(Infantry Columns)

We're foot—slog—slog—slog—sloggin' over Africa,
Foot—foot—foot—foot—sloggin' over Africa—
(Boots—boots—boots—boots—movin' up and down again!)
    There's no discharge in the war!

Seven—six—eleven—five—nine-an'-twenty mile to-day—
Four—eleven—seventeen—thirty-two the day before—
(Boots—boots—boots—boots—movin' up and down again!)
    There's no discharge in the war!

Don't—don't—don't—don't—look at what's in front of you.
(Boots—boots—boots—boots—movin' up an' down again),
Men—men—men—men—men go mad with watchin' 'em,
    An' there's no discharge in the war!

Try—try—try—try—to think o' something different—
Oh—my—God—keep—me from goin' lunatic!
(Boots—boots—boots—boots—movin' up an' down again!)
    There's no discharge in the war!

Count—count—count—count—the bullets in the bandoliers.
If—your—eyes—drop—they will get atop o' you.
(Boots—boots—boots—boots—movin' up and down again)—
    There's no discharge in the war!

We—can—stick—out—'unger, thirst, an' weariness,
But—not—not—not—not the chronic sight of 'em—
Boots—boots—boots—boots—movin' up an' down again,
    An' there's no discharge in the war!

'Tain't—so—bad—by—day because o' company,
But—night—brings—long—strings—o' forty thousand million
Boots—boots—boots—boots—movin' up an' down again.
    There's no discharge in the war!

I—'ave—marched—six—weeks in 'Ell an' certify
It—is—not—fire—devils—dark or anything,
But boots—boots—boots—boots—movin' up an' down again,
    An' there's no discharge in the war!

RUDYARD KIPLING.

425

INDEPENDENCE BELL—JULY 4, 1776

THERE WAS A TUMULT in the city
In the quaint old Quaker town,
And the streets were rife with people
Pacing restless up and down—
People gathering at corners,
Where they whispered each to each,
And the sweat stood on their temples
With the earnestness of speech.

As the bleak Atlantic currents
Lash the wild Newfoundland shore,
So they beat against the State House,
So they surged against the door;
And the mingling of their voices
Made the harmony profound,
Till the quiet street of Chestnut
Was all turbulent with sound.

"Will they do it?" "Dare they do it?"
"Who is speaking?" "What's the news?"
"What of Adams?" "What of Sherman?"
"Oh, God grant they won't refuse!"
"Make some way there!" "Let me nearer!"
"I am stifling!" "Stifle then!
When a nation's life's at hazard,
We've no time to think of men!"

So they surged against the State House,
While all solemnly inside,
Sat the Continental Congress,
Truth and reason for their guide,
O'er a simple scroll debating,
Which, though simple it might be,
Yet should shake the cliffs of England
With the thunders of the free.

Far aloft in that high steeple
Sat the bellman, old and gray,
He was weary of the tyrant
And his iron-sceptered sway;

So he sat, with one hand ready
On the clapper of the bell,
When his eye could catch the signal,
The long-expected news to tell.

See! See! The dense crowd quivers
Through all its lengthy line,
As the boy beside the portal
Hastens forth to give the sign!
With his little hands uplifted,
Breezes dallying with his hair,
Hark! with deep, clear intonation,
Breaks his young voice on the air.

Hushed the people's swelling murmur,
Whilst the boy crys joyously;
"Ring!" he shouts, "Ring! Grandpapa,
Ring! oh, ring for Liberty!"
Quickly, at the given signal
The old bellman lifts his hand,
Forth he sends the good news, making
Iron music through the land.

How they shouted! What rejoicing!
How the old bell shook the air,
Till the clang of freedom ruffled,
The calmly gliding Delaware!
How the bonfires and the torches
Lighted up the night's repose,
And from the flames, like fabled Phoenix,
Our glorious liberty arose!

That old State House bell is silent,
Hushed is now its clamorous tongue;
But the spirit it awakened
Still is living—ever young;
And when we greet the smiling sunlight
On the fourth of each July,
We will ne'er forget the bellman
Who, betwixt the earth and sky,
Rung out, loudly, "Independence";
Which, please God, shall never die!

UNKNOWN.

427

THE UNKNOWN SOLDIER

THERE'S A GRAVEYARD near the White House
  Where the Unknown Soldier lies,
And the flowers there are sprinkled
  With the tears from mother's eyes.

I stood there not so long ago
  With roses for the brave,
And suddenly I heard a voice
  Speak from out the grave:

'I am the Unknown Soldier,"
  The spirit voice began,
"And I think I have the right
  To ask some questions man to man.

"Are my buddies taken care of?
  Was their victory so sweet?
Is that big reward you offered
  Selling pencils on the street?

"Did they really win the freedom
  They battled to achieve?
Do you still respect that Croix de Guerre
  Above that empty sleeve?

"Does a gold star in the window
  Now mean anything at all?
I wonder how my old girl feels
  When she hears a bugle call.

"And that baby who sang
'Hello, Central, give me no man's land'—
Can they replace her daddy
  With a military band?

"I wonder if the profiteers
  Have satisfied their greed?
I wonder if a soldier's mother
  Ever is in need?

"I wonder if the kings, who planned it all
  Are really satisfied?
They played their game of checkers
  And eleven million died.

"I am the Unknown Soldier
  And maybe I died in vain,
But if I were alive and my country called,
  I'd do it all over again."

BILLY ROSE.

IN FLANDERS FIELDS

In Flanders fields the poppies blow
Between the crosses, row on row,
  That mark our place; and in the sky
  The larks, still bravely singing, fly
Scarce heard amid the guns below.

We are the Dead. Short days ago
We lived, felt dawn, saw sunset glow,
  Loved and were loved, and now we lie
  In Flanders fields.

Take up our quarrel with the foe:
To you from failing hands we throw
  The torch; be yours to hold it high.
  If ye break faith with us who die
We shall not sleep, though poppies grow
  In Flanders fields.

JOHN McCRAE.

REPLY TO IN FLANDERS FIELDS

Oh! sleep in peace where poppies grow;
The torch your falling hands let go
Was caught by us, again held high,
A beacon light in Flanders sky
That dims the stars to those below.
You are our dead, you held the foe,
And ere the poppies cease to blow,
We'll prove our faith in you who lie
  In Flanders Fields.

Oh! rest in peace, we quickly go
To you who bravely died, and know
In other fields was heard the cry,
For freedom's cause, of you who lie,
So still asleep where poppies grow,
In Flanders Fields.

As in rumbling sound, to and fro,
The lightning flashes, sky aglow,
The mighty hosts appear, and high
Above the din of battle cry,
Scarce heard amidst the guns below,
Are fearless hearts who fight the foe,
And guard the place where poppies grow.
Oh! sleep in peace, all you who lie
    In Flanders Fields.

And still the poppies gently blow,
Between the crosses, row on row.
The larks, still bravely soaring high,
Are singing now their lullaby
To you who sleep where poppies grow
In Flanders Fields.

JOHN MITCHELL.

ANOTHER REPLY TO *IN FLANDERS FIELDS*

IN FLANDERS FIELDS the cannons boom,
And fitful flashes light the gloom;
While up above, like eagles, fly
The fierce destroyers of the sky;
With stains the earth wherein you lie
Is redder than the poppy bloom,
    In Flanders Fields.
Sleep on, ye brave! The shrieking shell,
The quaking trench, the startling yell,
The fury of the battle hell
Shall wake you not, for all is well;
Sleep peacefully, for all is well.

430

Your flaming torch aloft we bear,
With burning heart and oath we swear
To keep the faith, to fight it through,
To crush the foe, or sleep with you,
    In Flanders Fields.

                        J. A. ARMSTRONG.

AMERICA'S ANSWER

REST YE in peace, ye Flanders dead.
The fight that ye so bravely led
We've taken up. And we will keep
True faith with you who lie asleep
With each a cross to mark his bed,
    In Flanders fields.

Fear not that we have died for naught.
The torch ye threw to us we caught.
Ten million hands will hold it high,
And Freedom's light shall never die!
We've learned the lesson that we taught
    In Flanders fields.

                        R. W. LILLIARD.

LAND OF THE FREE

AMERICA, O Power benign, great hearts revere your name,
You stretch your hand to every land, to weak and strong the same;
You claim no conquest of the sea, nor conquest of the field,
But conquest for the rights of man, that despots all shall yield.

Chorus:

    America, fair land of mine, home of the just and true,
    All hail to thee, land of the free, and the Red-White-and-Blue.

America, staunch, undismayed, your spirit is our might:
No splendor falls on feudal walls upon your mountain's height,
But shafts of Justice pierce your skies to light the way for all,
A world's great brotherhood of man, that cannot, must not fall.

America, in God we trust, we fear no tyrant's horde:
There's light that leads toward better deeds than conquest by the
    sword;
Yet our cause is just, if fight we must until the world be free
Of every menace, breed, or caste that strikes at Liberty.

America, home of the brave, our song in praise we bring—
Where Stars and Stripes the winds unfurl, 'tis there that tributes ring;
Our fathers gave their lives that we should live in Freedom's light—
Our lives we consecrate to thee, our guide the Might of Right.

ARTHUR NICHOLAS HOSKING

OLD IRONSIDES

[Written with reference to the proposed breaking up of the famous U. S. frigate
Constitution.]

Ay, TEAR her tattered ensign down!
    Long has it waved on high,
And many an eye has danced to see
    That banner in the sky;
Beneath it rung the battle-shout,
    And burst the cannon's roar:
The meteor of the ocean air
    Shall sweep the clouds no more!

Her deck, once red with heroes' blood,
    Where knelt the vanquished foe,
When winds were hurrying o'er the flood
    And waves were white below,
No more shall feel the victor's tread,
    Or know the conquered knee:
The harpies of the shore shall pluck
    The eagle of the sea!

O better that her shattered hulk
    Should sink beneath the wave!
Her thunders shook the mighty deep,
    And there should be her grave:
Nail to the mast her holy flag,
    Set every threadbare sail,
And give her to the god of storms,
    The lightning and the gale!

OLIVER WENDELL HOLMES.

THE BLUE AND THE GRAY

[The women of Columbus, Mississippi, strewed flowers alike on the graves of the Confederate and the National soldiers.]

By the flow of the inland river,
　Whence the fleets of iron have fled,
Where the blades of the grave grass quiver,
　Asleep are the ranks of the dead;—
　　Under the sod and the dew,
　　　Waiting the judgment day;—
　　Under the one, the Blue;
　　　Under the other, the Gray.

These in the robings of glory,
　Those in the gloom of defeat,
All with the battle blood gory,
　In the dusk of eternity meet;—
　　Under the sod and the dew,
　　　Waiting the judgment day;—
　　Under the laurel, the Blue;
　　　Under the willow, the Gray.

From the silence of sorrowful hours
　The desolate mourners go,
Lovingly laden with flowers
　Alike for the friend and the foe,—
　　Under the sod and the dew,
　　　Waiting the judgment day;—
　　Under the roses, the Blue;
　　　Under the lilies, the Gray.

So with an equal splendor
　The morning sun rays fall,
With a touch, impartially tender,
　On the blossoms blooming for all;—
　　Under the sod and the dew,
　　　Waiting the judgment day;—
　　'Broidered with gold, the Blue;
　　　Mellowed with gold, the Gray.

So, when the summer calleth,
　On forest and field of grain
With an equal murmur falleth
　The cooling drip of the rain;—

433

Under the sod and the dew,
  Waiting the judgment day;—
Wet with the rain, the Blue;
  Wet with the rain, the Gray.

Sadly, but not with upbraiding,
  The generous deed was done;
In the storm of the years that are fading,
  No braver battle was won;—
    Under the sod and the dew,
      Waiting the judgment day;—
    Under the blossoms, the Blue;
      Under the garlands, the Gray.

No more shall the war cry sever,
  Or the winding rivers be red;
They banish our anger forever
  When they laurel the graves of our dead!
    Under the sod and the dew,
      Waiting the judgment day;—
    Love and tears for the Blue,
      Tears and love for the Gray.

FRANCIS MILES FINCH.

THE MEN BEHIND THE GUNS

A CHEER and salute for the Admiral, and here's to the Captain bold,
And never forget the Commodore's debt when the deeds of might are
    told!
They stand to the deck through the battle's wreck when the great shells
    roar and screech—
And never they fear when the foe is near to practise what they preach:
But off with your hat and three times three for Columbia's true-blue
    sons,
The men below who batter the foe—the men behind the guns!

II

Oh, light and merry of heart are they when they swing into port once
    more,
When, with more than enough of the "green-back stuff," they start for
    their leave-o'-shore;

434

And you'd think, perhaps, that the blue-bloused chaps who loll along
    the street
Are a tender bit, with salt on it, for some fierce "mustache" to eat—
Some warrior bold, with straps of gold, who dazzles and fairly stuns
The modest worth of the sailor boys—the lads who serve the guns.

III

But say not a word till the shot is heard that tells the fight is on,
Till the long, deep roar grows more and more from the ships of "Yank"
    and "Don,"
Till over the deep and tempest's sweep of fire and bursting shell,
And the very air is a mad Despair in the throes of a living hell;
Then down, deep down, in the mighty ship, unseen by the midday suns,
You'll find the chaps who are giving the raps—the men behind the
    guns!

IV

Oh, well they know how the cyclones blow that they loose from their
    cloud of death,
And they know is heard the thunder-word their fierce ten-incher saith!
The steel decks rock with the lightning shock, and shake with the
    great recoil,
And the sea grows red with the blood of the dead and reaches for his
    spoil—
But not till the foe has gone below or turns his prow and runs,
Shall the voice of peace bring sweet release to the men behind the guns!

JOHN JEROME ROONEY.

JEANNETTE AND JEANNOT

You ARE GOING far away, far away from poor Jeannette;
There is no one left to love me now, and you, too, may forget.
But my heart will be with you, wherever you may go;
Can you look me in the face and say the same to me, Jeannot?

When you wear the jacket red and the beautiful cockade,
Oh! I fear that you'll forget all the promises you made;
With a gun upon your shoulder and your bayonet by your side,
You'll be taking some proud lady and making her your bride.

Or, when glory leads the way, you'll be madly rushing on,
Never thinking, if they kill you, that my happiness is gone;

435

If you win the day, perhaps a general you'll be;
Tho' I'm proud to think of that, what will become of me?

Oh! if I were Queen of France, or still better, Pope of Rome,
I'd have no fighting men abroad, no weeping maids at home;
All should be at peace; or if kings must show their might,
Why, let them who make the quarrel be the only men to fight.

CHARLES JEFFRIES.

Jeannot's Answer

Cheer up, cheer up! my own Jeanette, tho' far away I go,
In all the changes I may see I'll be the same Jeannot;
And if I win both fame and gold, ah! be not so unkind
To think I could forget you in the home I leave behind.

There's not a lady in the land, and if she were a queen,
Could win my heart from you, Jeannette, so true as you have been;
They must have gallant warriors; chance had cast the lot on me;
But, mind you, this soldier, love, must no deserter be.

Why, since the world began, the surest road to fame
Has been the field where men unknown might win themselves a name;
And well I know the brightest eyes have all the brighter shone,
When looking at some warrior bold, returned from battles won.

And you'd put an end to deeds which ladies love so well,
And have no tales of valor left for history to tell!
The soldier's is a noble trade, Jeannette; then rail no more,
Were only kings themselves to fight, there'd be an end to war!

CHARLES JEFFRIES.

BINGEN ON THE RHINE

A SOLDIER of the Legion lay dying in Algiers,
There was lack of woman's nursing, there was dearth of woman's tears;
But a comrade stood beside him, while his life-blood ebbed away,
And bent, with pitying glances, to hear what he might say.
The dying soldier faltered, and he took that comrade's hand,
And he said, "I nevermore shall see my own, my native land;
Take a message, and a token, to some distant friends of mine,
For I was born at Bingen,—at Bingen on the Rhine.

436

"Tell my brothers and companions, when they meet and crowd around
To hear my mournful story in the pleasant vineyard ground,
That we fought the battle bravely, and when the day was done
Full many a corpse lay ghastly pale beneath the setting sun.

"And 'midst the dead and dying were some grown old in wars,
The death-wound on their gallant breasts, the last of many scars;
But some were young, and suddenly beheld life's morn decline,
And one had come from Bingen, fair Bingen on the Rhine.

"Tell my mother that her other sons shall comfort her old age,
And I was aye a truant bird, that thought his home a cage,
For my father was a soldier, and even as a child
My heart leap'd forth to hear him tell of struggles fierce and wild;
And when he died, and left us to divide his scanty hoard,
I let them take whate'er they would, but kept my father's sword,
And with boyish love I hung it where the bright light used to shine
On the cottage-wall at Bingen—calm Bingen on the Rhine.

"Tell my sister not to weep for me, and sob with drooping head,
When the troops are marching home again with glad and gallant tread,
But to look upon them proudly, with a calm and steadfast eye,
For her brother was a soldier too, and not afraid to die.
And if a comrade seek her love, I ask her in my name
To listen to him kindly, without regret or shame,
And to hang the old sword in its place (my father's sword and mine),
For the honor of old Bingen—dear Bingen on the Rhine.

"There's another—not a sister: in the happy days gone by,
You'd have known her by the merriment that sparkled in her eye;
Too innocent for coquetry, too fond for idle scorning,
O friend, I fear the lightest heart makes sometimes heaviest mourning;

"Tell her the last night of my life (for ere the moon be risen
My body will be out of pain—my soul be out of prison),
I dream'd I stood with her, and saw the yellow sunlight shine
On the vineclad hills of Bingen—fair Bingen on the Rhine.

"I saw the blue Rhine sweep along—I heard, or seemed to hear,
The German songs we used to sing, in chorus sweet and clear,
And down the pleasant river, and up the slanting hill,
The echoing chorus sounded through the evening calm and still;
And her glad blue eyes were on me as we pass'd with friendly talk
Down many a path beloved of yore, and well-remember'd walk,
And her little hand lay lightly, confidingly in mine;
But we'll meet no more at Bingen—loved Bingen on the Rhine."

437

His voice grew faint and hoarser—his grasp was childish weak—
His eyes put on a dying look—he sigh'd and ceased to speak;
His comrade bent to lift him, but the spark of life had fled—
The soldier of the Legion in a foreign land was dead!
And the soft moon rose up slowly, and calmly she look'd down
On the red sand of the battle-field, with bloody corpses strown;
Yea, calmly on that dreadful scene her pale light seem'd to shine,
As it shone on distant Bingen—fair Bingen on the Rhine.

CAROLINE NORTON.

THE BIVOUAC OF THE DEAD

THE MUFFLED drum's sad roll has beat
   The soldier's last tattoo!
No more on life's parade shall meet
   The brave and fallen few.
On Fame's eternal camping ground
   Their silent tents are spread,
And glory guards with solemn round
   The bivouac of the dead.

No rumor of the foe's advance
   Now swells upon the wind,
Nor troubled thought of midnight haunts,
   Of loved ones left behind;
No vision of the morrow's strife
   The warrior's dreams alarms,
No braying horn or screaming fife
   At dawn to call to arms.

Their shivered swords are red with rust,
   Their plumèd heads are bowed,
Their haughty banner, trailed in dust,
   Is now their martial shroud—
And plenteous funeral tears have washed
   The red stains from each brow,
And the proud forms by battle gashed
   Are free from anguish now.

The neighing troop, the flashing blade,
   The bugle's stirring blast,
The charge,—the dreadful cannonade,
   The din and shout, are passed;

Nor war's wild notes, nor glory's peal
  Shall thrill with fierce delight
Those breasts that nevermore shall feel
  The rapture of the fight.

Like the fierce Northern hurricane
  That sweeps the great plateau,
Flushed with the triumph yet to gain,
  Come down the serried foe,
Who heard the thunder of the fray
  Break o'er the field beneath,
Knew the watchword of the day
  Was "Victory or death!"

Rest on, embalmed and sainted dead,
  Dear is the blood you gave—
No impious footstep here shall tread
  The herbage of your grave.
Nor shall your glory be forgot
  While Fame her record keeps,
Or honor points the hallowed spot
  Where valor proudly sleeps.

Yon marble minstrel's voiceless stone
  In deathless song shall tell,
When many a vanquished year hath flown,
  The story how you fell.
Nor wreck nor change, nor winter's blight,
  Nor time's remorseless doom,
Can dim one ray of holy light
  That gilds your glorious tomb.

THEODORE O'HARA.

I FIGHTS MIT SIGEL!

I MET HIM again, he was trudging along,
  His knapsack with chickens was swelling;
He'd "Blenkered" these dainties, and thought it **no wrong,**
  From some secessionist's dwelling.
"What regiment's yours? and under whose flag
  Do you fight?" said I, touching his shoulder;
Turning slowly around, he smilingly said,
  For the thought made him stronger and bolder;
    "I fights mit Sigel."

439

The next time I saw him his knapsack was gone,
  His cap and canteen were missing;
Shell, shrapnel, and grape, and the swift rifle ball
  Around him and o'er him were hissing.
How are you, my friend, and where have you been,
  And for what and for whom are you fighting?
He said, as a shell from the enemy's gun
  Sent his arm and his musket "a-kiting,"
      "I fights mit Sigel."

And once more I saw him and knelt by his side,
  His life blood was rapidly flowing;
I whispered of home, wife, children, and friends,
  The bright land to which he was going;
And have you no word for the dear ones at home,
  The "wee one," the father or mother?
"Yaw! yaw!" said he, "tell them! oh! tell them I fights"—
  Poor fellow! he thought of no other—
      "I fights mit Sigel."

We scraped out a grave, and he dreamlessly sleeps
  On the banks of the Shenandoah River;
His home and his kindred alike are unknown,
  His reward in the hands of the Giver.
We placed a rough board at the head of his grave,
  "And we left him alone in his glory,"
But on it we marked ere we turned from the spot,
  The little we knew of his story—
      "I fights mit Sigel."

                                    GRANT P. ROBINSON.

THE CHARGE OF THE LIGHT BRIGADE

HALF A LEAGUE, half a league,
  Half a league onward,
All in the valley of Death
  Rode the six hundred.
"Forward, the Light Brigade!
Charge for the guns," he said:
Into the valley of Death
  Rode the six hundred.

440

"Forward, the Light Brigade!"
Was there a man dismay'd?
Not tho' the soldier knew
  Someone had blunder'd:
Theirs not to make reply,
Theirs not to reason why,
Theirs but to do and die:
Into the valley of Death
  Rode the six hundred.

Cannon to right of them,
Cannon to left of them,
Cannon in front of them
  Volley'd and thunder'd;
Storm'd at with shot and shell,
Boldly they rode and well,
Into the jaws of Death,
Into the mouth of Hell
  Rode the six hundred.

Flash'd all their sabers bare,
Flash'd as they turn'd in air
Sabring the gunners there,
Charging an army, while
  All the world wonder'd:
Plung'd in the battery-smoke
Right thro' the line they broke;
Cossack and Russian
Reel'd from the saber-stroke
  Shatter'd and sunder'd.
Then they rode back, but not,
  Not the six hundred.

Cannon to right of them,
Cannon to left of them,
Cannon behind them
  Volley'd and thunder'd;
Storm'd at with shot and shell,
While horse and hero fell,
They that had fought so well
Came thro' the jaws of Death,
Back from the mouth of Hell,
All that was left of them,
  Left of six hundred.

When can their glory fade?
O the wild charge they made!
All the world wonder'd.
Honor the charge they made!
Honor the Light Brigade,
Noble six hundred!

ALFRED TENNYSON.

THE FIGHTING RACE

"READ OUT the names!" and Burke sat back,
　And Kelly drooped his head,
While Shea—they called him Scholar Jack—
　Went down the list of the dead.
Officers, seamen, gunners, marines,
　The crews of the gig and yawl,
The bearded man and the lad in his teens,
　Carpenters, coal passers—all.
Then, knocking the ashes from out his pipe,
　Said Burke in an offhand way:
"We're all in that dead man's list, by cripe!
　Kelly and Burke and Shea."
"Well, here's to the Maine, and I'm sorry for Spain,"
　Said Kelly and Burke and Shea.

"Wherever there's Kellys there's trouble," said Burke.
　"Wherever fighting's the game,
Or a spice of danger in grown man's work,"
　Said Kelly, "you'll find my name."
"And do we fall short," said Burke, getting mad,
　"When it's touch and go for life?"
Said Shea, "It's thirty-odd years, bedad,
　Since I charged to drum and fife
Up Marye's Heights, and my old canteen
　Stopped a rebel ball on its way;
There were blossoms of blood on our sprigs of green—
　Kelly and Burke and Shea—
And the dead didn't brag." "Well, here's to the flag!"
　Said Kelly and Burke and Shea.

442

"I wish 'twas in Ireland, for there's the place,"
  Said Burke, "that we'd die by right,
In the cradle of our soldier race,
  After one good stand-up fight.
My grandfather fell on Vinegar Hill,
  And fighting was not his trade;
But his rusty pike's in the cabin still,
  With Hessian blood on the blade."
"Aye, aye," said Kelly, "the pikes were great
  When the word was 'clear the way!'
We were thick on the roll in ninety-eight—
  Kelly and Burke and Shea."
"Well, here's to the pike and the sword and the like!"
  Said Kelly and Burke and Shea.

And Shea, the scholar, with rising joy,
  Said, "We were at Ramillies;
We left our bones at Fontenoy
  And up in the Pyrenees;
Before Dunkirk, on Landen's plain,
  Cremona, Lille, and Ghent;
We're all over Austria, France and Spain,
  Wherever they pitched a tent.
We've died for England from Waterloo
  To Egypt and Dargai;
And still there's enough for a corps or crew,
  Kelly and Burke and Shea."
'Well, here's to good honest fighting blood!"
  Said Kelly and Burke and Shea.

"Oh, the fighting races don't die out,
  If they seldom die in bed,
For love is first in their hearts, no doubt,"
  Said Burke; then Kelly said:
"When Michael, the Irish Archangel, stands,
  The Angel with the sword,
And the battle dead from a hundred lands
  Are ranged in one big horde,
Our line, that for Gabriel's trumpet waits,
  Will stretch three deep that day,
From Jehoshaphat to the Golden Gates—
  Kelly and Burke and Shea."
"Well, here's thank God for the race and the sod!"
  Said Kelly and Burke and Shea.

JOSEPH I. C. CLARKE.

YE MARINERS OF ENGLAND

YE MARINERS of England
That guard our native seas;
Whose flag has braved, a thousand years,
The battle and the breeze!
Your glorious standard launch again
To match another foe,
And sweep through the deep,
While the stormy winds do blow;
While the battle rages loud and long,
And the stormy winds do blow.

The spirits of your fathers
Shall start from every wave,
For the deck it was their field of fame,
And ocean was their grave:
Where Blake and mighty Nelson fell,
Your manly hearts shall glow,
As ye sweep through the deep,
While the stormy winds do blow;
While the battle rages loud and long,
And the stormy winds do blow.

Britannia needs no bulwarks,
No towers along the steep;
Her march is o'er the mountain-waves,
Her home is on the deep.
With thunders from her native oak,
She quells the floods below,—
As they roar on the shore,
When the stormy winds do blow;
When the battle rages loud and long
And the stormy winds do blow.

The meteor flag of England
Shall yet terrific burn;
Till danger's troubled night depart,
And the star of peace return.
Then, then, ye ocean warriors,
Our song and feast shall flow
To the fame of your name,
When the storm has ceased to blow;
When the fiery fight is heard no more,
And the storm has ceased to blow.

THOMAS CAMPBELL.

CANADIAN BOAT-SONG

LISTEN TO ME, as when ye heard our father
    Sing long ago the song of other shores—
Listen to me, and then in chorus gather
    All your deep voices, as ye pull your oars:

    Chorus:

Fair these broad meads—these hoary woods are grand;
    But we are exiles from our fathers' land.

From the lone shieling of the misty island
    Mountains divide us, and the waste of seas—
Yet still the blood is strong, the heart is Highland,
    And we in dreams behold the Hebrides.

Fair these broad meads—these hoary woods are grand;
    But we are exiles from our fathers' land.

We ne'er shall tread the fancy-haunted valley,
    Where 'tween the dark hills creeps the small clear stream,
In arms around the patriarch banner rally,
    Nor see the moon on royal tombstones gleam.

Fair these broad meads—these hoary woods are grand;
    But we are exiles from our fathers' land.

When the bold kindred, in the time long vanish'd,
    Conquer'd the soil and fortified the keep—
No seer foretold the children would be banish'd,
    That a degenerate lord might boast his sheep.

Fair these broad meads—these hoary woods are grand;
    But we are exiles from our fathers' land.

Come foreign rage—let Discord burst in slaughter!
    O then for clansmen true and stern claymore—
The hearts that would have given their blood like water,
    Beat heavily beyond the Atlantic roar.

Fair these broad meads, these hoary woods are grand;
    But we are exiles from our fathers' land.

CREDITED TO JOHN GALT, AND ALSO TO
JOHN WILSON ("CHRISTOPHER NORTH")

VIII.   HUMOR AND WHIMSEY

VAGABOND HOUSE

WHEN I HAVE a house . . . as I sometime may . . .
I'll suit my fancy in every way.
I'll fill it with things that have caught my eye
In drifting from Iceland to Molokai
It won't be correct or in period style,
But . . . oh, I've thought for a long, long while
Of all the corners and all the nooks,
Of all the bookshelves and all the books,
The great big table, the deep, soft chairs,
And the Chinese rug at the foot of the stairs;
It's an old, old rug from far Chow Wan
That a Chinese princess once walked on.

My house will stand on the side of a hill
By a slow, broad river, deep and still,
With a tall lone pine on guard near by
Where the birds can sing and the stormwinds cry.
A flagstone walk with lazy curves
Will lead to the door where a Pan's head serves
As a knocker there like a vibrant drum
To let me know that a friend has come;
And the door will squeak as I swing it wide
To welcome you to the cheer inside.

For I'll have good friends who can sit and chat
Or simply sit, when it comes to that,
By the fireplace where the fir logs blaze
And the smoke rolls up in a weaving haze.
I'll want a woodbox, scarred and rough,
For leaves and bark and odorous stuff

Like resinous knots and cones and gums
To chuck on the flames when winter comes;
And I hope a cricket will stay around,
For I love its creaky, lonesome sound.

There'll be driftwood powder to burn on logs,
And a shaggy rug for a couple of dogs—
Boreas, winner of prize and cup,
And Mickey, a lovable gutter pup.
Thoroughbreds, both of them, right from the start,
One by breeding, the other by heart.

There are times when only a dog will do
For a friend—when you're beaten, sick and blue,
And the world's all wrong; for he won't care
If you break and cry, or grouch and swear;
For he'll let you know as he licks your hands
That he's downright sorry—and understands.

I'll have on a bench a box inlaid
With dragon-plagues of milk-white jade
To hold my own particular brand
Of cigarettes brought from the Pharoah's land.
With a cloisonné bowl on a lizard's skin
To flick my cigarette ashes in,
And a squat blue jar for a certain blend
Of pipe tobacco. I'll have to send
To a quaint old chap I chanced to meet
In his fusty shop on a London street.

A long, low shelf of teak will hold
My best-loved books in leather and gold,
While magazines lie on a bowlegged stand
In a polyglot mixture close at hand.
I'll have on a table a rich brocade
That I think the pixies must have made
For the dull gold thread on blues and grays
Weaves the pattern of Puck—the Magic Maze.
On the mantelpiece I'll have a place
For a little mud god with a painted face,
That was given to me—oh, long ago,
By a Philippine maid in Olangapo.

Then—just in range of a lazy reach—
A bulging bowl of Indian beech

Will brim with things that are good to munch—
Hickory nuts to crack and crunch,
Big fat raisins and sun-dried dates
And curious fruits from the Malay Straits,
Maple sugar and cookies brown
With good hard cider to wash them down,
Wine-sap apples, pick of the crop,
And ears of corn to shell and pop,
With plenty of butter and lots of salt—
If you don't get filled it's not my fault.

And there where the shadows fall I've planned
To have a magnificent Concert Grand
With polished wood and ivory keys
For wild discordant rhapsodies,
For wailing minor Hindu songs,
For Chinese chants and clanging gongs,
For flippant jazz and for lullabies
And moody things that I'll improvise
To play the long gray dusk away
And bid good-by to another day.

Pictures—I think I'll have but three;
One in oil, of a wind-swept sea
With the flying scud and the waves whipped white—
(I know the chap who can paint it right)
In lapis blue and a deep jade green—
A great big smashing fine marine
That'll make you feel the spray in your face—
I'll hang it over my fireplace.

The second picture—a freakish thing—
Is gaudy and bright as a macaw's wing—
An impressionistic smear called "Sin,"
A nude on a striped zebra skin
By a Danish girl I knew in France.
My respectable friends will look askance
At the purple eyes and the scarlet hair,
At the pallid face and the evil stare
Of a sinister, beautiful vampire face.
I shouldn't have it about the place,
But I like—while I loathe—the beastly thing,
And that's the way one feels about sin.

451

The picture I love the best of all
Will hang alone on my study wall
Where the sunset's glow and the moon's cold gleam
Will fall on the face and make it seem
That the eyes in the picture are meeting mine,
That the lips are curved in the fine, sweet line
Of that wistful, tender, provocative smile
That has stirred my heart for a wondrous while.
It's the sketch of a girl who loved too well
To tie me down to that bit of Hell
That a drifter knows when he finds he's held
By the soft, strong chains that passions weld.

It was best for her and for me, I know,
That she measured my love and bade me go,
For we both have our great illusion yet
Unsoiled, unspoiled by a vain regret.
I won't deny that it makes me sad
To know that I've missed what I might have had.
It's a clean, sweet memory quite apart,
And I've been faithful—in my heart.

All these things I will have about,
Not a one could I do without,
Cedar and sandalwood chips to burn
In the tarnished bowl of a copper urn,
A paperweight of meteorite
That seared and scored the sky one night,
A Moro kris—my paper knife—
Once slit the throat of a Rajah's wife.

The beams of my house will be fragrant wood
That once in a teeming jungle stood
As a proud, tall tree where the leopards couched,
And the parrot screamed, and the black men crouched.
The roof must have a rakish dip
To shadowy eaves where the rain can drip
In a damp, persistent, tuneful way;
It's a cheerful sound on a gloomy day.
And I want a shingle loose somewhere
To wail like a banshee in despair
When the wind is high and the storm gods race,
And I am snug by my fireplace.

I hope a couple of birds will nest
Around the house. I'll do my best
To make them happy so every year
They'll raise their brood of fledglings here.
When I have my house I will suit myself,
And have what I'll call my "Condiment Shelf"
Filled with all manner of herbs and spice,
Curry and chutney for meats and rice,
Pots and bottles of extracts rare—
Onions and garlic will both be there—
And soyo and saffron and savory-goo
And stuff that I'll buy from an old Hindu.

Ginger and syrup in quaint stone jars,
Almonds and figs in tinseled bars,
Astrakhan caviar, highly prized,
And citron and orange peel crystallized,
Anchovy paste and poha jam,
Basil and chili and marjoram,
Pickles and cheeses from every land,
And flavors that come from Samarkand;
And hung with a string from a handy hook
Will be a dog-eared, well-thumbed book
That is pasted full of recipes
From France and Spain and the Caribbees—
Roots and leaves and herbs to use
For curious soups and odd ragouts.

I'll have a cook that I'll name Oh Joy,
A sleek, fat, yellow-faced Chinese boy
Who can roast a pig or mix a drink
(You can't improve on a slant-eyed Chink).
On the gray-stone hearth there'll be a mat
For a scrappy, swaggering yellow cat
With a war-scarred face from a hundred fights
With neighbors' cats on moonlight nights;
A wise old Tom who can hold his own
And make my dogs let him alone.

I'll have a window seat broad and deep
Where I can sprawl to read or sleep,
With windows placed so I can turn
And watch the sunsets blaze and burn

Beyond high peaks that scar the sky
Like bare white wolf fangs that defy
The very gods. I'll have a nook
For a savage idol that I took
From a ruined temple in Peru,
A demon chaser named Mang-Chu,
To guard my house by night and day
And keep all evil things away.

Pewter and bronze and hammered brass,
Old carved wood and gleaming glass,
Candles in polychrome candlesticks,
And peasant lamps in floating wicks,
Dragons in silk on a Mandarin suit,
In a chest that is filled with vagabond loot;
All of the beautiful, useless things
That a vagabond's aimless drifting brings.

Then, when my house is all complete,
I'll stretch me out on a window seat
With a favorite book and a cigarette,
And a long, cool drink that Oh Joy will get,
And I'll look about my bachelor nest
While the sun goes zooming down the west,
And the hot gold light will fall on my face
And make me think of some heathen place
That I've failed to see—that I've missed someway—
A place that I'd planned to find someday;
And I'll feel the lure of it drawing me,
Oh damn, I know what the end will be.

I'll go. And my house will fall away,
While the mice by night and the moths by day
Will nibble the covers off all my books,
And the spiders weave in the shadowed nooks,
And my dogs—I'll see that they have a home
While I follow the sun, while I drift and roam
To the ends of the earth like a chip on the stream,
Like a straw on the wind, like a vagrant dream;
And the thought will strike with a swift, sharp pain
That I probably never will build again
This house that I'll have in some far day.
Well—it's just a dream house, anyway.

DON BLANDING.

454

DRIED APPLE PIES

I LOATHE, abhor, detest, despise,
Abominate dried-apple pies.
I like good bread, I like good meat,
Or anything that's fit to eat;
But of all poor grub beneath the skies,
The poorest is dried apple pies.
Give me the toothache, or sore eyes,
But don't give me dried apple pies.
The farmer takes his gnarliest fruit,
'Tis wormy, bitter, and hard, to boot;
He leaves the hulls to make us cough,
And don't take half the peeling off.
Then on a dirty cord 'tis strung
And in a garret window hung,
And there it serves as roost for flies,
Until it's made up into pies.
Tread on my corns, or tell me lies,
But don't pass me dried-apple pies.

UNKNOWN.

THE MODERN BABY

"THE HAND that rocks the cradle"—but there is no such hand;
It is bad to rock the baby, they would have us understand;
So the cradle's but a relic of the former foolish days
When mothers reared their children in unscientific ways—
When they jounced them and they bounced them, these poor dwarfs
    of long ago—
The Washingtons and Jeffersons and Adamses, you know.

They warn us that the baby will possess a muddled brain
If we dandle him or rock him—we must carefully refrain;
He must lie in one position, never swayed and never swung,
Or his chance to grow to greatness will be blasted while he's young.
Ah! to think how they were ruined by their mothers long ago—
The Franklins and the Putnams and the Hamiltons, you know.

Then we must feed the baby by the schedule that is made,
And the food that he is given must be measured out or weighed.

455

He may bellow to inform us that he isn't satisfied,
But he couldn't grow to greatness if his wants were all supplied.
Think how foolish nursing stunted those poor weaklings, long ago—
The Shakespeares and the Luthers and the Buonapartes, you know.

We are given a great mission, we are here today on earth
To bring forth a race of giants, and to guard them from their birth,
To insist upon their freedom from the rocking that was bad
For our parents and their parents, scrambling all the brains they had.
Ah! If they'd been fed by schedule would they have been stunted so?
The Websters and the Lincolns and the Roosevelts, you know.

WILLIAM CROSWELL DOANE.

THE SYCOPHANTIC FOX AND THE GULLIBLE RAVEN

A RAVEN sat upon a tree,
    And not a word he spoke, for
His beak contained a piece of Brie,
    Or, maybe, it was Roquefort.
        We'll make it any kind you please—
        At all events it was a cheese.

Beneath the tree's umbrageous limb
    A hungry fox sat smiling;
He saw the raven watching him,
    And spoke in words beguiling:
        "J'admire," said he, "ton beau plumage,"
        (The which was simply persiflage.)

Two things there are, no doubt you know,
    To which a fox is used:
A rooster that is bound to crow,
    A crow that's bound to roost,
        And whichsoever he espies,
        He tells the most unblushing lies.

"Sweet fowl," he said, "I understand
    You're more than merely natty,
I hear you sing to beat the band
    And Adelina Patti.
        Pray render with your liquid tongue
        A bit from Götterdämmerung!"

456

This subtle speech was aimed to please
  The crow, and it succeeded;
He thought no bird in all the trees
  Could sing as well as he did.
    In flattery completely doused,
    He gave the "Jewel Song" from *Faust.*

But gravitation's law, of course,
  As Isaac Newton showed it,
Exerted on the cheese its force,
  And elsewhere soon bestowed it.
    In fact, there is no need to tell
    What happened when to earth it fell.

I blush to add that when the bird
  Took in the situation,
He said one brief, emphatic word,
  Unfit for publication.
    The fox was greatly startled, but
    He only sighed and answered "Tut."

The Moral is: A fox is bound
  To be a shameless sinner.
And also: When the cheese comes round
  You know it's after dinner.
    But (what is only known to few)
    The fox is after dinner, too.

GUY WETMORE CARRYL.

HELP WANTED

A LAW FIRM commanding
  Position of standing
Requires a general clerk—
  A man who's admitted
  To practice, and fitted
To handle diversified work;

  Must know the proceedings
  Relating to pleadings,
The ways of preparing a brief;
  Must argue with unction
  For writs of injunction
As well as for legal relief.

Must form corporations
And hold consultations,
Assuming a dignified mien;
Should read each decision
And legal provision
Wherever the same may be seen.

Must analyze cases
And get at their basis,
Should never be idle or slow;
Must manifest learning
In all things concerning
The matters referred to below:

Attachments and trials,
Specific denials,
Demurrers, replies and complaints,
Disbursements, expenses
And partial defenses,
Ejectments, replevins, distraints;

Estoppels, restrictions,
Constructive evictions,
Agreements implied and express,
Accountings, partitions,
Estates and commissions,
Incumbrances, fraud and duress.

Above are essentials,
The best of credentials
Required—and handsome physique;
Make prompt application,
Will pay compensation
Of seventeen dollars a week.

FRANKLIN WALDHEIM.

SORROWS OF WERTHER

WERTHER had a love for Charlotte
Such as words could never utter;
Would you know how first he met her?
She was cutting bread and butter.

458

Charlotte was a married lady,
  And a moral man was Werther,
And for all the wealth of Indies
  Would do nothing for to hurt her.

So he sighed and pined and ogled,
  And his passion boiled and bubbled,
Till he blew his silly brains out,
  And no more was by it troubled.

Charlotte, having seen his body
  Borne before her on a shutter,
Like a well-conducted person,
  Went on cutting bread and butter.

WILLIAM MAKEPEACE THACKERAY.

PLAIN LANGUAGE FROM TRUTHFUL JAMES

Popularly known as The Heathen Chinee

WHICH I WISH to remark—
  And my language is plain—
That for ways that are dark
  And for tricks that are vain,
The heathen Chinee is peculiar:
  Which the same I would rise to explain.

Ah Sin was his name;
  And I shall not deny
In regard to the same
  What that name might imply;
But his smile it was pensive and childlike,
  As I frequent remarked to Bill Nye.

It was August the third,
  And quite soft was the skies,
Which it might be inferred
  That Ah Sin was likewise;
Yet he played it that day upon William
  And me in a way I despise.

Which we had a small game,
  And Ah Sin took a hand:
It was euchre. The same
  He did not understand,

459

But he smiled, as he sat by the table,
   With the smile that was childlike and bland.

Yet the cards they were stocked
   In a way that I grieve,
And my feelings were shocked
   At the state of Nye's sleeve,
Which was stuffed full of aces and bowers,
   And the same with intent to deceive.

But the hands that were played
   By that heathen Chinee,
And the points that he made,
   Were quite frightful to see,—
Till at last he put down a right bower,
   Which the same Nye had dealt unto me.

Then I looked up at Nye,
   And he gazed upon me;
And he rose with a sigh,
   And said, "Can this be?
We are ruined by Chinese cheap labor,"—
   And he went for that heathen Chinee.

In the scene that ensued
   I did not take a hand,
But the floor it was strewed,
   Like the leaves on the strand,
With the cards that Ah Sin had been hiding
   In the game "he did not understand."

In his sleeves, which were long,
   He had twenty-four packs,—
Which was coming it strong,
   Yet I state but the facts;
And we found on his nails, which were taper,
What is frequent in tapers,—that's wax.

Which is why I remark,—
   And my language is plain,—
That for ways that are dark,
   And for tricks that are vain,
The heathen Chinese is peculiar,—
Which the same I am free to maintain.

FRANCIS BRET HARTE.

460

A PARODY ON *A PSALM OF LIFE*

LIFE IS REAL, life is earnest,
  And the shell is not its pen—
"Egg thou art, and egg remainest"
  Was not spoken of the hen.

Art is long and Time is fleeting,
  Be our bills then sharpened well,
And not like muffled drums be beating
  On the inside of the shell.

In the world's broad field of battle,
  In the great barnyard of life,
Be not like those lazy cattle!
  Be a rooster in the strife!

Lives of roosters all remind us,
  We can make our lives sublime,
And when roasted, leave behind us,
  Hen tracks on the sands of time.

Hen tracks that perhaps another
  Chicken drooping in the rain,
Some forlorn and henpecked brother,
  When he sees, shall crow again.

ATTRIBUTED TO OLIVER WENDELL HOLMES.

WHEN I GET TIME

WHEN I get time—
  I know what I shall do:
I'll cut the leaves of all my books
  And read them through and through.

When I get time—
  I'll write some letters then
That I have owed for weeks and weeks
  To many, many men.

When I get time—
  I'll pay those calls I owe,
And with those bills, those countless bills,
  I will not be so slow.

When I get time—
  I'll regulate my life
In such a way that I may get
  Acquainted with my wife.

When I get time—
  Oh glorious dream of bliss!
A month, a year, ten years from now—
  But I can't finish this—
I've no more time.

THOMAS L. MASSON.

Reprinted by permission from Doubleday, Doran & Company, Inc.

ART

THE HEN remarked to the mooley cow,
As she cackled her daily lay,
(That is, the hen cackled) "It's funny how
I'm good for an egg a day.
I'm a fool to do it, for what do I get?
My food and my lodging. My!
But the poodle gets that—he's the household pet,
And he never has laid a single egg yet—
Not even when eggs are high."

The mooley cow remarked to the hen,
As she masticated her cud,
(That is, the cow did) "Well, what then?
You quit, and your name is mud.
I'm good for eight gallons of milk each day,
And I'm given my stable and grub;
But the parrot gets that much, anyway,—
All she can gobble—and what does she pay?
Not a dribble of milk, the dub!"

But the hired man remarked to the pair,
"You get all that's coming to you.
The poodle does tricks, and the parrot can swear,
Which is better than you can do.

462

You're necessary, but what's the use
Of bewailing your daily part?
You're bourgeois—working's your only excuse;
You can't do nothing but just produce—
What them fellers does is ART!"

UNKNOWN.

STRICTLY GERM–PROOF

THE ANTISEPTIC BABY and the Prophylactic Pup
Were playing in the garden when the Bunny gamboled up;
They looked upon the Creature with a loathing undisguised;—
It wasn't Disinfected and it wasn't Sterilized.

They said it was a Microbe and a Hotbed of Disease;
They steamed it in a vapor of a thousand-odd degrees;
They froze it in a freezer that was cold as Banished Hope
And washed it in permanganate with carbolated soap.

In sulphureted hydrogen they steeped its wiggly ears;
They trimmed its frisky whiskers with a pair of hard-boiled shears;
They donned their rubber mittens and they took it by the hand
And 'lected it a member of the Fumigated Band.

There's not a Micrococcus in the garden where they play;
They bathe in pure iodoform a dozen times a day;
And each imbibes his rations from a Hygienic Cup—
The Bunny and the Baby and the Prophylactic Pup.

ARTHUR GUITERMAN.

THE MONKEY'S WEDDING

THE MONKEY married the Baboon's sister,
Smacked his lips and then he kissed her;
He kissed her so hard he raised a blister,
        She set up a yell.
The bridesmaid stuck on some court plaster,
It stuck so fast it couldn't stick faster;
Surely 'twas a bad disaster,
        But it soon got well.

What do you think the bride was dressed in?
White gauze veil and a green glass breast pin,
Red kid shoes—she was quite interesting—
    She was quite a belle.
The bridegroom swelled with a blue shirt collar,
Black silk stock that cost a dollar,
Large false whiskers, the fashion to follow;
    He cut a monstrous swell.

What do you think they had for supper?
Black-eyed peas and bread and butter,
Ducks in the duckhouse all in a flutter,
    Pickled oysters too;
Chestnuts raw and boiled and roasted,
Apples sliced and onions toasted,
Music in the corner posted,
    Waiting for the cue.

What do you think was the tune they danced to?
"The Drunken Sailor" sometimes "Jim Crow,"
Tails in the way, and some got pinched, too,
    'Cause they were too long.
What do you think they had for a fiddle?
An old banjo with a hole in the middle,
A tambourine made out of a riddle;
    And that's the end of my song.

                UNKNOWN.

DOAN'T YOU BE WHAT YOU AIN'T

[Written as a song for Marie Cahill. Music by Silvio Hein.]

DE SUNFLOWER ain't de daisy,
And de melon ain't de rose.
Why is dey all so crazy
To be sumpin' else dat grows?
Jes' stick to the place you's planted, and do de bes' you knows,
Be de sunflower or de daisy,
Be de melon or de rose.

De song thrush ain't de robin,
And de catbird ain't de jay.
Why is dey all a-throbbin' to outdo each other's lay?
Jes' sing de song God gave you, and let your heart be gay.
Be de song thrush or de robin,
Be de catbird or de jay.

Chorus:

Doan't ye be what you ain't,
Jes' you be what you is.
Ef a man is what he isn't,
Den he isn't what he is.
Ef you's jes' a little tadpole,
Doan't you try to be de frog.
Ef you's de tail doan't you try to wag de dog.
Jes' pass de plate ef you can't exhort and preach;
Ef you's jes' a little pebble,
Doan't ye try to be de beach.
Ef a man is what he isn't, den he isn't what he am,
And as sure as I'm a-talkin' he isn't worth a ——
Doan't ye be what you ain't,
Jes' you be what you is.
Ef a man is what he isn't,
Den he isn't what he is;
And as sure as I'm a-talkin',
He's gwyne to git his.

EDWIN MILTON ROYLE.

THE COUNTRY STORE

FAR OUT beyond the city's lights, away from din and roar,
The cricket chirps of summer nights beneath the country store;
The drygoods boxes ricked about afford a welcome seat
For weary tillers of the ground, who here on evenings meet.

A swinging sign of ancient make, and one above the door,
Proclaim that William Henry Blake is owner of the store;
Here everything from jam to tweed, from silks to ginghams bright,
Is spread before the folk who need from early morn till night.

Tea, sugar, coffee (browned or green), molasses, grindstones, tar,
Suspenders, peanuts, navy beans, and homemade vinegar,

Fine combs, wash ringers, rakes, false hair, paints, rice, and looking
    glasses,
Side saddles, hominy, crockery ware, and seeds for garden grasses.
Lawn mowers, candies, books to read, corn planter, household goods,
Tobacco, salt, and clover seed, horsewhips and knitted hoods,
Canned goods, shoe blacking, lime and nails, straw hats and carpet
    slippers,
Prunes, buttons, codfish, bridal veils, cranberries, clocks, and clippers

Umbrellas, candles, scythes and hats, caps, boots and shoes and bacon,
Thread, nutmegs, pins and Rough on Rats, for cash or produce taken;
Birdseed, face powder, matches, files, ink, onions and many more,
Are found in heaps and stacks and piles within the country store.

UNKNOWN.

CLARE DE KITCHEN

IN OLD KENTUCK in de arternoon,
We sweep de floor wid a bran-new broom,
And arter that we form a ring,
And dis de song dat we do sing:
Oh! Clare de kitchen, old folks, young folks,
Clare de kitchen, old folks, young folks,
Old Virginny never tire.

I went to de creek, I couldn't git across,
I'd nobody wid me but an old blind horse;
But Old Jim Crow came riding by,
Says he, old fellow, your horse will die.
        So clare, &c.

My horse fell down upon de spot,
Says he, "Don't you see his eyes is sot?"
So I took out my knife and off wid his skin,
And when he comes to life I'll ride him agin.
        So clare, &c.

A jay bird sot on a hickory limb,
He wink'd at me and I winked at him;
I pick'd up a stone and I hit his shin,
Says he, "You better not do dat agin."
        So clare, &c.

A bullfrog dress'd in soger's close
Went in de field to shoot some crows;
De crows smell powder and fly away,
De bullfrog mighty mad dat day.
          So clare, &c.

Den down I went wid Cato Moore,
To see de steamboat come ashore;
Every man for himself, so I pick'd up a trunk;
"Leff off," said de captain, "or I burn you wid a chunk."
          And clare, &c.

I hab a sweetheart in dis town,
She wears a yellow striped gown,
And when she walks de streets around,
De hollow of her foot make a hole in de ground.
          Now clare, &c.

Dis love is a ticklish ting, you know,
It makes a body feel all over so;
I put de question to coal-black Rose,
She as black as ten of spades, and got a lubby flat nose.
          So clare, &c.

Go away says she wid your cowcumber shin,
If you come here agin I stick you wid a pin;
So I turn on my heel and I bid her good bye,
And arter I was gone she began to cry.
          So clare, &c.

So now I'se up and off, you see,
To take a julep sangaree;
I'll sit upon a tater hill,
And eat a little whippoorwill.
          So clare, &c.

I wish I was back in Old Kentuck,
For since I left it I had no luck;
De gals so proud dey wont eat mush,
And w'en you go to court 'em dey say, "O hush."
          So clare, &c.

UNKNOWN.

467

THE PREACHER'S VACATION

THE OLD MAN went to meetin', for the day was bright and fair,
Though his limbs were very totterin', and 'twas hard to travel there;
But he hungered for the Gospel, so he trudged the weary way
On the road so rough and dusty, 'neath the summer's burning ray.

By and by he reached the building, to his soul a holy place;
Then he paused, and wiped the sweat drops off his thin and wrinkled
    face;
But he looked around bewildered, for the old bell did not toll,
And the doors were shut and bolted, and he did not see a soul.

So he leaned upon his crutches, and he said, "What does it mean?"
And he looked this way and that, till it seemed almost a dream;
He had walked the dusty highway, and he breathed a heavy sigh—
Just to go once more to meetin', ere the summons came to die.

But he saw a little notice, tacked upon the meetin' door,
So he limped along to read it, and he read it o'er and o'er.
Then he wiped his dusty glasses, and he read it o'er again,
Till his limbs began to tremble and his eyes began to pain.

As the old man read the notice, how it made his spirit burn!
"Pastor absent on vacation—church is closed till his return."
Then he staggered slowly backward, and he sat him down to think,
For his soul was stirred within him, till he thought his heart would
    sink.

So he mused along and wondered, to himself soliloquized—
"I have lived to almost eighty, and was never so surprised,
As I read that oddest notice, stickin' on the meetin' door,
'Pastor on vacation'—never heard the like before.

"Why, when I first jined the meetin', very many years ago,
Preachers traveled on the circuit, in the heat and through the snow;
If they got their clothes and vittels ('twas but little cash they got),
They said nothin' 'bout vacation, but were happy in their lot.

"Would the farmer leave his cattle, or the shepherd leave his sheep?
Who would give them care and shelter, or provide them food to eat?
So it strikes me very sing'lar when a man of holy hands
Thinks he needs to have vacation, and forsakes his tender lambs.

"Did St. Paul git such a notion? Did a Wesley or a Knox?
Did they in the heat of summer turn away their needy flocks?
Did they shut their meetin' house, just go and lounge about?
Why, they knew that if they did Satan certainly would shout.

"Do the taverns close their doors, just to take a little rest?
Why, 'twould be the height of nonsense, for their trade would be distressed.
Did you ever know it happen, or hear anybody tell,
Satan takin' a vacation, shuttin' up the doors of hell?

"And shall preachers of the gospel pack their trunks and go away,
Leavin' saints and dyin' sinners git along as best they may?
Are the souls of saints and sinners valued less than settlin' beer?
Or do preachers tire quicker than the rest of mortals here?

"Why it is I cannot answer, but my feelings they are stirred;
Here I've dragged my totterin' footsteps for to hear the Gospel Word,
But the preacher is a travelin' and the meetin' house is closed;
I confess it's very tryin', hard, indeed, to keep composed.

"Tell me, when I tread the valley and go up the shining height,
Will I hear no angels singin'—will I see no gleamin' light?
Will the golden harps be silent? Will I meet no welcome there?
Why, the thought is most distressin', would be more than I could bear

"Tell me, when I reach the city over on the other shore,
Will I find a little notice tacked upon the golden door,
Tellin' me 'mid dreadful silence, writ in words that cut and burn—
'Jesus absent on vacation, heaven closed till his return.'"

UNKNOWN.

A FROG WENT A–COURTING

A FROG went a-courting, away did ride, huh-huh.
A frog went a-courting, away did ride,
Sword and pistol by his side, huh-huh.

He rode up to Miss Mousie's door, huh-huh.
He rode up to Miss Mousie's door
With his coat all buttoned down before, huh-huh.

He took Miss Mousie on his knee, huh-huh.
He took Miss Mousie on his knee,
And he said my dear will you marry me, huh-huh.

Oh no! kind sir, I can't say that, huh-huh.
Oh no! kind sir, I can't say that,
You'll have to get the consent of my uncle rat, huh-huh.

Uncle rat he laughed and shook his fat side, huh-huh.
Uncle rat he laughed and shook his fat side,
To think that his niece would be a bride, huh-huh.

Oh, where shall the wedding breakfast be, huh-huh.
Oh, where shall the wedding breakfast be,
Way down in the woods in a hollow tree, huh-huh.

The first that came was a long-tailed rat, huh-huh.
The first that came was a long-tailed rat——
    Etc.

UNKNOWN.

[Other guests were enumerated, the names of which are not given. This was set to doggerel music and used as a nursery song. The HUH-HUH was a guttural expression giving assent to the statement just made.]

ANIMAL FAIR

I WENT to the animal fair,
The birds and beasts were there.
The big baboon, by the light of the moon,
Was combing his auburn hair.
The monkey, he got drunk,
And sat on the elephant's trunk.
The elephant sneezed and fell on his knees,
And what became of the monk, the monk?

UNKNOWN.

CAPTAIN JINKS

I'M CAPTAIN JINKS of the Horse Marines,
I feed my horse on corn and beans,
And sport young ladies in their teens,
     Though a captain in the army.
I teach young ladies how to dance,
How to dance, how to dance,
I teach young ladies how to dance,
     For I'm the pet of the army.

     Chorus:

Captain Jinks of the Horse Marines,
I feed my horse on corn and beans,
And often live beyond my means,
     Though a captain in the army.

I joined my corps when twenty-one,
Of course I thought it capital fun;
When the enemy came, of course I ran,
     For I'm not cut out for the army.
When I left home, mama she cried,
Mama she cried, mama she cried,
When I left home, mama she cried:
     "He's not cut out for the army."

The first time I went out to drill,
The bugle sounding made me ill;
Of the battle field I'd had my fill,
     For I'm not cut out for the army.
The officers they all did shout,
They all did shout, they all did shout,
The officers they all did shout:
     "Why, kick him out of the army."

                              UNKNOWN.

FINIGAN'S WAKE

TIM FINIGAN lived in Walker street—
     An Irish gintleman, mighty odd.
He'd a bit of a brogue, so neat and sweet,
     And to rise in the world, Tim carried a hod.

471

But Tim had a sort of tippling way;
  With a love of liquor Tim was born,
And, to help him through his work each day,
  Took a drop of the creature every morn.

  Chorus:

Whack! Hurrah! Now dance to your partners,
Welt the flure, your trotters shake;
Isn't all the truth I've told ye,
Lots of fun at Finigan's wake?

One morning Tim was rather full,
  His head felt heavy and it made him shake;
He fell from the ladder and broke his skull,
  So they carried him home, his corpse to wake.
They rolled him up in a nice clean sheet,
  And laid him out upon the bed,
With fourteen candles round his feet
  And a bushel of 'taters round his head.

His friends assembled at his wake,
  Missus Finigan called out for the lunch;
And first they laid in tay and cakes,
  Then pipes and tobacky and whisky punch.
Miss Biddy O'Neil began to cry:
  "Such a purty corpse did yez ever see!
Arrah! Tim mavourneen, and why did ye l'ave me?"
  "Hold your gob!" sez Judy Magee.

Then Peggy O'Connor took up the job:
  "Arrah, Biddy," says she, "ye're wrong, in sure."
But Judy gave her a belt in the gob,
  And left her sprawling on the flure.
Each side in war did soon engage;
  'Twas woman to woman and man to man;
Shillelah law was all the rage
  And a bloody ruction soon began.

Mickey Mulvaney raised his head,
  When a gallon of whisky flew at him;
It missed him, and, hopping on the bed,
  The liquor scattered over Tim.

472

"Och! he revives! See how he raises!"
  And Timothy, jumping from the bed,
Cries, while he lathers round like blazes,
  "Bad luck ter yer souls! D'ye think I'm dead?"

UNKNOWN.

HELL IN TEXAS

The devil, we're told, in hell was chained,
And a thousand years he there remained,
And he never complained, nor did he groan,
But determined to start a hell of his own
Where he could torment the souls of men
Without being chained to a prison pen.

So he asked the Lord if He had on hand
Anything left when He made the land.
The Lord said, "Yes, I had plenty on hand,
But I left it down on the Rio Grande.
The fact is, old boy, the stuff is so poor,
I don't think you could use it in hell any more."

But the devil went down to look at the truck,
And said if it came as a gift, he was stuck;
For after examining it careful and well
He concluded the place was too dry for hell.
So in order to get it off His hands
God promised the devil to water the lands.

For he had some water, or rather some dregs,
A regular cathartic that smelt like bad eggs.
Hence the deal was closed and the deed was given,
And the Lord went back to His place in Heaven.
And the devil said, "I have all that is needed
To make a good hell," and thus he succeeded.

He began to put thorns on all the trees,
And he mixed the sand with millions of fleas,
He scattered tarantulas along all the roads,
Put thorns on the cacti and horns on the toads;
He lengthened the horns of the Texas steers
And put an addition on jack rabbits' ears.

He put little devils in the broncho steed
And poisoned the feet of the centipede.
The rattlesnake bites you, the scorpion stings,
The mosquito delights you by buzzing his wings.
The sand burrs prevail, so do the ants,
And those that sit down need half soles on their pants

The devil then said that throughout the land
He'd manage to keep up the devil's own brand,
And all would be mavericks unless they bore
The marks of scratches and bites by the score.
The heat in the summer is a hundred and ten,
Too hot for the devil and too hot for men.

The wild boar roams through the black chaparral,
It's a hell of a place he has for a hell;
The red pepper grows by the bank of the brook,
The Mexicans use it in all that they cook.
Just dine with a Greaser and then you will shout,
"I've a hell on the inside as well as without."

UNKNOWN.

HOW PADDY STOLE THE ROPE

THERE WAS once two Irish labouring men; to England they came over;
They tramped about in search of work from Liverpool to Dover.
Says Pat to Mick, "I'm tired of this; we're both left in the lurch;
And if we don't get work, bedad, I'll go and rob a church."
"What, rob a church!" says Mick to Pat; how dare you be so vile?
There's something sure to happen as you're treading down the aisle.
But if you go I go with you; we'll get out safe, I hope;"
So, if you'll listen, I'll tell you here how Paddy stole the rope.

So off they went with theft intent, the place they wanted finding;
They broke into a country church which nobody was minding.
They scraped together all they could and then prepared to slope,
When Paddy cries out, "Hold on, Mick, what shall we do for rope?
We've got no bag to hold the swag, and e'er we get outside,
With something stout and strong, my lad, the bundle must be tied."
Just then he spies the old church bell, and quick as an antelope,
He scrambled up the belfry high to try and steal a rope.

Now when Paddy up the belfry got, "Ah-hah, bedad, but stop;
To get a piece that's long enough, I must climb up to the top."
So, like a sailor, up he went, and near the top, says he,
"I think the piece that's underneath quite long enough will be."
So, holding by one arm and leg, he drew his clasp knife out,
And right above his big fat head he cut the rope so stout,
He quite forgot it held him up, and, by the Holy Pope,
Down to the bottom of the church fell Paddy and the rope.

"Come out of that," says Mick to Pat, as he on the floor lay groaning,
"If that's the way you cut a rope, no wonder now your moaning.
I'll show you how to cut a rope, so just lend me the knife."
"Be very careful," cries out Pat, "or else you'll lose your life."
He clambered up the other rope, and, like an artful thief,
Instead of cutting it above, he cut it underneath.
The piece fell down and left poor Mick alone up there to cope;
Says he, "Bad luck unto the day when we came stealing rope."

Now with Paddy groaning on the floor and Mick hung up on high,
Says Pat, "Come down." "I can't," cried Mick, "for if I do, I die."
The noise soon brought the beadle round, the sexton and police,
And although they set poor Micky free, they gave them no release.
They marched them to the county jail where their conduct now they
    rue,
And if they'd got no work before, they've plenty now to do;
And for their ingenuity they now have larger scope
Than when they broke into a church to try and steal a rope.

UNKNOWN.

I HAD BUT FIFTY CENTS

I took my girl to a fancy ball;
It was a social hop;
We waited till the folks got out,
And the music it did stop.
Then to a restaurant we went,
The best one on the street;
She said she wasn't hungry,
But this is what she eat:
A dozen raw, a plate of slaw,
A chicken and a roast,
Some applesass, and sparagrass,
And soft-shell crabs on toast.

475

A big box stew, and crackers too;
Her appetite was immense!
When she called for pie,
I thought I'd die,
For I had but fifty cents.

She said she wasn't hungry
And didn't care to eat,
But I've got money in my clothes
To bet she can't be beat;
She took it in so cozy,
She had an awful tank;
She said she wasn't thirsty,
But this is what she drank:
A whisky skin, a glass of gin,
Which made me shake with fear,
A ginger pop, with rum on top,
A schooner then of beer,
A glass of ale, a gin cocktail;
She should have had more sense;
When she called for more,
I fell on the floor,
For I had but fifty cents.

Of course I wasn't hungry,
And didn't care to eat,
Expecting every moment
To be kicked into the street;
She said she'd fetch her family round,
And some night we'd have fun;
When I gave the man the fifty cents,
This is what he done:
He tore my clothes,
He smashed my nose,
He hit me on the jaw,
He gave me a prize
Of a pair of black eyes
And with me swept the floor.
He took me where my pants hung loose,
And threw me over the fence;
Take my advice, don't try it twice
If you've got but fifty cents!

UNKNOWN.

476

THE JAPANESE LOVERS

FANNY Foo-Foo was a Japanese girl,
　A child of the great Tycoon;
She wore her head bald, and her clothes were made
　Half petticoat, half pantaloon;
And her face was the color of lemon peel,
　And the shape of a tablespoon.

A handsome young chap was Johnny Hi-Hi;
　He wore paper-muslin clothes;
His glossy black hair on the top of his head
　In the shape of a shoe brush rose;
And his eyes slanted downward, as if some chap
　Had savagely pulled his nose.

Fanny Foo-Foo loved Johnny Hi-Hi,
　And when in the usual style
He popped, she blushed such a deep orange tinge
　You'd have thought she had too much bile,
If it hadn't been for her slant-eyed glance
　And her charming widemouthed smile.

And oft in the bliss of their newborn love
　Did these little Pagans stray
All around in spots, enjoying themselves
　In a strictly Japanese way,
She howling a song on a one-stringed lute,
　On which she thought she could play.

Often he'd climb to a high ladder's top,
　And quietly there repose,
As he stood on his head and fanned himself,
　While she balanced him on her nose,
Or else she would get in a pickle tub,
　And be kicked around on his toes.

The course of true love, even in Japan,
　Often runs extremely rough,
And the fierce Tycoon, when he heard of this,
　Used Japanese oaths so tough
That his courtiers' hair would have stood on end
　If they'd only had enough.

477

So the Tycoon buckled on both his swords,
  In his pistol placed a wad,
And went out to hunt for the truant pair,
  With his nerves well braced by a tod.
He found them enjoying their guileless selves
  On the top of a lightning rod.

Sternly he ordered the gentle Foo-Foo
  To "Come down out of that there!"
And he told Hi-Hi to go to a place—
  I won't say precisely where.
Then he dragged off his child, whose spasms evinced
  Unusual wild despair.

But the great Tycoon was badly fooled,
  Despite his paternal pains,
For John, with a toothpick, let all the blood
  Out of his jugular veins;
While with a back somersault over the floor
  Foo-Foo battered out her brains.

They buried them both in the Tycoon's lot
  Right under a dogwood tree,
Where they could list to the nightingale
  And the buzz of the bumblebee,
And where the mosquito's sorrowful chant
  Maddens the restless flea.

And often at night when the Tycoon's wife
  Slumbered as sound as a post,
His almond-shaped eyeballs glared on a sight
  That scared him to death, almost:
'Twas a bald-headed spectre flitting about
  With a paper-muslin ghost.

HORACE RUSSELL AND WILLIAM GREENE.

JONAH AND THE WHALE

About the year of one B. C.,
A gallant ship set out to sea,
To catch a whale and salt his tail,
To salt the end of his tail.

478

But when about a mile from shore
The ship began to dance,
Then every son of a sailorman,
Put on his working pants,
His pants, his pants, his working pants.

And down into the hold they went,
And over the pumps their backs they bent.
They pumped and pumped,
They thought they would drown,
The deck was too wet to sit down.

Then up spoke Mike O'Flaherty,
There's a Jonah on the boat, sez he;
So off they ran from Mike to Dan,
To find the Jonah Man.

And when upon the deck they came,
His "Nibs" a-smiling sat—
A-lighting a paper cigarette
In the crown of his derby hat,
His hat, his hat, his derby hat.

So they gave a whoop and they gave a yell
And overboard poor Jonah fell.
Sez Mike to Jim, " 'Tis better for him—
'Tis certainly better for him."

Just then a monster whale passed by,
And Jonah's trousers caught his eye.
"As I'm a goat, there's a lunch afloat,"
And he swallowed him into his throat.

Just about then the whale felt ill,
Sez he, "That lunch was poor,
For, judging by the way I feel,
I've swallowed a Jonah sure,
A Jonah, a Jonah, a Jonah sure."

Then Mike McGinty gave a call,
And he coughed up Jonah, pants and all,
'Twas on the spot ('tis not forgot),
McGinty's corner lot.

"Get out of here!" McGinty said;
"You can't stay here unless you're dead.
You'll hoodoo me and my familee,
My wife and familee."

So then he called his beautiful wife,
A mermaid fat and pale,
Who gave poor Jonah a terrible jag
With the end of her jagged tail,
Her jag, her jag, her jagged tail.

UNKNOWN.

JUDGED BY THE COMPANY ONE KEEPS

ONE NIGHT in late October,
When I was far from sober,
Returning with my load with manly pride,
My feet began to stutter,
So I lay down in the gutter,
And a pig came near and lay down by my side;
A lady passing by was heard to say:
"You can tell a man who boozes,
By the company he chooses,"
And the pig got up and slowly walked away.

UNKNOWN.

KAFOOZALUM

IN ANCIENT DAYS there lived a Turk,
A horrid beast within the East,
Who did the prophet's holy work
As Baba of Jerusalem.
He had a daughter sweet and smirk,
Complexion fair and dark blue hair,
With nothing 'bout her like a Turk
Except her name Kafoozalum.

  Chorus:

Oh, Kafoozalum, Kafoozalum, Kafoozalum.
Oh, Kafoozalum, the daughter of the Baba.

A youth resided near to she,
His name was Sam, a perfect lamb;
He was of ancient pedigree
And came from old Methusalem.
He drove a trade—and prospered well—
In skins of cats and ancient hats,
And, ringing at the Baba's bell,
He saw and loved Kafoozalum.

If Sam had been a Mussulman,
He might have sold the Baba old,
And, with a verse of Al Koran
Have managed to bamboozle him.
But oh dear, no, he tried to scheme,
Passed one night late the Baba's gate
And came up to the Turk's harem
To carry off Kafoozalum.

The Baba was about to smoke;
His slaves rushed in with horrid din;
"Mashallah, dogs your house have broke.
Come down, my lord, and toozle 'em!"
The Baba wreathed his face in smiles,
Came down the stair and witnessed there
A gentleman in three old tiles
A-kissing of Kafoozalum.

The pious Baba said no more
Than twenty prayers, then went upstairs,
And took his bowstring from the door
And came back to Kafoozalum.
The maiden and the youth he took,
And choked them both, a little loath,
Together threw them in the brook
Of Kedron in Jerusalem.

And so the ancient legend runs,
When night comes on in Lebanon,
And when the Eastern moonlight throws
Its shadows o'er Jerusalem,
Betwixt the wailing of the cats,
A sound there falls from ruined walls,
A ghost is seen in three old hats
A-kissing of Kafoozalum.

UNKNOWN.

481

METHUSELAH

METHUSELAH ate what he found on his plate,
And never, as people do now,
Did he note the amount of the calory count;
He ate it because it was chow.
He wasn't disturbed as at dinner he sat,
Devouring a roast or a pie,
To think it was lacking in granular fat
Or a couple of vitamins shy.
He cheerfully chewed each species of food,
Unmindful of troubles or fears
Lest his health might be hurt
By some fancy dessert;
And he lived over nine hundred years.

UNKNOWN.

MISS FOGGERTY'S CAKE

As I SAT by my window last evening,
  The letterman brought unto me
A little gilt-edged invitation
  Saying, "Gilhooley, come over to tea."

Sure I knew 'twas the Foggertys sent it,
  So I went for old friendship's sake,
And the first thing they gave me to tackle
  Was a slice of Miss Foggerty's cake.

Miss Martin wanted to taste it,
  But really there weren't no use,
For they worked at it over an hour
  And couldn't get none of it loose.

Till Foggerty went for a hatchet
  And Killey came in with a saw;
The cake was enough, by the powers,
  To paralyze any man's jaw.

In it were cloves, nutmegs and berries,
  Raisins, citron and cinnamon, too;
There were sugar, pepper and cherries,
  And the crust of it nailed on with glue.

Miss Foggerty, proud as a preacher,
   Kept winking and blinking away,
Till she fell over Flanigan's brogans
   And spilt a whole brewing of tay.

"O, Gilhooley," she cried, "you're not eating,
   Just take another piece for my sake."
"No thanks, Miss Foggerty," says I,
   "But I'd like the recipe for that cake."

McNulley was took with the colic,
   McFadden complained of his head,
McDoodle fell down on the sofa
   And swore that he wished he was dead.

Miss Martin fell down in hysterics,
   And there she did wriggle and shake,
While every man swore he was poisoned
   By eating Miss Foggerty's cake.

                    UNKNOWN.

THE PATTER OF THE SHINGLE

WHEN THE ANGRY PASSION gathering in my mother's face I see,
And she leads me to the bedroom, gently lays me on her knee,
Then I know that I will catch it, and my flesh in fancy itches
As I listen for the patter of the shingle on my breeches.

Every tingle of the shingle has an echo and a sting
And a thousand burning fancies into active being spring,
And a thousand bees and hornets 'neath my coattail seem to swarm,
As I listen to the patter of the shingle, oh, so warm.

In a splutter comes my father—who I supposed had gone—
To survey the situation and tell her to lay it on,
To see her bending o'er me as I listen to the strain
Played by her and by the shingle in a wild and weird refrain.

In a sudden intermission, which appears my only chance,
I say, "Strike gently, Mother, or you'll split my Sunday pants!"
She stops a moment, draws her breath, and the shingle holds aloft,
And says, "I had not thought of that, my son, just take them off."

Holy Moses and the angels! cast your pitying glances down,
And thou, O family doctor, put a good soft poultice on.
And may I with fools and dunces everlastingly commingle,
If I ever say another word when my mother wields the shingle!

UNKNOWN

CARMEN POSSUM

THE nox was lit by lux of Luna,
And 'twas a nox most opportuna
To catch a possum or a coona;
For nix was scattered o'er this mundus,
A shallow nix, et non profundus.
On sic a nox with canis unus,
Two boys went out to hunt for coonus.
The corpus of this bonus canis
Was full as long as octo span is,
But brevior legs had canis never
Quam had hic dog; et bonus clever,
Some used to say, in stultum jocum
Quod a field was too small locum
For sic a dog to make a turnus
Circum self from stem to sternus.
Unis canis, duo puer,
Nunquam braver, nunquam truer,
Quam hoc trio nunquam fuit,
If there was I never knew it.
This bonus dog had one bad habit,
Amabat much to tree a rabbit,
Amabat plus to chase a rattus,
Amabat bene tree a cattus.
But on this nixy moonlight night
This old canis did just right.
Nunquam treed a starving rattus,
Nunquam chased a starving cattus.
But sucurrit on, intentus
On the track and on the scentus,
Till he trees a possum strongum,
In a hollow trunkum longum.
Loud he barked in horrid bellum,
Seemed on terra vehit pellum.
Quickly ran the duo puer
Mors of possum to secure.
Quam venerit, one began

To chop away like quisque man.
Soon the axe went through the truncum
Soon he hit it all kerchunkum;
Combat deepens, on ye braves!
Canis, pueri et staves;
As his powers non longius tarry,
Possum potest, non pugnare.
On the nix his corpus lieth.
Down to Hades spirit flieth,
Joyful pueri, canis bonus,
Think him dead as any stonus.

Now they seek their pater's domo,
Feeling proud as any homo,
Knowing, certe, they will blossom
Into heroes, when with possum
They arrive, narrabunt story,
Plenus blood et plenior glory.
Pompey, David, Samson, Caesar,
Cyrus, Black Hawk, Shalmanezer!
Tell me where est now the gloria,
Where the honors of victoria?
Nunc a domum narrent story,
Plenus sanguine, tragic, gory.
Pater praiseth, likewise mater,
Wonders greatly younger frater.
Possum leave they on the mundus,
Go themselves to sleep profundus,
Somniunt possums slain in battle,
Strong as ursae, large as cattle.
When nox gives way to lux of morning,
Albam terram much adorning,
Up they jump to see the varmen,
Of the which this is the carmen.
Lo! possum est resurrectum!
Ecce pueri dejectum,
Ne relinquit track behind him,
Et the pueri never find him.
Cruel possum! bestia vilest,
How the pueros thou beguilest!
Pueri think non plus of Caesar,
Go ad Orcum, Shalmanezer,
Take your laurels, cum the honor,
Since ista possum is a goner!

UNKNOWN.

THE OPTIMIST

THE OPTIMIST fell ten stories.
At each window bar
He shouted to his friends:
"All right so far."

UNKNOWN.

TOWSER SHALL BE TIED TONIGHT

[A parody on *Curfew Must Not Ring Tonight*. See page 158]

SLOW THE KANSAS SUN was setting o'er the wheat fields far away,
Streaking all the air with cobwebs, at the close of one hot day;
And its last rays kissed the foreheads of a man and maiden fair,
He with whiskers short and frowzy, she with red and glist'ning hair;
He with jaws shut stern and silent, she with lips all cold and white,
Struggled to keep back the murmur, "Towser must be tied tonight."

"Papa," slowly spoke the maiden, "I am almost seventeen,
And I've got a real lover, though he's rather young and green;
But he has a horse and buggy, and a cow and thirty hens,
Boys that start out poor, dear Papa, make the best of honest men;
But if Towser sees and bites him, fills his heart with sudden fright,
He will never come again, pa: Towser must be tied tonight."

"Daughter," firmly spoke the farmer (every word pierced her young
heart
Like a carving knife through chicken, as it hunts a tender part),
"I've a patch of early melons, two of them are ripe today;
Towser must be loose to watch them, or they'll all be stole away.
I have hoed them late and early, (in dim morn and evening light)
Now they're grown I must not lose them. Towser won't be tied to-
night."

Then the old man ambled forward, opened wide the kennel door;
Towser bounded forth to meet him, as he oft had done before.
And the farmer stooped and loosed him from the dog chain short and
stout;
To himself he softly chuckled: "Bessie's fellow must look out."
But the maiden at the window saw the cruel teeth show white;
In an undertone she murmured, "Towser must be tied tonight."

Then the maiden's brow grew thoughtful, and her breath came short
    and thick,
Till she spied the family clothesline, and she whispered, "That's the
    trick."
From the kitchen door she glided with a plate of meat and bread;
Towser wagged his tail in greeting, knowing well he would be fed.
In his well-worn leather collar tied she then the clothesline tight,
All the time her white lips saying: "Towser must be tied tonight."

"There, old doggie," spoke the maiden. "You can watch the melon
    patch,
But the front gate's free and open when John Henry lifts the latch,
For the clothesline tight is fastened to the harvest-apple tree.
You can run and watch the melons, but the front gate you can't see."
Then her glad ears heard a buggy, and her eyes grew big and bright,
While her young heart said in gladness: "Towser, dog, is tied tonight."

Up the patch the young man saunters, with his eye and cheek aglow,
For he loves the red-haired maiden, and he aims to tell her so.
Bessie's roguish little brothers, in a fit of boyish glee,
Had untied the slender clothesline from the harvest-apple tree;
Then old Towser heard the footsteps, raised his bristle, fixed for fight.
"Bark away," the maiden whispers. "Towser, you are tied tonight."

Then old Towser bounded forward, past the open kitchen door;
Bessie screamed and quickly followed, but John Henry's gone before.
Down the path he speeds most quickly, for old Towser sets the pace,
And the maiden, close behind them, shows them she is in the race.
Then the clothesline—can she get it? And her eyes grow big and
    bright,
As she springs and grasps it firmly. "Towser shall be tied tonight."

Oftentimes a little minute forms the destiny of men.
You can change the fate of nations by the stroke of one small pen.
Towser made one last long effort, caught John Henry by his pants,
But John Henry kept on running, for he thought that his last chance;
But the maiden held on firmly, and the rope was drawn up tight;
But old Towser kept the garments, for he was not tied tonight.

Then the old man hears the racket; with long stride he soon is there,
While John Henry and the maiden, crouching, for the worst prepare.
At his feet John tells his story, shows his clothing soiled and torn;
And his face, so sad and pleading, yet so white and scared and worn,
Touched the old man's heart with pity, filled his eyes with misty light;
"Take her, boy, and make her happy. Towser shall be tied tonight."

UNKNOWN.

VAN AMBURGH'S MENAGERIE

VAN AMBURGH is the man that goes with all the shows;
He goes into the lion's den, and shows you all he knows;
He sticks his head in the lion's mouth, and keeps it there awhile,
And when he takes it out again, he greets you with a smile.

Chorus:

For the elephant now goes round, the band begins to play,
Those boys around the monkeys' cage, they'd better keep away.

This is the Arctic polar bear, oft called the iceberg's daughter,
Been known to eat three tubs of ice, then call for soda water;
She wades in the water up to her knees, not fearing any harm;
You may growl and grumble as much as you please, but she don't care
    a darn.

Next comes baboon Emmeline, catching flies and scratching her head;
Weeping and wailing all the day, because her husband's dead;
Poor weeping, wailing water lily, of all her friends bereft,
That monkey is thumbing his nose at her with his right paw over his
    left.

Next comes the anaconda boa constrictor, called the anaconda for
    brevity;
He can swallow an elephant as well as a toad, and is noted for his great
    longevity,
Can swallow himself, crawl through himself, come out with great
    facility,
Tie himself into a bowknot, snap his tail, and wink with great agility.

That hyena in the next cage, most wonderful to relate,
Got awful hungry the other night, and ate up his female mate;
Now, don't go near his cage, he'll hurt you, little boys,
For when he's mad he'll growl and bite, and make a horrible noise.
    Gr-rr-r——

Next comes the condor, an awful bird, from the highest mountain
    tops:
Been known to eat up little boys and then to smack his chops;
This performance can't go on—there's too much noise and confusion;
Those ladies giving those monkeys nuts will injure their constitution.

UNKNOWN.

WANTED—A MINISTER'S WIFE

AT LENGTH we have settled a pastor—
  I am sure I cannot tell why
The people should grow so restless,
  Or candidates grow so shy.
But after two years' searching
  For the "smartest" man in the land,
In a fit of desperation
  We took the nearest at hand.

And really he answers nicely
  To "fill the gap," you know,
To "run the machine" and "bring up arrears,"
  And make things generally go.
He has a few little failings,
  His sermons are commonplace quite,
But his manner is very charming,
  And his teeth are pearly white.

And, so, of all the "dear people,"
  Not one in a hundred complains,
For beauty and grace of manner
  Are so much better than brains;
But the parish have all concluded
  He needs a partner for life,
To shine, a gem, in the parlor:
  "Wanted—a minister's wife!"

Wanted—a perfect lady,
  Delicate, gentle, refined,
With every beauty of person,
  And every endowment of mind,
Fitted by early culture
  To move in fashionable life—
Please notice our advertisement:
  "Wanted—a minister's wife!"

Wanted—a thoroughbred worker,
  Who well to her household looks,
(Shall we see our money wasted
  By extravagant Irish cooks?)

Who cuts the daily expenses
  With economy sharp as a knife,
And washes and scrubs in the kitchen—
  "Wanted—a minister's wife."

A "very domestic person,"
  To callers she must not be "out";
It has such a bad appearance
  For her to be gadding about—
Only to visit the parish
  Every year of her life,
And attend the funerals and weddings—
  "Wanted—a minister's wife."

To conduct the "ladies meetings,"
  The "sewing circle" attend,
And when we have work for the soldiers
  Her ready assistance to lend:
To clothe the destitute children,
  Where sorrow and want are rife;
To hunt up Sunday-school scholars—
  "Wanted—a minister's wife!"

Careful to entertain strangers,
  Traveling agents and "such,"
Of this kind of "angels'" visits
  The deacons have had so much
As to prove a perfect nuisance,
  And hope these "plagues of their life"
Can soon be sent to the parson's—
  "Wanted—a minister's wife!"

A perfect pattern of prudence
  To all others, spending less,
But never disgracing the parish
  By looking shabby in dress.
Playing the organ on Sunday
  Would aid our laudable strife
To save the society's money—
  "Wanted—a minister's wife."

And when we have found the person;
  We hope, by working the two,
To lift our debt and build a new church—
  Then we shall know what to do;

For they will be worn and weary,
   Needing a change of life,
And so we'll advertise, "Wanted,
   A minister and his wife!"

UNKNOWN.

WILLIE THE WEEPER

LISTEN TO THE STORY of Willie the Weeper.
Willie the Weeper was a chimney sweeper.
He had the hop habit and he had it bad;
Listen and I'll tell you of a dream he had.

He went to a hop joint the other night,
Where he knew the lights were always shining bright,
And, calling for a chink to bring him some hop,
He started in smoking like he wasn't gonna stop.

After he'd smoked about a dozen pills,
He said, "This ought to cure all my aches and ills."
And turning on his side he fell asleep,
And dreamt he was a sailor on the ocean deep.

He played draw poker as they left the land,
And won a million dollars on the very first hand.
He played and he played till the crew went broke.
Then he turned around and took another smoke.

He came to the island of Siam,
Rubbed his eyes and said, "I wonder where I am,"
Played craps with the king and won a million more,
But had to leave the island cause the king got sore.

He went to Monte Carlo where he played roulette,
And couldn't lose a penny but won every bet—
Played and he played till the bank went broke.
Then he turned around and took another smoke.

Then he thought he'd better be sailing for home,
And chartered a ship and sailed away alone.
Ship hit a rock. He hit the floor.
Money was gone and the dream was o'er.

Now this is the story of Willie the Weeper;
Willie the Weeper was a chimney sweeper.
Someday a pill too many he'll take,
And dreaming he's dead, he'll forget to awake.

UNKNOWN.

THE BIRDS' BALL

SPRING ONCE SAID to the nightingale,
"I mean to give you birds a ball;
Pray, ma'am, ask the birdies all,
The birds and birdies, great and small."

Soon they came from bush and tree,
Singing sweet their song of glee,
Each one fresh from its cozy nest,
Each one dressed in its Sunday best.

Cuckoo and wren, they danc'd for life,
The raven waltzed with the yellowbird's wife;
The awkward owl and the bashful jay,
Wished each other "a very good day."

The woodpecker came from his hole in the tree,
And brought his bill to the company.
For the cherries ripe and the berries red,
'Twas a very long bill, so the birdies said.

They danced all day till the sun was low,
Till the mother birds prepared to go;
Then one and all, both great and small
Flew to their nest from the birdies' ball.

C. W. BARDEEN.

A BOSTON TOAST

[Written by Dr. Bossidy for an alumni dinner of Holy Cross College.]

AND THIS IS good old Boston,
   The home of the bean and the cod,
Where the Lowells talk to the Cabots,
   And the Cabots talk only to God.

JOHN C. BOSSIDY.

TO A LOUSE,

On Seeing One on a Lady's Bonnet at Church.

Ha! whare ye gaun, ye crawlin' ferlie?
Your impudence protects you sairly:
I canna say but ye strunt rarely
   Owre gauze an' lace;
Though, faith! I fear ye dine but sparely
   On sic a place.

Ye ugly, creepin', blastit wonner,
Detested, shunned by saunt an' sinner,
How dare you set your fit upon her,
   Sae fine a lady?
Gae somewhere else, and seek your dinner
   On some poor body.

Swith, in some beggar's haffet squattle;
There ye may creep and sprawl and sprattle
Wi' ither kindred, jumping cattle,
   In shoals and nations:
Whare horn nor bane ne'er daur unsettle
   Your thick plantations.

Now haud you there, ye're out o' sight,
Below the fatt'rels, snug an' tight;
Na, faith ye yet! ye'll no be right
   Till ye've got on it,
The very tapmost tow'ring height
   O' Miss's bonnet.

My sooth; right bauld ye set your nose out,
As plump and gray as ony grozet;
O for some rank, mercurial rozet,
   Or fell, red smeddum!
I'd gie you sic a hearty dose o't,
   Wad dress your droddum!

I wad na been surprised to spy
You on an auld wife's flannen toy;
Or aiblins some bit duddie boy,
   On 's wyliecoat;
But Miss's fine Lunardi, fie!
   How daur ye do 't?

493

O Jenny, dinna toss your head,
An' set your beauties a' abread!
Ye little ken what cursèd speed
   The blastie 's makin'!
Thae winks and finger-ends, I dread,
   Are notice takin'!

O wad some power the giftie gie us
To see oursel's as ithers see us!
It wad frae monie a blunder free us,
   And foolish notion:
What airs in dress an' gait wad lea'e us,
   And ev'n devotion!

ROBERT BURNS.

THE THREE WISE WOMEN

THREE WISE OLD WOMEN were they, were they,
Who went to walk on a winter day.
One carried a basket, to hold some berries;
One carried a ladder, to climb for cherries;
The third—and she was the wisest one—
Carried a fan to keep off the sun!

"Dear, dear!" said one. "A bear I see!
I think we'd better all climb a tree!"
But there wasn't a tree for miles around.
They were too frightened to stay on the ground;
So they climbed their ladder up to the top,
And sat there screaming, "We'll drop! We'll drop!"

But the wind was strong as wind could be,
And blew their ladder right out to sea!
Soon the three wise women were all afloat
In a leaky ladder, instead of a boat!
And every time the waves rolled in
Of course the poor things were wet to the skin.

Then they took their basket, the water to bail;
They put up their fan to make a sail;

But what became of the wise women then,
Whether they ever got home again,
Whether they saw any bears or no,
You must find out, for *I* don't know.

MRS. E. T. CORBETT.

THE THREE WISE COUPLES

THREE WISE OLD COUPLES were they, were they,
Who went to keep house together one day.
Upstairs and downstairs one couple ran,
He with his ulster, she with her fan.
"Fresh air!" cried the wife, "is the thing for me."
"Shut the windows—I'm freezing," said he.

The second couple, with basket and gun,
Went hunting for spiders, one by one.
Into the corners they poked and pried:
"There's one! I'll shoot him!" the husband cried,
While his wife exclaimed: "When the basket's full,
I can sell the spiders' webs for wool."

But the wisest couple of the three
Said: "We will a traveling circus be!"
"You," cried the wife, "the bear must play;
Up on the ladder you ought to stay,
And I'll carry the club, because, you know,
I'll have to beat you, your tricks to show."

So the man in the ulster was frozen stiff,
While his wife did nothing but fan and sniff.
The hunter was stung by a cross old spider,
As he very imprudently sat down beside her,
And his wife, who was gathering webs for wool,
Used him to make up a basket full.

But the man who learned the bear to play
Lived on the ladder for many a day.
He stole the club and he wouldn't come down,
So his poor wife carried him through the town,
And all the people said: "Let's go
To see the bear and the circus show!"

MRS. E. T. CORBETT.

THE OWL CRITIC

"Who stuffed that white owl?" No one spoke in the shop;
The barber was busy, and he couldn't stop;
The customers, waiting their turns, were reading
The *Daily,* the *Herald,* the *Post,* little heeding
The young man who blurted out such a blunt question;
Not one raised a head, or even made a suggestion;
    And the barber kept on shaving.

"Don't you see, Mister Brown,"
Cried the youth with a frown,
"How wrong the whole thing is,
How preposterous each wing is,
How flattened the head, how jammed down the neck is—
In short, the whole owl, what an ignorant wreck 'tis!

"I make no apology;
I've learned owleology,
I've passed days and nights in a hundred collections,
And cannot be blinded to any deflections
Arising from unskilful fingers that fail
To stuff a bird right, from his beak to his tail.
Mister Brown, Mister Brown!
Do take that bird down,
Or you'll soon be the laughing stock all over town!"
    And the barber kept on shaving.

"I've studied owls,
And other night fowls,
And I tell you
What I know to be true!
An owl cannot roost
With his limbs so unloosed;
No owl in this world
Ever had his claws curled,
Ever had his legs slanted,
Ever had his bill canted,
Ever had his neck screwed
Into that attitude.
He can't do it, because
'Tis against all bird laws.
Anatomy teaches,
Ornithology preaches,

An owl has a toe
That can't turn out so!
I've made the white owl my study for years,
And to see such a job almost moves me to tears!

"Mister Brown, I'm amazed
You should be so crazed
As to put up a bird
In that posture absurd!
To look at that owl really brings on a dizziness;
The man who stuffed him don't half know his business!"
  And the barber kept on shaving.
"Examine those eyes,
I'm filled with surprise
Taxidermists should pass
Off on you such poor glass;
So unnatural they seem
They'd make Audubon scream,
And John Burroughs laugh
To encounter such chaff.
Do take that bird down;
Have him stuffed again, Brown!"
  And the barber kept on shaving.

"With some sawdust and bark
I could stuff in the dark
An owl better than that.
I could make an old bat
Look more like an owl
Than that horrid fowl,
Stuck up there so stiff like a side of coarse leather;
In fact, about him there's not one natural feather."

Just then with a wink and a sly normal lurch,
The owl, very gravely, got down from his perch,
Walked round, and regarded his fault-finding critic,
(Who thought he was stuffed) with a glance analytic,
And then fairly hooted, as if he should say:
"Your learning's at fault, this time, anyway;
Don't waste it again on a live bird, I pray.
I'm an owl; you're another. Sir Critic, good-day!"
  And the barber kept on shaving.

JAMES T. FIELDS

497

TO MY NOSE

KNOWS HE that never took a pinch,
  Nosey, the pleasure thence which flows?
Knows he the titillating joys
    Which my nose knows?
O nose, I am as proud of thee
As any mountain of its snows;
I gaze on thee, and feel that pride
    A Roman knows!

ALFRED A. FORRESTER (ALFRED CROWQUILL).

THE YARN OF THE NANCY BELL

(From the *Bab Ballads*)

'T WAS ON THE SHORES that round our coast
  From Deal to Ramsgate span,
That I found alone, on a piece of stone,
  An elderly naval man.

His hair was weedy, his beard was long,
  And weedy and long was he;
And I heard this wight on the shore recite,
  In a singular minor key:

"O, I am a cook and a captain bold,
  And the mate of the Nancy brig,
And a bo'sun tight, and a midshipmite,
  And the crew of the captain's gig."

And he shook his fists and he tore his hair,
  Till I really felt afraid,
For I couldn't help thinking the man had been drinking,
  And so I simply said:

"O elderly man, it's little I know
  Of the duties of men of the sea,
And I'll eat my hand if I understand
  How you can possibly be

498

"At once a cook and a captain bold,
  And the mate of the Nancy brig,
And a bo'sun tight, and a midshipmite,
  And the crew of the captain's gig!"

Then he gave a hitch to his trousers, which
  Is a trick all seamen larn,
And having got rid of a thumping quid
  He spun this painful yarn:

" 'T was in the good ship Nancy Bell
  That we sailed to the Indian sea,
And there on a reef we come to grief,
  Which has often occurred to me.

"And pretty nigh all o' the crew was drowned
  (There was seventy-seven o' soul);
And only ten of the Nancy's men
  Said 'Here' to the muster-roll.

"There was me, and the cook, and the captain bold,
  And the mate of the Nancy brig,
And the bo'sun tight, and a midshipmite,
  And the crew of the captain's gig.

"For a month we'd neither wittles nor drink,
  Till a-hungry we did feel,
So we drawed a lot, and, accordin', shot
  The captain for our meal.

"The next lot fell to the Nancy's mate,
  And a delicate dish he made;
Then our appetite with the midshipmite
  We seven survivors stayed.

"And then we murdered the bo'sun tight,
  And he much resembled pig;
Then we wittled free, did the cook and me,
  On the crew of the captain's gig.

"Then only the cook and me was left,
  And the delicate question, 'Which
Of us two goes to the kettle?' arose,
  And we argued it out as sich.

"For I loved that cook as a brother, I did,
  And the cook he worshipped me;
But we'd both be blowed if we'd either be stowed
  In the other chap's hold, you see.

" 'I'll be eat if you dines off me,' says Tom.
  'Yes, that,' says I, 'you'll be.
I'm boiled if I die, my friend,' quoth I;
  And 'Exactly so,' quoth he.

"Says he: 'Dear James, to murder me
  Were a foolish thing to do,
For don't you see that you can't cook me,
  While I can—and will—cook you?'

"So he boils the water, and takes the salt
  And the pepper in portions true
(Which he never forgot), and some chopped shalot,
  And some sage and parsley too.

" 'Come here,' says he, with a proper pride,
  Which his smiling features tell;
" 'T will soothing be if I let you see
  How extremely nice you'll smell.'

"And he stirred it round, and round, and round,
  And he sniffed at the foaming froth;
When I ups with his heels, and smothers his squeals
  In the scum of the boiling broth.

"And I eat that cook in a week or less,
  And as I eating be
The last of his chops, why I almost drops,
  For a wessel in sight I see.

"And I never larf, and I never smile,
  And I never lark nor play;
But I sit and croak, and a single joke
  I have—which is to say:

"O, I am a cook and a captain bold
  And the mate of the Nancy brig,
And a bo'sun tight, and a midshipmite,
  And the crew of the captain's gig!"

WILLIAM SCHWENCK GILBERT.

500

ELEGY ON THE DEATH OF A MAD DOG

GOOD PEOPLE ALL, of every sort,
  Give ear unto my song;
And if you find it wondrous short,
  It cannot hold you long.

In Islington there was a man
  Of whom the world might say,
That still a godly race he ran—
  Whene'er he went to pray.

A kind and gentle heart he had,
  To comfort friends and foes:
The naked every day he clad—
  When he put on his clothes.

And in that town a dog was found,
  As many dogs there be,
Both mongrel, puppy, whelp, and hound,
  And curs of low degree.

This dog and man at first were friends;
  But when a pique began,
The dog, to gain his private ends,
  Went mad, and bit the man.

Around from all the neighboring streets
  The wondering neighbors ran,
And swore the dog had lost his wits,
  To bite so good a man!

The wound it seemed both sore and sad
  To every Christian eye:
And while they swore the dog was mad,
  They swore the man would die.

But soon a wonder came to light,
  That showed the rogues they lied:—
The man recovered of the bite,
  The dog it was that died!

OLIVER GOLDSMITH.

THE FROST

THE FROST looked forth, one still, clear night,
And he said, "Now I shall be out of sight,
So through the valley and over the height,
   In silence I'll take my way.
I will not go like that blustering train,
The wind and the snow, the hail and the rain,
Who make so much bustle and noise in vain,
   But I'll be as busy as they!"

Then he went to the mountain, and powdered its crest,
He climbed up the trees, and their boughs he dressed
With diamonds and pearls, and over the breast
   Of the quivering lake he spread
A coat of mail, that it need not fear
The downward point of many a spear
That he hung on its margin, far and near,
   Where a rock could rear its head.

He went to the windows of those who slept,
And over each pane like a fairy crept:
Wherever he breathed, wherever he stepped,
   By the light of the moon were seen
Most beautiful things. There were flowers and trees,
There were bevies of birds and swarms of bees,
There were cities, thrones, temples, and towers, and these
   All pictured in silver sheen!

But he did one thing that was hardly fair,—
He peeped in the cupboard, and finding there
That all had forgotten for him to prepare,
   "Now, just to set them thinking,
I'll bite this basket of fruit," said he;
"This costly pitcher I'll burst in three,
And the glass of water they've left for me
   Shall '*tchick!*' to tell them I'm drinking."

HANNAH FRANCES GOULD.

TROUBLE IN THE "AMEN CORNER"

'TWAS A STYLISH CONGREGATION, that of Theophrastus Brown,
And its organ was the finest and the biggest in the town;
And the chorus—all the papers favorably commented on it,
For 'twas said each female member had a forty-dollar bonnet.

Now in the "amen corner" of the church sat Brother Eyer,
Who persisted every Sabbath day in singing with the choir;
He was poor, but genteel looking, and his heart as snow was white,
And his face beamed with sweetness when he sung with all his might.

His voice was cracked and broken; age had touched his vocal cords.
And nearly every Sunday he would mispronounce the words
Of the hymns, and 'twas no wonder; he was old and nearly blind,
And the choir rattling onward always left him far behind.

The chorus stormed and blustered, Brother Eyer sang too slow,
And then he used the tunes in vogue a hundred years ago;
At last the storm cloud burst and the church was told, in fine,
That the brother must stop singing, or the choir would resign.

Then the pastor called together in the lecture room one day
Seven influential members, who subscribe more than they pay,
And having asked God's guidance in a printed prayer or two
They put their heads together to determine what to do.

They debated, thought, suggested, till at last "dear Brother York,"
Who last winter made a million on a sudden rise in pork,
Rose and moved that a committee wait at once on Brother Eyer,
And proceed to rake him lively "for disturbin' of the choir."

Said he: "In that 'ere organ I've invested quite a pile,
And we'll sell it if we cannot worship in the latest style;
Our Philadelphy tenor tells me 'tis the hardest thing
For to make God understand him when the brother tries to sing.

"We've got the biggest organ, the best-dressed choir in town,
We pay the steepest sal'ry to our pastor, Brother Brown;
But if we must humor ignorance because it's blind and old—
If the choir's to be pestered, I will seek another fold."

Of course the motion carried, and one day a coach-and-four,
With the latest style of driver, rattled up to Eyer's door.

And the sleek, well-dressed committee, Brothers Sharkey, York and
    Lamb,
As they crossed the humble portal took good care to miss the jamb.

They found the choir's great trouble sitting in his old armchair,
And the summer's golden sunbeams lay upon his thin white hair,
He was singing "Rock of Ages" in a voice both cracked and low,
But the angels understood him, 'twas all he cared to know.

Said York: "We're here, dear brother, with the vestry's approbation,
To discuss a little matter that affects the congregation";
"And the choir, too," said Sharkey, giving Brother York a nudge.
"And the choir, too!" he echoed, with the graveness of a judge.

"It was the understanding when we bargained for the chorus,
That it was to relieve us, that is, do the singing for us;
If we rupture the agreement, it is very plain, dear brother,
It will leave our congregation and be gobbled by another.

"We don't want any singing except that what we've bought!
The latest tunes are all the rage; the old ones stand for naught;
And so we have decided—are you listening, Brother Eyer?—
That you'll have to stop your singin', for it flurrytates the choir."

The old man slowly raised his head, a sign that he did hear,
And on his cheeks the trio caught the glitter of a tear;
His feeble hands pushed back the locks white as the silky snow,
As he answered the committee in a voice both sweet and low:

"I've sung the Psalms of David for nearly eighty years;
They've been my staff and comfort and calmed life's many fears;
I'm sorry I disturb the choir, perhaps I'm doing wrong,
But when my heart is filled with praise I can't keep back a song.

"I wonder if beyond the tide that's breaking at my feet,
In the far-off heavenly temple, where the Master I shall greet—
Yes, I wonder when I try to sing the songs of God up higher
If the angel band will chide me for disturbing Heaven's choir."

A silence filled the little room; the old man bowed his head:
The carriage rattled on again, but Brother Eyer was dead!
Yes, dead! his hand has raised the veil the future hangs before us,
And the Master dear had called him to the everlasting chorus.

The choir missed him for a while, but he was soon forgot!
A few churchgoers watched the door; the old man entered not.
Far away, his voice no longer cracked, he sings his heart's desires,
Where there are no church committees and no fashionable choirs!

THOMAS CHALMERS HARBAUGH.

MY DAD'S DINNER PAIL

PRESERVE that old kettle, so blackened and worn;
It belonged to my father before I was born;
It hung in a corner beyant on a nail—
'Twas the emblem of labor, my dad's dinner pail.

Chorus:

It glistened like silver, so sparkling and bright;
I am fond of the trifle that held his wee bite;
In summer or winter, in snow, rain or hail,
I've carried that kettle, my dad's dinner pail.
When the bell rang for mealtime my father'd come down—
He'd eat with the workmen about on the ground;
He'd share with the laborer and he'd go bail,
You would never reach the bottom of dad's dinner pail.
If the day should be rainy my father'd stop home,
And he'd polish his kettle as clane as a stone;
He'd joke with my mother and me he would whale
If I put a finger on dad's dinner pail.
There's a place for the coffee and also for bread,
The corned beef and praties, and oft it was said:
"Go fill it with porter, with beer or with ale;"
The drink would taste sweeter from dad's dinner pail.

EDWARD HARRIGAN.

GOOD FORTUNE

GOOD FORTUNE is a giddy maid,
    Fickle and restless as a fawn;
She smooths your hair; and then the jade
    Kisses you quickly, and is gone.

But Madam Sorrow scorns all this;
    She shows no eagerness for flitting,
But with a long and fervent kiss
    Sits by your bed—and brings her knitting.

HEINRICH HEINE. *Translated by Louis Untermeyer.*

THE WORRIED SKIPPER

"I HATES TO THINK of dyin'," says the skipper to the mate;
"Starvation, shipwrecks, heart disease I loathes to contemplate.
I hates to think of vanities and all the crimes they lead to,"
    Then says the mate,
    With looks sedate,
"Ye doesn't reely need to."

"It fills me breast with sorrer," says the skipper with a sigh,
"To conjer up the happy days what careless has slipped by;
I hates to contemplate the day I ups and left me Mary."
    Then says the mate,
    "Why contemplate,
If it ain't necessary?"

"Suppose that this here vessel," says the skipper, with a groan,
"Should lose 'er bearin's, run away, and hump upon a stone;
Suppose she'd shiver and go down, when save ourselves we couldn't."
    The mate replies,
    "Oh, blow me eyes!
Suppose, ag'in, she shouldn't?"

"The chances is ag'in us," says the skipper in dismay;
"If fate don't kill us out and out, it gits us all some day.
So many perish of old age, the death rate must be fearful,"
    "Well," says the mate,
    "At any rate,
We might as well die cheerful."

"I read in them statistic books," the nervous skipper cries,
"That every minute by the clock some feller ups and dies;
I wonder what disease they gits that kills in such a hurry,"
    The mate he winks
    And says, "I thinks
They mostly dies of worry."

"Of certain things," the skipper sighs, "me conscience won't be rid,
And all the wicked things I done I sure should not have did;
The wrinkles on me inmost soul compel me oft to shiver."
  "Yer soul's fust-rate,"
  Observes the mate;
"The trouble's with yer liver."

                      WALLACE IRWIN.

SIGNS OF RAIN

FORTY REASONS FOR NOT ACCEPTING AN INVITATION OF A FRIEND TO MAKE
AN EXCURSION WITH HIM.

1 THE HOLLOW WINDS begin to blow,
2 The clouds look black, the glass is low;
3 The soot falls down, the spaniels sleep,
4 And spiders from their cobwebs peep.
5 Last night the sun went pale to bed,
6 The moon in halos hid her head;
7 The boding shepherd heaves a sigh,
8 For see, a rainbow spans the sky!
9 The walls are damp, the ditches smell,
10 Closed is the pink-eyed pimpernel.
11 Hark how the chairs and tables crack!
12 Old Betty's nerves are on the rack;
13 Loud quacks the duck, the peacocks cry,
14 The distant hills are seeming nigh.
15 How restless are the snorting swine!
16 The busy flies disturb the kine;
17 Low o'er the grass the swallow wings,
18 The cricket, too, how sharp he sings!
19 Puss on the hearth, with velvet paws,
20 Sits wiping o'er her whiskered jaws;
21 Through the clear streams the fishes rise,
22 And nimbly catch the incautious flies.
23 The glowworms, numerous and light,
24 Illumed the dewy dell last night;
25 At dusk the squalid toad was seen,
26 Hopping and crawling o'er the green;
27 The whirling dust the wind obeys,
28 And in the rapid eddy plays;
29 The frog has changed his yellow vest,

30 And in a russet coat is dressed.
31 Though June, the air is cold and still,
32 The mellow blackbird's voice is shrill;
33 My dog, so altered in his taste,
34 Quits mutton bones on grass to feast;
35 And see yon rooks, how odd their flight!
36 They imitate the gliding kite,
37 And seem precipitate to fall,
38 As if they felt the piercing ball.
39 'T will surely rain; I see with sorrow,
40 Our jaunt must be put off to-morrow.

DR. EDWARD JENNER.

THE PESSIMIST

NOTHING TO DO but work,
  Nothing to eat but food;
Nothing to wear but clothes
  To keep one from going nude.

Nothing to breathe but air,
  Quick as a flash 'tis gone;
Nowhere to fall but off,
  Nowhere to stand but on.

Nothing to comb but hair,
  Nowhere to sleep but in bed;
Nothing to weep but tears,
  Nothing to bury but dead.

Nothing to sing but songs;
  Ah, well, alas! alack!
Nowhere to go but out,
  Nowhere to come but back.

Nothing to see but sights,
  Nothing to quench but thirst;
Nothing to have but what we've got;
  Thus thro' life we are cursed.

Nothing to strike but a gait;
  Everything moves that goes.
Nothing at all but common sense
  Can ever withstand these woes.

BEN KING.

THE LEGEND OF THE ADMEN

HEAR THE LEGEND of the Admen
Ere they conquered all creation.

In the Prophylactic forest,
On the shores of Coca Cola
Dwelt the Moxies in their wigwams—
Old Sapolio, the chieftain,
Pebeco, the grizzled prophet,
And the warriors, young and eager.

In the lodge of the old chieftain
With Uneeda, more than mother,
And Victrola, old and feeble,
Lived the warmest of the maidens,
Musterole, Sapolio's daughter—
Musterole, the Sunkist Chiclet.

All the young men sought her favor
Left their trophies at her wigwam,
Brought her Thermos skins for raiment,
Brought her Tarvia for ointment;
And sweet Musterole smiled on them—
Smiled on Vaseline and Pointex,
Smiled on Danderine and Jello,
Smiled on Listerine and Valspar—
Smiled but left them unrequited,
For her love she gave to no one—
Frigidaire alone she gave them.

Then from Multibestos mountains
From the tribe of the Texacos,
Came the young chief, Instant Postum.

Mightiest hunter in the forest,
All superb in strength and beauty.
He it was who trapped the Kodak,
He, who shot the great Sears-Roebuck.
Eversharp his trusty hatchet,
Every Arrow had a Hotpoint.
On him gazed the Moxie maidens—
Nujol poured her glowing glances,
Bold Carbona sought to win him,
Zonite brought him luscious Pyrene;
But for Musterole yearned Postum.

Through the fields of ripe Wheatena
Hand in hand the lovers wandered.
Seated then upon the White Rock,
By the rippling Cuticura—
Safe beneath Palmolive shadows
From the boughs they picked the Grapenuts,
There, they saw the sun descending.

Naught cared Postum for the night winds
Blowing through the Holeproof forest;
Musterole was there beside him.
To his bosom quick he drew her,
Held her to his manly bosom—
Whispered words with love a burning,
Told her how he'd caught the Sealpax,
Told her how he'd slain Bull Durham,
Told her how he'd trapped Ampico—
Boasted of his father's tepee,
With its sides of Mentholatum
And its rugs of soft Socony.

To him, Musterole aquiver,
Listened and her heart gave answer.
All the warmth of love she gave him
Gave her Rubberset affection
Gave her heart to Instant Postum.
Thus he won her—thus he took her.

Passed the years in quick succession;
Little Fairies came to bless them—
Gold-Dust twins and bright BVD,
Little Beechnut, Wrigley Spearmint,
Vici Kid and Pluto Water
Filled the wigwam with their laughter.

So they lived in happy union
Safe in peace and strong in warfare;
And their progeny continues,
Finds a place in town and hamlet
Known and loved by every mortal—
All the tribes are held in honor.

This the legend I have told you.

EVERETT W. LORD.

SOCRATES SNOOKS

MISTER SOCRATES SNOOKS, a lord of creation,
The second time entered the married relation:
Xantippe Caloric accepted his hand,
And they thought him the happiest man in the land.
But scarce had the honeymoon passed o'er his head,
When one morning to Xantippe Socrates said:
"I think, for a man of my standing in life,
This house is too small, as I now have a wife;
So, as early as possible, carpenter Carey
Shall be sent for to widen my house and my dairy."

"Now, Socrates, dearest," Xantippe replied,
"I hate to hear everything vulgarly *my'd*;
Now, whenever you speak of your chattels again,
Say, *our* cowhouse, *our* barnyard, *our* pigpen."
"By your leave, Mrs. Snooks, I will say what I please
Of *my* houses, *my* lands, *my* gardens, *my* trees."
"Say *our*," Xantippe exclaimed in a rage.
"I won't, Mrs. Snooks, though you ask it an age!"

Oh, woman! though only a part of man's rib,
If the story in Genesis don't tell a fib,
Should your naughty companion e'er quarrel with you,
You are certain to prove the best man of the two.
In the following case this was certainly true;
For the lovely Xantippe just pulled off her shoe,
And laying about her, all sides at random,
The adage was verified—"Nil desperandum."

Mister Socrates Snooks, after trying in vain,
To ward off the blows which descended like rain—
Concluding that valor's best part was discretion—
Crept under the bed like a terrified Hessian;
But the dauntless Xantippe, not one whit afraid,
Converted the siege into a blockade.

At last, after reasoning the thing in his pate,
He concluded 'twas useless to strive against fate:
And, so, like a tortoise protruding his head,
Said, "My dear, may we come out from under *our* bed?"
"Ha! ha!" she exclaimed, "Mr. Socrates Snooks,
I perceive you agree to my terms by your looks;
Now, Socrates—hear me—from this happy hour,
If you'll only obey me, I'll never look sour."

'Tis said the next Sabbeth, ere going to church,
He chanced for a clean pair of trousers to search;
Having found them, he asked, with a few nervous twitches,
"My dear, may we put on our new Sunday breeches?"

FITZ HUGH LUDLOW.

FIN DE SIÈCLE

THIS LIFE'S A HOLLOW bubble,
    Don't you know?
Just a painted piece of twouble,
    Don't you know?
We come to earth to cwy,
We gwow oldeh and we sigh,
Oldeh still and then we die,
    Don't you know?

It is all a howwid mix,
    Don't you know?
Business, love and politics,
    Don't you know?
Clubs and pawties, cliques and sets,
Fashions, follies, sins, wegwets,
Stwuggle, stwife and cigawettes.
    Don't you know?

And we wowwy through each day,
    Don't you know?
In a sort of, kind of way,
    Don't you know?
We are hungry, we are fed,
Some few things are done and said,
We are tihed, we go to bed,
    Don't you know?

Business, oh, that's beastly twade,
    Don't you know?
Something's lost or something's made,
    Don't you know?
And you wowwy, and you mope,
And you hang youah highest hope
On the pwice, pe'haps of soap,
    Don't you know?

Politics! oh, just a lawk,
    Don't you know?
Just a nightmeah in the dawk,
    Don't you know?
You pe'spiah all day and night,
And afteh all the fight,
Why, pe'haps the w'ong man's wight,
    Don't you know?

Society? Is dwess,
    Don't you know?
And a sou'ce of much distwess,
    Don't you know?
To determine what to weah,
When to go and likewise wheah,
And how to pawt youah haih,
    Don't you know?

Love? Oh yes. You meet some gi'l,
    Don't you know?
An' you get in such a whi'l,
    Don't you know?
Then you kneel down on the fioah
And imploah and adoah—
And it's all a beastly boah,
    Don't you know?

So theah's weally nothing in it,
   Don't you know?
And we live just for the minute,
   Don't you know?
For when you've seen and felt,
Dwank and eaten, heahd and smelt,
Why all the cawds are dealt,
   Don't you know?

You've one consciousness, that's all,
   Don't you know?
And one stomach, and it's small,
   Don't you know?
You can only weah one tie,
One eyeglass in youah eye,
And one coffin when you die.
   Don't you know?

EDMUND VANCE COOKE.

WHAT THE CHOIR SANG ABOUT THE NEW BONNET

A FOOLISH LITTLE MAIDEN bought a foolish little bonnet,
With a ribbon and a feather and a bit of lace upon it;
And that the other maidens of the little town might know it,
She thought she'd go to meeting next Sunday just to show it.

But though the little bonnet was scarce larger than a dime
The getting of it settled proved to be a work of time;
So when 'twas fairly tied all the bells had stopped their ringing,
And when she came to meeting, sure enough, the folks were singing.

So the foolish little maiden stood and waited at the door,
And she shook her ruffles out behind and smoothed them out before.
"Hallelujah, hallelujah!" sang the choir above her head—
"Hardly knew you! Hardly knew you!" were the words she thought
   they said.

This made the little maiden feel so very, very cross
That she gave her little mouth a twist, her little head a toss;
For she thought the very hymn they sang was all about her bonnet,
With the ribbon and the feather and the bit of lace upon it.

And she would not wait to listen to the sermon or the prayer,
But pattered down the silent street and hurried up the stair
Till she'd reached her little bureau, and in a bandbox on it,
Had hidden safe from critic's eye her foolish little bonnet.

Which proves, my little maidens, that each of you will find
In every Sabbath service but an echo of your mind,
And that the little head that's filled with silly little airs
Will never get a blessing from sermons or from prayers.

M. T. MORRISON.

RIDING DOWN FROM BANGOR

RIDING DOWN from Bangor, on an eastern train,
After weeks of hunting in the woods of Maine,
Quite extensive whiskers, beard, moustache as well,
Sat a fellow student, tall and slim and swell.

Empty seat behind him, no one at his side,
Into eastern village then the train did glide.
Enter aged couple, take the hindmost seat;
Enter village maiden, beautiful, petite.

Blushingly she faltered, "Is this seat engaged?"
Sees the aged couple properly enraged.
Student, quite ecstatic, sees her ticket through.
Thinks of the long tunnel, thinks what he will do.

Pleasantly they chatted; how the cinders fly!
Till the student fellow got one in his eye.
Maiden, sympathetic turns herself about,
"May I, if you please, sir, try to get it out?"

Then the student fellow feels a gentle touch,
Hears a gentle murmur, "Does it hurt you much?"
Whiz! Slap! Bang! into the tunnel, quite
Into glorious darkness, black as Egypt's night.

Out into the daylight glides that eastern train,
Student's hair is ruffled just the merest grain;
Maiden seems all blushes, when then and there appeared
A tiny little earring in that horrid student's beard.

LOUIS SHREVE OSBORNE.

A MODEST WIT

A SUPERCILIOUS NABOB of the East—
  Haughty, being great—purse-proud, being rich—
A governor, or general, at the least,
  I have forgotten which—

Had in his family a humble youth,
  Who went from England in his patron's suite,
An unassuming boy, in truth
  A lad of decent parts, and good repute.

This youth had sense and spirit;
  But yet, with all his sense,
  Excessive diffidence
Obscured his merit.

One day, at table, flushed with pride and wine,
  His Honor, proudly free, severely merry,
Conceived it would be vastly fine
  To crack a joke upon his secretary.

"Young man," he said, "by what art, craft, or trade,
  Did your good father gain his livelihood?"
"He was a saddler, sir," Modestus said,
  "And in his time was reckoned good."

"A saddler, eh! and taught you Greek
  Instead of teaching you to sew!
Pray, why did not your father make
  A saddler, sir, of you?"

Each parasite, then, as in duty bound,
  The joke applauded, and the laugh went round.

At length Modestus, bowing low,
  Said (craving pardon, if too free he made),
"Sir, by your leave, I fain would know
  Your father's trade!"

"My father's trade! By heaven, that's too bad!
My father's trade? Why, blockhead, are you mad?
  My father, sir, did never stoop so low—
  He was a gentleman, I'd have you know."

"Excuse the liberty I take,"
  Modestus said, with archness on his brow,
"Pray, why did not your father make
  A gentleman of you?"

SEELECK OSBORN.

KAISER & CO.

DER KAISER auf der Vaterland
Und Gott on high, all dings gommand;
Ve two, ach, don'd you understandt?
  Meinself—und Gott.

He reigns in heafen, und always shall,
Und mein own embire don'd vas small;
Ein noble bair, I dink you call
  Meinself—und Gott.

While some mens sing der power divine,
Mein soldiers sing "Der Wacht am Rhein,"
Und drink der healt in Rhenish wein
  Auf me—und Gott.

Dere's France dot swaggers all aroundt,
She ausgespieldt—she's no aggoundt;
To mooch ve dinks she don'd amoundt,
  Meinself—und Gott.

She vill not dare to fight again,
But if she should, I'll show her blain,
Dot Elsass und (in French) Lorraine
  Are mine—und Gott's.

Von Bismarck vas a man of might,
Und dought he was glean oud auf sight,
But, ach! he vas nicht goot to fight
  Mit me—und Gott.

Ve knock him like ein man auf straw,
Ve let him know whose vill vas law,
Und dot ve don'd vould standt his jaw,
  Meinself—und Gott.

517

Ve send him oudt in big disgrace,
Ve giff him insuldt to his face,
Und put Caprivi in his place,
   Meinself—und Gott.

Und ven Caprivi get svelled headt,
Ve very bromptly on him set,
Und told him to get up and get—
   Meinself—und Gott.

Dere's Grandma dinks she's nicht shmall beer—
Mit Boers und dings she interfere;
She'll learn none runs dis hemisphere
   But me—und Gott.

She dinks, goot fräu, some ships she's got,
Und soldiers mit der sgarlet coat,
Ach! we could knock dem—pouf! like dot,
   Meinself—und Gott.

Dey say dat badly fooled I vas
At Betersburg by Nicholas,
Und dat I act shust like ein ass,
   Und dupe; Herr Gott!

Vell, maybe yah und maybe nein,
Und maybe czar mit France gombine,
To take dem lands about der Rhein
   From me—und Gott.

But dey may try dat leedle game,
Und make deir breaks; but all der same
Dey only vill ingrease der fame
   Auf me—und Gott.

In dimes of peace, brebared for wars,
I bear der helm und spear ouf Mars,
Und care nicht for den dousandt czars—
   Meinself—und Gott.

In short, I humor efery whim,
Mit aspect dark und visage grim;
Gott pulls mit me und I mit him—
   Meinself—und Gott.

                 ALEXANDER MACGREGOR ROSE.

TEDDY UNT ME UNT GOTT
(A revision)

DER KAISER of dis Vaterlandt
Unt Gott on high all dings commandt—
Eggsept, of course, you understandt,
  Dare's Teddy.

It used to be dot me unt Gott
Could run der vorldt as vell as not;
But now of help ve get a lot
  From Teddy.

Who told us two unt two makes four,
Unt neffer either less or more,
Unt all about our ancient lore?
  Vy Teddy.

Who sait to me, "I like you, Bill?"
Who helped me not to keep right still
Unt talk of animals to kill?
  Dot Teddy.

Who told me vat mein army needs,
Unt how vords doesn't count mit deeds?
Who valks unt talks der vile he reads?
  Dot Teddy.

Who told me dings I neffer knew?
Who told me vat I ought to do
Unt how to say "Dee-lighted!" too?
  Dot Teddy.

Dare iss no bleak unt lonesome spot
Vich ve don't cheer—I tell you dot!—
Der vorldt iss bossed by me unt Gott—
  Unt Teddy.

UNKNOWN.

DE FUST BANJO

Go 'way, fiddle! folks is tired o' hearin' you a-squawkin'.
Keep silence fur yo' betters! don't you heah de banjo talkin'?
About de 'possum's tail she's gwine to lecter—ladies, listen!
About de ha'r whut isn't dar, an' why de ha'r is missin':

"Dar's gwine to be a' oberflow," said Noah, lookin' solemn—
Fur Noah tuk de *Herald,* an' he read de ribber column—
An' so he sot his hands to wuk a-clarin' timber patches,
An' 'lowed he's gwine to build a boat to beat de steamah Natchez.

Ol' Noah kep' a-nailin' an' a-chippin' an' a-sawin',
An' all de wicked neighbors kep' a-laughin' an a-pshawin';
But Noah didn' min' 'em, knowin' whut wuz gwine to happen,
An' forty days an' forty nights de rain it kep' a-drappin'.

Now, Noah had done cotched a lot ob eb'ry sort o' beas'es—
Ob all de shows a-trabbelin', it beat 'em all to pieces!
He had a Morgan colt an' seb'ral head o' Jarsey cattle—
An' druv 'em board de Ark as soon's he heered de thunder rattle.

Den sech anoder fall ob rain! It come so awful hebby,
De ribber riz immejitly, an' busted troo de lebbee;
De people all wuz drownded out—'cep' Noah an' de critters,
An' men he' hired to wuk de boat—an' one to mix de bitters.

De Ark she kep' a-sailin' an' a-sailin' *an'* a-sailin';
De lion got his dander up, an' like to bruk de palin';
De sarpints hissed; de painters yelled; tel', whut wid all de fussin',
You c'u'dn't hardly heah de mate a-bossin' 'roun' an' cussin'.

Now Ham, de only nigger whut wuz runnin' on de packet,
Got lonesome in de barber shop, an' c'u'dn't stan' de racket;
An' so, fur to amuse hese'f, he steamed some wood an' bent it,
An' soon he had a banjo made—de fust dat was invented.

He wet de ledder, stretched it on; made bridge an' screws an' aprin;
An' fitted in a proper neck—'twuz berry long an' tap'rin';
He tuk some tin, an' twisted him a thimble fur to ring it:
An' den de mighty question riz: how wuz he gwine to string it?

De 'possum had as fine a tail as dis dat I's a-singin';
De ha'r's so long an' thick an' strong—des fit fur banjo stringin';
Dat nigger shaved 'em off as short as washday-dinner graces,
An' sorted ob 'em by de size—f'om little E's to bases.

He strung her, tuned her, struck a jig,—'twuz "Nebber min' de wed-
    der,"—
She soun' like forty-lebben bands a-playin' all togedder:
Some went to pattin'; some to dancin': Noah called de figgers;
An Ham he sot an' knocked de tune, de happiest ob niggers!

Now, sence dat time—it's mighty strange—dere's not de slightes'
    showin'
Ob any ha'r at all upon de 'possum's tail a-growin';
An' curyus, too, dat nigger's ways: his people nebber los' 'em—
Fur whar you finds de nigger—dar's de banjo an' de 'possum!

                                        IRWIN RUSSELL.

THE BLIND MEN AND THE ELEPHANT

IT WAS SIX MEN of Indostan
    To learning much inclined,
Who went to see the elephant
    (Though all of them were blind),
That each by observation
    Might satisfy his mind.

The First approached the elephant,
    And, happening to fall
Against his broad and sturdy side,
    At once began to bawl:
"God bless me! but the elephant
    Is nothing but a wall!"

The Second, feeling of the tusk,
    Cried: "Ho! what have we here
So very round and smooth and sharp?
    To me 'tis mighty clear
This wonder of an elephant
    Is very like a spear!"

521

The Third approached the animal,
    And, happening to take
The squirming trunk within his hands,
    Thus boldly up and spake:
"I see," quoth he, "the elephant
    Is very like a snake!"

The Fourth reached out his eager hand,
    And felt about the knee:
"What most this wondrous beast is like
    Is mighty plain," quoth he;
" 'Tis clear enough the elephant
    Is very like a tree."

The Fifth, who chanced to touch the ear,
    Said: "E'en the blindest man
Can tell what this resembles most;
    Deny the fact who can,
This marvel of an elephant
    Is very like a fan!"

The Sixth no sooner had begun
    About the beast to grope,
Than, seizing on the swinging tail
    That fell within his scope,
"I see," quoth he, "the elephant
    Is very like a rope!"

And so these men of Indostan
    Disputed loud and long,
Each in his own opinion
    Exceeding stiff and strong,
Though each was partly in the right.
    And all were in the wrong!

So, oft in theologic wars
    The disputants, I ween,
Rail on in utter ignorance
    Of what each other mean,
And prate about an elephant
    Not one of them has seen!

                    JOHN GODFREY SAXE.

522

THE GAME OF LIFE

THERE'S A GAME much in fashion—I think it's called Euchre
(Though I never have played it, for pleasure or lucre),
In which, when the cards are in certain conditions,
The players appear to have changed their positions,
And one of them cries, in a confident tone,
"I think I may venture to go it alone!"

While watching the game, 'tis a whim of the bard's
A moral to draw from that skirmish of cards,
And to fancy he finds in the trivial strife
Some excellent hints for the battle of Life,
Where—whether the prize be a ribbon or throne—
The winner is he who can go it alone!

When great Galileo proclaimed that the world
In a regular orbit was ceaselessly whirled,
And got—not a convert—for all of his pains,
But only derision and prison and chains,
"It moves, for all that!" was his answering tone,
For he knew, like the Earth, he could go it alone!

When Kepler, with intellect piercing afar,
Discovered the laws of each planet and star,
And doctors, who ought to have lauded his name,
Derided his learning, and blackened his fame,
"I can wait!" he replied, "till the truth you shall own";
For he felt in his heart he could go it alone!

Alas! for the player who idly depends,
In the struggle for life, upon kindred or friends;
Whatever the value of blessings like these,
They can never atone for inglorious ease,
Nor comfort the coward who finds, with a groan,
That his crutches have left him to go it alone!

There's something, no doubt, in the hand you may hold;
Health, family, culture, wit, beauty, and gold
The fortunate owner may fairly regard
As, each in its way, a most excellent card;
Yet the game may be lost, with all these for your own,
Unless you've the courage to go it alone!

In battle or business, whatever the game,
In law or in love, it is ever the same;
In the struggle for power, or the scramble for pelf,
Let this be your motto—Rely on yourself!
For, whether the prize be a ribbon or throne,
The victor is he who can go it alone!

JOHN GODFREY SAXE.

AN OVERWORKED ELOCUTIONIST

ONCE THERE was a little boy whose name was Robert Reese;
And every Friday afternoon he had to speak a piece.
So many poems thus he learned, that soon he had a store
Of recitations in his head and still kept learning more.

And now this is what happened: He was called upon one week
And totally forgot the piece he was about to speak.
His brain he cudgeled. Not a word remained within his head!
And so he spoke at random, and this is what he said:

"My beautiful, my beautiful, who standest proudly by,
It was the schooner Hesperus—the breaking waves dashed high!
Why is this Forum crowded? What means this stir in Rome?
Under a spreading chestnut tree, there is no place like home!

When freedom from her mountain height cried, 'Twinkle, little star,'
Shoot if you must this old gray head, King Henry of Navarre!
Roll on, thou deep and dark blue castled crag of Drachenfels,
My name is Norval, on the Grampian Hills, ring out, wild bells!

If you're waking, call me early, to be or not to be,
The curfew must not ring tonight! Oh, woodman, spare that tree!
Charge, Chester, charge! On, Stanley, on! and let who will be clever!
The boy stood on the burning deck, but I go on forever!"

His elocution was superb, his voice and gestures fine;
His schoolmates all applauded as he finished the last line.
"I see it doesn't matter," Robert thought, "what words I say,
So long as I declaim with oratorical display."

CAROLYN WELLS.

SLEEPIN' AT THE FOOT O' THE BED

DID YE ever sleep at the foot o' the bed
  When the weather wuz whizzin' cold,
When the wind wuz a-whistlin aroun' the house
  An' the moon wuz yeller ez gold,
An give yore good warm feathers up
  To Aunt Lizzie and Uncle Fred—
Too many kinfolks on a bad, raw night
  And you went to the foot o' the bed—
  Fer some dern reason the coldest night o' the season
An' you wuz sent to the foot o' the bed.

I could allus wait till the old folks et
  An' then eat the leavin's with grace,
The teacher could keep me after school,
  An' I'd still hold a smile on my face,
I could wear the big boys' wore-out clothes
  Er let sister have my sled,
But it allus did git my nanny goat
  To have to sleep at the foot o' the bed;
  They's not a location topside o' creation
That I hate like the foot o' the bed.

'Twuz fine enough when the kinfolks come—
  The kids brought brand-new games,
You could see how fat all the old folks wuz,
  An' learn all the babies' names,
Had biscuits an' custard and chicken pie,
  An' allus got Sunday fed,
But you knowed dern well when night come on
  You wuz headed fer the foot o' the bed;
  You couldn't git by it, they wuz no use to try it,
You wuz headed fer the foot o' the bed.

They tell me that some folks don't know whut it is
  To have company all over the place,
To rassel fer cover thru a long winter night
  With a big foot settin' in your face,
Er with cold toenails a-scratchin' yore back
  An' a footboard a-scrubbin' yore head;

525

I'll tell the wide world you ain't lost a thing
   Never sleepin' at the foot o' the bed;
    You can live jest as gladly an' die jest as sadly
'N' never sleep at the foot o' the bed.

I've done it, an' I've done it a many uv a time
   In this land o' brave an' the free,
An' in this all-fired battle uv life
   It's done left its mark upon me,
Fer I'm allus a-strugglin' around at the foot
   Instead of forgin' ahead,
An' I don't think it's caused by a doggone thing
   But sleepin' at the foot o' the bed;
    I've lost all my claim on fortune an' fame,
A-sleepin' at the foot o' the bed.

LUTHER PATRICK.

A MAXIM REVISED

LADIES, to this advice give heed—
In controlling men:
If at first you don't succeed,
Why, cry, cry again.

UNKNOWN.

I KISSED YOU

[Parody on *You Kissed Me,* by Josephine Slocum Hunt. See page 44]

I KISSED YOU, I own, but I did not suppose
That you, through the papers, the deed would disclose,
Like free-loving cats, when on ridgepoles they meet—
When their squalls of "You kissed me!" disturb the whole street.
I kissed you. The impulse as suddenly came
As that cold-looking cloud is transformed into flame;
My act was the lightning that glances and thrills,
And yours the loud thunder that blabs to the hills.

I kissed you. As kissed the poor Cyprian boy
In dreams, his Diana, so cold and so coy,
And foolishly fancied—encircling your charms—
A maid—not a matchbox—was clasped in my arms.
I kissed you. The zephyr on tiptoe passed by,
The moon with a kerchief cloud hid her soft eye;
From the bough that swayed o'er us, all silvered with dew,
With a half-smothered titter the katydid flew.

I kissed you. All nature to counterfeit sleep,
Half promised our secret so sacred to keep;
No ubiquitous press correspondent peeped through
The leaves. I was "interviewed" only by you.
I kissed you. Then, scared at my boldness, I deemed
You had fainted, or else you would surely have screamed:
But no, you not only all censure forebore,
But, like Oliver Twist, are now asking for "more."

I kissed you. All others may do it who choose,
But I to repeat the performance refuse.
On your lips I will never again print a smack;
By the press or by note, you may send that one back.
I kissed you. The poetess Sappho of old,
Like you, was so warm that her Pharon grew cold;
So she ended her love and her life in a pet—
I presume there are equal facilities yet.

UNKNOWN.

527

IX. MEMORY AND GRIEF

PRAYER FOR A VERY NEW ANGEL

God, God, be lenient her first night there.
  The crib she slept in was so near my bed;
Her blue-and-white wool blanket was so soft,
  Her pillow hollowed so to fit her head.

Teach me that she'll not want small rooms or me
When she has You and Heaven's immensity!

I always left a light out in the hall.
  I hoped to make her fearless in the dark;
And yet, she was so small—one little light,
  Not in the room, it scarcely mattered. Hark!

No, no; she seldom cried! God, not too far
For her to see, this first night, light a star!

And in the morning, when she first woke up,
  I always kissed her on her left cheek where
The dimple was. And oh, I wet the brush.
  It made it easier to curl her hair.

Just, just tomorrow morning, God, I pray,
When she wakes up, do things for her my way!

VIOLET ALLEYN STOREY.

BACHELOR HALL

It seems like a dream—that sweet wooing of old—
Like a legend of fairies on pages of gold—
Too soon the sweet story of loving was closed,
Too rudely awakened the soul that reposed;
I kissed the white lips that lay under the pall,
And crept back to you, lonely Bachelor Hall.

Mine eyes have grown dim and my hair has turned white,
But my heart beats as warmly and gaily tonight
As in days that are gone and years that are fled—
Though I fill up my flagon and drink to the dead;
For over my senses sweet memories fall,
And the dead is come back to old Bachelor Hall.

I see her fair face through a vapor of tears,
And her sweet voice comes back o'er the desert of years,
And I hear, oh, so gently, the promises she spoke,
And a soft spirit hand soothes the heart that is broke;
So I fill up the flagon, and drink—that is all—
To the dead and the dying of Bachelor Hall.

EUGENE FIELD.

HE IS NOT DEAD

I cannot say, and I will not say
That he is dead. He is just away.
With a cheery smile, and a wave of the hand,
He has wandered into an unknown land
And left us dreaming how very fair
It needs must be, since he lingers there.
And you—oh, you, who the wildest yearn
For an old-time step, and the glad return,
Think of him faring on, as dear
In the love of There as the love of Here.
Think of him still as the same. I say,
He is not dead—he is just away.

JAMES WHITCOMB RILEY.

564

OUT OF THE HITHERWHERE

Out of the hitherwhere into the yon—
The land that the Lord's love rests upon,
Where one may rely on the friends he meets,
And the smiles that greet him along the streets,
Where the mother that left you years ago
Will lift the hands that were folded so,
And put them about you, with all the love
And tenderness you are dreaming of.

Out of the hitherwhere into the yon—
Where all the friends of your youth have gone—
Where the old schoolmate who laughed with you
Will laugh again as he used to do,
Running to meet you, with such a face
As lights like a moon the wondrous place
Where God is living, and glad to live
Since He is the Master and may forgive.

Out of the hitherwhere into the yon—
Stay the hopes we are leaning on—
You, Divine, with Your merciful eyes
Looking down from far-away skies,
Smile upon us and reach and take
Our worn souls Home for the old home's sake—
And so, Amen—for our all seems gone
Out of the hitherwhere into the yon.

JAMES WHITCOMB RILEY.

THE HOUSE WITH NOBODY IN IT

Whenever I walk to Suffern along the Erie track
I go by a poor old farmhouse with its shingles broken and black.
I suppose I've passed it a hundred times, but I always stop for a minute
And look at the house, the tragic house, the house with nobody in it.

I never have seen a haunted house, but I hear there are such things;
That they hold the talk of spirits, their mirth and sorrowings.
I know this house isn't haunted, and I wish it were, I do;
For it wouldn't be so lonely if it had a ghost or two.

533

This house on the road to Suffern needs a dozen panes of glass,
And somebody ought to weed the walk and take a scythe to the grass.
It needs new paint and shingles, and the vines should be trimmed and
   tied;
But what it needs the most of all is some people living inside.

If I had a lot of money and all my debts were paid,
I'd put a gang of men to work with brush and saw and spade.
I'd buy that place and fix it up the way it used to be,
And I'd find some people who wanted a home and give it to them
   free.

Now a new house standing empty, with staring window and door,
Looks idle, perhaps, and foolish, like a hat on its block in the store.
But there's nothing mournful about it; it cannot be sad and lone
For the lack of something within it that it has never known.

But a house that has done what a house should do, a house that has
   sheltered life,
That has put its loving wooden arms around a man and his wife,
A house that has echoed a baby's laugh and held up his stumbling feet
Is the saddest sight, when it's left alone, that ever your eyes could meet.

So whenever I go to Suffern along the Erie track
I never go by the empty house without stopping and looking back;
Yet it hurts me to look at the crumbling roof and the shutters fallen
   apart,
For I can't help thinking the poor old house is a house with a broken
   heart.

JOYCE KILMER.

VERSES WRITTEN IN 1872

THOUGH HE that, ever kind and true,
Kept stoutly step by step with you,
Your whole long, gusty lifetime through,
   Be gone a while before—
Be now a moment gone before—
Yet doubt not; soon the season shall restore
   Your friend to you.

He has but turned the corner—still
He pushes on with right good will
Through mire and marsh, by heugh and hill
   That selfsame arduous way—
That selfsame, upland, hopeful way,
That you and he, through many a doubtful **day**
   Attempted still.

He is not dead—this friend—not dead,
But in the path we mortals tread
Got some few trifling steps ahead,
   And nearer to the end;
So that you, too, once past the bend,
Shall meet again, as face to face, this **friend**
   You fancy dead.

Push gaily on, brave heart, the while
You travel forward mile by mile,
He loiters, with a backward smile,
   Till you can overtake;
And strains his eyes to search his wake,
Or, whistling as he sees you through the **brake,**
   Waits on a stile.

ROBERT LOUIS STEVENSON.

MY SON

God GAVE my son in trust to me;
Christ died for him, and he should be
A man for Christ. He is his own,
And God's and man's; not mine alone.
He was not mine to "give." He gave
Himself that he might help save
All that a Christian should revere,
All that enlightened men hold dear.

"To feed the guns!" O torpid soul!
Awake, and see life as a whole,
When freedom, honor, justice, right,
Were threatened by the despot's **might;**
With heart aflame and soul alight

535

He bravely went for God to fight
Against base savages, whose pride
The laws of God and man defied,
Who slew the mother and her child,
Who maidens pure and sweet defiled;
He did not go "to feed the guns."
He went to save from ruthless Huns
His home and country, and to be
A guardian of democracy.

"What if he does not come?" you say;
Ah well, my sky would be more gray,
But through the clouds the sun would shine
And vital memories be mine.
God's test of manhood is, I know,
Not "Will he come?" but "Did he go?"
My son well knew that he might die.
And yet he went with purpose high,
To fight for peace, and overthrow
The plans of Christ's relentless foe.
He dreaded not the battle field;
He went to make fierce vandals yield.
If he come not again to me
I shall be sad; but not that he
Went like a man—a hero true—
His part unselfishly to do.

My heart will feel exultant pride
That for humanity he died.

"Forgotten grave!" The selfish plea
Awakes no deep response in me.
For, though his grave I may not see,
My boy will ne'er forgotten be,
My real son can never die;
'Tis but his body that may lie
In foreign land, and I shall keep
Remembrance food, forever, deep
Within my heart of my true son
Because of triumphs that he won.
It matters not where anyone
May lie and sleep when work is done.

It matters not where some men live,
If my dear son his life must give.
Hosannas I will sing for him,
E'en though my eyes with tears be dim.
And when the war is over, when
His gallant comrades come again
I'll cheer them as they're marching by,
Rejoicing that they did not die.
And when his vacant place I see
My heart will bound with joy that he
Was mine so long—my fair young son,
And cheer for him whose work is done.

JAMES D. HUGHES.

NO FUNERAL GLOOM

No FUNERAL GLOOM, my dears, when I am gone,
Corpse-gazings, tears, black raiment, graveyard grimness.
Think of me as withdrawn into the dimness,
Yours still, you mine.
Remember all the best of our past moments and forget the rest,
And so to where I wait come gently on.

ELLEN TERRY.

ALONG THE ROAD

I WALKED a mile with Pleasure;
    She chattered all the way,
But left me none the wiser
    For all she had to say.

I walked a mile with Sorrow
    And ne'er a word said she;
But oh, the things I learned from her
    When Sorrow walked with me!

ROBERT BROWNING HAMILTON.

LUCY

SHE DWELT among the untrodden ways
   Beside the springs of Dove;
A maid whom there were none to praise,
   And very few to love.

'A violet by a mossy stone
   Half hidden from the eye!
Fair as a star, when only one
   Is shining in the sky.

She lived unknown, and few could know
   When Lucy ceased to be;
But she is in her grave, and O,
   The difference to me!

                WILLIAM WORDSWORTH.

THE OLD FAMILIAR FACES

I HAVE HAD playmates, I have had companions,
In my days of childhood, in my joyful school-days;
All, all are gone, the old familiar faces.

I have been laughing, I have been carousing,
Drinking late, sitting late, with my bosom cronies;
All, all are gone, the old familiar faces.

I loved a Love once, fairest among women:
Closed are her doors on me, I must not see her,—
All, all are gone, the old familiar faces.

I have a friend, a kinder friend has no man,
Like an ingrate, I left my friend abruptly;
Left him, to muse on the old familiar faces.

Ghost-like I paced round the haunts of my childhood,
Earth seemed a desert I was bound to traverse,
Seeking to find the old familiar faces.

Friend of my bosom, thou more than a brother,
Why wert not thou born in my father's dwelling?
So might we talk of the old familiar faces.

How some they have died, and some they have left me,
And some are taken from me; all are departed;
All, all are gone, the old familiar faces.

CHARLES LAMB.

JOSEPH RODMAN DRAKE

[Died in New York, September, 1820]

GREEN be the turf above thee,
  Friend of my better days!
None knew thee but to love thee,
  Nor named thee but to praise.

Tears fell, when thou wert dying,
  From eyes unused to weep,
And long, where thou art lying,
  Will tears the cold turf steep.

When hearts, whose truth was proven,
  Like thine, are laid in earth,
There should a wreath be woven
  To tell the world their worth;

And I, who woke each morrow
  To clasp thy hand in mine,
Who shared thy joy and sorrow,
  Whose weal and woe were thine,

It should be mine to braid it
  Around thy faded brow,
But I've in vain essayed it,
  And feel I cannot now.

While memory bids me weep thee,
  Nor thoughts nor words are free,
The grief is fixed too deeply
  That mourns a man like thee.

FITZ-GREENE HALLECK.

DOUGLAS, DOUGLAS, TENDER AND TRUE

COULD YE come back to me, Douglas, Douglas,
   In the old likeness that I knew,
I would be so faithful, so loving, Douglas,
   Douglas, Douglas, tender and true.

Never a scornful word should grieve ye,
   I'd smile on ye sweet as the angels do,
Sweet as your smile on me shone ever,
   Douglas, Douglas, tender and true.

O, to call back the days that are not!
   My eyes were blinded, your words were few;
Do you know the truth now up in heaven,
   Douglas, Douglas, tender and true?

I never was worthy of you, Douglas;
   Not half worthy the like of you;
Now all men beside seem to me like shadows—
   I love *you,* Douglas, tender and true.

Stretch out your hand to me, Douglas, Douglas,
   Drop forgiveness from heaven like dew,
As I lay my heart on your dead heart, Douglas,
   Douglas, Douglas, tender and true.

                DINAH MARIA MULOCK CRAIK.

MEMORY

MY CHILDHOOD'S HOME I see again,
   And sadden with the view;
And still, as memory crowds my brain,
   There's pleasure in it, too.

O memory! thou midway world
   'Twixt earth and paradise,
Where things decayed and loved ones lost
   In dreamy shadows rise,

And, freed from all that's earthly, vile,
  Seem hallowed, pure and bright,
Like scenes in some enchanted isle
  All bathed in liquid light.

As dusky mountains please the eye
  When twilight chases day;
As bugle notes that, passing by,
  In distance die away;

As, leaving some grand waterfall,
  We, lingering, list its roar—
So memory will hallow all
  We've known but know no more.

Near twenty years have passed away
  Since here I bid farewell
To woods and fields, and scenes of play,
  And playmates loved so well.

Where many were, but few remain
  Of old familiar things,
But seeing them to mind again
  The lost and absent brings.

The friends I left that parting day,
  How changed, as time has sped!
Young childhood grown, strong manhood gray;
  And half of all are dead.

I hear the loved survivors tell
  How nought from death could save,
Till every sound appears a knell
  And every spot a grave.

I range the fields with pensive tread,
  And pace the hollow rooms,
And feel (companion of the dead)
  I'm living in the tombs.

ABRAHAM LINCOLN.
[When thirty-seven years old.]

'TIS THE LAST ROSE OF SUMMER

'TIS THE LAST rose of Summer,
 Left blooming alone;
All her lovely companions
 Are faded and gone;
No flower of her kindred,
 No rosebud is nigh,
To reflect back her blushes,
 Or give sigh for sigh!

I'll not leave thee, thou lone one,
 To pine on the stem;
Since the lovely are sleeping,
 Go sleep thou with them.
Thus kindly I scatter
 Thy leaves o'er the bed
Where thy mates of the garden
 Lie scentless and dead.

So soon may I follow,
 When friendships decay,
And from Love's shining circle
 The gems drop away!
When true hearts lie withered,
 And fond ones are flown,
Oh! who would inhabit
 This bleak world alone?

THOMAS MOORE.

ANNABEL LEE

IT WAS MANY and many a year ago,
 In a kingdom by the sea,
That a maiden there lived whom you may know
 By the name of Annabel Lee;
And this maiden she lived with no other thought
 Than to love and be loved by me.

542

I was a child and she was a child,
  In this kingdom by the sea;
But we loved with a love that was more than love,
  I and my Annabel Lee;
With a love that the winged seraphs of heaven
  Coveted her and me.

And this was the reason that, long ago,
  In this kingdom by the sea,
A wind blew out of a cloud, chilling
  My beautiful Annabel Lee;
So that her high-born kinsman came
  And bore her away from me,
To shut her up in a sepulcher
  In this kingdom by the sea.

The angels, not half so happy in heaven,
  Went envying her and me.
Yes, that was the reason—as all men know,
  In this kingdom by the sea—
That the wind came out of the cloud by night,
  Chilling and killing my Annabel Lee.

But our love it was stronger far than the love
  Of those that were older than we,
  Of many far wiser than we.
And neither the angels in heaven above,
Nor the demons down under the sea,
Can ever dissever my soul from the soul
  Of the beautiful Annabel Lee:

For the moon never beams without bringing me dreams
  Of the beautiful Annabel Lee;
And the stars never rise but I feel the bright eyes
  Of the beautiful Annabel Lee;
And so, all the night-tide, I lie down by the side
Of my darling, my darling, my life, and my bride,
  In the sepulcher there by the sea,
  In her tomb by the sounding sea.

EDGAR ALLAN POE.

THE CLOSED DOOR

I NEVER CROSSED your threshold with a grief
  But that I went without it; never came
Heart hungry but you fed me, eased the blame,
  And gave the sorrow solace and relief.

I never left you but I took away
  The love that drew me to your side again
Through that wide door that never could remain
  Quite closed between us for a little day.

Oh! Friend, who gave and comforted, who knew
  So overwell the want of heart and mind,
Where may I turn for solace now, or find
  Relief from this unceasing loss of you?

Be it for fault, for folly, or for sin,
  Oh! terrible my penance, and most sore
To face the tragedy of that closed door
  Whereby I pass and may not enter in.

THEODOSIA GARRISON

DEATH IS A DOOR

DEATH IS ONLY an old door
  Set in a garden wall;
On gentle hinges it gives, at dusk
  When the thrushes call.

Along the lintel are green leaves,
  Beyond the light lies still;
Very willing and weary feet
  Go over that sill.

There is nothing to trouble any heart;
  Nothing to hurt at all.
Death is only a quiet door
  In an old wall.

NANCY BYRD TURNER

THE COUNTRY DOCTOR

THERE'S A GATHERING in the village, that has never been outdone
Since the soldiers took their muskets to the war of '61,
And a lot of lumber wagons near the church upon the hill,
And a crowd of country people, Sunday dressed and very still.
Now each window is pre-empted by a dozen heads or more,
Now the spacious pews are crowded from the pulpit to the door;
For with coverlet of blackness on his portly figure spread,
Lies the grim old country doctor, in a massive oaken bed,
    Lies the fierce old country doctor,
    Lies the kind old country doctor,
Whom the populace considered with a mingled love and dread.

Maybe half the congregation, now of great or little worth,
Found this watcher waiting for them, when they came upon the earth;
This undecorated soldier, of a hard, unequal strife,
Fought in many stubborn battles with the foes that sought their life.
In the nighttime or the daytime, he would rally brave and well,
Though the summer lark was fifing or the frozen lances fell;
Knowing, if he won the battle, they would praise their Maker's name,
Knowing, if he lost the battle, then the doctor was to blame.
    'Twas the brave old virtuous doctor,
    'Twas the good old faulty doctor,
'Twas the faithful country doctor—fighting stoutly all the same.

When so many pined in sickness he had stood so strongly by,
Half the people felt a notion that the doctor couldn't die;
They must slowly learn the lesson how to live from day to day,
And have somehow lost their bearings—now this landmark is away.
But perhaps it still is better that his busy life is done;
He has seen old views and patients disappearing, one by one;
He has learned that Death is master both of science and of art;
He has done his duty fairly and has acted out his part.
    And the strong old country doctor,
    And the weak old country doctor
Is entitled to a furlough for his brain and for his heart.

           WILL M. CARLETON

MY TRUNDLE BED

As I RUMMAGED thro' the attic,
  List'ning to the falling rain
As it patter'd on the shingles
  And against the windowpane,
Peeping over chests and boxes
  Which with dust were thickly spread,
Saw I in the farthest corner
  What was once—my trundle bed.
So I drew it from the recess
  Where it had remained so long,
Hearing all the while the music
  Of my mother's voice in song,
As she sang in sweetest accents
  What I since have often read:
"Hush, my dear, lie still and slumber;
  Holy angels guard thy bed."

As I listen'd, recollections
  That I thought had been forgot
Came, with all the gush of mem'ry,
  Rushing, thronging to the spot;
And I wander'd back to childhood,
  To those merry days of yore,
Where I knelt beside my mother
  By this bed, upon the floor.
Then it was, with hands so gently
  Placed upon my infant head,
That she taught my lips to utter
  Carefully the words she said;
Never can they be forgotten,
  Deep are they in memory riven:

"Hallowed be thy name, O, Father,
  Father! Thou who are in Heaven."
Years have pass'd, and that dear mother
  Long hast moulder'd 'neath the sod,
And I trust her sainted spirit
  Revels in the home of God;
But that scene at summer twilight
  Never has from mem'ry fled,
And it comes in all its freshness
  When I see my trundle bed.

This she taught me, then she told me
Of its import, great and deep,
After which I learned to utter
"Now I lay me down to sleep";
Then it was, with hands uplifted
And in accents soft and mild,
That my mother asked Our Father:
"Father, do Thou bless my child."

J. G. BAKER.

ON THE THRESHOLD

I AM STANDING on the threshold of eternity at last,
As reckless of the future as I have been of the past;
I am void of all ambition, I am dead of every hope;
The coil of life is ended; I am letting go the rope.

I have drifted down the stream of life till weary, sore oppressed;
And I'm tired of all the motion and simply want a rest.
I have tasted all the pleasures that life can hold for man.
I have scanned the whole world over till there's nothing left to scan.

I have heard the finest music, I have read the rarest books,
I have drunk the purest vintage, I have tasted all the cooks;
I have run the scale of living and have sounded every tone,
There is nothing left to live for and I long to be alone.

Alone and unmolested where the vultures do not rave,
And the only refuge left me is the quiet, placid grave;
I am judge and jury mingled, and the verdict that I give
Is, that minus friends and money it is foolishness to live.

In a day or two my body will be found out in the lake;
The coroner will get a fee; and the printer get a "take";
The usual verdict—"Suicide, from causes yet unknown."
And Golgotha draws another blank, a mound without a stone.

To change the usual verdict I will give the reason now,
Before the rigid seal of death is stamped upon my brow.
'Tis the old familiar story of passion, love and crime,
Repeated thru the ages since Cleopatra's time.

547

A woman's lips, a woman's eye—a siren all in all,
A modern Circe fit to cause the strongest men to fall;
A wedded life, some blissful years, and poverty drops in
With care and doubt and liquor from whisky down to gin.

The story told by Tolstoi in comparison to mine
Is moonlight unto sunlight, as water unto wine;
The jealous pangs I suffered, the sleepless nights of woe
I pray no other mortal may ever undergo.

But I've said enough, I fancy, to make the reason plain—
Enough to show the causes of a shattered heart and brain;
What wonder then that life holds not a single thread to bind
A wish or hope to live for, an interest in mankind.

Already dead but living, a fact that I regret,
A man without desire excepting to forget;
And since there is denied me one, why should I linger here,
A dead leaf from the frost of a long-forgotten year?

So au revoir, old cronies; if there's a meeting place beyond,
I'll let you know in spirit, and I know you will respond;
I'm going now, old comrades, to heaven or to hell;
I'll let you know which shortly—farewell, a long farewell.

UNKNOWN.

TWENTY YEARS AGO

I've wander'd to the village, Tom, I've sat beneath the tree,
Upon the school-house play-ground, which shelter'd you and me;
But none were there to greet me, Tom, and few were left to know,
That play'd with us upon the grass some twenty years ago.

The grass is just as green, Tom—barefooted boys at play,
Were sporting just as we did then, with spirits just as gay;
But the "master" sleeps upon the hill, which, coated o'er with snow,
Afforded us a sliding-place, just twenty years ago.

The old school-house is alter'd some, the benches are replaced
By new ones, very like the same our penknives had defaced;
But the same old bricks are in the wall, the bell swings to and fro,
It's music, just the same, dear Tom, 'twas twenty years ago.

The boys were playing some old game, beneath the same old tree—
I do forget the name just now; you've play'd the same with me
On that same spot; 'twas play'd with knives, by throwing so and so,
The loser had a task to do, there, just twenty years ago.

The river's running just as still, the willows on its side
Are larger than they were, Tom, the stream appears less wide;
But the grapevine swing is ruin'd now where once we play'd the beau,
And swung our sweethearts—"pretty girls"—just twenty years ago.

The spring that bubbled 'neath the hill, close by the spreading beech,
Is very low—'twas once so high that we could almost reach;
And kneeling down to get a drink, dear Tom, I even started so!
To see how much that I am changed since twenty years ago.

Near by the spring, upon an elm, you know I cut your name,
Your sweetheart's just beneath it, Tom, and you did mine the same—
Some heartless wretch had peel'd the bark, 'twas dying sure but slow,
Just as the one whose name was cut, died twenty years ago.

My lids have long been dry, Tom, but tears came in my eyes,
I thought of her I loved so well—those early broken ties—
I visited the old churchyard, and took some flowers to strew
Upon the graves of those we loved, some twenty years ago.

Some are in the churchyard laid, some sleep beneath the sea,
But few are left of our old class, excepting you and me,
And when our time is come, Tom, and we are call'd to go,
I hope they'll lay us where we play'd, just twenty years ago.

DILL ARMOR SMITH.

THE LONG AGO

OH! A WONDERFUL STREAM is the river of Time,
    As it runs through the realm of tears,
With a faultless rhythm and a musical rhyme,
And a broader sweep and a surge sublime,
    And blends with the ocean of years!

How the winters are drifting like flakes of snow,
    And the summers like buds between,
And the ears in the sheaf—so they come and they go,
On the river's breast, with its ebb and flow,
    As it glides in the shadow and sheen!

There's a magical Isle in the river of Time,
　Where the softest of airs are playing;
There's a cloudless sky and tropical clime,
And a song as sweet as a vesper chime,
　And the Junes with the roses are staying.

And the name of this Isle is Long Ago,
　And we bury our treasures there;
There are brows of beauty, and bosoms of snow,
There are heaps of dust—but we loved them so!
　There are trinkets and tresses of hair.

There are fragments of song that nobody sings,
　And a part of an infant's prayer;
There's a lute unswept, and a harp without strings,
There are broken vows and pieces of rings,
　And the garments she used to wear.

There are hands that are waved when the fairy shore
　By the mirage is lifted in air;
And we sometimes hear through the turbulent roar,
Sweet voices heard in the days gone before,
　When the wind down the river is fair.

Oh! remembered for aye be that blessed Isle,
　All the day of life till night;
When the evening comes with its beautiful smile,
And our eyes are closing to slumber awhile,
　May that greenwood of soul be in sight!

BENJAMIN F. TAYLOR.

FARE THEE WELL!

FARE THEE WELL! and if for ever,
　Still for ever, fare thee well:
Even though unforgiving, never
　'Gainst thee shall my heart rebel.

Would that breast were bared before thee
　Where thy head so oft hath lain,
While that placid sleep came o'er thee
　Which thou ne'er canst know again!

Would that breast, by thee glanced over,
  Every inmost thought could show!
Then thou wouldst at last discover
  'Twas not well to spurn it so.

Though the world for this commend thee,—
  Though it smile upon the blow,
Even its praises must offend thee,
  Founded on another's woe:

Though my many faults defaced me,
  Could no other arm be found,
Than the one which once embraced me,
  To inflict a cureless wound?

Yet, oh yet, thyself deceive not:
  Love may sink by slow decay,
But by sudden wrench, believe not
  Hearts can thus be torn away:

Still thine own its life retaineth,—
  Still must mine, though bleeding, beat;
And the undying thought which paineth
  Is—that we no more may meet.

These are words of deeper sorrow
  Than the wail above the dead;
Both shall live, but every morrow
  Wake us from a widowed bed.

And when thou wouldst solace gather,
  When our child's first accents flow,
Wilt thou teach her to say "Father!"
  Through his care she must forego?

When her little hands shall press thee,
  When her lip to thine is pressed,
Think of him whose prayer shall bless thee,
  Think of him thy love had blessed!

Should her lineaments resemble
  Those thou nevermore mayst see,
Then thy heart will softly tremble
  With a pulse yet true to me.

All my faults perchance thou knowest,
  All my madness none can know;
All my hopes, where'er thou goest,
  Wither, yet with *thee* they go.

Every feeling hath been shaken;
  Pride, which not a world could bow,
Bows to thee,—by thee forsaken,
  Even my soul forsakes me now:

But 'tis done: all words are idle,—
  Words from me are vainer still;
But the thoughts we cannot bridle
  Force their way without the will.

Fare thee well!—thus disunited,
  Torn from every nearer tie,
Seared in heart, and lone, and blighted,
  More than this I scarce can die.

LORD BYRON.

LADY BYRON'S REPLY TO LORD BYRON'S
FARE THEE WELL

YES, FAREWELL, farewell forever,
  Thou thyself hast fix'd our doom,
Bade hope's sweetest blossoms wither,
  Never more for me to bloom.

"Unforgiving," thou hast call'd me,
  Didst thou ever say "Forgive?"
For the wretch whose wiles enthrall'd thee,
  Thou didst seem alone to live.

Short the span which time has given
  To complete thy love's decay;
By unhallowed passions driven,
  Soon thy heart was taught to stray.

Love for me that feeling tender
  Which so well thy verse can show,
From my arms why didst thou wander,
  My endearment why forgo?

Wrapt in dreams of joy abiding
  On thy breast my head hath lain,
In thy love and truth confiding,
  Bliss I cannot know again.

When thy heart by me "glanc'd over"
  First displayed the guilty stain,
Would these eyes have closed forever,
  Ne'er to weep thy crimes again.

But by Heaven's recording spirit,
  May that wish forgotten be,
Life, though now a load, I'd bear it,
  For the babe I've borne to thee.

In whose lovely features (let me
  All my weakness here confess,
While the struggling tears permit me)
  All her father's I can trace.

His, whose image never leaves me,
  Whose remembrance, yet, I prize,
Who this bitterest feeling gives me,
  Still to love where I despise.

With regret and sorrow rather,
  When our child's first accents flow,
I shall teach her to say "Father,"
  But his fault she ne'er shall know.

Whilst tomorrow and tomorrow,
  Take me to a widowed bed,
In another's arms no sorrow
  Wilt thou feel!—no tear wilt shed!

For the world's applause I sought not
  When I tore myself from thee,
Of its praise or blame, I thought not;
  What is praise or blame to me!

He in whom my soul delighted
  From his heart my image drove.
With contempt my truth requited
  And preferred a wanton's love.

553

Thou art proud, and mark me, Byron,
　I've a soul proud as thine own,
Soft to love, but hard as iron,
　When despite on me is thrown.

But farewell! I'll not upbraid thee
　Never, never wish thee ill;
Wretched tho' thy crimes have made me,
　If thou canst—be happy still.

SORROW

Count each affliction, whether light or grave,
　God's messenger sent down to thee; do thou
　With courtesy receive him, rise and bow;
And, ere his shadow pass thy threshold, crave
Permission first his heavenly feet to lave;
　Then lay before him all thou hast; allow
　No cloud of passion to usurp thy brow,
　Or mar thy hospitality; no wave
Of mortal tumult to obliterate
　Thy soul's marmoreal calmness.
　　Grief should be
Like joy, majestic, equable, sedate,
　Confirming, cleansing, raising, making free;
Strong to consume small troubles; to commend
Great thoughts, grave thoughts, thoughts lasting to the end.

SIR AUBREY DE VERE.

NOT THOU BUT I

It must have been for one of us, my own,
To drink this cup and eat this bitter bread,
Had not my tears upon thy face been shed,
Thy tears had dropped on mine; if I alone
Did not walk now, thy spirit would have known
My loneliness, and did my feet not tread
This weary path and steep, thy feet had bled
For mine, and thy mouth had for mine made moan;
And so it comforts me, yea, not in vain

To think of thy eternity of sleep,
To know thine eyes are tearless though mine weep;
And when this cup's last bitterness I drain,
One thought shall still its primal sweetness keep—
Thou hadst the peace and I the undying pain.

PHILIP BOURKE MARSTON.

IF I SHOULD DIE TONIGHT

If I SHOULD DIE tonight,
My friends would look upon my quiet face,
Before they laid it in its resting place,
And deem that death had left it almost fair,
And laying snow-white flowers against my hair,
Would smooth it down with tearful tenderness,
And fold my hands with lingering caress—
Poor hands, so empty and so cold tonight!

If I should die tonight,
My friends would call to mind with loving thought
Some kindly deed the icy hand had wrought;
Some gentle word the frozen lips had said;
Errands on which the willing feet had sped.
The memory of my selfishness and pride,
My hasty words, would all be put aside,
And so I should be loved and mourned tonight.

If I should die tonight,
Even hearts estranged would turn once more to me,
Recalling other days remorsefully.
The eyes that chill me with averted glance
Would look upon me as of yore, perchance
Would soften in the old familiar way;
For who would war with dumb, unconscious clay?
So I might rest, forgiven of all tonight.

O friends, I pray tonight
Keep not your kisses for my dead, cold brow;
The way is lonely, let me feel them now.
Think gently of me; I am travel worn;
My faltering feet are pierced with many a thorn.
Forgive, O hearts estranged, forgive, I plead!
When dreamless rest is mine I shall not need
The tenderness for which I long tonight.

ARABELLA EUGENIA SMITH.

555

A CRY FROM THE CANADIAN HILLS

[Written as a tribute to the author's brother, Private Frank Leveridge, a member of the 39th Canadian Battalion who died of wounds in France, 1916.]

Laddie, little laddie, come with me over the hills,
Where blossom the white May lilies, and the dogwood and daffodils;
For the Spirit of Spring is calling to our spirits that love to roam
Over the hills of home, laddie, over the hills of home.

Laddie, little laddie, here's a hazel and meadow rue,
And wreaths of the rare arbutus, a-blowing for me and you;
And cherry and bilberry blossoms, and hawthorn as white as foam,
We'll carry them all to Mother, laddie, over the hills at home.

Laddie, little laddie, the winds have many a song,
And blithely and bold they whistle to us as we trip along;
But your own little song is sweeter, your own with its merry trills;
So, whistle a tune as you go, laddie, over the windy hills.

Laddie, little laddie, 'tis time that the cows were home;
Can you hear the klingle-klangle of their bell in the greenwood gloam?
Old Rover is waiting, eager to follow the trail with you;
Whistle a tune as you go, laddie, whistle a tune as you go.

Laddie, little laddie, there's a flash of a bluebird's wing;
O hush! If we wait and listen we may hear him caroling.
The vesper song of the thrushes, and the plaint of the whippoorwills—
Sweet, how sweet is the music, laddie, over the twilit hills.

Brother, little brother, your childhood is passing by,
And the dawn of a noble purpose I see in your thoughtful eye.
You have many a mile to travel and many a task to do;
Whistle a tune as you go, laddie, whistle a tune as you go.

Laddie, soldier laddie, a call comes over the sea,
A call to the best and bravest in the land of liberty,
To shatter the despot's power, to lift up the weak that fall.
Whistle a song as you go, laddie, to answer your country's call.

Brother, soldier brother, the Spring has come back again,
But her voice from the windy hilltops is calling your name in vain;
For never shall we together 'mid the birds and the blossoms roam,
Over the hills of home, brother, over the hills of home.

Laddie! Laddie! Laddie! "Somewhere in France" you sleep,
Somewhere 'neath alien flowers and alien winds that weep;
Bravely you marched to battle, nobly your life laid down,
You unto death were faithful, laddie; yours is the victor's crown.

Laddie! Laddie! Laddie! How dim is the sunshine grown,
As Mother and I together speak softly in tender tone!
And the lips that quiver and falter have ever a single theme,
As we list for your dear, lost whistle, laddie, over the hills of dream.

Laddie, beloved laddie! How soon should we cease to weep
Could we glance through the golden gateway whose keys the angels
    keep!
Yet love, our love that is deathless, can follow you where you roam,
Over the hills of God, laddie, the beautiful hills of Home.

LILLIAN LEVERIDGE.

THE QUEEN'S LAST RIDE

THE QUEEN is taking a drive today;
They have hung with purple the carriage way;
They have dressed with purple the royal track
Where the Queen goes forth and never comes back.

Let no man labor as she goes by,
On her last appearance to mortal eye.
With heads uncovered let all men wait
For the Queen to pass in her regal state.

Army and navy shall lead the way
For that wonderful coach of the Queen's today;
Kings and Princes and Lords of the land
Shall ride behind her, a humble band.
And over the city and over the world
Shall flags of all nations be half-mast furled
For the silent lady of royal birth
Who is riding away from the courts of earth—
Riding away from the world's unrest
To a mystical goal on a secret quest.

Though in regal splendor she drives through town,
Her robes are simple—she wears no crown.
And yet she wears one; for. widowed no more,
She is crowned with the love that has gone before,
And crowned with the love she has left behind
In the hidden depths of each thinking mind.

Uncover your heads, lift your hearts on high,
The Queen in silence is driving by.

ELLA WHEELER WILCOX.

X. NATURE

TREES

[For Mrs. Henry Mills Alden]

I THINK that I shall never see
A poem lovely as a tree.

A tree whose hungry mouth is prest
Against the earth's sweet flowing breast;

A tree that looks at God all day,
And lifts her leafy arms to pray;

A tree that may in Summer wear
A nest of robins in her hair;

Upon whose bosom snow has lain;
Who intimately lives with rain.

Poems are made by fools like me,
But only God can make a tree.

JOYCE KILMER.

MY GARDEN IS A PLEASANT PLACE

MY GARDEN is a pleasant place
Of sun glory and leaf grace.
There is an ancient cherry tree
Where yellow warblers sing to me,

And an old grape arbor, where
A robin builds her nest, and there
Above the lima beans and peas
She croons her little melodies,
Her blue eggs hidden in the green
Fastness of that leafy screen.
Here are striped zinnias that bees
Fly far to visit; and sweet peas,
Like little butterflies newborn,
And over by the tasseled corn
Are sunflowers and hollyhocks,
And pink and yellow four-o'clocks.
Here are hummingbirds that come
To seek the tall delphinium—
Songless bird and scentless flower
Communing in a golden hour.

There is no blue like the blue cup
The tall delphinium holds up,
Not sky, nor distant hill, nor sea,
Sapphire, nor lapis lazuli.

My lilac trees are old and tall;
I cannot reach their bloom at all.
They send their perfume over trees
And roofs and streets, to find the bees.

I wish some power would touch my ear
With magic touch, and make me hear
What all the blossoms say, and so
I might know what the winged things know.
I'd hear the sunflower's mellow pipe,
"Goldfinch, goldfinch, my seeds are ripe!"
I'd hear the pale wistaria sing,
"Moon moth, moon moth, I'm blossoming!"

I'd hear the evening primrose cry,
"Oh, firefly! come, firefly!"
And I would learn the jeweled word
The ruby-throated hummingbird
Drops into cups of larkspur blue,
And I would sing them all for you!

My garden is a pleasant place
Of moon glory and wind grace.
O friend, wherever you may be,
Will you not come to visit me?
Over fields and streams and hills,
I'll pipe like yellow daffodils,
And every little wind that blows
Shall take my message as it goes.
A heart may travel very far
To come where its desires are,
Oh, may some power touch my ear,
And grant me grace, and make you hear!

LOUISE DRISCOLL.

FAR FROM THE MADDING CROWD

IT SEEMS TO ME I'd like to go
Where bells don't ring, nor whistles blow,
Nor clocks don't strike, nor gongs sound,
And I'd have stillness all around.

Not real stillness, but just the trees,
Low whispering, or the hum of bees,
Or brooks faint babbling over stones,
In strangely, softly tangled tones.

Or maybe a cricket or katydid,
Or the songs of birds in the hedges. hid,
Or just some such sweet sound as these,
To fill a tired heart with ease.

If 'tweren't for sight and sound and smell,
I'd like the city pretty well,
But when it comes to getting rest,
I like the country lots the best.

Sometimes it seems to me I must
Just quit the city's din and dust,
And get out where the sky is blue,
And say, now, how does it seem to you?

NIXON WATERMAN.

GOD, THE ARTIST

GOD, WHEN YOU THOUGHT of a pine tree,
  How did you think of a star?
How did you dream of a damson West
  Crossed by an inky bar?
How did you think of a clear brown pool
  Where flocks of shadows are?

God, when you thought of a cobweb,
  How did you think of dew?
How did you know a spider's house
  Had shingles, bright and new?
How did you know we human folk
  Would love them as we do?

God, when you patterned a bird song,
  Flung on a silver string,
How did you know the ecstasy
  That crystal call would bring?
How did you think of a bubbling throat
  And a darling speckled wing?

God, when you chiseled a raindrop,
  How did you think of a stem
Bearing a lovely satin leaf
  To hold the tiny gem?
How did you know a million drops
  Would deck the morning's hem?

Why did you mate the moonlit night
  With the honeysuckle vines?
How did you know Madeira bloom
  Distilled ecstatic wines?
How did you weave the velvet dusk
  Where tangled perfumes are?
God, when you thought of a pine tree,
  How did you think of a star?

ANGELA MORGAN.

THE PATH THAT LEADS TO NOWHERE

THERE'S A PATH that leads to Nowhere
　　In a meadow that I know,
Where an inland river rises
　　And the stream is still and slow;
There it wanders under willows
　　And beneath the silver green
Of the birches' silent shadows
　　Where the early violets lean.

Other pathways lead to Somewhere,
　　But the one I love so well
Had no end and no beginning—
　　Just the beauty of the dell,
Just the windflowers and the lilies
　　Yellow striped as adder's tongue,
Seem to satisfy my pathway
　　As it winds their sweets among.

There I go to meet the Springtime,
　　When the meadow is aglow,
Marigolds amid the marshes,
　　And the stream is still and slow;
There I find my fair oasis,
　　And with carefree feet I tread
For the pathway leads to Nowhere,
　　And the blue is overhead.

All the ways that lead to Somewhere
　　Echo with the hurrying feet
Of the Struggling and the Striving,
　　But the way I find so sweet
Bids me dream and bids me linger—
　　Joy and Beauty are its goal;
On the path that leads to Nowhere
　　I have sometimes found my soul.

CORINNE ROOSEVELT ROBINSON.

OCTOBER'S BRIGHT BLUE WEATHER

O suns and skies and clouds of June,
   And flowers of June together,
Ye cannot rival for one hour
   October's bright blue weather.

When loud the humblebee makes haste,
   Belated, thriftless vagrant,
And Golden Rod is dying fast,
   And lanes with grapes are fragrant;

When Gentians roll their fringes tight,
   To save them for the morning,
And chestnuts fall from satin burrs
   Without a sound of warning;

When on the ground red apples lie
   In piles like jewels shining,
And redder still on old stone walls
   Are leaves of woodbine twining;

When all the lovely wayside things
   Their white-winged seeds are sowing,
And in the fields, still green and fair,
   Late aftermaths are growing;

When springs run low, and on the brooks,
   In idle golden freighting,
Bright leaves sink noiseless in the hush
   Of woods, for winter waiting;

When comrades seek sweet country haunts,
   By twos and twos together,
And count like misers, hour by hour,
   October's bright blue weather.

O suns and skies and flowers of June,
   Count all your boasts together,
Love loveth best of all the year
   October's bright blue weather.

HELEN HUNT JACKSON.

THE SPELL OF THE YUKON

I WANTED the gold, and I sought it;
  I scrabbled and mucked like a slave.
Was it famine or scurvy—I fought it;
  I hurled my youth into a grave.
I wanted the gold, and I got it—
  Came out with a fortune last fall—
Yet somehow life's not what I thought it,
  And somehow the gold isn't all.

No! There's the land. (Have you seen it?)
  It's the cussedest land that I know,
From the big, dizzy mountains that screen it
  To the deep, deathlike valleys below.
Some say God was tired when He made it;
  Some say it's a fine land to shun;
Maybe; but there's some as would trade it
  For no land on earth—and I'm one.

You come to get rich (damned good reason);
  You feel like an exile at first;
You hate it like hell for a season,
  And then you are worse than the worst.
It grips you like some kinds of sinning;
  It twists you from foe to a friend;
It seems it's been since the beginning;
  It seems it will be to the end.

I've stood in some mighty-mouthed hollow
  That's plumb-full of hush to the brim;
I've watched the big, husky sun wallow
  In crimson and gold, and grow dim,
Till the moon set the pearly peaks gleaming,
  And the stars tumbled out, neck and crop;
And I've thought that I surely was dreaming,
  With the peace o' the world piled on top.

The summer—no sweeter was ever;
  The sunshiny woods all athrill;
The grayling aleap in the river,
  The bighorn asleep on the hill.
The strong life that never knows harness;
  The wilds where the caribou call;
The freshness, the freedom, the farness—
  O God! how I'm stuck on it all.

The winter! the brightness that blinds you,
  The white land locked tight as a drum,
The cold fear that follows and finds you,
  The silence that bludgeons you dumb.
The snows that are older than history,
  The woods where the weird shadows slant;
The stillness, the moonlight, the mystery,
  I've bade 'em good-bye—but I can't.

There's a land where the mountains are nameless,
  And the rivers all run God knows where;
There are lives that are erring and aimless,
  And deaths that just hang by a hair;
There are hardships that nobody reckons;
  There are valleys unpeopled and still,
There's a land—oh, it beckons and beckons,
  And I want to go back—and I will.

They're making my money diminish;
  I'm sick of the taste of champagne.
Thank God! when I'm skinned to a finish
  I'll pike to the Yukon again.
I'll fight—and you bet it's no sham-fight;
  It's hell!—but I've been there before;
And it's better than this by a damsite—
  So me for the Yukon once more.

There's gold, and it's haunting and haunting;
  It's luring me on as of old;
Yet it isn't the gold that I'm wanting
  So much as just finding the gold.
It's the great, big, broad land 'way up yonder,
  It's the forests where silence has lease;
It's the beauty that thrills me with wonder,
  It's the stillness that fills me with peace.

ROBERT W. SERVICE.

A SCANDAL AMONG THE FLOWERS

A WOODLAND SPRITE of the rakish kind
  Suddenly made up his mind
That he had been so good through Lent
  He'd just start out on pleasure bent.

568

He flittered around from flower to flower,
And told them love tales by the hour.
But the posies tired and sought repose—
All but one little budded rose.
And she, poor, silly little dear,
Turned to the Sprite a willing ear.
He kissed her velvet pin-white lips,
And fingered her dress with his finger tips,
He flattered her gown, admired her taste,
From her moss-green cap to her sylphlike waist.
He told of a duel he had fought
With a bandit bee he had caught
While robbing a rose of its honeydew,
And with his sword he ran it through.
Then what did the little rosebud do?
Why, she laid her head on the Sprite's broad breast,
And then, ah well, you know the rest;
It was the same old story in a different light,
For the bud gave birth to the rose that night.
You'll all condemn this naughty elf
Who thought so much of his selfish self,
But he did the manly, spritely thing,
And presented the bud with a wedding ring.
And now, instead of one, they say
The little bud was a whole bouquet.

CHARLES S. TAYLOR.

TO A FAT LADY SEEN FROM THE TRAIN

O why do you walk through the fields in gloves,
    Missing so much and so much?
O fat white woman, whom nobody loves,
Why do you walk through the fields in gloves,
When the grass is soft as the breast of doves
    And shivering-sweet to the touch?
O why do you walk through the fields in gloves,
    Missing so much and so much?

FRANCES CORNFORD.

DID YOU EVER HEAR AN ENGLISH SPARROW SING?

WHAT? an English sparrow sing?
  Insignificant brown thing,
So common and so bold, 'twould surely bring
  Tears of laughter to the eyes
  Of the superficial wise
To suggest that that small immigrant could sing.

'Twas the bleakest wintry day,
  Earth, sky, water, all were gray,
Of the universe old Boreas seemed king,
  As he swept across the lake,
  But his empire was at stake,
When that little English sparrow dared to sing.

Not a friend on earth had I,
  No horizon to my sky,
No faith that there could be another spring.
  Cold the world as that gray wall
  Of the Auditorium tall
Where I heard that little English sparrow sing.

On the shelving of one stone
  He was cuddling all alone;
Oh, the little feet knew bravely how to cling!
  As from out the tuneful throat
  Came the sweetest, springlike note,
And I truly heard an English sparrow sing.

You may talk for all your days
  In the thrush and bluebirds' praise
And all your other harbingers of spring,
  But I've never heard a song
  Whose echoes I'd prolong
Like that I heard that English sparrow sing.

Oh, my heart's a phonograph
  That will register each laugh
And all happy sounds that from the joy-bells ring,
  So if cloudy days should come,
  In my hours of darkest gloom
I'm sure I'll hear that English sparrow sing.

BERTHA JOHNSTON.

WHO LOVES A GARDEN

Who loves a garden
Finds within his soul
Life's whole;
He hears the anthem of the soil
While ingrates toil;
And sees beyond his little sphere
The waving fronds of heaven, clear.

LOUISE SEYMOUR JONES.

THE RAINBOW

My heart leaps up when I behold
    A Rainbow in the sky:
So was it when my life began;
So is it now I am a Man;
So be it when I shall grow old,
    Or let me die!
The Child is Father of the Man;
And I could wish my days to be
Bound each to each by natural piety.

WILLIAM WORDSWORTH.

I SAW GOD WASH THE WORLD

I saw God wash the world last night
    With his sweet showers on high,
And then, when morning came, I saw
    Him hang it out to dry.

He washed each tiny blade of grass
    And every trembling tree;
He flung his showers against the hill,
    And swept the billowing sea.

The white rose is a cleaner white,
    The red rose is more red,
Since God washed every fragrant face
    And put them all to bed.

There's not a bird, there's not a bee
   That wings along the way
But is a cleaner bird and bee
   Than it was yesterday.

I saw God wash the world last night.
   Ah, would He had washed me
As clean of all my dust and dirt
   As that old white birch tree.

WILLIAM L. STIDGER.

FRAGMENT

FLOWER in the crannied wall,
I pluck you out of the crannies,
I hold you here, root and all, in my hand,
Little flower—but *if* I could understand
What you are, root and all, and all in all,
I should know what God and man is.

ALFRED TENNYSON.

DAFFODILS

I WANDERED lonely as a cloud
   That floats on high o'er vales and hills,
When all at once I saw a crowd,—
   A host of golden daffodils
Beside the lake, beneath the trees,
Fluttering and dancing in the breeze.

Continuous as the stars that shine
   And twinkle on the Milky Way,
They stretched in never-ending line
   Along the margin of a bay:
Ten thousand saw I, at a glance,
Tossing their heads in sprightly dance.

The waves beside them danced, but they
   Outdid the sparkling waves in glee;
A poet could not but be gay
   In such a jocund company;
I gazed—and gazed—but little thought
What wealth the show to me had brought.

For oft, when on my couch I lie,
   In vacant or in pensive mood,
They flash upon that inward eye
   Which is the bliss of solitude;
And then my heart with pleasure fills,
And dances with the daffodils.

WILLIAM WORDSWORTH.

XI.   ANIMALS

TO MY SETTER, SCOUT

You ARE a tried and loyal friend;
        The end
    Of life will find you leal, unweary
Of tested bonds that naught can rend,
    And e'en though years be sad and dreary
Our plighted friendship will extend.

A truer friend man never had;
        'Tis sad
    That 'mongst all earthly friends the fewest
Unfaithful ones should be clad
    In canine lowliness; yet truest
They, be their treatment good or bad.

Within your eyes methinks I find
        A kind
    And thoughtful look of speechless feeling
That mem'ry's loosened cords unbind,
    And let the dreamy past come stealing
Through your dumb, reflective mind.

Scout, my trusty friend, can it be
        You see
    Again, in retrospective dreaming,
The run, the woodland and the lea,
    With past autumnal streaming
O'er every frost-dyed field and tree?

Or do you see now once again
        The glen
  And fern, the highland and the thistle,
And do you still remember when
    We heard the bright-eyed woodcock whistle
Down by the rippling shrub-edged fen?

I see you turn a listening ear
        To hear
  The quail upon the flower-pied heather;
But, doggie, wait till uplands sere
    And then the autumn's waning weather
Will bring the sport we hold so dear.

Then we will hunt the loamy swale
        And trail
  The snipe, their cunning wiles o'ercoming,
And oft will flush the bevied quail,
    And hear the partridge slowly drumming
Dull echoes in the leaf-strewn dale.

When wooded hills with crimson light
        Are bright
  We'll stroll where trees and vines are growing,
And see birds warp their southern flight
    At sundown, when the Day King's throwing
Sly kisses to the Queen of Night.

When shadows fall in life's fair dell,
        And knell
  Of death comes with the autumn's ev'n
To separate us, who can tell
    But that, within the realm of heaven,
We both together there will dwell?

FRANK H. SELDON.

THE CURATE THINKS YOU HAVE NO SOUL

THE CURATE thinks you have no soul;
  I know that he has none. But you,
Dear friend, whose solemn self-control,
  In our foursquare familiar pew,

Was pattern to my youth—whose bark
   Called me in summer dawns to rove—
Have you gone down into the dark
   Where none is welcome—none may love?
I will not think those good brown eyes
   Have spent their life of truth so soon;
But in some canine paradise
   Your wraith, I know, rebukes the moon,
And quarters every plain and hill,
   Seeking his master . . . As for me,
This prayer at least the gods fulfill:
   That when I pass the flood and see
Old Charon by the Stygian coast
   Take toll of all the shades who land,
Your little, faithful, barking ghost
   May leap to lick my phantom hand.

ST. JOHN LUCAS.

BISHOP DOANE ON HIS DOG

I AM QUITE SURE he thinks that I am God—
Since he is God on whom each one depends
For life, and all things that His bounty sends—
My dear old dog, most constant of all friends;
Not quick to mind, but quicker far than I
To Him whom God I know and own; his eye,
Deep brown and liquid, watches for my nod;
He is more patient underneath the rod
Than I, when God His wise corrections sends.

He looks love at me, deep as words e'er spake;
And from me never crumb nor sup will take
But he wags thanks with his most vocal tail;
And when some crashing noise wakes all his fear,
He is content and quiet, if I am near,
Secure that my protection will prevail.
So, faithful, mindful, thankful, trustful, he
Tells me what I unto my God should be.

GEORGE WASHINGTON DOANE.

EPITAPH TO A DOG

NEAR this spot
Are deposited the Remains
of one
Who possessed Beauty
Without Vanity,
Strength without Insolence,
Courage without Ferocity,
And all the Virtues of Man
Without his Vices.

This Praise, which would be unmeaning flattery
If inscribed over Human Ashes,
Is but a just tribute to the Memory of
"Boatswain," a Dog
Who was born at Newfoundland,
May, 1803,
And died at Newstead Abbey
Nov. 18, 1808.

When some proud son of man returns to earth,
Unknown to glory, but upheld by birth,
The sculptor's art exhausts the pomp of woe,
And storied urns record who rests below.
When all is done, upon the tomb is seen,
Not what he was, but what he should have been.
But the poor dog, in life the firmest friend,
The first to welcome, foremost to defend,
Whose honest heart is still his master's own,
Who labors, fights, lives, breathes for him alone,
Unhonored falls, unnoticed all his worth,
Denied in heaven the soul he held on earth—
While man, vain insect! hopes to be forgiven,
And claims himself a sole exclusive heaven.

Oh man! thou feeble tenant of an hour,
Debased by slavery, or corrupt by power—
Who knows thee well must quit thee with disgust,
Degraded mass of animated dust!
Thy love is lust, thy friendship all a cheat,
Thy smiles hypocrisy, thy words deceit!
By nature vile, ennobled but by name,
Each kindred brute might bid thee blush for shame.

Ye, who perchance behold this simple urn,
Pass on—it honors none you wish to mourn.
To mark a friend's remains these stones arise;
I never knew but one—and here he lies.

Lord Byron's tribute to "Boatswain," on a monument in the garden of Newstead
Abbey.

RAGS

WE CALLED him "Rags." He was just a cur,
  But twice, on the Western Line,
That little old bunch of faithful fur
  Had offered his life for mine.

And all that he got was bones and bread,
  Or the leavings of soldier grub,
But he'd give his heart for a pat on the head,
  Or a friendly tickle and rub.

And Rags got home with the regiment,
  And then, in the breaking away—
Well, whether they stole him, or whether he went,
  I am not prepared to say.

But we mustered out, some to beer and gruel,
  And some to sherry and shad,
And I went back to the Sawbones School,
  Where I still was an undergrad.

One day they took us budding M. D.s
  To one of those institutes
Where they demonstrate every new disease
  By means of bisected brutes.

They had one animal tacked and tied
  And slit like a full-dressed fish,
With his vitals pumping away inside
  As pleasant as one might wish.

I stopped to look like the rest, of course,
  And the beast's eyes leveled mine;
His short tail thumped with a feeble force,
  And he uttered a tender whine.

It was Rags, yes, Rags! who was martyred there,
  Who was quartered and crucified,
And he whined that whine which is doggish prayer
  And he licked my hand—and died.

And I was no better in part nor whole
  Than the gang I was found among,
And his innocent blood was on the soul
  Which he blessed with his dying tongue.

Well! I've seen men go to courageous death
  In the air, on sea, on land!
But only a dog would spend his breath
  In a kiss for his murderer's hand.

And if there's no heaven for love like that,
  For such four-legged fealty—well!
If I have any choice, I tell you flat,
  I'll take my chance in hell.

EDMUND VANCE COOKE.

TO A DOG

So, BACK again?
              —And is your errand done,
Unfailing one?
How quick the gray world, at your morning look,
Turns wonder book!
Come in—O guard and guest;
Come, O you breathless, from a lifelong quest!
Search my heart; and if a comfort be,
Ah, comfort me.
You eloquent one, you best
Of all diviners, so to trace
The weather gleams upon a face;
With wordless, querying paw,
Adventuring the law!
You shaggy Loveliness,
What call was it?—What dream beyond a guess,
Lured you, gray ages back,
From that lone bivouac
Of the wild pack?—
Was it your need or ours? The calling trail
Of Faith that should not fail?

Of hope dim understood?—
That you should follow our poor humanhood,
Only because you would!
To search and circle—follow and outstrip,
Men and their fellowship;
And keep your heart no less,
Your to-and-fro of hope and wistfulness,
Through all world-weathers and against all odds!

Can you forgive us, now?—
Your fallen gods?

JOSEPHINE PRESTON PEABODY.

I THINK I KNOW NO FINER THINGS THAN DOGS

THOUGH PREJUDICE perhaps my mind befogs,
I think I know no finer things than dogs:
The young ones, they of gay and bounding heart,
Who lure us in their games to take a part,
Who with mock tragedy their antics cloak
And, from their wild eyes' tail, admit the joke;
The old ones, with their wistful, fading eyes,
They who desire no further paradise
Than the warm comfort of our smile and hand,
Who tune their moods to ours and understand
Each word and gesture; they who lie and wait
To welcome us—with no rebuke if late.
Sublime the love they bear; but ask to live
Close to our feet, unrecompensed to give;
Beside which many men seem very logs—
I think I know no finer things than dogs.

HALLY CARRINGTON BRENT.

BUM

HE'S A LITTLE DOG, with a stubby tail, and a mother-eaten coat of tan,
    And his legs are short, of the wabbly sort;
I doubt if they ever ran;
And he howls at night, while in broad daylight he sleeps like a bloom-
        in' log,
And he likes the food of the gutter breed; he's a most irregular dog.

583

I call him Bum, and in total sum he's all that his name implies,
For he's just a tramp with a highway stamp that culture cannot dis-
guise;
And his friends, I've found, in the streets abound, be they urchins or
dogs or men;
Yet he sticks to me with a fiendish glee. It is truly beyond my ken.

I talk to him when I'm lonesome-like, and I'm sure that he under-
stands
When he looks at me so attentively and gently licks my hands;
Then he rubs his nose on my tailored clothes, but I never say nought
thereat,
For the good Lord knows I can buy more clothes, but never a friend
like that!

W. DAYTON WEDGEFARTH.

THE POWER OF THE DOG

THERE IS SORROW enough in the natural way
From men and women to fill our day;
And when we are certain of sorrow in store,
Why do we always arrange for more?
Brothers and Sisters, I bid you beware
Of giving your heart to a dog to tear.

Buy a pup and your money will buy
Love unflinching that cannot lie—
Perfect passion and worship fed
By a kick in the ribs or a pat on the head.
Nevertheless it is hardly fair
To risk your heart for a dog to tear.

When the fourteen years which Nature permits
Are closing in asthma, or tumour, or fits,
And the vet's unspoken prescription runs
To lethal chambers or loaded guns,
Then you will find—it's your own affair—
But . . . you've given your heart to a dog to tear.

When the body that lived at your single will,
With its whimper of welcome, is stilled (how still!);
When the spirit that answered your every mood
Is gone—wherever it goes—for good,
You will discover how much you care,
And will give your heart to a dog to tear.

584

We've sorrow enough in the natural way,
When it comes to burying Christian clay.
Our loves are not given, but only lent,
At compound interest of cent per cent.
Though it is not always the case, I believe,
That the longer we've kept 'em, the more do we grieve:
For, when debts are payable, right or wrong,
A short-time loan is as bad as a long—
So why in—Heaven (before we are there)
Should we give our hearts to a dog to tear?

RUDYARD KIPLING.

SUPPLICATION OF THE BLACK ABERDEEN

I PRAY! My little body and whole span
Of years is Thine, my Owner and my Man.
For Thou hast made me—unto Thee I owe
This dim, distressed half-soul that hurts me so,
Compact of every crime, but, none the less,
Broken by knowledge of its naughtiness.
Put me not from Thy Life—'tis all I know.
If Thou forsake me, whither shall I go?

Thine is the Voice with which my Day begins:
Thy Foot my refuge, even in my sins.
Thine Honour hurls me forth to testify
Against the Unclean and Wicked passing by.
(But when Thou callest they are of Thy Friends,
Who readier than I to make amends?)
I was Thy Deputy with high and low—
If Thou dismiss me, whither shall I go?

I have been driven forth on gross offence
That took no reckoning of my penitence.
And, in my desolation—faithless me!—
Have crept for comfort to a woman's knee!
Now I return, self-drawn, to meet the just
Reward of Riot, Theft and Breach of Trust.
Put me not from Thy Life—though this is so.
If Thou forsake me, whither shall I go?

585

Into The Presence, flattening while I crawl—
From head to tail, I do confess it all.
Mine was the fault—deal me the stripes—but spare
The Pointed Finger which I cannot bear!
The Dreadful Tone in which my Name is named.
That sends me 'neath the sofa-frill ashamed!
(Yet, to be near Thee, I would face that woe.)
If Thou reject me, whither shall I go?

Can a gift turn Thee? I will bring mine all—
My Secret Bone, my Throwing-Stick, my Ball.
Or wouldst Thou sport? Then watch me hunt awhile,
Chasing, not after conies, but Thy Smile,
Content as breathless on the turf I sit,
Thou shouldst deride my little legs and wit—
Ah! Keep me in Thy Life for a fool's show!
If Thou deny me, whither shall I go? . . .

Is the Dark gone? The Light of Eyes restored?
The Countenance turned meward, O my Lord?
The Paw accepted, and—for all to see—
The Abject Sinner throned upon the Knee?
The Ears bewrung, and Muzzle scratched because
He is forgiven, and All is as It was?
Now am I in Thy Life, and since 'tis so—
That Cat awaits the Judgment. May I go?

RUDYARD KIPLING.

MY DOG

I HAVE no dog, but it must be
Somewhere there's one belongs to me—
A little chap with wagging tail,
And dark brown eyes that never quail,
But look you through, and through, and through,
With love unspeakable and true.

Somewhere it must be, I opine,
There is a little dog of mine
With cold black nose that sniffs around
in search of what things may be found
In pocket or some nook hard by
Where I have hid them from his eye.

Somewhere my doggie pulls and tugs
The fringes of rebellious rugs,
Or with the mischief of the pup
Chews all my shoes and slippers up,
And when he's done it to the core,
With eyes all eager, pleads for more.

Somewhere upon his hinder legs
My little doggie sits and begs,
And in a wistful minor tone
Pleads for the pleasures of the bone—
I pray it be his owner's whim
To yield, and grant the same to him.

Somewhere a little dog doth wait;
It may be by some garden gate.
With eyes alert and tail attent—
You know the kind of tail that's meant–
With stores of yelps of glad delight
To bid me welcome home at night.

Somewhere a little dog is seen,
His nose two shaggy paws between,
Flat on his stomach, one eye shut
Held fast in dreamy slumber, but
The other open, ready for
His master coming through the door.

JOHN KENDRICK BANGS.

A MALEMUTE DOG

You can't tell me God would have Heaven
So a man couldn't mix with his friends—
That we are doomed to meet disappointment
When we come to the place the trail ends.

That would be a low-grade sort of Heaven,
And I'd never regret a damned sin
If I rush up to the gates white and pearly,
And they don't let my malemute in.

For I know it would never be homelike,
  No matter how golden the strand,
If I lose out that pal-loving feeling
  Of a malemute's nose on my hand.

PAT O'COTTER.

THE LITTLE CAT ANGEL

THE GHOST of a little white kitten
Crying mournfully, early and late,
Distracted St. Peter, the watchman,
As he guarded the heavenly gate.
"Say, what do you mean," said his saintship,
"Coming here and behaving like that?"
"I want to see Nellie, my missus,"
Sobbed the wee little ghost of a cat.
"I know she's not happy without me,
Won't you open and let me go in?"
"Begone," gasped the horrified watchman,
"Why the very idea is a sin;
I open the gate to good angels,
Not to stray little beggars like you."
"All right," mewed the little white kitten,
"Though a cat I'm a good angel, too."
Amazed at so bold an assertion,
But aware that he must make no mistake,
In silence, St. Peter long pondered,
For his name and repute were at stake,
Then placing the cat in his bosom
With a "Whist now, and say all your prayers,"
He opened the heavenly portals
And ascended the bright golden stairs.
A little girl angel came flying,
"That's my kitty, St. Peter," she cried.
And, seeing the joy of their meeting,
Peter let the cat angel abide.

This tale is the tale of a kitten
Dwelling now with the blessed above,
It vanquished grim Death and High Heaven
For the name of the kitten was Love.

LEONTINE STANFIELD.

IN MEMORIAM—LEO: A YELLOW CAT

IF TO YOUR TWILIGHT land of dream—
  Persephone, Persephone,
Drifting with all your shadow host—
Dim sunlight comes, with sudden gleam
And you lift veilèd eyes to see
Slip past a little golden ghost,
That wakes a sense of springing flowers,
Of nesting birds, and lambs newborn,
Of spring astir in quickening hours,
And young blades of Demeter's corn;
For joy of that sweet glimpse of sun,
O Goddess of unnumbered dead,
Give one soft touch—if only one—
To that uplifted, pleading head!
Whisper some kindly word, to bless
A wistful soul who understands
That life is but one long caress
Of gentle words and gentle hands.

MARGARET SHERWOOD.

LEO TO HIS MISTRESS

(Answer)

DEAR MISTRESS, do not grieve for me
Even in such sweet poetry.
Alas! It is too late for that,
No mistress can recall her cat.
Eurydice remained a shade
Despite the music Orpheus played;
And pleasures here outlast, I guess,
Your earthly transitoriness.

You serious denizens of Earth
Know nothing of Elysian mirth;
With other shades I play or doze
And wash, and stretch, or rub my nose.

589

I hunt for mice, or take a nap
Safe in Iphigenia's lap.
At times I bite Achilles' heel
To learn if shadow heroes squeal,
And should he turn to do me hurt,
I hide beneath Cassandra's skirt.

But should he smile, no creature bolder,
I lightly bounce upon his shoulder,
Then leap to fair Electra's knee
Or scamper with Antigone.
I chase the rolling woolen ball
Penelope has just let fall,
And crouch when Meleager's cheer
Awakes the shades of trembling deer.
I grin when Stygian boys, beguiled,
Stare after Helen, Ruin's child;
Or should these placid pastimes fail
I play with Cerberus's tail.
At last I purr and spit and spatter
When kind Demeter fills my platter.

And yet, in spite of all of this,
I sometimes yearn for earthly bliss,
To hear you calling "Leo!" when
The glorious sun awakens men;
Or hear your "Good night, Pussy" sound
When starlight falls on mortal ground;
Then, in my struggles to get free,
I almost scratch Persephone.

HENRY DWIGHT SEDGWICK.

I AM THE CAT

In Egypt they worshiped me—
    I am the Cat.
Because I bend not to the will of man
    They call me a mystery.
When I catch and play with a mouse,
    They call me cruel,

Yet they take animals to keep
   In parks and zoos, that they may gape at them.
Nay, more, they persecute their own human creatures;
They shoot, they hang, they torture them,
   Yet dare to call me cruel.
Could they but see themselves
  As I, the Cat, see them,
These human creatures, bereft of all freedom,
   Who follow in the ruts others made
Long ages gone!
   Who have rings in their noses,
Yet know it not.
   They hate me, the Cat,
Because, forsooth, I do not love them.
   Do they love me?
They think all animals are made for their pleasure,
   To be their slaves.
And, while I kill only for my needs,
   They kill for pleasure, power and gold,
And then pretend to a superiority!
   Why should I love them?
I, the Cat, whose ancestors
   Proudly trod the jungle,
Not one ever tamed by man.
   Ah, do they know
That the same immortal hand
   That gave them breath, gave breath to me?
But I alone am free—
   I am THE CAT.

LEILA USHER.

THE ARAB'S FAREWELL TO HIS HORSE

My BEAUTIFUL! my beautiful! that standest meekly by,
With thy proudly arch'd and glossy neck, and dark and fiery eye,
Fret not to roam the desert now, with all thy wingèd speed;
I may not mount on thee again,—thou'rt sold, my Arab steed!
Fret not with that impatient hoof,—snuff not the breezy wind,—
The farther that thou fliest now, so far am I behind:
The stranger hath thy bridle-rein,—thy master hath *his* gold,—
Fleet-limb'd and beautiful, farewell; thou'rt sold, my steed, thou'rt sold.

Farewell! those free, untired limbs full many a mile must roam,
To reach the chill and wintry sky which clouds the stranger's home;
Some other hand, less fond, must now thy corn and bread prepare,
The silky mane I braided once, must be another's care!
The morning sun shall dawn again, but never more with thee
Shall I gallop through the desert paths, where we were wont to be;
Evening shall darken on the earth, and o'er the sandy plain
Some other steed, with slower step, shall bear me home again.

Yes, thou must go! the wild, free breeze, the brilliant sun and sky,
Thy master's home,—from all of these my exiled one must fly;
Thy proud dark eye will grow less proud, thy step become less fleet,
And vainly shalt thou arch thy neck, thy master's hand to meet.
Only in sleep shall I behold that dark eye, glancing bright;—
Only in sleep shall hear again that step so firm and light;
And when I raise my dreaming arm to check or cheer thy speed,
Then must I, starting, wake to feel—thou'rt *sold*, my Arab steed!

Ah! rudely, then, unseen by me, some cruel hand may chide,
Till foam-wreaths lie, like crested waves, along thy panting side:
And the rich blood that's in thee swells, in thy indignant pain,
Till careless eyes, which rest on thee, may count each started vein.
Will they ill use thee? If I thought—but no, it cannot be,—
Thou art so swift, yet easy curb'd; so gentle, yet so free;
And yet, if haply, when thou'rt gone, my lonely heart should yearn,—
Can the hand which casts thee from it now command thee to return?

Return! alas! my Arab steed! what shall thy master do,
When thou, who wast his all of joy, hast vanish'd from his view?
When the dim distance cheats mine eye, and through the gathering
    tears,
Thy bright form, for a moment, like the false mirage appears;
Slow and unmounted shall I roam, with weary step alone,
Where, with fleet step and joyous bound, thou oft hast borne me on;
And sitting down by that green well, I'll pause and sadly think,
"It was here he bow'd his glossy neck when last I saw him drink!"

When last I saw thee drink!—Away! the fever'd dream is o'er,—
I could not live a day, and *know* that we should meet no more!
They tempted me, my beautiful!—for hunger's power is strong,—
They tempted me, my beautiful! but I have loved too long.
Who said that I had given thee up? who said that thou wast sold?
'Tis false,—'tis false! my Arab steed! I fling them back their gold!
Thus, *thus,* I leap upon thy back, and scour the distant plains;
Away! who overtakes us now shall claim thee for his pains!

CAROLINE NORTON.

XII. VARIOUS THEMES

THE MAN WITH THE HOE

Written After Seeing the Painting by Millet

God made man in His own image, in the image of God made He him.—GENESIS.

Bowed by the weight of centuries he leans
Upon his hoe and gazes on the ground,
The emptiness of ages in his face,
And on his back the burden of the world.
Who made him dead to rapture and despair,
A thing that grieves not and that never hopes,
Stolid and stunned, a brother to the ox?
Who loosened and let down this brutal jaw?
Whose was the hand that slanted back this brow?
Whose breath blew out the light within this brain?

Is this the Thing the Lord God made and gave
To have dominion over sea and land,
To trace the stars and search the heavens for power,
To feel the passion of Eternity?
Is this the Dream He dreamed who shaped the suns
And pillared the blue firmament with light?
Down all the stretch of hell to its last gulf
There is no shape more terrible than this—
More tongued with censure of the world's blind greed—
More filled with signs and portents for the soul—
More fraught with menace to the universe.

What gulfs between him and the seraphim!
Slaves of the wheel of labor, what to him
Are Plato and the swing of Pleiades?
What the long reaches of the peaks of song,

The rift of dawn, the reddening of the rose?
Through this dread shape the suffering ages look;
Time's tragedy is in that aching stoop;
Through this dread shape humanity betrayed,
Plundered, profaned, and disinherited,
Cried protest to the Judges of the World,
A protest that is also prophecy.

O masters, lords, and rulers in all lands,
Is this the handiwork you give to God,
This monstrous thing distorted and soul-quenched?
How will you ever straighten up this shape,
Touch it again with immortality;
Give back the upward looking and the light;
Rebuild in it the music and the dream;
Make right the immemorial infamies,
Perfidious wrongs, immedicable woes?

O masters, lords, and rulers in all lands,
How will the Future reckon with this Man?
How answer his brute question in that hour
When whirlwinds of rebellion shake the world?
How will it be with kingdoms and with kings—
With those who shaped him to the thing he is—
When this dumb Terror shall reply to God,
After the silence of the centuries?

EDWIN MARKHAM.

THE FEMALE OF THE SPECIES

1911

WHEN THE HIMALAYAN peasant meets the he-bear in his pride,
He shouts to scare the monster, who will often turn aside;
But the she-bear thus accosted rends the peasant tooth and nail,
For the female of the species is more deadly than the male.

When Nag the basking cobra hears the careless foot of man,
He will sometimes wriggle sideways and avoid it as he can;
But his mate makes no such motion where she camps beside the trail,
For the female of the species is more deadly than the male.

When the early Jesuit fathers preached to Hurons and Choctaws,
They prayed to be delivered from the vengeance of the squaws.
'Twas the women, not the warriors, turned those stark enthusiasts
    pale,
For the female of the species is more deadly than the male.

Man's timid heart is bursting with the things he must not say,
For the Woman that God gave him isn't his to give away;
But when the hunter meets with husband, each confirms the other's
    tale—
The female of the species is more deadly than the male.

Man, a bear in most relations—worm and savage otherwise,—
Man propounds negotiations, Man accepts the compromise.
Very rarely will he squarely push the logic of a fact
To its ultimate conclusion in unmitigated act.

Fear, or foolishness, impels him, ere he lay the wicked low,
To concede some form of trial even to his fiercest foe.
Mirth obscene diverts his anger! Doubt and Pity oft perplex
Him in dealing with an issue—to the scandal of The Sex!

But the Woman that God gave him, every fibre of her frame
Proves her launched for one sole issue, armed and engined for the same;
And to serve that single issue, lest the generations fail,
The female of the species must be deadlier than the male.

She who faces Death by torture for each life beneath her breast
May not deal in doubt or pity—must not swerve for fact or jest.
These be purely male diversions—not in these her honour dwells.
She the Other Law we live by, is that Law and nothing else.

She can bring no more to living than the powers that make her great
And the Mother of the Infant and the Mistress of the Mate!
And when Babe and Man are lacking and she strides unclaimed to
    claim
Her right as femme (and baron), her equipment is the same.

She is wedded to convictions—in default of grosser ties;
Her contentions are her children, Heaven help him who denies!—
He will meet no suave discussion, but the instant, white-hot, wild,
Wakened female of the species warring as for spouse and child.

Unprovoked and awful changes—even so the she-bear fights,
Speech that drips, corrodes, and poisons—even so the cobra bites,
Scientific vivisection of one nerve till it is raw,
And the victim writhes in anguish—like the Jesuit with the squaw!

So it comes that Man the coward, when he gathers to confer
With her fellow-braves in council, dare not leave a place for her
Where, at war with Life and Conscience, he uplifts his erring hands
To some God of Abstract Justice—which no woman understands.

And Man knows it! Knows, moreover, that the Woman that God gave
  him
Must command but may not govern—shall enthral but not enslave him.
And She knows, because She warns him, and Her instincts never fail,
That the Female of Her Species is more deadly than the Male.

RUDYARD KIPLING.

THE VAMPIRE

A FOOL there was and he made his prayer
(Even as you and I!)
To a rag and a bone and a hank of hair,
(We called her the woman who did not care),
But the fool he called her his lady fair—
(Even as you and I!)

Oh, the years we waste and the tears we waste,
And the work of our head and hand
Belong to the woman who did not know
(And now we know that she never could know)
And did not understand!

A fool there was and his goods he spent,
(Even as you and I!)
Honour and faith and a sure intent
(And it wasn't the least what the lady meant),
But a fool must follow his natural bent
(Even as you and I!)

Oh, the toil we lost and the spoil we lost
And the excellent things we planned
Belong to the woman who didn't know why
(And now we know that she never knew why)
And did not understand!

598

The fool was stripped to his foolish hide,
(Even as you and I!)
Which she might have seen when she threw him aside—
(But it isn't on record the lady tried)
So some of him lived but the most of him died—
(Even as you and I!)

"And it isn't the shame and it isn't the blame
That stings like a white-hot brand—
It's coming to know that she never knew why
(Seeing, at last, she could never know why)
And never could understand!"

RUDYARD KIPLING.

A WOMAN'S ANSWER TO *THE VAMPIRE*

A FOOL there was, and she lowered her pride,
    (Even as you and I),
To a bunch of conceit in a masculine hide—
We saw the faults that could not be denied,
But the fool saw only his manly side,
    (Even as you and I).

Oh, the love she laid on her own heart's grave,
With care of her head and hand,
Belongs to the man who did not know,
(And now she knows that he never could know),
And did not understand.

A fool there was and her best she gave,
    (Even as you and I),
Of noble thoughts, of gay and grave,
(And all were accepted as due to the knave),
But the fool would never her folly save—
    (Even as you and I).

Oh, the stabs she hid, which the Lord forbid,
Had ever been really planned,
She took from the man who didn't know why,
(And now she knows he never knew why),
And did not understand.

The fool was loved while the game was new
  (Even as you and I),
And when it was played, she took her cue,
(Plodding along as most of us do),
Trying to keep his faults from view
  (Even as you and I).

And it isn't the ache of the heart, or its break
That stings like a white-hot brand—
It's learning to know that she raised the rod,
And bent her head to kiss the rod
For one who could not understand.

FELICIA BLAKE.

OLD TESTAMENT CONTENTS

In Genesis, the world was made;
  In Exodus, the march is told;
Leviticus contains the Law;
  In Numbers are the tribes enrolled.

In Deuteronomy again,
  We're urged to keep God's law alone;
And these five Books of Moses make
  The oldest holy writing known.

Brave Joshua to Canaan leads;
  In Judges, oft the Jews rebel;
We read of David's name in Ruth
  And First and Second Samuel.

In First and Second Kings we read
  How bad the Hebrew state became;
In First and Second Chronicles
  Another history of the same.

In Ezra, captive Jews return,
  And Nehemiah builds the wall;
Queen Esther saves her race from death.
  These books "Historical" we call.

In Job we read of patient faith;
  In Psalms are David's songs of praise;
The Proverbs are to make us wise;
  Ecclesiastes next portrays,

How fleeting earthly pleasures are;
  The Song of Solomon is all
About true love, like Christ's; and these
  Five books "Devotional" we call.

Isaiah tells of Christ to come,
  While Jeremiah tells of woe,
And in his Lamentations mourns
  The Holy City's overthrow.

Ezekiel speaks of mysteries;
  And Daniel foretells kings of old;
Hosea over Israel grieves;
  In Joel blessings are foretold.

In Amos, too, are Israel's woes;
  And Obadiah's sent to warn;
While Jonah shows that Christ should die
  And Micah where he should be born.

In Nahum Nineveh is seen;
  Habakkuk tells of Chaldea's guilt;
In Zephaniah are Judah's sins;
  In Haggai the Temple's built.

Then Zechariah speaks of Christ,
  And Malachi of John, his sign;
The Prophets number seventeen,
  And all the books are thirty-nine.

Matthew, Mark, Luke and John
  Tell what Christ did in every place;
The Acts tell what the Apostles did,
  And Romans how we're saved by grace.

Corinthians instruct the Church;
  Galatians shows us faith alone;
Ephesians, true love, and in
  Philippians God's grace is shown.

Colossians tells us more of Christ,
   And Thessalonians of the end;
In Timothy and Titus both
   Are rules for pastors to attend.

Philemon, Christian friendship shows.
   Then Hebrews clearly tell how all
The Jewish law prefigured Christ;
   And these Epistles are by Paul.

James shows that faith by works must live,
   And Peter urges steadfastness;
While John exhorts to Christian love,
   For those who have it God will bless.

Jude shows the end of evil men,
   And Revelation tells of Heaven.
This ends the whole New Testament
   And all the books are twenty-seven.

UNKNOWN.

NAMES AND ORDER OF THE BOOKS OF THE OLD TESTAMENT

THE GREAT JEHOVAH speaks to us,
In Genesis and Exodus,
Leviticus and Numbers see,
Followed by Deuteronomy.
Joshua and Judges sway the land,
Ruth gleans a sheaf with trembling hand,
Samuel and numerous kings appear,
Whose Chronicles we wondering hear;
Ezra and Nehemiah now
Esther the beauteous mourner show;
Job speaks in sighs, David in Psalms,
The Proverbs teach to scatter alms.
Ecclesiastes then comes on,
And the sweet song of Solomon.
Isaiah, Jeremiah then
With Lamentations takes his pen.
Ezekiel, Daniel, Hosea's lyres
Swell Joel, Amos, Obadiah's.

Next Jonah, Micah, Nahum come,
And lofty Habakkuk finds room,
Rapt Zephaniah, Haggai calls,
While Zechariah builds the walls;
And Malachi, with garments rent,
Concludes the ancient Testament.

UNKNOWN.

OUR PRESIDENTS

FIRST STANDS the lofty Washington,
That noble, great, immortal one.
The elder Adams next we see,
And Jefferson comes number three;
Then Madison is fourth you know,
The fifth one on the list, Monroe;
The sixth, then Adams comes again,
And Jackson seventh in the train.
Van Buren eighth upon the line
And Harrison counts number nine.
The tenth is Tyler in his turn,
And Polk the eleventh, as we learn.
The twelfth is Taylor in rotation,
The thirteenth Fillmore in succession;
The fourteenth, Pierce, has been selected,
Buchanan, fifteenth is elected;
Sixteenth, Lincoln rules the nation;
Johnson, seventeenth, fills the station;
As the eighteenth Grant two terms serves;
Nineteenth, Hayes our honor preserves;
Twentieth, Garfield becomes our head;
Twenty-first, Arthur succeeds the dead;
Then Cleveland next was selected;
Twenty-third, Harrison's elected;
Twenty-fourth, Cleveland is recalled;
Twenty-fifth, McKinley twice installed;
Twenty-sixth, Roosevelt, strenuous, firm;
Taft, twenty-seventh, serves his term;
Twenty-eighth, Wilson holds the place,
A nation's problems has to face.

UNKNOWN.

THE HISTORY OF THE U. S.

IN FOURTEEN HUNDRED NINETY-TWO, Columbus sailed the ocean blue
And found this land, land of the Free, beloved by you, beloved by me.

And in the year sixteen and seven, good Captain Smith thought he'd
reach Heav'n,
And then he founded Jamestown City, alas, 'tis gone, oh, what a pity.

'Twas in September sixteen nine, with ship, Half Moon, a real Dutch
sign,
That Henry Hudson found the stream, the Hudson River of our
dream.

In sixteen twenty pilgrims saw our land that had no unjust law.
Their children live here in this day, proud citizens of U. S. A.

In sixteen hundred eighty-three, good William Penn stood 'neath a
tree
And swore that unto his life's end he would be the Indian's friend.

In seventeen hundred seventy-five good Paul Revere was then alive;
He rode like wild throughout the night, and called the Minute Men
to fight.

Year seventeen hundred seventy-six, July the fourth, this date please fix
Within your minds, my children dear, for that was Independence
Year.

Two other dates in your mind fix—Franklin born in seventeen six,
And Washington first said "Boo-Hoo" in seventeen hundred thirty-
two.

In that same year, on a bitter night at Trenton was an awful fight,
But by our brave George Washington the battle was at last well won.

In seventeen hundred seventy-nine, Paul Jones, who was a captain fine,
Gained our first naval victory fighting on the big, wide sea.

And in the year eighteen and four, Lewis and Clark both went before,
And blazed for us the Oregon Trail where men go now in ease by rail.

In eighteen hundred and thirteen on great Lake Erie could be seen
Our Perry fight the Union Jack and drive it from our shores far back.

In eighteen hundred and sixty-one an awful war was then begun
Between the brothers of our land, who now together firmly stand.

In eighteen hundred sixty-three each slave was told that he was free
By Lincoln with whom few compare in being kind and just and fair.

In eighteen hundred eighty-one at Panama there was begun
By good De Lesseps, wise and great, the big canal, now our ships' gate.

At San Juan, eighteen ninety-eight, our brave Rough Riders lay in wait,
And on the land brought victory, while Dewey won it on the sea.

In nineteen hundred and fifteen was shown a panoramic screen
At San Francisco's wondrous fair; all peoples were invited there.

But cruel war in that same year kept strangers from our land o' cheer,
And nineteen seventeen brought here the war that filled our hearts
    with fear.

Thank God in nineteen eighteen Peace on the earth again was seen,
And we are praying that she'll stay forever in our U. S. A.

WINIFRED SACKVILLE STONER.

ENGLAND'S SOVEREIGNS IN VERSE

Norman Kings

William the Conqueror long did reign;
William, his son, by an arrow was slain;
Henry the First was a scholar bright;
Stephen was king without any right.

Plantagenet

Henry the Second, Plantagenet's scion;
Richard the First was as brave as a lion;
John, though a tyrant, the Charter signed;
Henry the Third had a weakly mind.
Edward the First conquered Cambria dales;
Edward the Second was born Prince of Wales;
Edward the Third humbled France in its pride;
Richard the Second in prison died.

HOUSE OF LANCASTER

Henry the Fourth for himself took the crown;
Henry the Fifth pulled the French king down;
Henry the Sixth lost his father's gains.

HOUSE OF TUDOR

Edward of York laid hold of the reins;
Edward the Fifth was killed with his brother;
Richard the Third soon made way for another.
Henry the Seventh was frugal of means;
Henry the Eighth had a great many queens.
Edward the Sixth reformation began;
Cruel Queen Mary prevented the plan.
Wise and profound were Elizabeth's aims.

STUART LINE

England and Scotland were joined by King James.
Charles found the people a cruel corrector;
Oliver Cromwell was called Lord Protector;
Charles the Second was hid in an oak,
James the Second took Popery's yoke.
William and Mary were offered the throne,
Anne succeeded and reigned alone.

HANOVERIAN KINGS

George the First from Hanover came;
George the Second kept up the name;
George the Third was loved in the land,
George the Fourth was polite and grand;
William the Fourth had no heir of his own,
So Queen Victoria ascended the Throne.

When good Queen Victoria's long reign was o'er
Edward the Seventh the English crown wore;
George the Fifth rules the vast realm of England today
And "God Save the King!" all his subjects' hearts say.

UNKNOWN.

KINGS OF FRANCE

THE FIRST KING was Pharamond; after him came
The race Merovingian, unworthy of fame;
Then Pepin the Little, and Charlemagne, great,
Victorious, kingly, in church and in state.
First Louis, Charles first, then two Louis more;
Charles; Endes, Count of Paris, whose reign was soon o'er;
Charles the Simple; Raoul de Burgoyne, rarely known,
One after another ascended the throne.

Then Louis the Fourth, who was named "L'Outre Mer,"
Then Louis the Sluggard came; after, Lothaire;
Hugh Capet, and Robert, and Henry then came;
First Philip, two Louis, and Philip whose name
Was Augustus; then Louis the Lion; and one
Called Louis the Saint, for the good he had done.
Two Philips, tenth Louis, fifth Philip came on,
And then Charles the Fourth, the sixth Philip, and John;
Charles fifth, sixth and seventh, when Joan d'Arc came
To rescue the country from sorrow and shame.

Then Louis Eleventh, perfidious king;
Charles Eighth, whose adventures let history sing;
Twelfth Louis, first Francis, and then Henry came;
Then Francis, whose wife is so well known to fame
As Mary of Scotland; Charles Ninth on whose head
Is the blood of Bartholemew's Protestant dead.
Two Henrys, five Louis, one king but in name,
For Terror was monarch till Buonaparte came.
Then Louis Eighteenth and Charles Tenth the grandson
Of Louis Fifteenth, but his reign was soon done.
Then Louis Philippe and Napoleon Third,
Who, often successful, more frequently erred.
The throne is now vacant, and no one can tell
The name of the next, so I'll bid you farewell.

MARY W. LINCOLN.

LET ME GROW LOVELY

Let me grow lovely, growing old—
  So many fine things do;
Laces, and ivory, and gold,
  And silks need not be new;

And there is healing in old trees,
  Old streets a glamour hold;
Why may not I, as well as these,
  Grow lovely, growing old?

KARLE WILSON BAKER.

GROWING OLDER

A little more tired at the close of day,
A little more anxious to have our way,
A little less ready to scold and blame,
A little more care for a brother's name;
And so we are nearing the journey's end,
Where time and eternity meet and blend.

A little less care for bonds or gold,
A little more zeal for the days of old;
A broader view and a saner mind,
And a little more love for all mankind;
And so we are faring down the way
That leads to the gates of a better day.

A little more love for the friends of youth,
A little more zeal for established truth,
A little more charity in our views,
A little less thirst for the daily news;
And so we are folding our tents away
And passing in silence at close of day.

A little more leisure to sit and dream,
A little more real the things unseen,
A little nearer to those ahead,
With visions of those long loved and dead;
And so we are going where all must go—
To the place the living may never know.

A little more laughter, a few more tears,
And we shall have told our increasing years.
The book is closed and the prayers are said,
And we are part of the countless dead;
Thrice happy, then, if some soul can say,
"I live because of their help on the way."

R. G. WELLS.

WHAT IS CHARM?

CHARM is the measure of attraction's power
To chain the fleeting fancy of an hour
And rival all the spell of Beauty's dower.

A subtle grace of heart and mind that flows
With tactful sympathy; the sweetest rose,
If not the fairest, that the garden knows.

A quick responsiveness in word and deed,
A dignity and stateliness at need,
The will to follow or the art to lead.

She to whom this most gracious gift is known
Has life's great potent factor for her own,
And rules alike the cottage and the throne.

LOUISA CARROLL THOMAS.

ECHOES

To W. A.

OR EVER the knightly years were gone
    With the old world to the grave,
I was a King in Babylon
    And you were a Christian Slave.

I saw, I took, I cast you by,
    I bent and broke your pride.
You loved me well, or I heard them lie,
    But your longing was denied.
Surely I knew that by and by
    You cursed your gods and died.

And a myriad suns have set and shone
  Since then upon the grave
Decreed by the King in Babylon
  To her that had been his Slave.

The pride I trampled is now my scathe,
  For it tramples me again.
The old resentment lasts like death,
  For you love, yet you refrain.
I break my heart on your hard unfaith,
  And I break my heart in vain.

Yet not for an hour do I wish undone
  The deed beyond the grave,
When I was a King in Babylon
  And you were a Virgin Slave.

WILLIAM ERNEST HENLEY.

WHO HAS KNOWN HEIGHTS

WHO HAS KNOWN heights and depths shall not again
  Know peace—not as the calm heart knows
  Low, ivied walls; a garden close;
And though he tread the humble ways of men
He shall not speak the common tongue again.

Who has known heights shall bear forevermore
  An incommunicable thing
  That hurts his heart, as if a wing
  Beat at the portal, challenging;
And yet—lured by the gleam his vision wore—
Who once has trodden stars seeks peace no more.

MARY BRENT WHITESIDE.

THE GARDEN OF PROSERPINE

HERE, WHERE THE WORLD is quiet,
  Here, where all trouble seems
Dead winds' and spent waves' riot
  In doubtful dreams of dreams;

I watch the green field growing
For reaping folk and sowing,
For harvest time and mowing,
   A sleepy world of streams.

I am tired of tears and laughter,
   And men that laugh and weep,
Of what may come hereafter
   For men that sow to reap:
I am weary of days and hours,
Blown buds of barren flowers,
Desires and dreams and powers
   And everything but sleep.

Here life has death for neighbor,
   And far from eye or ear
Wan waves and wet winds labor,
   Weak ships and spirits steer;
They drive adrift, and whither
They wot not who make thither;
But no such winds blow hither,
   And no such things grow here.

No growth of moor or coppice,
   No heather-flower or vine,
But bloomless buds of poppies,
   Green grapes of Proserpine,
Pale beds of blowing rushes
Where no leaf blooms or blushes,
Save this whereout she crushes
   For dead men deadly wine.

Pale, without name or number,
   In fruitless fields of corn,
They bow themselves and slumber
   All night till light is born;
And like a soul belated,
In hell and heaven unmated,
By cloud and mist abated
   Comes out of darkness morn.

Though one were strong as seven,
   He too with death shall dwell,
Nor wake with wings in heaven,
   Nor weep for pains in hell;

Though one were fair as roses,
His beauty clouds and closes;
And well though love reposes,
  In the end it is not well.

Pale, beyond porch and portal,
  Crowned with calm leaves, she stands
Who gathers all things mortal
  With cold immortal hands;
Her languid lips are sweeter
Than love's who fear to greet her
To men that mix and meet her
  From many times and lands.

She waits for each and other,
  She waits for all men born;
Forgets the earth her mother,
  The life of fruits and corn;
And spring and seed and swallow,
Take wing for her and follow
Where summer song rings hollow
  And flowers are put to scorn.

There go the loves that wither,
  The old loves with wearier wings;
And all dead years draw thither,
  And all disastrous things;
Dead dreams of days forsaken,
Blind buds that snows have shaken,
Wild leaves that winds have taken,
  Red strays of ruined springs.

We are not sure of sorrow,
  And joy was never sure;
To-day will die to-morrow;
  Time stoops to no man's lure;
And love, grown faint and fretful
With lips but half regretful
Sighs, and with eyes forgetful
  Weeps that no loves endure.

From too much love of living,
  From hope and fear set free,
We thank with brief thanksgiving
  Whatever gods may be

That no life lives forever;
That dead men rise up never;
That even the weariest river
    Winds somewhere safe to sea.

Then star nor sun shall waken,
    Nor any change of light:
Nor sound of waters shaken
    Nor any sound or sight:
Nor wintry leaves nor vernal,
Nor days nor things diurnal;
Only the sleep eternal
    In an eternal night.

ALGERNON CHARLES SWINBURNE.

THREE GATES

IF YOU ARE TEMPTED to reveal
A tale to you someone has told
About another, make it pass,
Before you speak, three gates of gold.
These narrow gates: First, "Is it true?"
Then, "Is it needful?" In your mind
Give truthful answer. And the next
Is last and narrowest, "Is it kind?"
And if to reach your lips at last
It passes through these gateways three,
Then you may tell the tale, nor fear
What the result of speech may be.

FROM THE ARABIAN.

THE OLD ASTRONOMER TO HIS PUPIL

REACH ME down my Tycho Brahe, I would know him when we meet,
When I share my later science, sitting humbly at his feet;
He may know the law of all things, yet be ignorant of how
We are working to completion, working on from then to now.

Pray remember that I leave you all my theory complete,
Lacking only certain data for your adding, as is meet,
And remember men will scorn it, 'tis original and true,
And the obloquy of newness may fall bitterly on you.

But, my pupil, as my pupil you have learned the worth of scorn,
You have laughed with me at pity, we have joyed to be forlorn.
What for us are all distractions of men's fellowship and smiles;
What for us the Goddess Pleasure with her meretricious smiles!

You may tell that German College that their honor comes too late,
But they must not waste repentance on the grizzly savant's fate.
Though my soul may set in darkness, it will rise in perfect light;
I have loved the stars too fondly to be fearful of the night.

SARAH WILLIAMS.

THE SIDEWALKS OF NEW YORK

Down IN FRONT of Casey's old brown wooden stoop
On a Summer's evening we formed a merry group;
Boys and girls together, we would sing and waltz
While the "Ginnie" played the organ
On the sidewalks of New York.

That's where Johnny Casey and little Jimmie Crowe,
With Jakey Krause, the baker, who always had the dough,
Pretty Nellie Shannon, with a dude as light as cork,
First picked up the waltz-step
On the sidewalks of New York.

Things have changed since those times,
Some are up in "G,"
Others they are wand'rers, but they all feel just like me.
They'd part with all they've got could they but once more walk
With their best girl and have a twirl
On the sidewalks of New York.

East side, west side, all round the town,
The tots sang "Ring-a-rosie," "London Bridge is falling down";
Boys and girls together, me and Mamie Rorke
Tripped the light fantastic
On the sidewalks of New York.

CHARLES B. LAWLOR AND JAMES W. BLAKE.

THE WOMAN I AM

The woman I am
   Hides deep in me
Beneath the woman
   I seem to be.

She hides away
   From the stranger's eye—
She is not known
   To the passers-by.

She goes her way,
   The woman I seem,
But the woman I am
   Withdraws to dream!

The woman I seem
   Goes carelessly—
When love goes by
   Does not seem to see.

But the woman I am
   Knows sudden fear . . .
And hides more deeply
   When love draws near!

For love might look closely
   Perhaps . . . and see
Her beneath the woman
   I seem to be!

GLEN ALLEN

CHARITY

There is so much good in the worst of us,
And so much bad in the best of us,
That it ill behoves any of us
To find fault with the rest of us.

UNKNOWN

LIFE'S A GAME

THIS LIFE is but a game of cards,
Which everyone must learn;
Each shuffles, cuts, and deals the deck,
And then a trump does turn;
Some show up a high card,
While others make it low,
And many turn no cards at all—
In fact, they cannot show.

When hearts are up we play for love,
And pleasure rules the hour;
Each day goes pleasantly along,
In sunshine's rosy bower.
When diamonds chance to crown the pack,
That's when men stake their gold,
And thousands then are lost and won,
By gamblers, young and old.

When clubs are trump look out for war,
On ocean and on land,
For bloody deeds are often done
When clubs are held in hand.
At last turns up the darkened spade,
Held by the toiling slave,
And a spade will turn up trump at last
And dig each player's grave.

UNKNOWN.

DAYS OF BIRTH

MONDAY'S CHILD is fair of face,
Tuesday's child is full of grace,
Wednesday's child is full of woe,
Thursday's child has far to go,
Friday's child is loving and giving,
Saturday's child works for its living,
And a child that's born on the Sabbath day
Is fair and wise and good and gay.

UNKNOWN.

THE FESTAL BOARD

COME TO THE FESTAL board tonight,
For bright-eyed beauty will be there,
Her coral lips in nectar steeped
And garlanded her hair.

Come to the festal board tonight,
For there the joyous laugh of youth
Will ring those silvery peals which speak
Of bosoms pure and stainless truth.

Come to the festal board tonight,
For friendship there with stronger chain
Devoted hearts already bound
For goodwill will bind again.

I went.
Nature and art their stores outpoured,
Joy beamed in every kindling glance;
Love, friendship, youth and beauty smiled.
What could that evening's bliss enhance?

We parted.
And years have flown, but where are now
The guests who round that table met?
Riseth their sun as gloriously
As on the banquets we it set?

How holds the chain which friendship wove?
It broke and soon the hearts it bound
Were widely sundered, and for peace
Envy and strife and blood were found.

The merriest laugh which then was heard
Has changed its tones to maniac screams,
As half-quenched memory kindles up
Glimmerings of guilt in feverish dreams.

And where, is she whose diamond eyes
Golconda's purest gems outshone,
Whose roseate lips of Eden breathed—
Say, where is she, the beauteous one?

617

Beneath yon willows' drooping shade,
With eyes all dim and lips all pale,
She sleeps in peace. Read on her urn,
"Broken Heart." This tells her tale.

And where is he, that tower of strength,
Whose fate with hers for life was joined;
How beats his heart, once honor's throne,
How high has soared his daring mind?

Go to the dungeon's gloom tonight,
His wasted form, his aching head,
And all that now remains of him
Lies shuddering in a felon's bed.

Ask you if all these woes the cause—
The festal board, the enticing bowl
More often came, and reason fled,
And maddened passions spurned control.

Learn wisdom there. The frequent feast
Avoid. For there with stealthy tread
Temptation walks to lure you on
Till death at last—the banquet spread.

Then shun Ovlum the enchanted cup,
Tho more its draught like joy appears;
Ere long it will be fanned by sighs,
And sadly mixed with blood and tears.

UNKNOWN.

THE GATE AT THE END OF THINGS

SOME PEOPLE say the world's all a stage
  Where each plays a part in life;
While others proclaim that life is quite real,
  Its joys, its battles, its strife.
Some say it's a joke, we should laugh it along,
  Should smile at the knocks and stings;
Whatever is true just take this from me,
  There's a gate at the end of things.

Don't try to kid yourself with the thought,
  You can do as you please all the while;
Don't think you can kick the poor fellow who's down,
  While you climb to the top of the pile.
Don't go back on your pal, just because he won't know,
  Oh, in his eyes you may be a king;
Some day he will see you just as you are,
  At the gate at the end of things.

Don't think you fool all the folks all the while,
  You may do it sometimes, that is true;
They will find you out in the end every time,
  The only one you fool is you.
If you see a man down, why, give him a hand,
  And find how much pleasure it brings,
To know you are ready to meet all mankind,
  At the gate at the end of things.

Don't let your head swell 'cause your bank roll is large
  And your clothes are the latest style;
There is many a prince walking round in rags,
  May have you beaten a mile.
Just try to remember as through life you go,
  If you're square you're as good as a king,
And you won't have to crawl through a hole in the wall,
  At the gate at the end of things.

If you've got a wife, as most fellows have,
  Remember what she's been to you,
When prosperity smiles, treat her like a pal,
  She's the one that has stuck to you;
Don't look for the girl from the Great White Way,
  Who wears diamonds, fine clothes and those things;
Think how you'd feel to meet your little girl,
  At the gate at the end of things.

Live like a man, it don't cost any more,
  To act on the square and be right.
It's reward enough to know you're a man,
  To hear people say, "He's white."
You can look everybody straight in the eye,
  And your voice has sincerity's ring;
Then you're ready to go and pass through with the bunch,
  At the gate at the end of things.

UNKNOWN.

THE HEART OF A GIRL IS A WONDERFUL THING

WHAT IS THE HEART of a girl?
Is it something that's given to swing?
Oh! Be it whatever it may,
The heart of a girl is a wonderful thing.

What a precious gift man can obtain,
And it's something that to him brings
Love, joy and perhaps fame—
'Tis the heart of a girl, a wonderful thing.

If you be a gambler, or maybe a cheat,
When a girl comes along, ah then,
If she gives you her heart, you'll fall at her feet,
For the heart of a girl is a wonderful thing.

A heart that's wonderful and true,
A heart that's ready to sing,
Except that heart there's nothing for you,
For the heart of a girl is a wonderful thing.

If you want to be happy and gay,
Listen to me, my friend,
Get the heart of a girl of today,
For it is a wonderful thing.

It will wipe away all sadness,
It will wipe away all pain;
It will bring you joy and gladness,
For the heart of a girl is a wonderful thing!

UNKNOWN.

THE LEVEL AND THE SQUARE

WE MEET upon the Level and we part upon the Square,
What words of precious meaning those words Masonic are!
Come, let us contemplate them! They are worthy of a tho't;
In the very walls of Masonry the sentiment is wrought!

We meet upon the Level, though from every station come
The rich man from his palace and the poor man from his home.
For the rich must leave their wealth and state outside the Mason's
    door,
And the poor man finds his best respect upon the Checkered Floor.

We act upon the Plumb,—'tis the order of our Guide—
We walk upright in every way and lean to neither side;
Th' All-Seeing Eye that reads our hearts doth bear us witness true,
That we still try to honor God and give each man his due.

We part upon the Square, for the word must have its due,
We mingle with the multitude, a faithful band and true,
But the influence of our gatherings in Masonry is green,
And we long upon the Level to renew the happy scene.

There is a world where all are equal, we are hurrying to it fast,
We shall meet upon the Level when the Gates of Death are past;
We shall stand before the Orient and our Master will be there,
To try the blocks we offer with His own unerring square.

We shall meet upon the Level there, but never thence depart,
There's a Mansion, 'tis all ready for each trusting, faithful heart,
There's a Mansion and a welcome and a multitude is there;
Who have met upon the Level and been tried upon the Square.

Let us meet upon the Level then while laboring patient here,
Let us meet and let us labor though the labor be severe;
Already in the western sky the signs bid us prepare
To gather up our working tools and part upon the Square.

Hands round! Ye faithful brotherhood, the bright fraternal chain,
We part upon the Square below and meet in Heaven again;
And the words of precious meaning, those words Masonic are:
"We meet upon the Level and we part upon the Square."

ROBERT MORRIS.

IS IT REALLY WORTH THE WHILE?

Sometimes, old pal, in the morning,
When the dawn is cold and gray,
And I lie in the perfumed blankets
Thinking thoughts that I dare not say,

I think of the stunts of the night before
And smile a feeble smile
  And say to myself the hundredth time
Is it really worth the while?

  I pick up the morning papers
And see where some saintly man
  Who never got stewed in all his life,
Who never said hell nor damn,
  Who never stayed out till the wee small hours,
Or courted a gay soubrette,
  But preached on the evils of drinking,
The wine and the cigarette—

"Cut off in the prime of life,"
The headlines glibly say;
  Or "He went to meet his Maker"
And "He's passed the Great White Way."
  They bury him deep while a few friends weep,
And the world moves on without a sigh,
  And the saintly man is forgotten soon
Even as you and I.

  Then I say to myself "Well, Bill, old scout,
When it's time to take the jump
  And you reach that place where the best and worst
Must bump the eternal bump,
  You can smile to yourself and chuckle,
Though the path be exceedingly hot,
  When you were on earth you were going some,
Now is that an unholy thought?"

  So I arise and attach a cracked ice band
To the crown of my battered hat,
  And saunter forth for a gold gin fizz—
She's a great old world at that;
  And I go on my way rejoicing—
What's the use to complain or sigh
  Go the route, old scout, and be merry,
For tomorrow you may die.

UNKNOWN.

MONEY AND A FRIEND

I ONCE HAD money and a friend;
  Of either, thought I store.
I lent my money to my friend
  And took his word therefor.
I sought my money from my friend,
  Which I had wanted long.
I lost my money and my friend;
  Now was that not a wrong?

UNKNOWN.

HE WHO KNOWS

He who knows not, and knows not that he knows not, is a fool, shun
  him;
He who knows not, and knows that he knows not, is a child, teach
  him.
He who knows, and knows not that he knows, is asleep, wake him.
He who knows, and knows that he knows, is wise, follow him.

PERSIAN PROVERB.

SIX FEET OF EARTH

I'LL SING YOU a song of the world and its ways,
  And the many strange people we meet—
From the rich man who rolls in his millions of wealth,
  To the struggling wretch on the street.
But a man, tho' he's poor, and in tatters and rags,
  We should never affect to despise;
But think of the adage, remember, my friends,
  That six feet of earth makes us all of one size.

There's the rich man with thousands to spare if he likes,
  But he haughtily holds up his head,
And who thinks he's above the mechanic who toils,
  And is honestly earning his bread;
But his gold and his jewels he can't take away,
  To the world up above, when he dies;
For death levels all, and conclusively shows
  That six feet of earth makes us all of one size.

There's many a coat that is tatter'd and torn,
　　That beneath lies a true, honest heart,
But because he's not dress'd like his neighbors in style,
　　Why, "Society" keeps them apart.
For on one Fortune smiles while the other one fails,
　　Yes, no matter what venture he tries;
But time calls them both to the grave in the end,
　　And six feet of earth makes us all of one size.

Then when you once see a poor fellow that tries
　　To baffle the world and its frown,
Let us help him along, and perchance he'll succeed—
　　Don't crush him because he is down.
For a cup of cold water, in charity given,
　　Is remembered with joy in the skies;
We are all but human, we have all got to die,
　　And six feet of earth makes us all of one size.

UNKNOWN.

TO A SKELETON

BEHOLD THIS RUIN! 'Twas a skull
Once of ethereal spirit full.
This narrow cell was Life's retreat,
This space was Thought's mysterious seat.
What beauteous visions fill'd this spot!
What dreams of pleasure long forgot!
Nor hope, nor joy, nor love, nor fear,
Have left one trace of record here.

Beneath this mouldering canopy
Once shone the bright and busy eye,
But start not at the dismal void,—
If social love that eye employ'd,
If with no lawless fire it gleam'd,
But through the dews of kindness beam'd,
That eye shall be forever bright
When stars and sun are sunk in night.

Within this hollow cavern hung
The ready, swift, and tuneful tongue;
If Falsehood's honey it disdain'd,
And when it could not praise was chain'd;

If bold in Virtue's cause it spoke,
Yet gentle concord never broke,—
This silent tongue shall plead for thee
When Time unveils Eternity!

Say, did these fingers delve the mine?
Or with the envied rubies shine?
To hew the rock or wear a gem
Can little now avail to them.
But if the page of Truth they sought,
Or comfort to the mourner brought,
These hands a richer meed shall claim
Than all that wait on Wealth and Fame.

Avails it whether bare or shod
These feet the paths of duty trod?
If from the bowers of Ease they fled,
To seek Affliction's humble shed;
If Grandeur's guilty bribe they spurn'd,
And home to Virtue's cot return'd,—
These feet with angel wings shall vie,
And tread the palace of the sky!

ANNA JANE VARDHILL.

MAN'S INHUMANITY TO MAN

Many and sharp the numerous ills
    Inwoven with our frame;
More pointed still, we make ourselves
    Regret, remorse and shame;
And man, whose heaven-erected face
    The smiles of love adorn,
Man's inhumanity to man,
    Makes countless thousands mourn.

ROBERT BURNS.

THE INDIAN HUNTER

Oh, why does the white man follow my path,
Like the hound on the tiger's track?
Does the flush of my dark cheek waken his wrath—
Does he covet the bow at my back?

525

He has rivers and seas where billows and breeze
Bear riches to him alone;
And the sons of the wood never plunge in the flood,
Which the white man calls his own.

Why, then, should he come to the streams where none
But the red man dares to swim?
Why, why should he wrong the hunter—one
Who never did harm to him?

The Father above thought fit to give
The white man corn and wine;
There are golden fields where he may live,
But the forest shades are mine.

The eagle hath its place of rest;
The wild horse—where to dwell;
And the spirit that gave the bird its nest
Made me a home as well.

Then back! go back from the red man's track;
For the hunter's eyes grow dim,
To find that the white man wrongs the one
Who never did harm to him.

ELIZA COOK.

RETIREMENT

I PRAISE the Frenchman,* his remark was shrewd,
How sweet, how passing sweet is solitude!
But grant me still a friend in my retreat,
Whom I may whisper, Solitude is sweet.

WILLIAM COWPER.

HY-BRASAIL—THE ISLE OF THE BLEST

ON THE OCEAN that hollows the rocks where ye dwell
A shadowy land has appeared, as they tell;
Men thought it a region of sunshine and rest,
And they called it Hy-Brasail, the isle of the blest.

*La Bruyère, says Bartlett.

From year unto year on the ocean's blue rim,
The beautiful spectre showed lovely and dim;
The golden clouds curtained the deep where it lay,
And it looked like an Eden, away, far away!

A peasant who heard of the wonderful tale,
In the breeze of the Orient loosened his sail;
From Ara, the holy, he turned to the West,
For though Ara was holy, Hy-Brasail was blest.
He heard not the voices that called from the shore—
He heard not the rising wind's menacing roar;
Home, kindred, and safety he left on that day,
And he sped to Hy-Brasail, away, far away!

Morn rose on the deep, and that shadowy isle,
O'er the faint rim of distance reflected its smile;
Noon burned on the wave, and that shadowy shore
Seemed lovelily distant and faint as before;
Lone evening came down on the wanderer's track,
And to Ara again he looked timidly back;
Oh, far on the verge of the ocean it lay,
Yet the Isle of the Blest was away, far away!

Rash dreamer, return. O, ye winds of the main,
Bear him back to his own peaceful Ara again.
Rash fool! for a vision of fanciful bliss,
To barter thy calm life of labour and peace.
The warning of reason was spoken in vain;
He never revisited Ara again!
Night fell on the deep, amidst tempest and spray,
And he died on the waters, away, far away!

GERALD GRIFFIN.

EAT AND WALK

THERE'S A THREE-PENNY Lunch on Dover Street
With a cardboard sign in the window: EAT.

Three steps down to the basement room,
Two gas jets in a sea of gloom;

Four-square counter, stove in the center,
Heavy odor of food as you enter;

A kettle of soup as large as a vat,
Potatoes, cabbage, morsels of fat

Bubbling up in a savory smoke—
Food for the gods when the gods are broke.

A wrecked divinity serving it up,
A hunk of bread and a steaming cup;

Three penny each, or two for a nickel;
An extra cent for a relish of pickle.

Slopping it up, no time for the graces—
Why should they care, these men with faces

Gaunt with hunger, battered with weather,
In walking the streets for days together?

No delicate sipping, no leisurely talk—
The rule of the place is Eat and Walk.

JAMES NORMAN HALL.

WHENAS IN SILKS MY JULIA GOES

WHENAS IN SILKS my Julia goes,
Then, then, me thinks, how sweetly flowes
That liquefaction of her clothes.

Next, when I cast mine eyes and see
That brave vibration each way free,
O how that glittering taketh me!

ROBERT HERRICK.

TO THE VIRGINS

GATHER ye rosebuds while ye may,
  Old Time is still a flying;
And this same flower that smiles to-day
  To-morrow will be dying.

The glorious lamp of Heaven, the sun,
　　The higher he's a getting,
The sooner will his race be run,
　　And nearer he's to setting.

The age is best which is the first,
　　When youth and blood are warmer;
But being spent, the worse and worst
　　Times still succeed the former.

Then be not coy, but use your time,
　　And, while ye may, go marry;
For having lost but once your prime,
　　You may forever tarry.

ROBERT HERRICK.

DUTY

I slept and dreamed that life was Beauty:
I woke and found that life was Duty:
Was then thy dream a shadowy lie?
Toil on, sad heart, courageously,
And thou shalt find thy dream to be
A noonday light and truth to thee.

ELLEN S. HOOPER.

WHO HATH A BOOK

Who hath a book
　　Has friends at hand,
And gold and gear
　　At his command;

And rich estates,
　　If he but look,
Are held by him
　　Who hath a book.

Who hath a book
　　Has but to read
And he may be
　　A king indeed;

His Kingdom is
His inglenook;
All this is his
Who hath a book.

WILBUR D. NESBIT.

LINES ON THE BACK OF A CONFEDERATE NOTE

REPRESENTING nothing on God's earth now,
   And naught in the waters below it,
As the pledge of a nation that's dead and gone,
   Keep it, dear friends, and show it.

Show it to those who will lend an ear
   To the tale that this trifle can tell,
Of a liberty born of a patriot's dream,
   Of a storm-cradled nation that fell.

Too poor to possess the precious ores,
   And too much of a stranger to borrow,
We issued today our promise to pay
   And hoped to redeem on the morrow.

The days rolled by and the weeks became years,
   But our coffers were empty still.
Coin was so rare that the treasury'd quake
   If a dollar dropped into the till.

But the faith that was in us was strong indeed,
   And our poverty well we discerned,
And this little note represented the pay
   That our suffering veterans earned.

They knew it had hardly a value in gold,
   Yet as gold each soldier received it.
It gazed in our eyes with a promise to pay,
   And every true soldier believed it.

But our boys thought little of price or of pay,
   Or of bills that were long past due;
We knew if it brought us our bread today,
   'Twas the best our poor country could do.

Keep it; it tells all our history over,
　　From the birth of the dream to its last:
Modest and born of the Angel of Hope,
　　Like our hope of success it has passed.

MAJOR SAMUEL ALROY JONAS.

WHAT CONSTITUTES A STATE?

What constitutes a State?
Not high-raised battlement or labored mound,
　　Thick wall or moated gate;
Not cities proud with spires and turrets crowned;
　　Not bays and broad-armed ports,
Where, laughing at the storm, rich navies ride;
　　Not starred and spangled courts,
Where low-browed baseness wafts perfume to pride.
　　No:—men, high-minded men,
With powers as far above dull brutes endued
　　In forest, brake, or den,
As beasts excel cold rocks and brambles rude,—
　　Men who their duties know,
But know their rights, and, knowing, dare maintain,
　　Prevent the long-aimed blow,
And crush the tyrant while they rend the chain;
　　These constitute a State;
And sovereign law, that State's collected will,
　　O'er thrones and globes elate
Sits empress, crowning good, repressing ill.
　　Smit by her sacred frown,
The fiend, Dissension, like a vapor sinks;
　　And e'en the all-dazzling crown
Hides his faint rays, and at her bidding shrinks.
　　Such was this heaven-loved isle,
Than Lesbos fairer and the Cretan shore!
　　No more shall freedom smile?
Shall Britons languish, and be men no more?
　　Since all must life resign,
Those sweet rewards which decorate the brave
　　'T is folly to decline,
And steal inglorious to the silent grave.

SIR WILLIAM JONES.

OH! WHY SHOULD THE SPIRIT OF MORTAL BE PROUD?

OH! WHY SHOULD the spirit of mortal be proud?
Like a swift-fleeting meteor, a fast-flying cloud,
A flash of the lightning, a break of the wave,
Man passeth from life to his rest in the grave.

The leaves of the oak and the willow shall fade,
Be scattered around, and together be laid;
And the young and the old, and the low and the high
Shall molder to dust and together shall die.

The infant a mother attended and loved;
The mother that infant's affection who proved;
The husband that mother and infant have blessed—
Each, all, are away to their dwellings of rest.

The maid on whose cheek, on whose brow, in whose eye,
Shone beauty and pleasure—her triumphs are by;
And the memory of those who loved her and praised
Are alike from the minds of the living erased.

The hand of the king that the scepter hath borne;
The brow of the priest that the miter hath worn;
The eye of the sage, and the heart of the brave,
Are hidden and lost in the depth of the grave.

The peasant whose lot was to sow and to reap;
The herdsman who climbed with his goats up the steep;
The beggar who wandered in search of his bread,
Have faded away like the grass that we tread.

The saint who enjoyed the communion of heaven;
The sinner who dared to remain unforgiven;
The wise and the foolish, the guilty and just,
Have quietly mingled their bones in the dust.

So the multitude goes, like the flowers or the weed
That withers away to let others succeed;
So the multitude comes, even those we behold,
To repeat every tale that has often been told.

632

For we are the same our fathers have been;
We see the same sights our fathers have seen;
We drink the same stream, and view the same sun,
And run the same course our fathers have run.

The thoughts we are thinking our fathers would think;
From the death we are shrinking our fathers would shrink;
To the life we are clinging they also would cling;
But it speeds for us all, like a bird on the wing.

They loved, but the story we cannot unfold;
They scorned, but the heart of the haughty is cold;
They grieved, but no wail from their slumbers will come;
They joyed, but the tongue of their gladness is dumb.

They died, aye! they died; and we things that are now,
Who walk on the turf that lies over their brow,
Who make in their dwelling a transient abode,
Meet the things that they met on their pilgrimage road.

Yea! hope and despondency, pleasure and pain,
We mingle together in sunshine and rain;
And the smiles and the tears, the song and the dirge,
Still follow each other, like surge upon surge.

'Tis the wink of an eye, 'tis the draught of a breath,
From the blossom of health to the paleness of death,
From the gilded saloon to the bier and the shroud—
Oh! why should the spirit of mortal be proud?

WILLIAM KNOX.

DRIFTING SANDS AND A CARAVAN

DRIFTING SANDS *and a caravan, the desert's endless space.*
Lustrous eyes 'neath Eastern skies, and a woman's veiled face.

Brigands bold on their Arab steeds, trampling all in their wake,
From out of the mystic Eastern lore one page from the book we take.

633

The sands of time move slowly in the hourglass of life,
But not on the desert's drifting sands, where bloodshed is and strife.
Out from the cruel, lashing sting of the world's merciless hate,
The soul of a man to the desert came to grapple its chance with Fate.
Ruthless, daring, brutal and suave the outer husk became,
But deep down in his innermost heart the man was just the same.
So the drama unfolded for you is set where in days of old
Eastern kings of culture and wealth lay buried in tombs of gold.

Drifting sands and a caravan, the desert's endless space.
Lustrous eyes 'neath Eastern skies, and a woman's veilèd face.

YOLANDE LANGWORTHY.

THE SHIP

A KING, a pope, and a kaiser,
  And a queen—most fair was she—
Went sailing, sailing, sailing,
  Over a sunny sea.
And amid them sat a beggar,
  A churl of low degree;
And they all went sailing, sailing,
  Over the sunny sea.

And the king said to the kaiser,
  And his comrades fair and free,
"Let us turn adrift this beggar,
  This churl of low degree,
For he taints the balmy odors
  That blow to you and me,
As we travel—sailing, sailing,
  Over the sunny sea."

"The ship is mine," said the beggar—
  That churl of low degree—
"And we're all of us sailing, sailing,
  To the grave o'er the sunny sea;
And you may not and you cannot
  Get rid of mine, or me;
No! not for your crowns and sceptres—
  And my name is Death!" quoth he.

CHARLES MACKAY.

634

I SAW THREE SHIPS

I saw three ships come sailing in,
  On Christmas day, on Christmas day,
I saw three ships come sailing in,
  On Christmas day, in the morning.

Pray, whither sailed those ships all three,
  On Christmas day, on Christmas day?
Pray, whither sailed those ships all three
  On Christmas day, in the morning.

Oh, they sailed into Bethlehem,
  On Christmas day, on Christmas day;
Oh, they sailed into Bethlehem,
  On Christmas day, in the morning.

And all the bells on earth shall ring,
  On Christmas day, on Christmas day;
And all the bells on earth shall ring,
  On Christmas day, in the morning.

And all the angels in heaven shall sing,
  On Christmas day, on Christmas day;
And all the angels in heaven shall sing,
  On Christmas day, in the morning.

And all the souls on earth shall sing
  On Christmas day, on Christmas day;
And all the souls on earth shall sing
  On Christmas day, in the morning.

UNKNOWN.

LITTLE THINGS

Little drops of water,
  Little grains of sand,
Make the mighty ocean
  And the pleasant land.

635

Thus the little minutes,
  Humble though they be,
Make the mighty ages
  Of eternity.

JULIA A. FLETCHER.

LIFE

THEY TOLD ME that Life could be just what I made it—
  Life could be fashioned and worn like a gown;
I, the designer; mine the decision
  Whether to wear it with bonnet or crown.

And so I selected the prettiest pattern—
  Life should be made of the rosiest hue—
Something unique, and a bit out of fashion,
  One that perhaps would be chosen by few.

But other folks came and they leaned o'er my shoulder;
  Somebody questioned the ultimate cost;
Somebody tangled the thread I was using;
  One day I found that my scissors were lost.

And somebody claimed the material faded;
  Somebody said I'd be tired ere 'twas worn;
Somebody's fingers, too pointed and spiteful,
  Snatched at the cloth, and I saw it was torn.

Oh! somebody tried to do all of the sewing,
  Wanting always to advise or condone.
Here is my life, the product of many;
  Where is that gown I could fashion—alone?

NAN TERRELL REED.

MOTHER SHIPTON'S PROPHECIES

OVER A WILD and stormy sea
Shall a noble sail,
Who to find will not fail
A new and fair countree,
From whence he shall bring:

636

A Herb and a root
That all men shall suit,
And please both the plowman and the king;
And let them take no more than measure,
But shall have the even pleasure,
In the belly and the brain.
Carriages without horses shall go,
And accidents fill the world with woe.
Primrose Hill in London shall be
And in its centre a Bishop's See.
Around the world thoughts shall fly
In the twinkling of an eye.
Waters shall yet more wonders do;
How strange, yet shall be true,
The world upside down shall be,
And gold found at the root of a tree.
Through hills men shall ride
And no horse or ass by their side,
Under water men shall walk,
Shall ride, shall sleep, and talk;
In the air men shall be seen,
In white, in black, and in green.
A great man shall come and go—
Three times shall lovely France
Be led to play a bloody dance;
Before her people shall be free
Three tyrant rulers shall she see;
Three times the people's hope is gone,
Three rulers in succession see,
Each springing from different dynasty.
Then shall the worser fight be done,
England and France shall be as one.
The British Olive next shall twine
In marriage with the German vine.
Men shall walk over rivers and under rivers.
Iron in the water shall float,
As easy as a wooden boat;
Gold shall be found, and found (shown?)
In a land that's not now known.
Fire and water shall more wonders do.
England shall at last admit a Jew; (foe?)
The Jew that was held in scorn
Shall of a Christian be born and born.
A house of glass shall come to pass
In England, but alas!

War will follow with the work,
In the land of Pagan and Turk,
And State and State in fierce strife,
Will seek each other's life.
But when the North shall divide the South,
An eagle shall build in the lion's mouth.
Taxes for blood and for war,
Will come to every door.
All England's sons that plough the land,
Shall be seen, book in hand;
Learning shall so ebb and flow,
The poor shall most learning know.
Waters shall flow where corn shall grow,
Corn shall grow where waters doth flow.
Houses shall appear in the vales below,
And covered by hail and snow;
The world then to an end shall come
In Eighteen Hundred and Eighty-one."

[Martha Shipton was born near Knaresborough, July 1488, and baptized as Ursula Sonthiel: married an artisan named Toby Shipton, settled in York, England, and started prophesying, dying about 1561. Her prophecies were regarded as pure fiction, being put in shape from time to time by scribes for commercial purposes. The accepted version given above is said to have been the work of one Charles Hindley, and was published about 1862, and, as related, "caused great anxiety" to many persons who expected the end of the world in 1881.]

OWED TO NEW YORK

VULGAR of manner, overfed,
Overdressed and underbred,
Heartless, Godless, hell's delight,
Rude by day and lewd by night;
Bedwarfed the man, o'ergrown the brute,
Ruled by boss and prostitute:
Purple-robed and pauper-clad,
Raving, rotting, money-mad;
A squirming herd in Mammon's mesh,
A wilderness of human flesh;
Crazed by avarice, lust and rum,
New York, thy name's "Delirium."

BYRON RUFUS NEWTON.

CITY ROOFS

(From the Metropolitan Tower)

Roof-tops, roof-tops, what do you cover?
Sad folk, bad folk, and many a glowing lover;
Wise people, simple people, children of despair—
Roof-tops, roof-tops, hiding pain and care.

Roof-tops, roof-tops, O what sin you're knowing,
While above you in the sky the white clouds are blowing,
While beneath you, agony and dolor and grim strife
Fight the olden battle, the olden war of Life.

Roof-tops, roof-tops, cover up their shame—
Wretched souls, prisoned souls too piteous to name;
Man himself hath built you all to hide away the stars—
Roof-tops, roof-tops, you hide ten million scars.

Roof-tops, roof-tops, well I know you cover
Many solemn tragedies, and many a lonely lover;
But, ah! you hide the good that lives in the throbbing city—
Patient wives, and tenderness, forgiveness, faith, and pity.

Roof-tops, roof-tops, this is what I wonder:
You are thick as poisonous plants, thick the people under;
Yet roofless and homeless, and shelterless they roam,
The driftwood of the town who have no roof-tops, and no home!

CHARLES HANSON TOWNE.

RETRIBUTION

"The mills of the gods grind late, but they grind fine."
GREEK POET.

Though the mills of God grind slowly, yet they grind exceeding small;
Though with patience he stands waiting, with exactness grinds he all.

F. VON LOGAU.
Translated by Henry Wadsworth Longfellow

639

QUARRELLING

Let dogs delight to bark and bite,
  For God hath made them so;
Let bears and lions growl and fight,
  For 'tis their nature too.

But, children, you should never let
  Your angry passions rise;
Your little hands were never made
  To tear each other's eyes.

WATTS.

THE MEN THAT DON'T FIT IN

There's a race of men that don't fit in,
  A race that can't stay still;
So they break the hearts of kith and kin,
  And they roam the world at will.
They range the field and they rove the flood,
  And they climb the mountain's crest;
Theirs is the curse of the gypsy blood,
  And they don't know how to rest.

If they just went straight they might go far;
  They are strong and brave and true;
But they're always tired of the things that are,
  And they want the strange and new.
They say: "Could I find my proper groove,
  What a deep mark I would make!"
So they chop and change, and each fresh move
  Is only a fresh mistake.

And each forgets, as he strips and runs
  With a brilliant, fitful pace,
It's the steady, quiet, plodding ones
  Who win in the lifelong race.
And each forgets that his youth has fled,
  Forgets that his prime is past,
Till he stands one day, with a hope that's dead,
  In the glare of the truth at last.

He has failed, he has failed; he has missed his chance;
    He has just done things by half.
Life's been a jolly good joke on him,
    And now is the time to laugh.
Ha, ha! He is one of the Legion Lost;
    He was never meant to win;
He's a rolling stone, and it's bred in the bone;
    He's a man who won't fit in.

ROBERT W. SERVICE.

THE MONEYLESS MAN

Is THERE no secret place on the face of the earth,
Where charity dwelleth, where virtue has birth,
Where bosoms in mercy and kindness will heave,
When the poor and the wretched shall ask and receive?
Is there no place at all, where a knock from the poor
Will bring a kind angel to open the door?
Ah, search the wide world wherever you can,
There is no open door for the Moneyless Man!

Go, look in yon hall where the chandelier's light
Drives off with its splendor the darkness of night,
Where the rich hanging velvet in shadowy fold
Sweeps gracefully down with its trimmings of gold,
And the mirrors of silver take up and renew
In long-lighted vistas the 'wildering view.
Go there! at the banquet, and find, if you can,
A welcoming smile for a Moneyless Man!

Go, look in yon church of the cloud-reaching spire,
Which gives to the sun his same look of red fire,
Where the arches and columns are gorgeous within,
And the walls seem as pure as a soul without sin;
Walk down the long aisle, see the rich and the great
In the pomp and pride of their worldly estate;
Walk down in your patches and find, if you can,
Who opens a pew to a Moneyless Man!

Go, look in the banks, where Mammon has told
His hundreds and thousands of silver and gold;
Where, safe from the hands of the starving and poor,
Lies pile upon pile of the glittering ore!

641

Walk up to their counters—ah, there you may stay
Till your limbs grow old, till your hairs grow grey,
And you'll find at the banks not one of the cian
With money to lend to a Moneyless Man!

Go, look to yon judge, in his dark, flowing gown,
With the scales wherein law weighteth equity down;
Where he frowns on the weak and smiles on the strong
And punishes right whilst he justifies wrong;
Where juries their lips to the Bible have laid,
To render a verdict—they've already made:
Go there, in the courtroom and find, if you can,
Any law for the cause of a Moneyless Man!

Then go to your hovel—no raven has fed
The wife who has suffered too long for her bread.
Kneel down by her pallet, and kiss the death frost
From the lips of the angel your poverty lost,
Then turn in your agony upward to God,
And bless, while it smites you, the chastening rod,
And you'll find, at the end of your life's little span,
There's a welcome above for a Moneyless Man!

MAJOR HENRY T. STANTON.

THE LOVELY RIVERS AND LAKES OF MAINE

O, THE LOVELY RIVERS and lakes of Maine!
I am charmed with their names, as my song will explain;
Aboriginal muses inspire my strain,
While I sing the bright rivers and lakes of Maine—
From Cupsuptic to Cheputmatticook,
From Sagadahock to Pohenegamook—
            'gamook, 'gamook,
                Pohenegamook,
From Sagadahock to Pohenegamook.

For light serenading the "Blue Moselle,"
"Bonnie Doon" and "Sweet Avon" may do very well;
But the rivers of Maine, in their wild solitudes,
Bring a thunderous sound from the depth of the woods:
The Aroostook and Chimmenticook,

The Chimpanaoc and Chinquassabamtook—
      'bamtook, 'bamtook,
        Chinquassabamtook,
The Chimpassoc and Chinquassabamtook,
Behold how they sparkle and flash in the sun!
The Mattewamkeag and the Mussungun;
The kingly Penobscot, the wild Woolastook,
Kennebec, Kennebago and Sebasticook;
The pretty Presumpscut and gay Tulanbic;
The Ess'quilsagook and little Schoodic—
        Schoodic, Schoodic;
          The little Schoodic;
The Ess'yuilsagook and little Schoodic.

Yes, yes, I prefer the bright rivers of Maine
To the Rhine or the Rhone or the Saône or the Seine;
These may do for the Cockney, but give me some nook
On the Ammonoosuc or the Wytopadiook.
On the Umsaskis or the Ripogenis,
The Ripogenis or the Piscataquis—
        'aquis, 'aquis,
          The Piscataquis.

"Away down South," the Cherokee
Has named his river the Tennessee,
The Chattahoochee and the Ocmulgee,
The Congaree and the Ohoopee;
But what are they, or the Frenchy Detroit,
To the Passadumkeag or the Wassatoquoit—
        'toquoit, 'toquoit,
          The Wassatoquoit,
To the Passadumkeag or the Wassatoquoit—

Then turn to the beautiful lakes of Maine
(To the Sage of Auburn be given the strain,
The statesman whose genius and bright fancy makes
The earth's highest glories to shine in its lakes);
What lakes out of Maine can we place in the book
With the Matagomon and the Pangokomook
        'omook, 'omook,
          The Pangokomook.
With the Matagomon and the Pangokomook?

Lake Leman, or Como, what care I for them,
When Maine has the Moosehead and Pangokwahem,
And, sweet as the dews in the violet's kiss,
Wallahgosqueqamook and Telesimis;
And when I can share in the fisherman's bunk
On the Moosetuckmaguntic or Mol'tunkamunk—
        'amunk, 'amunk,
          Or Mol'tunkamunk,
On the Moosetuckmaguntic or Mol'tunkamunk?

And Maine has the Eagle Lakes, Cheppawagan,
And the little Sepic and the little Scapan,
The spreading Sebago, the Congomgomoc,
The Milliemet and Motesoinloc,
Caribou and the fair Anmonjenegamook,
Oquassac and rare Wetokenebacook—
        'acook, 'acook,
          Wetokenebacook,
Oquassac and rare Wetokenebacook.

And there are the Pokeshine and Patquongomis;
And there is the pretty Coscomgonnosis,
Romantic Umbagog and Pemadumook,
The Pemadumook and the old Chesuncook,
Sepois and Moosteuck; and take care not to miss
The Umbazookskus or the Sysladobsis
        'dobsis, 'dobsis,
          The Sysladobsis.
The Umbazookskus or the Sysladobsis.

O, give me the rivers and lakes of Maine,
In her mountains or forests or fields of grain,
In the depth of the shade or the blaze of the sun,
The lakes of Schoodic and the Basconegun,
And the dear Waubasoos and the clear Aquessuc,
The Cosbosecontic and Millenkikuk—
        'kikuk, 'kikuk,
          The Millenkikuk,
The Cosbosecontic and Millenkikuk!

GEORGE B. WALLIS.

LIFE'S SCARS

THEY SAY the world is round, and yet
  I often think it square,
So many little hurts we get
  From corners here and there.
But one great truth in life I've found,
  While journeying to the West—
The only folks who really wound
  Are those we love the best.

The man you thoroughly despise
  Can rouse your wrath, 'tis true;
Annoyance in your heart will rise
  At things mere strangers do;
But those are only passing ills;
  This rule all lives will prove;
The rankling wound which aches and thrills
  Is dealt by hands we love.

The choicest garb, the sweetest grace,
  Are oft to strangers shown;
The careless mien, the frowning face,
  Are given to our own.
We flatter those we scarcely know,
  We please the fleeting guest,
And deal full many a thoughtless blow
  To those who love us best.

Love does not grow on every tree,
  Nor true hearts yearly bloom.
Alas for those who only see
  This cut across a tomb!
But, soon or late, the fact grows plain
  To all through sorrow's test:
The only folks who give us pain
  Are those we love the best.

                    ELLA WHEELER WILCOX.

LIFTING AND LEANING

THERE ARE TWO KINDS of people on earth today,
Just two kinds of people. no more, I say.

Not the good and the bad, for 'tis well understood
The good are half bad and the bad are half good.

Not the happy and sad, for the swift-flying years
Bring each man his laughter and each man his tears.

Not the rich and the poor, for to count a man's wealth
You must first know the state of his conscience and health.

Not the humble and proud, for in life's busy span
Who puts on vain airs is not counted a man.

No! the two kinds of people on earth I mean
Are the people who lift and the people who lean.

Wherever you go you will find the world's masses
Are ever divided in just these two classes.

And, strangely enough, you will find, too, I ween,
There is only one lifter to twenty who lean.

In which class are you? Are you easing the load
Of overtaxed lifters who toil down the road?

Or are you a leaner who lets others bear
Your portion of worry and labor and care?

ELLA WHEELER WILCOX.

A CHIP ON HIS SHOULDER

HE ALWAYS HAS something to grumble about,
  Has the man with a chip on his shoulder;
The world to the dogs is going, no doubt,
  To the man with a chip on his shoulder;
The clouds are too dark, the sun is too bright.
No matter what happens, it is never right;
When peace is prevailing he is spoiling to fight,
  The man with a chip on his shoulder.

UNKNOWN.

OUR LIPS AND EARS

IF YOU your lips would keep from slips,
    Five things observe with care:
Of whom you speak, to whom you speak,
    And how and when and where.

If you your ears would save from jeers,
    These things keep meekly hid:
Myself and I, and mine and my,
    And how I do and did.

UNKNOWN.

EMPTIES COMING BACK

have you ever sat by the railroad track
and watched the emptys cuming back?
lumbering along with a groan and a whine,—
smoke strung out in a long gray line
belched from the panting injun's stack
    —just emptys cuming back.

i have—and to me the emptys seem
like dreams i sometimes dream—
of a girl—or munney—or maybe fame—
my dreams have all returned the same,
swinging along the homebound track
    —just emptys cuming back.

ANGELO DE PONCIANO.

A WISE OLD OWL

A WISE OLD OWL lived in an oak;
The more he saw the less he spoke;
The less he spoke the more he heard:
Why can't we all be like that bird?

EDWARD HERSEY RICHARDS.

[Said to have been quoted by the American millionaire, Rockefeller, September 1915, when questioned about a War Loan from America to the Entente Allies.]

HORSE SENSE

A HORSE can't pull while kicking.
This fact I merely mention.
And he can't kick while pulling,
Which is my chief contention.

Let's imitate the good old horse
And lead a life that's fitting;
Just pull an honest load, and then
There'll be no time for kicking.

UNKNOWN.

THE YEAR'S AT THE SPRING

THE YEAR'S at the spring
And the day's at the morn;
Morning's at seven;
The hillside's dew-pearled;
The lark's on the wing;
The snail's on the thorn:
God's in his heaven—
All's right with the world!

ROBERT BROWNING.

INDEX BY AUTHORS

INDEX BY AUTHORS

INDEX BY AUTHORS

651

INDEX BY AUTHORS

INDEX BY FIRST LINES

INDEX BY FIRST LINES